Selected Writings

SELECTED WRITINGS

1974–1999

RICHARD MABEY

Chatto & Windus
LONDON

Published by Chatto & Windus 1999

2 4 6 8 10 9 7 5 3 1

First published in Great Britain in 1999 by
Chatto & Windus
Random House, 20 Vauxhall Bridge Road,
London SW1V 2SA

Random House Australia (Pty) Limited
20 Alfred Street, Milsons Point, Sydney,
New South Wales 2061, Australia

Random House New Zealand Limited
18 Poland Road, Glenfield,
Auckland 10, New Zealand

Random House South Africa (Pty) Limited
Endulini, 5A Jubilee Road, Parktown 2193, South Africa

Random House UK Limited Reg. No. 954009

A CIP catalogue record for this book
is available from the British Library

ISBN 1–85619–779–4

Papers used by Random House UK Limited are natural,
recyclable products made from wood grown in sustainable forests.
The manufacturing processes conform to the environmental
regulations of the country of origin.

Printed and bound in Great Britain by
Biddles Ltd, Guildford.

For Mike Curtis

CONTENTS

Contents

GENIUS LOCI

Spring Fever (1978)

I'm afraid it must be a chronic affliction. Every year I fret away the damp and birdless days of early April, wondering if they will ever come back. And every May I wake one morning to a clear sky alive with swifts and martins, and am cured in a minute. It does not last. Come next spring, I am looking out of the window at the chill north-easterlies ruffling the primroses and thinking mournfully about the birds held up on the other side of the Channel, each of us, in our different ways, trapped by our expectations.

We seem to make a more heartfelt response to the coming of spring than to any other season. The first green film on the hawthorns, or a swallow on Easter Day, can lift the spirits far more than is explicable by a simple relief that winter is past. Perhaps our biological roots are deeper than we think, and we recognise these natural tokens as part of an annual renewal in which we still share.

When I was at school our talisman was the chiffchaff. For the first few days of the Easter holidays we would comb the woods for them, trying to push our personal first dates further and further back into March. It was about as devout as a game of conkers, and it was only years later that I learned to appreciate the sweet and subtle triumph in that first new voice of spring. The bird that touched me most then – as now – was the swift. But no random swift would do. No precociously early date would make up for a bird in the wrong place at the wrong time. *My* first swift had to fly above a high meadow I crossed on the way to afternoon cricket on the first day of May. I trudged up the hill with my bike, gazing into the air and holding my blazer collar for luck, aching for a glimpse of those careering crescent wings.

Swifts have become as important to us as nightingales were to the Romantics, but I'm not sure I can fully explain the spell they hold over me. There is, of course, the thrill of their mass chases round the housetops, and the poignancy of their life styles, so completely aerial that a young swift spends three years entirely on the wing (covering 3,000,000 miles) between fledging and first breeding. But the real reasons, what I feel when I see them back again, aren't anything like as rational and objective as this. They have to do with renewal again, and with the extraordinary sense of privilege that comes from having such cryptic, remote birds returning, every year, to spend the best three months of the summer in *our* parish.

Meanwhile, whilst we're waiting, the resident birds make their own welcome diversions. There is a pair of collared doves that appears regularly on our lawn in the first mild days of January. There are mistle thrushes that skirl through the gales of February from the lime trees down the lane, and not long after, the first real dawn chorus. And in early March there is almost always a spell of mild weather that will be all we see of spring for the next four or five weeks. Larks sing, pussy willows buzz with yellow-dusted bees. Last year, I remember, it began at the very start of the month with a day of bizarre manifestations: a brimstone butterfly in the back garden, a frog in the front, and a French partridge, under the cherry tree, that sprinted down the lawn and vanished along our drive.

They carry on the spring, the inexorable thread of new life. Yet on bleak mid-April days, how one longs for the return of the summer birds, for the reassurance that comes from long-awaited arrivals. Our first pair of local swallows always returns at this time, to a site they have clung to with such persistence and magnanimity that it makes you ashamed of all those sceptical proverbs. This solitary pair helps make many people's summers. They nest by the railway station, under a bridge which carries the main line to Euston over a busy road. They have survived not just the traffic but the rebuilding of the bridge, and in the evenings they swoop over the heads of the homebound commuters and fly the 100 yards to the moat of our Norman castle, where their ancestors probably hunted for midges nearly a thousand years ago.

But these swallows are exceptional in moving into their summer quarters so early. Most other migrants are biding their time near patches of open water, waiting for a change in the weather. Sometimes, when the cold winds hold on beyond the end of April, I have seen gatherings of martins, swifts and swallows so many thousands strong over a nearby reservoir that the surface of the water seemed to be boiling with them. It is a breathtaking sight, but it cannot compare with that moment in early May when the wind veers round to the south, and the birds come home, back to the streets and steeples.

W. H. Hudson once wrote about 'birds at their best'. I think he had in mind these moments when a bird seems to belong utterly to a particular landscape. I remember a wood warbler I saw in a Chiltern beechwood one spring. It was the first warm day of May and you could still see the sky through the thin-leaved lattice of the branches. Primroses were in flower, and blackcaps and garden warblers singing in the undergrowth. And in their midst – the soloist to their chorus – was a single wood warbler, in full tremulous song. It was on a thin beech sapling, not 12 feet from me, and even without binoculars I could see its throat shaking with every note of that falling, clear-water song, and seeming in the filtered sunlight to be the same translucent green as the young beech leaves. A bird at its best, and undeniably in its place.

And with the spring fully settled, I feel a need to see the summer birds 'in their places'. I suppose it is a kind of beating of the bounds, not just of the parish itself, but of my internal map of haunts and memories, a way of confirming the continuity in my own life as much as in the landscape. The track I follow is always the same. I go up the hill to the wood where I searched for chiffchaffs when I was a boy, cross a narrow valley where swallows hawk over a farm pond, and climb to a patch of chalk scrub that is always thronging with warblers. I stay here till dusk. Sometimes a sparrowhawk glides down the valley, sometimes a woodcock on its roding circuit, both, like me, checking out their territories. And high in the night sky, beyond human sight, the parish swifts cruise above the sodium lights, home for the summer.

Richard Mabey's Hertfordshire (1982)

The trouble with Hertfordshire is that it has a low profile and earns low loyalties. There is no quintessential county landscape, no great range of hills or heaths. There is no Hertfordshire cheese, sheep, hot-pot or pudding (though there is Hertfordshire puddingstone, a glacial relic which pops up here and there and consists of a conglomeration of rough stones held together by natural cement). You will need to talk to a life-long inhabitant for first-hand memories of an authentic local industry. Hertfordshire-persons don't even have any oddball qualities for people to make jokes about. The nearest thing to a piece of county mythology I have heard is Bernard Miles' laconic tale of a family tombstone that was 'the finest piece of sharpening stone in all Hertfordshire', which he would relate in a dry and measured accent exactly halfway between Wessex round and Norfolk flat. But then Bernard Miles, I hardly need add, also lived just over the border, in Middlesex.

Having no sharply defined character of its own, Herts is apt to take on the contours and hues of its more distinct neighbours. Much of the south of the county, for instance, seems little more than a dense and busy carapace of north London, whilst the extreme east is as olde-world as Essex. It depends on your point of view. Drive down from the rural north, along the Great North Road through Stevenage, or the Old Roman Ermine Street (now the A10) through Hoddesdon, and Herts appears as a long, low industrial estate, a working suburbia of compact electronics factories, garden centres, office complexes and gravel pits landscaped for anglers and weekend sailors. Wind your way westwards from the North Circular, through Bushey, Oxhey and Chorleywood, and it is a thickening vista of beechwoods and gorse-covered commons.

If you actually live here you may not have a view at all of the county as such. It is hardly firm enough ground to grow roots in. Herts is more a kind of temporary mooring, a place to commute from, to pause in on the way to somewhere else, to leave behind at the end of a working life. Through traffic has been one of its burdens since prehistoric times. The county's oldest road, the Icknield Way, was in use as the main route between Wessex and the Wash four thousand years ago. It was taken along the chalk ridge on the extreme north-west edge of the county to bypass the densely wooded claylands that covered its centre. Since then Herts has been criss-crossed by the Grand Union Canal, four main railway

6

lines, and bits of five motorways. Most of the proposed sites for the third London Airport have been just a few miles one side or other of its boundary.

All these facilities for hectic toing and froing reflect the looming presence of the capital, which has been the major force in shaping Hertfordshire's character for more than a thousand years. With nothing particular to act as a counterbalance – a coastline, for example, as have those other suburban counties, Essex and Kent – London exerts its influence in much the same way as a magnet affects iron filings, giving a slant, a kind of metropolitan restlessness, to everything from house prices to insect life (Herts has more species of flea than any other county in England). Looked at the other way, we live at the edge of the capital's shadow, where urban stresses become faint and muddled. The first vague memories of my life are of the grim wartime struggles being acted out to the south, which to my uncomprehending infant eyes seemed more like a circus than a world war. There were distant dog-fights and languid barrage balloons in the day, and searchlights playing about the sky at night. The morning after an air-raid I would toddle out on to the lawn to gather the thin strips of metal foil the bombers had dropped to confuse our radar. They lay amongst the dew and daisies like gossamer. Once a bomb was off-loaded into a nearby field, blowing a chip off our greenhouse wall and leaving a vast crater. For years afterwards I assumed that all the dells and holes with which West Herts is pitted (ancient and innocent marl diggings for the most part) were caused by German bombs.

These are the kinds of incongruity and distortion that London's proximity can nurture. It gives much of the countryside a vulnerable, unsettled look, and encourages the towns to fray at the edges. Hertfordshire is the county where, in the 1920s, a fig tree sprouted out of a tomb in Watford cemetery, and, with a pattern of growth scarcely less remarkable, the first garden cities were created in Letchworth and Welwyn.

But I am making it sound like so much puddingstone, all quirky lumps set in rather bland dough. Although the constant contrast of old and new, urban and rural, sometimes seems like a huge topographical cartoon – as where the Euston–Birmingham Intercity line has to mount a mighty embankment to clear the marshy edges and triple moat of Berkhamsted's Norman castle – it can also be startling enough to make your heart beat faster. Drive into Hemel Hempstead New Town on the A4251 in mid-May, and look at the golden blaze of Boxmoor's buttercup meadows wedged between road and railway. Or out of Baldock on a winter's afternoon, up the graciously broad medieval market street, east into the Icknield Way, and past the Victorian maltings on your left, to find yourself, suddenly and unexpectedly, in a vast East Anglian vista of limitless chalky fields, shining as the low sun is reflected off flints and furrows.

This point is one of the gateways through Hertfordshire's chief internal boundary, between the light, chalky soils of the north and east, and the heavier clays of the south and west. The arable fields that stretch for miles around Royston and Buntingford and into Cambridgeshire and Essex, with scarcely a hedge or bank between them, are the latest developments in a pattern of agriculture that was set by neolithic farmers. Since the forest was easier to clear on the light soils than on the clay, this is where most of the major early settlements clustered and grew. By Domesday the pattern was fixed: 'woodlands with swine' are concentrated in the west and 'ploughteams' in the north and east. If the woodland settlements meant a pastoral economy with a multitude of scattered, self-sufficient smallholdings, the cornlands were the strongholds of the open field system and of highly organised and cooperative nucleated villages. These, sadly, were all too vulnerable to human disease and crop failure, and to the bureaucratic 'improvements' of Parliamentary Enclosure during the eighteenth and nineteenth centuries. The rationalised landscape of rectangular fields and dead straight roads that resulted led inevitably to the huge, hedgeless prairies and similarly huge machines that are the current fashion in arable organisation.

As a landscape it is too airy to be oppressive, but I find it lonely as well as featureless, and full of melancholy echoes. This is not the first time these now very open fields have been drained of people. The region is littered with the sites of deserted medieval villages, abandoned during prolonged periods of bad harvest or plague. On an inside wall of the great tower of St Mary's Church in Ashwell (where the open field system survived into the twentieth century) an anonymous reporter has scratched a bleak graffito about the march of the Black Death. It is as chilling a cry out of the past as I have ever read: '1350, wretched, wild, distracted. The dregs of the mob alone survive to tell the tale. At the end of the second [outbreak of plague] was a mighty wind. St Maurus thunders in all the world.'

Villages were also commonly deserted or rearranged because of the whims of 'improving' landowners, and an outlandish example of this is Ayot St Lawrence, probably Hertfordshire's best-known village because of its association with Bernard Shaw. In 1778 Sir Lionel Lyte, director of the Bank of England, London tobacconist and local squire, decided to pull down the village's modest medieval church and build something more in keeping with the spirit of the age. The Bishop stopped him before he had finished demolishing old St Lawrence, but Lyte continued with his other plans and as a result there now stands on the edge of this tiny village a large and stunning Palladian Temple. It was – and is – a working folly, used for worship, though the unfortunate villagers had to make a wide detour, approaching the building from the back and entering by a side door so as not to spoil the view from the House.

Shaw himself regarded it as a monstrosity, though his own piece of early twentieth-century Det. ('Shaw's Corner') is hardly an architectural jewel. GBS's somewhat churlish tastes, however, received their comeuppance at the hands of Hertfordshire's *genius loci*. It is a bizarre story. In 1931 Shaw began an acrimonious correspondence with Islington Council over their refuse tip at Wheathampstead, which is just one mile, as the wind blows, from Ayot. Shaw quoted Exodus on plagues of flies, and compared the smoking tip to the volcano of Stromboli. The council denied his charges. The tip, meanwhile, apparently favouring Judges 14 ('out of the strong came forth sweetness') as its text, was taking matters into its own hands, and the following year an apple tree of prolific blossom and unknown pedigree grew out of Islington's rubbish. In 1936 it produced one single, gigantic fruit weighing a pound and a half, which Shaw's cook tricked him into eating in a stew. After the war, grafts from this wilding were grown successfully on a commercial scale, and are still sometimes known as Shaw's Pippin.

Ayot, strictly, is over the Hitchin–Hertford line and in the county's western woodland zone. This is my own patch of Herts, especially where the claylands merge with the Chilterns in the extreme west. I find it a very agreeable countryside, compact and manageable but always surprising. It is a landscape of dips and folds, ponds and Ends, and straggling commons that have probably never been enclosed since they were first grazed in the Iron Age. Above all there are the woods. Too many have become uniform smudges of conifer for my taste, but there aren't many high places where you can't stand amongst trees and look at a continuous line of woodland on the next scarp. In autumn they are as colourful as the woodlands of the Weald. Beech is both wild and planted, but there are cherry, field maple and hornbeam in abundance too, mottling the beech's rusts and coppers with crimson, orange and lemon in autumn.

One of the most striking woods – and by now one of the most familiar in Britain – is the beech hanger that sweeps down the hill behind the much-filmed village of Aldbury, with its commuters' cottages clustered round pond and green and stocks. There is also a mansion called Stocks in the village, where the Playboy Club's Bunny Girls used to be trained. It isn't, I should hastily add, named after the local bondage instrument, but after the old word for an area of stumps, or cleared woodland. And this, really, is the key to the landscape of West Herts. It was cleared and enclosed by individual effort direct from the forest. Hence the tangle of narrow, banked lanes and paths joining isolated farmhouses, the greens that served as night-time refuges for stock or as grazing stations along droveways, and the continuously changing mosaic of wood and clearing.

It was this personalised mixture that so moved Cobbett when he rode between Redbourn and Hemel Hempstead in 1822: ' . . . the sort of corn, the sort of underwood and timber, the shape and size of the fields, the height of the hedgerows, the height of the trees, all continually varying. Talk of *pleasure-grounds* indeed! What that man ever invented, under the name of pleasure-grounds, can equal these fields in Hertfordshire?' So close were these do-it-yourself landscapes to the ideal of pastoral wilderness that when Capability Brown came to create 'landskip' parks at Ashridge, Beechwood, Digswell, Moor Park and Youngsbury, he remarked of one of them, 'Nature has done so much, little was wanting, but enlarging the River.'

I suspect both Brown and Cobbett would be shocked at the degree to which the variety that so impressed them has been levelled down. Yet a streak of wildness still plays across these western frontier lands. At the beginning of the century much of this western protuberance of Herts was owned by the Rothschilds. They bought Tring Park in 1786, and many of the villages round about are graced by the distinctive gabled cottages they built for their workers. But the Rothschilds were eccentric explorers and animal collectors as well as farmers and financiers. One was famous for riding about Tring in a cart drawn by zebras, and dotting the Park with enclosures full of exotic animals. But the enclosures weren't quite secure enough. Rothschild's edible dormouse, the glis-glis, now spends the winters snoozing in local lofts, and the summers munching the tops off beech saplings. Rothschild's giant catfish, introduced from central Europe, still haunt the depths of Tring Reservoirs, which, with true Herts contrariness, were the first wholly man-made lakes to be declared a National Nature Reserve.

Even the capital of the region, the elegant cathedral city of St Albans, has pagan leanings. St Albans was founded in AD 950 by the abbot Wulsin, on the site of the Roman town of Verulamium. But before that the area was a stronghold of a tribe of Belgic Celts known as the Catuvellauni. They lived in Prae Wood, about a mile west of the present city, and by all accounts were wealthy and artistic, and pioneers of benign alternative technologies. They fought off the Roman chariots with an awesome (and still surviving) system of 40-foot-deep ditches, but were finally beaten in 54 BC. It's encouraging to see that their spiritual ancestors have been gaining ground recently against the vestiges of Roman authoritarianism. 'Snorbens', as the new Herts Celts call their city, quite properly remembering their roots are pre-Christian, is a bright and innovative community, full of peace groups, poets, live-music pubs and all manner of modern friends of the earth. This was the birthplace of the wood-burning stove revival and the Campaign for Real Ale, but it is saved from being too folksily precious by the best Chinese and Indian take-aways in the area. It even has a thoroughgoing Catuvellaunian in the shape of Ginger Mills, the wildman of St Albans, who lives in a van at the edge of the city and amazes the earnest brass-rubbing tourists throughout the summer. My friend Jeff Cloves wrote a broadsheet poem about 'this spangled aboriginal stomping among the brittle relics of Centurions and Abbots', and says: 'Ginge, like the true artist he is, was buying copies from me at a tanner and selling them for two bob.'

This area of Herts seems always to have been environmentally conscious, and it was an upsurge of concern amongst the urban middle class that led to the saving of much of the commonland in the west of the county, typified by the famous estates of Ashridge (now owned by the National Trust). By the middle of the nineteenth century Parliamentary Enclosure had put paid to many commons at Watford, Bushey, Barnet, and Wigginton, but it was becoming clear that the remainder had a vital role to play as places for the recreation of the new urban multitudes. So when Lord Brownlow rather dubiously fenced off 400 acres of Berkhamsted Common it was not so much the dispossessed graziers who fought back as the new commuters, led by Augustus Smith, Lord of the Isles of Scilly. In March 1866 he imported a gang of 130 London navvies, who marched up from the station and tore down the three miles of iron railings. There followed a great open-air celebration by the townspeople, a fifteen-verse ballad in *Punch*, a lawsuit for damages by Brownlow, and an immediate and successful countersuit for illegal enclosure by Smith. It was a famous and decisive victory and it subsequently became increasingly difficult to enclose commons near towns. Hertfordshire has 186 registered commons and village greens, of enormous variety. Berkhamsted Common, with its ancient pollard beeches and sweeps of birch and gorse, is one of the largest in the Home Counties. Chipperfield has a cricket pitch set in a holly wood. Roughdown and Sheethanger Commons, at Hemel Hempstead, are on an outcrop of chalk, and support not just a roller-coaster of a golf course, but a flock of Soay sheep, which graze amongst wild orchids within sight of the John Dickinson paper factory.

So many of Hertfordshire's commons have courses that golf, with its suburban social codes and skills, might be reckoned the county sport – were it not for the extraordinary, burgeoning popularity of horse-riding. In many of the wealthier areas, round Flaunden, Bovingdon and Little Gaddesden, for instance, it's believed that the population of ponies now exceeds that of people. Along with them has come a new (and not always welcome) landscape of oil-barrel jumps and bare, fenced fields around the village perimeters.

But all these developments are a kind of apotheosis of the Hertfordshire paradox. A split-level house amongst the trees near a fairway, a pony and a paddock for the children, a good motorway link with London – this, for an increasing number of people, is the recipe for the Good Life.

It had all been anticipated, of course. In the late eighteenth and early nineteenth centuries *nouveau riche* industrialists and merchants chose Hertfordshire as a convenient retreat from the City. And by 1848, what is now the Lea Valley Park was already a recreation area for the metropolis. One guidebook (to Rye House, in the Valley) commented that 'so numerous have been the visitors to this pleasant place, that the Directors of the Great Eastern Railway Company have erected a station within a few yards of the spot'. The railway companies bowed gratefully to the growing popularity of the county, began buying development land along their extending lines, and by 1920 were set to create the first generation of commuters. 'The song of the nightingales for which the neighbourhood is renowned...' ran a Metropolitan Railway Company advert in 1920, 'the network of translucent rivers traversing the peaceful valley render Rickmansworth a Mecca to the city man pining for the country and pure air.'

Ebenezer Howard's garden cities at Letchworth and Welwyn were based on the same dream, and if they seem unexceptional now, it is partly because their curving, tree-lined roads and wide verges have become routine features of up-market suburban development; and partly because they gave birth in their turn to the feckless and artificially grafted new towns at Hemel Hempstead, Hatfield and Stevenage. At their worst, these are as shabby and heartless as inner-city tower blocks, a cheapskate New Jerusalem to have offered London's overspill. But at their best they can have moments of unexpected charm, and are the one area where you may finally pin down Hertfordshire's amorphous county spirit. E. M. Forster called the county 'England meditative'. In modern jargon I suppose we might say that it was 'soft' – low on definition, open to impression. So you can move about in these fringelands, neither town nor country, and invent a personal county identity as you go. You might hear medieval carols ringing around a pedestrian precinct; or watch a deer scuttle out of a villa garden in Sunnyside Avenue. This is the animal that gave the county its name, after all, though now, of course, it's not the royal red beast, but the diminutive Asian muntjac that has spread from Knebworth, where they have a rock-music festival next to the deer park.

Damp Humours (1974)

Otmoor is an area of rough, wet pastureland just east of Oxford and has a small claim to fame in that its chequered network of dykes is believed to have given Lewis Carroll the idea for the chessboard scene in *Through the Looking-Glass*. I must admit that my first glimpse of this boggy plain suggested something much less orderly – a semi-wasteland, ragged and unfinished.

I was in rural conference with some publishing colleagues at the time – an indulgence we allowed ourselves every summer. We always called it our 'retreat'; but this was the first time our hotel had actually once been a priory. Out on the edge of this lonely moor, embattled with ancient trees and walled gardens, it seemed an ideal spot for a spell of the contemplative life.

But it was mid-June, and blazing hot. Even when we were forced out into the garden, the spotted flycatchers flicking about our tables were just as tantalisingly soporific as the lime-shaded lawn had looked through the lounge window. What a way to spend a summer afternoon!

After dinner, in the spare hour we had before the late-night session began, I'd had enough, and trudged off to these 4 square miles of marshland which looked so invitingly odd on the map, stuck out there in the shires.

I couldn't have picked a better time for my first visit to Otmoor. The dusk made its outlines obscure and slightly sinister. The fields, such as I could see of them in the gloom, bristled with sedges and rushes. There were tufts of bramble and osier, rattling with the interminable reelings of grasshopper warblers. The trees were short and sparse, a few craggy willows and decaying elms in scattered belts along the field edges. Bulky and hunched silhouettes that they were in this failing light, they seemed on the point of collapsing under their own weight into the ground. One, close to me, actually had, and on it a little owl was bobbing, eyes glaring into the tussocks. Minutes before I had to dash back for that last session it flew down into the grass for a kill.

I walked out on to the moor every early morning for the rest of our stay, along hedges that were brimming with singing blackcaps and garden warblers. Once I heard a few bars from a nightingale. And I came to grips with Otmoor's basic humour: its immutable, inescapable wetness. I went into breakfast every morning drenched to the knees.

Otmoor did not seem as brooding on those early-morning walks as it had during that first twilight visit; nor has it on the occasions I have been back since. There is only a hint now of the forbidding presence the 'great swamp' must have possessed when they rang a bell every winter's evening from the tower of St Mary's in Charlton to guide benighted travellers across the waste. Many of the fenny fields have been enclosed and drained, and the duck which used to haunt the floodwater in thousands during the winter are now more often counted in dozens. In some ways Otmoor is no more than a distillation of the surrounding landscape, an Oxfordshire pasture taken to its limits. The dykes are deeper, the willows more stunted, the grass coarser, the horizon more uncompromisingly flat.

Yet the 'damp vapours' which the inhabitants used to blame for their continuous debility aren't that easily exorcised. Otmoor lies in a bowl formed by 450 feet of impenetrable clay, and the water is ineradicable, turning every untended corner and undredged dyke into a lush tangle of rushes and teasel. Leland, visiting the site of yet another Otmoor priory in the sixteenth century (the medieval Abbey of Oddington, which the rheumatic monks vacated after a few months), described it as 'more fitted for an ark than a monastery'.

And Otmoor's 'seven towns' still circle the moor warily, like shoreline villages on an inland sea. They seem to face away from the waste. Walk 100 yards down any of the tracks that lead from them into the moor and they have vanished from sight.

That any of Otmoor's character survives is the result of the doggedness of its inhabitants, who for centuries have been battling against absentee landowners, road builders, and water companies, who have all cast covetous eyes on its rich and empty acres. In the eleventh century Otmoor was the common pasture of all the surrounding villages, and many cottagers made quite adequate incomes by putting out geese. The old winding dykes and tracks lined with pollard willows that are now all that remains of the moor in many parts, were set down by these anonymous commoners. But in the early nineteenth century one of the largest landlords, the Duke of Marlborough, successfully petitioned for a Parliamentary Enclosure Award for almost the entire moor, including schemes for extensive drainage and fencing. It was one of the most unjust enactments of this sorry episode in English agricultural history, and the cottagers and smaller commoners found either that they could not establish their ancient rights by law and so received no allotments in compensation, or, having received an allotment, could not meet the enormous legal and fencing costs.

In September 1829 there was a mass uprising against the enclosure. More than a thousand people marched round the seven-mile boundary of the moor, tearing down all the fences. The Yeomanry arrived and the Riot Act was read, but the commoners refused to disperse. Forty-four of them were arrested and sent off to Oxford jail. In Oxford it happened to be the day of the St Giles Fair, and there a great crowd attacked the troops and rescued the prisoners. Back on the moor itself, the cattle were turned out to graze in common again.

But though the commoners fought on, both in law and in the fields, for another decade, the Enclosure was eventually imposed by force. And ironically, to round off this sad story of armed occupation, Otmoor has recently been used as a bombing range, 'a marked advance', as W. G. Hoskins drily observed, 'over the simple common grazing of the Dark Ages'.

I last visited Otmoor with a friend one gloomy February morning. We saw more cattle than birds, but the old swamp was lurking behind the electric fence. It trapped our car as we were parking, a small levy for two centuries of abuse. As my friend remarked as she shook yet another ball of sodden clay off her boots, it did put new meaning into the phrase 'bound to the soil'.

The New Forest (1979)

This year [1979] the New Forest celebrates what is believed to be its nine hundredth birthday. I have to put it like that as no one is sure exactly when William the Conqueror annexed this considerable tract of southern England as a hunting estate. More than 500 square miles of woodland, heath and bog may have been involved, yet not a single document exists concerning the exact date or extent of afforestation. It's mentioned in Domesday, so presumably was well established by 1086; but the entry ('*in Nova Foresta et circa eam*') is notorious for its complexity and ambiguity, and it still leaves great doubts about where, precisely, the forest boundaries were, which villages were put under forest law, and what restrictions these laws put upon agriculture. This much later it is possible to be rather more certain about a few matters – for instance, that the Forest has shrunk to 145 square miles, 105 of which are in 'public' or Crown ownership. But beyond that the old familiar muddles begin to appear. The geology of south-west Hampshire and the tenacity of its inhabitants have repeatedly confounded the ambitions of planners, land-grabbers, despots, agricultural improvers, tidiers, enclosers and developers of every complexion. As a result, the New Forest survives as a testament to the virtues and viability of the common use of land and as almost the only remaining stretch of lowland Britain where there is still the illusion of an ancient wilderness. It is also a unique remnant of Norman England, and if William – whose first monumental act of appropriation ironically helped make all later attempts unsuccessful – were to return, he would probably be able to find his way about without much difficulty.

My first encounter with the New Forest was on a camping holiday when I was about fifteen. It seemed to me then an awesome and hostile place, pitted with bogs, blanketed with scorching airs, wet and hot in ways that had more to do with imagined jungles than old England. Later, when I became more familiar with it, I began to appreciate its extraordinary variety of textures, and how these were reflections of the way the Forest had been seen and used by others. I remember seeing my first red deer here and, one autumn, the herds of pigs that are let out to forage when there is a good acorn crop, in the exercise of a right that still has only the old Norman word 'pannage' to describe it. I doubt if there is another place in England where the King's beasts and the com- moners' still run together in the woods. It is midsummer dusks that I relish the most: the bog myrtle that spices the air in every damp valley, and the sweeter scent of lesser butterfly orchids on the grassy plains by Set Thorns; and the hot evenings when nightjars loll about on the dusty tracks through the heather, flitting always just a few yards ahead of you. Sometimes, if it is early enough in the summer, you may glimpse their breathtaking courtship displays, in which they skim and float over the surface of the heather, clapping their wings above their backs.

And at all times and seasons, there is that sense of a quiet tension between the wood and the heath: the stands of great beeches, now nearing their maturity, and the new, self-sown thickets of holly, birch and oak springing up on the heaths; yet the ponies and cattle staking their territory too, eating the woods back. In valleys like those near Berry Wood and Matley Bog the scene is uncannily like Maurice Wilson's reconstructions of Stone Age landscapes; only the animals have changed.

These are very partial images of the New Forest, the view of a casual visitor. It is easy to forget that as well as being a national treasure, it is also the working, common pasture of hundreds of local smallholders. Peter Tate is a local (though not a grazier) and his pleasantly discursive book *The New Forest: 900 Years After* covers many less usual, more parochial aspects. He is especially good on the Forest's tough little ponies, which are easy to look on as nothing more than attractive ornaments or schoolgirls' playthings, rather than as vital components of the whole Forest ecosystem. They have been here since 1208 and play a fundamental role in keeping the heaths and plains open. It is sad to read of the numbers being shipped for their meat to Belgium (where their unborn foals are regarded as a delicacy) and that they and the Forest alike may be suffering from overstocking. I can forgive Peter Tate many of his rather breathless journalistic excesses for the sake of his pleas for what he calls the Forest's 'little lawn-mowers'.

The ponies appear many times in the book. They stray on to the village cricket pitches, and PSP (ponies stopped play) is a recognised abbreviation in Forest scorebooks. They used to mingle, and no doubt breed, with the gypsies' horses, when the New Forest was a stronghold of the 'lost tribe' and a Romany was respected as a kind of honorary commoner. The best-known chronicler of local gypsy life (and probably half Romany herself) was Juliette de Bairacli Levy, who had her own unique vision of the Forest. Peter Tate quotes her description of a bizarre swim in a flooded pond: 'The entire base . . . being grass, it is possible, when the rains have given the water sufficient depth, to swim there slowly and gaze down upon flowers like mer-things shining at the bottom.'

There are so many New Forests, so many harvests taken from them. There are arboreta, working gravel pits, golf courses and a model-aircraft flying area. It is the intricate system of mutual checks and balances between the multitude of different users of the Forest that has helped it survive against all the odds. For nine centuries the resolute (some would say stubborn) defence of their rights by all interested parties – and, indeed, by the soil itself, which is reckoned to be almost the poorest in Europe – has prevented any single faction gaining absolute control. Various kings tried to enclose the open heath and establish timber plantations, but were repeatedly blocked by the commoners, who succeeded in keeping the bulk of their grazing land open. Today it is the commoners who wish to improve the productivity of the heaths (especially the undrained boggy ones) and who are being restrained by conservationists who have the interest of marsh gentians and smooth snakes at heart. Nobody is completely satisfied, but then no one is ignored either.

The worst threat the Forest has ever faced resulted, typically, in an even stronger network of safeguards. In the late 1960s the Forestry Commission, which had become the Crown's executors in the Forest in 1923, drew up a plan for 'phasing out' the broadleaf trees of the 'Ancient and Ornamental Woodlands' and replacing them with quick-growing conifers. In 1970, after a nerveless piece of espionage, a group of local environmentalists exposed the Commission's plan. There was a national outcry, which led the Minister of Agriculture to draw up a mandate whose major objectives were that: 'The New Forest is to be regarded as a national heritage and priority given to the conservation of its traditional character . . . The Ancient and Ornamental Woodlands are to be conserved without regard to timber production objectives.' The affair played an important role in the revision of Forestry Commission policy nationally, and led to a new strategy for controlling tourist use of the Forest. It was a typical piece of Forest balancing, a way of safeguarding the 'national heritage' at the same time as reminding the nation that people and animals had a job of work to do here.

The long evolution of the New Forest has never had the orderliness and sense of direction beloved by modern planners. It has been quarrelsome, compromised and laboriously slow. In fact, the jostling for position and 'demonstration of presence' by New Foresters is like nothing so much as the way animals sort out their territorial claims over a stretch of land – which is perhaps the most appropriate style for the custodians of such an anciently wild habitat. In the future more conventional, so-called 'rational' planning is probably inevitable, given the increasing pressures on the Forest. But the authorities would do well to remember that it was not planning but a kind of organic evolution that was responsible for the Forest's variety, and probably the chief reason why it has survived. For it is, when you think about it, a complete anomaly: besieged by Southampton's expanding petrochemical complexes to the east, by Bournemouth's ribbon development to the south, by the Ministry of Defence to the north-west, it remains the largest and most luxuriant semi-natural landscape in north-western Europe. Despite the dubious airs surrounding it, its trees carry a collection of lichens (exceptionally sensitive to atmospheric pollution) unrivalled in southern Britain. It has demonstrated that even under conditions of quite intense grazing, native woodlands will regenerate, provided they have enough room; and that when there is room, it is possible to combine public access with the experience of solitude. Millions of people visit the Forest every year, yet it's still possible to walk for a whole day and not see another soul.

Many small faults could be found with the management of the Forest, and its future immunity from oil or mineral extraction is by no means secure. But for the moment it remains perhaps the finest working example of an alternative route to efficient resource use, where diversity rather than size of output is the goal. It might, of course, be possible to drench the whole area with fertilisers, clear the trees and plant out carrots. (Indeed, one of the first agribusinessmen, Arthur Young, wanted to do just that.) But it would be a costly and wasteful fate for a stretch of land that grows so many other things with scarcely any input at all. It may be hard to put a price on the multitude of products of the Forest cooperative, but they make an impressive list: 18,000 acres of timber, and nearly 10,000 more of superb ancient trees; 5,000 head of stock; 1,000,000 'camper-nights' a year; cicadas, wild gladioli, free-range pigs, a gypsy floating in a pond . . .

A Tide in the Affairs (1981)

I was nearly eighteen before I succeeded in getting as far north as the Norfolk coast. One summer a friend whose father had a converted lifeboat moored at Blakeney invited a group of us to spend a few days there. We went up in his Land Rover, eight of us, scrabbling about in the back like over-excited puppies. For all of us, East Anglia was something of an unknown quantity. It had a reputation as a bit of an outback, on the way to nowhere, and as its prospects began to unfold before us north of Newmarket, it looked like a very strange country indeed. American bomber bases glinted ominously in distant heaths. Asparagus grew in sandy fields. The roads were lined with stunted pine windbreaks, unlike any hedges I had ever seen. Then, further on, there were no margins at all, and the great washes of sugar beet and barley broke abruptly against the flint walls of medieval churches. When we swung into the long straight reach of the Icknield Way, north of Brandon, Justin, our driver and host, sensing our excitement but also aware of the responsibility of having such a gathering of greenhorns in his charge, hunched down towards the dashboard and showed us how he could change into four-wheel drive with his foot.

We saw more kicking out – and the same mixture of nonchalance and authority – that evening in a Blakeney pub. One of the regulars was Crow, a ruddy-faced village elder, yarner and Jack-of-all-trades, whom we came to adulate in a rather silly way as a local 'character'. He, of course, made merciless fun of us by acting out the role for all his worth. That night he showed us a natty trick he had with the bar skittles. He would aim the ball somewhere between the door-knob and the photograph of the pre-war lifeboat crew that hung on the wall, and on the backswing give it a flick with his foot that made it swoop round and knock every skittle flat. Crow was in his late fifties then, the same age as most of the lifeboatmen in the photo. The picture had been taken after a momentous rescue in which conditions had been so terrible that the men's hands had been frozen solid to the oars. Norfolk, that evening, looked like a place where one might have to flex all manner of undiscovered muscles.

Yet even on those first visits the place sounded old chords. It was the first time I had gone tribal since I was a child in the early fifties. I was with another gang then and we spent our school holidays in the grounds of a demolished eighteenth-century mansion behind our road. We went out there first thing, built camps up trees and in holes in the ground, churned milk on upturned bicycles, baked potatoes in wood fires, fought off invaders from the council estate on the far side of the park, and then went home for tea. We used it as our common, and always referred to it, rather imperiously, as 'The Field'. Everywhere else, just as airily, was 'Up the Top'. And up the top, in ecstatic daydreaming on the hills to the south of our road, was where I spent most of the remainder of my youth. It was a patch of country that I clung to like a secret code, full of touchstones and private vistas that had to be visited in a precise and rigid sequence. It was right enough for a brooding adolescent, but when Norfolk arrived I was glad to be back with some company again, and with a landscape that seemed to have some of the perennial new-mintedness of those childhood mornings in The Field.

We spent that first Norfolk night, as we were to spend many more in the years to come, crammed into the eccentric cavities of the old lifeboat (which was called, for reasons beyond any fathoming, *Dilemma X*). The lucky few had bunks, the rest of us found what spaces we could under tables and in the wheelhouse. In the morning I wriggled stiffly out of my own cranny near the bilges, found a porthole, and looked out on the sight that has kept me in thrall to this coastline ever since: a high tide swirling in over a mile of saltmarsh and lapping the concrete quay where we were moored. There was not a single point of stillness. Terns hovered above the water and spikes of sea-lavender bent and bounced under the tide-race. Even the mud was alive, and slid out of the receding water with the moist shine of a new-born animal.

Saltmarshes don't fit into our conventional views about landscape. They are neither sea nor dry land. Most of the time they have the comfortably timeless look of old pastureland, yet twice a day they are reshaped by the sea. The men who go out on them to dig for lugworm and mussels also live odd hybrid existences, hunter-gathering in season, odd-jobbing on farms and gardens in the summer. They use the language of land-workers to describe the mudflats, and talk of fields and valleys and ditches; yet they know that no tractor could drag them out if they were caught by tides that come in faster than a person can walk.

The local ferrymen showed their indifference to the shifting contours of Blakeney Channel by bringing in their boats at the lowest possible water, holding the tiller with one hand and rolling a cigarette ('wibbling' they called it) with the other. We were altogether more timid when it came to the sea, and one trip up the spout on *Dilemma* per visit was quite enough. Even then we didn't venture out to the open sea, but to the Pit, a natural haven formed and sheltered by the long shingle spit known as Blakeney Point.

The Point was an enchanted oasis of lagoons and shifting sand-dunes, where seals basked and the air was full of the clamour of oyster-catchers and redshank. Even when rain hung over the mainland this 3-mile-long peninsula often lay under its own mysteriously clear strip of blue sky. It was our Coral Island, and on hot days I can still conjure up the coconut and honey scent of the sea-pinks and tree lupins. (Once or twice, walking over the marshes at nearby Stiffkey, I have seen a true mirage of the Point. It floated high above the horizon, stretched by the heat haze so that its dunes looked like the walls of a Moorish castle.) When the tide went out it left little pools, not more than two or three feet deep, and warm enough to doze in. Occasionally we would see a great flock of terns swirling like ticker-tape above one of these pools, and raining down after the shoal of whitebait that had been stranded there. We never bothered to try and catch fish ourselves, but we grubbed for cockles and cooked bundles of marsh samphire (wrapped in silver foil – we were no purists) over drift-wood fires.

But though we thought sometimes of spending whole days and nights out there, curled up under the dunes, the fantasy of being castaways was never strong enough to keep us from the sociable pleasures of the main-land in the evenings. So when the tide was right we would row back to *Dilemma*, on to the flats on the landward side of the Pit, and then walk to the pub at Morston across a mile of glassy mud and rickety plank bridges, with black mud squirting between our toes. It was a hilarious, slithery journey even in the daylight, and how we used to make it back after closing-time I do not know. Justin, never one to shirk his captain's responsibilities, wouldn't allow us to use torches in case we dropped them and fell away ourselves with night blindness (some of the creeks under those bridges were 10 feet deep). So if there was no moon the only light was the phosphorescence that rippled about our feet as we splashed into the shallow water. Sometimes we could see our last footprints glowing for a brief instant in the damp sand behind us, as long-lived a trace as anyone leaves here. I learned much later that it was partly these marsh-lights that Justin thought had given samphire, the plant which grew in these muds, its name. Never having had a reason to see the word written, he thought it was 'sand-fire'.

In wintertime the Point was too wild and wind-torn for our tastes, but we still haunted the marshes north of Morston, and took long, tacking walks along the sea-walls. At New Year the sky here is often the purest, sharpest blue, and is etched with vast flights of wintering birds – wild geese, wigeon, flocks of waders swirling like smoke over the distant slack water with their pale underwings flashing in the sun as they turn.

I've never understood those who find marshes desolate places. They can be remorselessly hard, especially in winter, but they are never oppressive. They are too open for that. If you look east or west along these flats you can sometimes see for a dozen miles, up to the edge of the Wash, if you are lucky. The view would swallow you if it were not for the rim of the sea itself. It is a shifting edge, but it puts a comforting limit to things. On the tideline, you know where you are. Stand by it and look due north and there is nothing between you and the Arctic Circle. The North Sea here is as dark as anywhere in Britain, and the locals still often refer to it by its stark ancient name, the German Ocean.

Yet turn round and look inland and you could be in the Chilterns. In the mile or so that lies between the sea and the coast road the marshes gradually assemble themselves. Nearest you are the bare sands and the plastic, shifting muds; then the pastel wash of the first plants, the silver wormwood and lilac sea-lavenders; then the claimed land locked up behind the sea-walls; and finally, backed up against the low swell of the coastal hills, the little villages with their mighty churches, as compact and bright as if they were tucked in a secure inland valley.

It's hard to feel lonely where there is a tide. Whatever else it may be, it is reliable. A tide will come in, always more or less on time, and always, eventually, recede. The signs the spent water leaves on the sand and mudflats are like vanishing footprints. They are soft-edged, fleeting, curiously tidy. Perhaps it is this husbanding by the sea that gives marshy landscapes what affinities they have with more slowly moulded sceneries inland. It is as if a whole round of seasons – or a whole generation of farming – were enacted twice a day.

Every few years the sea breaks in more savagely, but even then the changes are transient. Early in 1976 a great storm breached sea-walls right along the coast and all the shoreline habitats – beaches, sand, mudflats, saltings – were thrown together in a mad jumble. The sea sprayed tongues of shingle far into the marsh and hollowed out muddy pools in the middle of the beach. In many places the rows of sea-blite bushes that grow along the margin between beach and mud were completely buried by shingle. But by August that year their shoots had already started to reappear above the surface. I dug down below one of these new sprigs, down to the old and already decaying parent plants, and saw the new shoots, pallid but indomitable, pushing their way up through more than 2 feet of heavy pebbles.

These harsh conditions demand a measure of adaptability from everything that lives here. Once or twice a year, when high spring tides are boosted by north-easterly winds, the seaward edge of Blakeney floods. In the summer everyone gathers round the quay to see the tide in, and it becomes a kind of coastal village green. The car park attendant's booth bobs free and floats off, the bus stop is moved, and as the water starts lapping the steps of the knitwear store in the High Street, the more adventurous boat-people go shopping in their tenders. This narrow street is steep enough to give a view over the whole quay and out into the Pit, and you can see how the tide drives everything remorselessly before it – spectators, cars, boats and all – like flecks of spindrift on the shore. When Blakeney Channel was wider and the quay used commercially, the cargoes had to be edged down this slope in carts braked by backward-facing horses. Steep land, high water: the influence of the elements of a landscape can be ineluctable. I've watched a bulldozer, clearing up flotsam after one of these flood tides, run gently out of control down the hill and over the edge of the quay. And once, when we were trundling a piano down the street to the pub, it began to move so fast that the wheels glowed hot and hissed in the puddles.

The tribe has broken up now and its members gone their separate ways, and when I come back to this stretch of Norfolk I am usually by myself. But the marsh landscapes are as familiar company as they ever were. I still follow the old route up – past the airfields and squat pines, along the road from Fakenham that edges, maddeningly slowly, towards the coast. Then through the gorse and heather of Salthouse Heath, which lies on a ridge of sandy gravels dumped here by the last ice-sheet. You see the first glint of water, then as you tip sharply down through the narrow strip of arable fields, the marsh suddenly fills the whole horizon, criss-crossed with silver dykes. You feel age and time falling away. Where you stand was the coastline five hundred years ago. What you are looking at now is a sight that has never been seen exactly so before, nor ever will be again.

I drive as fast as I dare to Morston, kick off my shoes and run out over the mud towards that thin blue line that hangs over the tide's edge, and wonder why I have ever left.

Paper Dreams (1981)

During the early seventies I lived part-time in a cottage about five miles from the Suffolk coast. The East Anglian interior proved to be a revelation. Despite the great agricultural changes of the past hundred years the skeleton of its earlier landscapes – an intricate network of boundary banks, green lanes and remote woods – was still largely intact. I soon became a compulsive mapworm. Whenever I was unable to be out east myself, I would browse endlessly over the Ordnance Survey sheets, plotting walks, trying to imagine the shape and character of unknown, unvisited corners, and sometimes just taking a sheer impractical delight in the abstracted patterns on the map.

There were some powerfully evocative patches. The lattice-work of lanes and contour lines around Rattlesden and Poystreet Green reminded me of the bumpy surfaces of a leaded window and I was sure that if I ever saw it first-hand, the landscape would have just the same capricious pattern of light and shade. Further east was the lonely Saints' country, south of Bungay, where thirteen saintly parishes – including eight different South Elmhams – were threaded together by the yellow byroads like a melancholy concrete poem.

I began to understand what had moved Edward Thomas to write the second of his 'Household Poems', just before he left for the Front in 1915. He was teaching map-reading in Essex at the time, and was so entranced by the field and village names on the local Ordnance Survey sheets – 'Wingle Tye and Margaretting Tye, and Skreen, Gooshays, and Cockerells' – that he felt they were the present he would most like to leave his son.

I was just as captivated by the place names of my more northerly corner of East Anglia: Maggotbox and Poppylots, and Mellis, Occold and Rishangles. Why was there another Gretna Green, by a medieval priory just outside Eye? What had happened at High Wrong Corner near Thetford and, not many miles away, induced the normally unsentimental North-folk to honour a patch of damp scrub by a field dyke with the name of Shropham Tuzzy Muzzy?

There are answers, of course, and just occasionally some of this incidental poetry is apt to disappear when you visit places in the flesh. But the sense maps give of being clues to endless layers of historical riddles is their most compelling feature, even when you are looking at quite straightforward information. On the most popular maps, the 1:50,000 series, you can uncover old ridgeways, new footpaths, icehouses and dove-cotes, battlefields, burial mounds, mills and mines, quarries and gorges, where rivers begin and where they can be forded. On larger maps, such as the 1:25,000 series, you can trace the boundaries not just of your own parish but of individual fields, and see whether these are marked by dykes or shelter belts. On the 1:10,000 maps (roughly six inches to a mile) even individual trees are sometimes marked.

As well as placing all these features, maps give them names. And the names have meanings which are related to the place – either as it is, or as it was. Go back a hundred and fifty years (this is the kind of time travel you can do with maps) and you may find the wood that gave a village name the suffix 'holt', or the common pasture that has given a housing estate the incongruous label of 'green'. Sometimes the stories behind the names turn out to be wonderfully convoluted. When the 1803 Enclosure Map for Donnington in Buckinghamshire was being scanned recently it was found to show a streamside plot called Frogcup Meadow. Although there no longer appears to be a parish called Donnington, this is superficially no more or less cryptic than most nineteenth-century field names. But a sharp-witted historical ecologist realised that 'frogcup' could well be what a city surveyor, unused to Bucks dialects, might make of the local name for that rare and beautiful water-meadow flower, the snake's-head fritillary. This has been variously written down as crawcup, crowcup, fro'cup and frockup (and take your pick as to whether this last one means frock-cup or frock-up). But Vale of Aylesbury citizens who could remember where and when the flower grew locally insist that the correct rendering is *frawcup*. This is the local, inverted pronunciation of Ford-cup – the flower that grew most plentifully in the hamlet of Ford. Ford is next to a village now called Dinton, which was presumably Donnington. It is also the site of a meadow in which fritillaries could be found right up until the fifties, when it was ploughed for the first time. The field boundaries and stream courses on the modern OS and 1803 maps match up exactly and show that this plant, which now occurs in only a score of old hayfields in the whole of England, had grown at this one site for at least a hundred and fifty years.

The early nineteenth-century Enclosure Maps and the Tithe Apportion-ment maps that were produced at about the same time are the largest and most meticulous charts that still survive from this period. They were hand-drawn on fabric or parchment, and it was unusual for more than one or two copies to be made. They are sometimes kept in vicarages, but most have now been transferred to various public record offices. I can remember my first glimpse of our local Tithe Map in the Herts Record

Office. It was all of 6 feet long, and you had to view it piece by piece, holding down the unrolled sections with polished stones.

I'm sure this map's size had something to do with its impact. So did its accuracy and neatness. But what touched me most of all was its intimacy. This was no piece of impersonal surveying. One hundred and fifty years ago a man had tramped round my own favourite woods and fields, and in a tidy copperplate hand had marked in their names and shapes and eccentricities in a way that made them instantly recognisable.

The hand-drawn Tithe Maps are a reminder that maps are made by people, at particular moments in history and often for quite particular purposes. For the county of Suffolk, the first comprehensive map was produced by Joseph Hodskinson in 1783. This was fifty years before the OS began introducing more rigorous survey techniques, but the map is very accurate, and its distances are rarely more than three per cent out. It won Hodskinson the praise of the agricultural reformer Arthur Young (who lived near Bury St Edmunds) and a gold medal from the Royal Society for the Encouragement of Arts, Manufacture and Commerce.

The original proposals were first published in 1776, so the whole project took seven years to complete. This is a long while compared with most eighteenth-century maps, and was probably connected with the fact that the surveying and printing had to be paid for by advance subscriptions. The conditions are set out in the 'Proposals', and include an undertaking that on the payment of a one-guinea subscription fee 'The Noblemen's and Gentlemen's Names shall be engraved at their Seats on the Map . . . as well as the Number of Maps they subscribe for'.

And there they are, making collectively what amounts to the first vanity advertisement for some now very familiar stately homes: Earl Cornwallis at West Stow, Richard Savage Lloyd at Hintlesham Hall, the Earl of Bristol at Ickworth, down to Arthur Young himself and the thinly inked garden of one Revd Nicholas Bacon. Heveningham Hall, the seat of William Gerrard Vanneck, looks especially resplendent. The grounds had been landscaped by Capability Brown just the previous year and great attention has been paid to the drawing of the new lakes, islands and carriage drives.

It's no wonder that the large estates are one of Hodskinson's most painstaking and detailed features: putting someone quite literally on the map is one of the most convincing (and rewarding) forms of flattery. The need to attract subscriptions probably also accounts for the conspicuous care which has been taken over the depiction of the county's commons. The last quarter of the eighteenth century was a time when Enclosure by Parliamentary Award was gathering pace across England. But in the eastern counties most of the open arable fields had been enclosed piecemeal in medieval times, and agricultural improvers had to concentrate their attention on appropriating common pastures, heaths, peat-fens and woods. Any map which detailed these areas (and Arthur Young believed there were 100,000 acres of such 'waste' land in Suffolk) would be of the greatest interest to ambitious landlords.

The highlighting of the commons could hardly be called bias. But it's an instance of the way that the social functions of maps can affect their emphases. The fact is that maps show not just what is 'there', but also the outlines of their makers' social and intellectual landscapes. Although they use naturalistic codes ('outdoor' colours, miniaturised windmills and churches, for example), maps are necessarily selective. No map smaller than life size can escape the use of simplification and symbol, or avoid some kind of point of view; and the details that result can fix an edition absolutely in its period.

In the most widely used modern maps (the 1:50,000 series) the outstanding example of highlighting is the roads. In terms of position these are shown as accurately as they ever will be within the limits of surveying techniques. But their width is out of all proportion to their real size. Even minor roads are drawn at a scale that would make them about fifty yards wide. This, of course, is a reflection not just of the geographical importance of modern roads, but of the fact that this is where most of us use maps *from*.

Roads and tracks are a significantly well-drawn feature of the first edition OS, which is not so surprising when you consider the origins of the Ordnance Survey. It was set up in 1791 to provide the British Army with accurate maps of the south coast during a period when French invasion seemed imminent. Its early years coincided with a period of great social and economic upheaval. Agriculture was in a state of revolution, there was bitterness and uprising in the countryside and wholesale migrations to the expanding cities, and the authorities clearly thought it was in their interest to have a clear picture of these unstable territories.

Given their social and political roles, these maps had to be as topically accurate as was practicable. You can consequently learn a good deal about the detailed changes in the landscape by comparing them with modern maps, or with the modern landscape itself. You will, of course, see a great number of roads and buildings that were not there at the beginning of the last century, and even, perhaps, a number of timber plantations. But in the countryside the story has largely been one of loss, and you're more likely to notice what has gone – a demolished farmstead or a drained fen. Long-established features like this often leave some persistent trace in the landscape long after they have vanished, and amongst the most exciting discoveries to be made with old maps is unravelling the origins of these remains. A narrow pool near a stream, for instance, may turn out to be a vanished mill-leat, or the hammer pond of a seventeenth-century furnace. A huge, reversed bank-and-ditch may be the boundary of a medieval deer park.

These remnants have become known as landscape 'ghosts', which nicely suggests the previous existence of something more substantial as well as a mysterious modern presence. In my own parish the best ghosts are botanical – some clumps of wood anemone that survive, stubbornly and quite untypically, along unploughed edges of an arable field and in some grassy road islands nearby. I'd always been mystified by their origins until I saw (on the first edition OS) that they were growing on the site of a wood that had been cleared over fifty years ago.

The 'Tyes' that Edward Thomas rhapsodised over in East Anglia are also a kind of ghost, the residue of small, self-contained settlements on what was once commonland. Typically they are a cluster of houses at the junction of several roads with the tapering, fan-like pattern that tracks form on unfenced land. On the first OS maps you can often see the 'green' that was the Tye's original 'home range'.

Geoffrey Grigson even managed to track down the kiln where the bricks for his Wiltshire house were made. The 1828 OS map showed kilns some five miles away, and on some hard, flat ground near the overgrown clay-pits he was able to find bricks which exactly matched those in his house.

The OS still regards itself as a contemporary service, and its paramount duty as the recording of *useful* information. And this, of course, ensures that future historians will find our maps as valuable as we find those of the last century. Maps are documentary evidence and of no value as historical records unless they accurately reflect the needs and attitudes of the period in which they were made.

To this end the OS works with several consultative committees, repre-senting every kind of user, from casual walkers to government departments and nationalised industries. Their advice helps shape the current codes with which the cartographers work, which decree, for example, how a milestone should be differentiated from a milepost, and which post offices merit having their letter boxes annotated with 'LB'. The consultative committees have recently recommended that the new edition of the 1:50,000 series should carry again those tiny representational trees which show whether a wood is broad-leaved or coniferous. These were taken out to reduce clutter a few years ago, but users have pleaded successfully for them to be put back.

The Ordnance Survey is also guided by the importance of usefulness when it comes to the vexed question of 'correct' place names. Although there are occasional requests that maps should use traditional (which often means archaic) names for places and features, the OS insists that a map's duty is to record common usage. If there is a dispute it normally accepts the word of the landowner or tenant, as the person most likely to determine the currency. But the owner must sign a form (and these are available for public scrutiny) to testify that the name originates with him or her. Although the OS retains the right to have the last word, it makes determined efforts to keep to this policy. There is a story that some of the obscure Gaelic place names in the far north of Scotland, diligently obtained from local citizens and inscribed on the map, are rather less than decent in translation!

True or not, I find this a cheering tribute to the Ordnance Survey's strongly democratic character. Their surveyors aren't alone amongst public servants in having the authority to go where they wish on private land, but they are unusual in using the information they gather for such a public document, which is increasingly a work of art and history as well as geography. I like to think that OS maps reflect the belief that at a fundamental level the surface of the land is a common heritage. Every one of us has the right to consult the National Map, and every one of us, in some small way, is featured on it.

The Tides of March (1982)

I first read about the tidal woods on the Fal estuary in *A Nature Conservation Review*,* a weighty compendium of the 'biological sites of national importance to nature conservation in Britain' not given to travel agents' flights of fancy. But I sensed a rather special excitement in its restrained account of strange natural ceremonials under the Cornish full moon: 'The site is a complex of saltings, salt marsh, carr and . . . fine natural transition to alder-willow woodland still tidal at the equinoxes, a habitat type now almost extinct in Europe . . . 120 species of flowering plants and ferns, many not normally associated with the inter-tidal zone . . . Mature oak trees survive occasional flooding with water showing as much as one-tenth sea water salinity.'

A high tide in a springtime wood: it sounded faintly preposterous, like a cornfield on a mountain top. But then we will persist in glamorising the spring. Against all experience we forget that it's as much a time for a great rearranging of the hemisphere's air and water as it is the season for breaking buds. In Cornwall, especially, spring can be tumultuous. It brings gales which race capriciously up the peninsula from the south-west, hard on the tails of incoming eels and swallows which have crossed whole oceans in the hope of a quiet summer here. Walter White, who walked from London to Land's End in 1854, found the wind all but took over his senses. The gales, he marvelled, 'carried the salt spray ten miles inland, so that it may be tasted on window-panes, and the blades of corn'.

Seven thousand years ago, when most of lowland England was cloaked in trees, sea-lashed woods must have been much commoner. But they would have been urgent, fleeting places. Trees don't take kindly to provinces of hurtling gales and shifting sands. Little clumps would have 'got away' here and there on the highest level of dunes, in pockets of earth caught in cliff faces, or on the more stable banks of silted estuaries; thickets of willow, blackthorn, oak, taking their chances for ten, maybe fifty years. Then there would be a run of winter floods, or a landslip, and the shoreline would be scoured clean again. Today they do not even have these brief chances. If a patch of ground is secure enough to grow trees, even temporarily, it will be worth someone's while to commandeer it for crops or villas.

* Ed. D. A. Ratcliffe, Cambridge University Press, 1977.

Yet you can wind your way inland through the jumble of creeks that fray the edges of the river between Feock and Truro, and every one is fringed with glistening silt right up to the trees. You have to travel north-east along the route of the Fal for ten miles from the estuary mouth before the river is narrow enough to be crossed by a stone bridge. If you look upstream here, between the steeply wooded sides of the valley, you can believe for a moment that you are on an ordinary West Country river. But something is not quite right. Either the woods are too steep or the flood-plain between them is too flat. They meet in an unnaturally sharp boundary, and along it there is a white encrustation on the lower branches of the oaks. Is it lichen, or salt? Follow its line and you can see how the dip between the tilted oakwoods is being steadily taken over by young willows and alders. You have the uneasy feeling that you are too low down, or that the smooth sward of marshland grasses is deceptively, and probably dangerously, high.

If you turn round and face towards the sea, there still isn't much comfort in the prospect. The river broadens out more quickly than the woods and they meet sharply half a mile away. You are in the mouth of a natural bottle that is filling with water. In front of the incoming tide curlews and shelduck are taking flight. You cannot see them, but their lilting calls seem to be coming from the woods, as if these marshland birds had taken to the trees. Do they know something you don't?

I should mention one more thing. The water that trickles thinly out of the woods, broadens into a surge beneath the bridge, then begins to spread like a stain across the estuarine grasses, is the colour of clotted cream.

The mould for this bizarre landscape was set even before the Ice Ages began. That would have been a satisfying time to have been a Cornish-person, with the rest of southern England still languishing under the sea, and forests of wild rhododendron and magnolia growing on the site of modern shrubberies. Between them flowed the fledgling rivers Fal and Helford, well-behaved freshwater streams then, presumably, with quiet banks of reed and water-mint.

Then, about two million years ago, the southern coast of Cornwall subsided, and its river estuaries drowned in the sea. They have been tidal ever since, and woods have had little chance of forming below the high-water mark. Except, that is, on the Fal. This labyrinthine natural drain, gathering most of its water from heavy rains washing through the china-clay beds below Bodmin, and having to funnel through steep-sided valleys on its way to the sea, has swung between flooding and silting as far back as the Middle Ages. But by the beginning of the nineteenth century the silt was certainly winning, and the woods were on the march across the flood-plain. The willows that still flourish there used to be cut to make local crab and lobster pots.

In the middle of the nineteenth century silting was speeded up still further by the china-clay works at St Austell, which were discharging enough sediment to colour the Fal and most of its tributaries white. It is a rich sediment, and since 1878 the valley wood has been able to extend nearly three miles from Tregony to the bridge at Ruan Lanihorne. This is the most truly tidal of the local woods. But every creek and low-lying corner has some trace of this ancient mix of trees and sea. West of Ruan the road corkscrews up through Lamorran Wood, fording a point where brackish water seeps over and under the tarmac. The sea itself lies just a hundred yards into the wood, lapping a bank of Cornish elms and primroses. Then, just past Lamorran, it fills a creek that runs parallel with the road, and changes in colour from kaolin white to livid Amazonian green as you move further inland.

From here on the lanes bury themselves deeper in the woods. You glimpse flashes of yellow behind dry-stone walls, where cultivated daffodils are growing in field patterns scarcely changed since Celtic times. Scarlet-flowered tree rhododendrons, escaped from isolated country houses' gardens, light up the leafless woods as they may have done a million years ago.

You cannot reach every stretch of estuarine wood. At St Michael Penkevil the road ends with great finality at a church on an intricately walled mound, and with every other exit from the hamlet blocked by estate gates. Beyond one of them, so my map said, lay another landscape curiosity: an estuarine deer park. I imagined the animals gazing at the white water like creatures in a Watteau painting. At Philleigh the paths down to Borlase and Pelgerran woods were much too muddy to tramp. Both water and sap, it seemed, were rising. In the village a well-outfitted, white-haired tramp strode out east for summer quarters. A barn owl floated across the lane behind him. And in the churchyard of St Filii de Eglosros they were giving the grass and wild garlic its first mow of the year.

So the next afternoon, the first of spring, I went to the most truly tidal wood, sat on a badger track and waited for the equinoctial high water. There was a cold wind out on the open marsh, but in amongst the twisted oak coppice and heather it was warm and still. In summer I imagine it could be quite stifling. Buzzards floated above the wood, and as the tide began to turn, invisible curlews piped overhead. When it came, the high tide was not quite the dramatic mix of wood and water that I had hoped for. It lapped milkily and rather sedately round the golden saxifrage and yellow flag, but never seemed to *flood* the wood.

But that night I was woken by rain and spray lashing my seafront hotel.

A south-westerly gale had blown up and was driving the tide over St Mawes quay. The highest waves were spraying the second-storey windows. Down at Ruan, it had been a night of devastation. A film of white clay lay over the whole of the valley, and the sea had even reached the lower levels of the oakwood. A windblown tidemark of twine and polystyrene flotsam lay tangled up with the lowest primroses. I had read of another surprise flood-tide in October 1963. The animal inhabitants of the valley had had to improvise a mass escape, with spiders and beetles climbing to the tops of tall plants, bugs hopping across the surface of the water, and voles (pursued by flocks of predatory gulls) swimming for their lives. I thought of them that night fleeing on rafts of detergent bottles. It would have been funny if it was not so tragic.

It rained mercilessly on the drive back, until the sun came out over the Thames at Henley on a meeker kind of spring. Cornwall, as they say, is still a foreign country.

Oxford: City of Greening Spires (1983)

'It is typical of Oxford,' said Charles Ryder to Sebastian on their return from Brideshead, 'to start the new year in autumn.' Typical, too, that the city's oldest monument isn't some august monastic foundation but the pleasantly scruffy stretch of pastureland known as Port Meadow; and that this home of lost causes and high brows should have begun the popularisation of Morris dancing, after it was rediscovered, alive and kicking, amongst the Headington 'Quarry Roughs' whose ancestors had dug out the building stone for the colleges.

Oxford has a hopelessly ambivalent relationship with all things earthy and natural. Famous for a bracing and sceptical intellectual climate, it is also notorious for dank and enervating airs. Its acres of lawn and water generate an almost irresistible aura of perpetual garden-partying, yet you still feel that your attention should be concentrated on higher things, like Gothic cornices or the Logical Positivists. (And 'Is paying attention an action or a state of mind?' is just the sort of question they like to wrangle over.)

When I was 'up', as the apt expression goes, I was so overawed by the headiness of it all that I quite forgot I was a country boy who'd spent most of his youth mooching about the hedges with pockets full of squashed plants and Romantic poetry. My rural roots grew back, I'm glad to say, but surprised me by putting out some strong tendrils towards this beguiling city. Now I'm beginning to believe that Oxford's tolerance of almost any flight of fancy – when by rights it ought to feel prickly and unsettled from so many clashes of class and opinion – has a lot to do with being infiltrated by forms of life vastly older than the crustiest fellow or Bodleian incunabulum.

If you stand on a high point near the outskirts of the city and the sun is bright enough to pick out its honey-coloured stonework, Oxford looks like a collection of so many village churches. The vaunted spires seem to be growing out of a continuous thicket of green, a huge rectory garden. It isn't a mirage. Both city and university are embedded in an ancient, intricate and often ecclesiastical countryside. If your view is from the west, it would be over the ragged flats of Port Meadow, which was well organised as common grazing long before Domesday. The Freemen of Oxford still put out cattle on it, and it is one of the last stretches of grass in lowland England never to have felt the plough.

Another is the group of hayfields tucked alongside the A40 to the north. Pixey and Yarnton Meads are a unique survival of a communal system of land tenure that flourished in the Middle Ages. They are what is known as 'lot-meadows'. The local commoners don't own any particular strip, but simply the right to take a certain proportion of the hay crop. What they literally possess is a share in a number of ancient cherrywood balls inscribed with names like Watery Molly, Perry and Dunn (probably corruptions of medieval family names). Up until a few years ago the balls were still ceremonially drawn by lot to decide who had which strips of hay that summer.

In the thirteenth century the meadows were nominally owned by Godstow Nunnery, whose shell survives in a field near the Trout Inn. In this territory near the city boundaries you soon become aware of the influence of the female church in the Middle Ages. The meadowland in nearby Binsey, for instance, was the property of St Frideswide, an eighth-century princess who is the patron saint of the university. To the east of the city is the imposing bulk of Brasenose Wood, given to the Prioress of Littlemore by Henry III as a source of fuel for the priory. Now it is part of Shotover Country Park, and Oxford City Council manage it with great sensitivity as the kind of coppice-with-standards that the Prioress no doubt ran – and use the cut wood in rustic architecture all over the city.

It was out of – and over – this complex alloy of theology and husbandry that there grew the jumble of cloisters, quadrangles, halls, laboratories, temples to Christ and memorials to Lord Nuffield that together make up *Universitas Oxoniensis*. No wonder that reminders of the old order sometimes shoot back up between the seams. Amongst the ruins of the nunnery at Godstow there grows one of the few surviving English colonies of a curious plant called birthwort. Because its yellow flowers look something like a uterus in shape, birthwort was popular as a gynaecological herb, and was introduced to monastic physic gardens in the twelfth century. (It does indeed speed up labour, and one distinguished Oxford botanist, the late E. F. Warburg, believed that its presence at so many nunneries may have hidden a multitude of little sins!)

Oxford is infused by greenery as well as lapped by it. Plants scale the walls, arch over the alleyways, spring out of the thinnest cracks in the stonework. Sometimes they even force their way through it. In the 1880s a root of the ivy that then covered Magdalen Tower found its way into the college wine cellar, broached the cork in a bottle of port, and drank the lot.

All this lush and promiscuous growth helps soften the edges of a city which is a labyrinth of nooks and crannies. It turns backyards into courtyards, and waste plots into improvised gardens. And what makes so many of these patches doubly exciting is that you only catch sight of them as tantalising flashes: a fellows' garden sparkling through a half-open gate; dark shrubs straining against the railings at the end of a one-way street; something very like a clump of young trees growing out of the *top* of a pollard willow . . . Then your punt floats on, the gate closes, the traffic lights change. In the busiest part of St Aldate's Street, one architect in tune with the spirit of the place has generously designed a courtyard gate with a large port-hole cut out of its middle.

Oxford's alleys and walled lanes are crucial to this sense of a city insinuated, though they had a rather bad image in the past. Thomas Hardy's Jude saw them as an impossibly decrepit framework for 'modern thought' – 'obscure alleys, apparently never trodden now by the foot of man . . . their extinct air being accentuated by the rottenness of the stones'. Max Beerbohm called New College Lane a 'grim ravine', and though I suppose this is topographically accurate, it is precisely the lane's quality as a kind of overground underpass that makes it the most dramatic back-way through the city. Its secret, I suspect, lies in the tall walls not *quite* cutting off the world outside. They are crowned with self-seeded snap-dragons, wallflowers and tiny yew trees, and just above and behind these, the mysterious tops of things: a row of runner beans, a frieze of gargoyles round an invisible quad. A hand appears, picks a bean, and vanishes again. There is one corner in the lane where the angles of the half-hidden roofs and trees seem to break all the rules of perspective. It is like looking at one of those two-dimensional geometric illusions and you begin to appreciate how Lewis Carroll, otherwise a mathematics tutor called C. L. Dodgson, was able to conjure up the quirky world of Alice here.

As well as these stone arteries, there are the waterways. Oxford is surrounded and penetrated by rivers and sits on a bed of impervious clay. It is under siege by water, which at the slightest excuse reclaims its old territories, flooding meadows and lawns alike, and sometimes seeping up through the pavements. When the Cherwell is in full spate, the crush of punts by Magdalen Bridge looks like a scene from Hong Kong harbour. I remember one February day when even the ducks could not swim against the current, and Magdalen gardens were graced by the spectacle of snowdrops flowering underneath the water.

The college gardens are, of course, the pride and glory of green Oxford. There are forty assorted colleges and halls, and probably four times that number of discrete gardens. There are knot gardens, herb gardens, formal French gardens, and all manner of scholarly garden conceits. In New College there used to be a living sundial, with the numbers clipped out of box, and a continuous avenue of trees each with its bottom limbs grafted on to those of its neighbours. In University College there is still one bewitching corner where a solitary bush of deadly nightshade grows against an inscrutably worn stone.

Worcester College is famous for its swans and lily-decked ponds, Wadham for its wildness, St John's for its rockery (into which various Presidents have slipped plants gathered on their Aegean holidays). Trinity has long shaded lawns, much used for croquet and play-reading – though for enterprising employment of grassy space it would be hard to beat the occasion on which a full symphony orchestra, including live cannon, played the 1812 Overture in Christ Church's Tom Quad.

If you wander through the modest gateway of St Edmund Hall, into the little paved courtyard with its pots of bright red geraniums hanging from the walls, you might be forgiven for thinking you had strayed into a discreetly modernised coaching inn. In New College it is more like a castle, with dense herbaceous beds banked up to the massive wall the college shares with the city. The medieval city wall reappears (now rather sadly scoured of wild flowers) as one of the boundaries of Merton College gardens, and along its top runs an avenue of lime trees and a rose-lined lovers' walk. Next to Merton is Corpus Christi, with the most delightfully bizarre garden of all. Corpus has a reputation as something of an ark, having given sanctuary at various times to a vast swarm of bees (which were reputedly faithful to the Professor of Rhetoric's roof until Cromwell dissolved the monarchy), a mascot fox in memory of the college founder Richard Fox, three tame owls, and two tortoises painted with the college colours. And in the front quad, Charles Turnbull's elaborate 1605 sundial is topped off with a pelican. So you may be prepared for the botanical follies that greet you in the surrounding beds, and for a herbaceous border that might contain – to pick just a couple of square yards – sweet peas, sweet corn, pansies, passion flowers, borage, rue and a cabbage. This cheerful greengrocer's mix (which looks, I must stress, wonderfully exuberant and not at all contrary) continues as you move into further quads, past little thickets of catmint, gooseberry, climbing roses and lovingly hoed urban weeds, until you reach a kind of summit near the city wall, where a potting shed and bed of pumpkins look almost directly into the elaborate east window of Christ Church Cathedral's Lady Chapel. It is not really as incongruous as it sounds, and this is the way that plants must have jostled together in monastic gardens, before they were so rigidly separated into the useful and the decorative. (Much like George Eliot's description of her perfect garden, where 'you gathered a moss rose one moment and a bunch of currants the next; you were in a delicious fluctuation between the scent of jasmine and the juice of gooseberries'.)

The most celebrated and serene of all Oxford's gardens is at Magdalen

College, whose emblem, fittingly, is a madonna lily. Magdalen's hundred acres are in a more orthodox style than the conceits of Corpus and New College, and may remind you of the grounds of several stately homes; but no other college has anything quite like its wistaria-draped cloisters and its riverside walks, and especially its deer park amongst the trees.

The deer seem to get tamer by the year and have taken to loitering winsomely near the railing when there are tourists about. Perhaps they have a herd memory of the time when it was a favourite undergraduate prank to intoxicate them with lumps of sugar soaked in port – though I suspect this is a rather better type of snack than they are being fed at present.

As for the long circular walk around Magdalen Meadow, it is so wild and bosky that you may find it hard to believe you are only half a mile from the city centre. But then the college's great tower floats into view between the trees, you notice blue alpine anemones amongst the white native wood aremones and snakeflowers in the grass, and remember where you are. Such gentle and artful deceptions are the essence of Oxford's landscape, and much of their charm is due to the fun they make of labels like 'wild' and 'domesticated'. It would be a brave person indeed who tried such categorisation on the plants in the vicinity of Magdalen Meadow. From the huge trusses of mistletoe that make the poplars look as if they are in mid-winter leaf, down to the meekest creeping periwinkle, they are all growing with wild abandon; but are quite likely to have nipped in here from the Botanic Gardens, just across the High Street.

This, founded in 1621, is the oldest botanic garden in Britain; and being small, decorous and high-walled is the most tranquil of sanctuaries in which to pass a summer's afternoon. But it has a long history of escapes, including the one and only flower to be named after the city, the Oxford ragwort. Linnaeus introduced this European species to the Gardens in the mid-eighteenth century, and its downy seeds appear to have made their breakout sometime during the 1790s. They soon arrived at the station, and appeared to find the wide swath of ground that had been cut out to accommodate the Great Western Railway much like their rocky native terrain. Using the spreading road and rail systems as its own freeways, the footloose ragwort (which had been disparagingly named *Senecio squalidus*) rapidly colonised the rest of England. The Victorian botanist Claridge Druce once wrote about a railway journey he shared with a party of its seeds, which floated into his carriage at Oxford and out again at Tilehurst, 20 miles down the line.

Such is the casual way that many Oxford products spread themselves about, and the ragwort might be considered the city's most apt botanical emblem – were it not now strewn so liberally across the whole of urban

Britain. All manner of plants have been suggested for this honour, especially some of the city's notable trees. The gigantic oak against which Magdalen was built, and which could reputedly shade 3,456 men, fell down with 'a violent rushing noise and a shock felt throughout the College' on the night of 29 June 1789. But the youngish sycamore jutting into the High Street, which the town planner Thomas Sharp called the most important single tree in Europe, is still standing. So – though only just, given the tipsy angles at which their trunks grow – are the ancient mulberry trees with which so many of the colleges have been endowed since the time of James I, and whose fruit still occasionally finds its way into High Table sorbets. Horse chestnuts would also have to be highly listed. Luscious trees spread over many of the alleys, especially the cobbled lane between Brasenose and Exeter Colleges. And Christ Church Meadow would be a bleaker place without its chestnuts now that the great elms in the Broad Walk have gone.

But individual trees, I think, are too mortal and too recently arrived to qualify as Oxford's companion plants. We need proof of a more continuous presence, and of roots in a dimmer past. Godstow's birthwort is just the kind of thing, and by no means the only obstinate floral relic of ancient ecclesiastical habits (heresies are easier to root out than some of these herbs). The snake's-head fritillary, whose mottled purple bell-flowers colour parts of Magdalen Meadow in late April, may be another – although it is popularly supposed to be wild, and has been the most celebrated flower in Oxford poetry. What is odd is that it wasn't recorded here until 1785. It's hardly conceivable that such striking and gregarious blooms weren't noticed if they were already growing here – even allowing for the fact that the Professor of Botany in the late eighteenth century was the somnolent Humphrey Sibthorp, who only gave one lecture in forty years. The most convincing explanation of their origins that I have heard is that they were introduced to the Meadow from genuinely wild colonies in Ducklington in the Windrush valley. The living of the church here was in the patronage of Magdalen College, and it's quite possible that an incumbent (paying an all too rare visit to his parish) took a fancy to the fritillaries and carried a few bulbs back to Oxford.

But my own choice for an emblem would be the greater celandine. It is an unprepossessing plant, rather like a small-flowered yellow poppy, but it grows in almost every corner of the city, at the edges of car parks, on ancient walls, in waste plots and at the foot of exclusive college staircases. Its leaves are also unmistakably carved on the shrine to St Frideswide, which dates from 1289 and now sits in the Lady Chapel at Christ Church. It's an unusual plant to find portrayed on sacred medieval stonework, and its presence here may not be a coincidence.

Greater celandine was anciently introduced to Britain from southern Europe, as a physic herb. The orange latex which can be squeezed from its leaves was used as a caustic, to cauterise warts and – harrowing thought – to clean 'away slimie things that cleave about the ball of the eie'. Now Frideswide, as well as being the patron saint of the university, also happens to be a benefactress of the blind and was canonised chiefly for summoning up a holy well whose water had curative powers for the eyes. (The story would make a wonderful plot for a romantic novel: Frideswide was the daughter of an eighth-century Mercian princess and went into hiding for three years to avoid an arranged marriage. Her luckless suitor subsequently went blind and Frideswide, in an act of contrition, entered holy orders. Then up sprang the well, at Binsey, just downriver from Oxford.)

I like to think that the celandine was carved on her shrine as a pagan tribute to the supposed power of her well. Eyewash, perhaps. But the shrine is worth a look anyway. Its carvings are amongst the finest representational portraits of plants that survive from the thirteenth century, and there are beautiful and precise figures of ivy, columbine, hop, maple, sycamore (the earliest known representation in Britain), jack-in-the-green hawthorn and both species of native oak.

The fabric of Oxford has always been decked up as much by its citizens as by nature itself. All over the city flowers have been carved on stonework and painted on the walls of dining-halls. Gardens have been planted up wherever there is space, from the foot of St Mary's Church, eight centuries old, to the yard of the Turf Tavern with its log-burning brazier.

And no wonder, for there are still tensions in this city which need easing. It is still a place of privilege, and Town and Gown are still wary of each other's territories. As for the cloister-and-quad model – the archetype of civilised pedestrian precincts and housing estates – it has been all but ignored in most of the city's ghastly new developments.

It would be hard to prove the good done by Oxford's greenery, but it helps to provide some reassuring continuity in a city that is forever replacing much of its younger generation. And the parks and rivers are great social levellers, Oxford's commons in a way. A punt on the overgrown reaches of the Cherwell is no place to stand on your dignity, and it is hard to lounge about in flower-draped alleys with anything other than goodwill. Above all, exuberant growth puts pomposity and logic in their place. As Jan Morris, in her incomparable book about the city, writes about the siting of that supreme scientific monument to plants, the Botanic Gardens: 'The designers so arranged things that if you stand with your back to the urn beside the southern wall, and look down the central pathway to the ornamental gate, over the lily pond, through the ceremonial pillars and across the fountain – if you look down this bower of the Age of Reason, Magdalen Tower is *not* framed in the centre of the great gateway.'*

* *Oxford*, Faber & Faber, 1965.

A Dales Diary (1985)

I spent most of the bleakest June in recent memory [1985] on location in the Yorkshire Dales, making a documentary with a team from the BBC's Natural History Unit. The result – *White Rock, Black Water* – is a personal view of limestone country, which delves into geology, botany, history and the human uses of this landscape, both traditional and novel.

What was fascinating was how the business of film-making itself became a kind of model of the new uses that are emerging for rural landscapes. Films are usually offered to their audiences like manna, materialising from unknown sources and invisible hands. In fact, natural history documentary filming is both a kind of rural craft – needing the most intimate knowledge of local material – and a species of tourism, sometimes even voyeurism. For weeks the crew have to live out this awkward, bipartisan role in the closest physical contact with their locations. Like their wild subjects, they have to feed, rest, escape the weather. And, also like their subjects, they do not always enjoy being involved in a film.

This is a diary I kept during those unsettled weeks trying to capture the relationship between what happened in front of and behind the camera. It begins in blissful May sunshine.

30 May
First day's filming. We begin at the top, having climbed up Ingleborough's 2,500 feet for a windswept view of the whole of the western Dales. (The locals call Ingleborough simply 'The Hill', as if there wasn't another one worth a mention.) With hundredweights of gear to carry, the haul has taken us about five hours. On the top, we meet a student from south London who *cycled* up the other side in twenty minutes. We slip him a fiver and film him for our closing sequences, careering about the rocks on his eighteen-gear mountain bike.

We wonder if a film team can find its niche and adapt as easily.

31 May
Heatwave continues. We begin again, this time at rock bottom, and film a fossilised shingle beach that was laid down on an ancient sea's edge just before the limestone. By noon we wouldn't have minded becoming fossilised sun-bathers on it, but the limestone pavements, great cracked slabs of rock scoured flat by the glaciers, are a pretty good beach substitute.

The globe flowers and bird's-eye primroses, weeks behind only a few days ago, are racing into full bloom in the heat.

1 June

We're grateful for the cool of Weathercote Cave, part of the great network of underground chambers eaten out of the limestone by water. Turner painted in here, amazed by the spectacle of a waterfall in a cave, in the sunlight (the roof had fallen in). On his second visit, in 1816, the weather was so appallingly wet that the cave was half full of water, and he had to be content to sketch from the top. But he added a small rainbow in the spray when he came to paint the finished watercolour.

We are luckier. We find a spot near the bottom of the cave, under the fine spray from the falls, where the rainbow would suddenly flip on its side and completely surround you at chest height, like a slipped halo. One other bonus: spotted flycatchers, on this balmy day, swooping down into the roof of the cave and catching midges in the sunbeams.

Later we climb Norber, where a spectacular and sinister range of ancient sandstone rocks was swept up on top of the limestone by the last glacier. Now they perch on worn limestone plinths like the wreckage of a huge megalithic temple. But there are early purple orchids in the grass, curlews keening, and a view that stretches to the Lancashire coast.

We are all frisky from the exhilarating air and work until dusk piecing together the story of Norber – then racing down to the pub, wind- and sun-burnt already, to drink away the sunset among the swifts rocketing around the stone cottages. This is always, in such blissful weather, the best moment of the day, but bought at a price. Most hotels in Yorkshire don't serve food after 8 p.m. So we live off pub snacks and wine-bar nick-nacks.

2 June

A Sunday. We have the morning off and, in the afternoon, film a couple of young drystone-walling champions from Feizor. It is extraordinary, the things that people will do for the BBC: they demolished 20 feet of perfectly good wall just to build it up for us again.

3 June

Still blazing hot. We are working feverishly before the weather breaks, as it surely must, and already have a third of the film in the can. Today it is aerial shots from a helicopter, to show the structure of the limestone country, the pattern of valley meadows and scree and high terraces that we began to glimpse from Ingleborough. Your presenter, neither an adventurous soul nor a fan of privileged high-tech views of the world, is reduced to a state of sullen terror by the prospect of his first vertical trip. But the views are awesome. From above, the limestone is a dazzling white engraving that stretches from horizon to horizon. And it turns out not to be my day to be added to the scree.

Not so, sadly, for the female swallow whose corpse we found on the helicopter landing field (part of a garage forecourt). She had been hawking with her mate over the next-door hay meadows and had not seen the full-length plate glass surrounds of the garage showroom. Her mate kept flying back and settling uncomprehendingly by the body. I wished, for the umpteenth time in my life, that I had the slightest inkling of a bird's view of the world, of what bafflement and grief might mean to a bereaved swallow. Do birds need to mourn or just to forget? In the end the male tried desperately to revive his dead partner by attempting to mate with her. I could bear it no longer and decided to bury her away in the corner of the field.

4 June

This is hard country. The roads are littered with dead sheep and birds. There have been three tragic accidents since we were here: a pot-holer falling into the blackness of Gaping Gill, a walker and dog run down on the road, a child killed in a ravine near Thornton Force waterfall. These things happen when a new population of urban people, desperate for contact with nature, move for the first time into a landscape that is still comparatively wild and teeming with life. It is a culture shock for both sides. I hope that what we film will not hide the sheer rawness of life up here.

This morning we film around the Ingleton Falls, close to where the child was killed. It is a soft, humid day, and everything seems shaped or touched by the presence of water. We film a wood warbler, with its shaking throat and tumbling liquid song, and the sapphire glow of wood forget-me-nots in the flushed hollows. We have a treat at lunchtime – wine cooled in the rushing stream. But the danger – a persistent shadow of slithery rock and dark water – is never far from our consciousness.

5 June

The weather breaks, and for the next three days we are twiddling our thumbs, snatching odd shots of Ingleborough looming out of the mist and drizzle. The chill of the north wind is breathtaking. Twice we are driven back into our cars, even in our full weather gear, to sit gazing at the Yorkshire summer through the windscreen. We marvel that the lapwing chicks, newly hatching in the meadows, seem entirely capable of surviving the cold.

Fortunately, our weekend break begins on the seventh. So we miss a couple of days of frustration.

10 June

We return to learn that there was a blizzard on top of Malham Moor on the 8th, with snowploughs called out. The weather is still unsettled and cool, and we are not sorry to be spending the night down Ingleborough Cave. This is a vast and labyrinthine cavern that was once the drainage channel for most of the water caught by the Hill. Now it is a show cave, open to the public, which is why we must film there at night. It is full of the most extraordinary stalactites, huge, bloated masses of redeposited calcium carbonate looking like bellows, sides of meat, shower curtains – and smaller ones as curly as pigs' tails.

We also find curious signs of life: albino shrimps, washed in with floodwaters, that are now a quite distinct and well-adapted race, fungi on apple cores and ferns growing by the electric light bulbs. For our benefit, the cave has been specially lit by a hyper-efficient team of Leeds sparks (they trundle their gear around in wheelbarrows on the cave floor). The manager of the cave marvels dreamily at how his treasures are transformed by these mega-watts, and is scribbling figures on the back of envelopes. I marvel at how rapidly my claustrophobia is retreating as I am persuaded into nooks and crannies that even glacial meltwaters must have found rather pressurising.

We emerge just before dawn, to a drizzly night, far colder than the cave, and a life-saving bottle of bourbon, brought by Vicky, our production assistant.

11 June

The rest of the week continues cold, dark and drizzly. We can grab only a minute or two of film each day, and for the first time we begin to worry if we will finish on schedule. The frustration begins to exaggerate all the normally trivial and overlooked irritations caused by living and working together so intensively. Even the swifts have vanished, and we each retreat into our private worries and escapes. Richard the cameraman astonishes everyone by his skill – and stamina – at bar-billiards, and I become convinced we are suffering from malnutrition.

15 June

Not a bad morning back on the limestone pavements. It is bewildering, trying to decide what to film. Every crack and hollow is different. Drifts of lily-of-the-valley, globe flowers, ferns, baneberry, bonsaied ash trees, the first few bloody crane's-bill.

We unpack a canny piece of equipment for this sequence – the arm, a contraption for swinging the camera over and into the limestone rocks. Unfortunately, it has arrived without a balance-weight, and wonders of improvisation are done with two rucksacks and a pile of limestone boulders. We wonder if this is a 'damaging operation' under the SSSI regulations. In the afternoon, the weather closes in yet again, and Sue the camera assistant, not one for wasting time or opportunities, wangles her way into hang-gliding with a swarm of local enthusiasts taking advantage of the wind.

16 June

A Sunday. Surely only in Yorkshire would they think of holding a brass-band concert by the side of a waterfall. But it works wonderfully. The great chasm worn out by Hardraw Force is a natural amphitheatre, with astonishing acoustics and, for good measure, a choir of resident jackdaws. Bands have been playing here for more than a century, and there is a huge crowd of good-humoured supporters and friends sprawling among the banks of red campion and wood cranesbill. Bob the sound-man passes his fiftieth different recording of water, and if it all looks on film as good as it sounds and feels, it will be the perfect closing sequence for the film.

18 June

But not for the filming. Today comes the crunch, when we begin to have more film left to shoot than time to shoot it in. The weather forecast is dismal, but it has been infuriatingly misleading for days, and mouthing prayers, we drive up to Moughton Fell. This is a very special place: the ultimate limestone landscape, a vast, high plateau of shattered rock that is not worth filming unless the atmosphere is right.

But for once our luck is in. We become absorbed in this bizarre, invigorating wilderness, with its clattering, rocking stones, its stunted junipers, its dwarf woods growing in cracks, its strange, sharks' teeth cairns – all, this fortunate morning, bathed in a spectral Hebridean light from the racing clouds.

We snatch some lunch at 3.30 p.m., and spot that a patch of brilliant sunlight appears to be hanging over Thornton Force waterfall, scene of a crucial and so far unfinished sequence. But it may be an illusion, and we've only got three precious hours of daylight left. Caroline, our producer, makes a courageous decision, and we speed off towards it.

For miles a vast black cloud teases us, seemingly perched quite maliciously right over Ingleborough. But when we arrive it proves to be over the next-door peak, Whernside, and our Hill and falls are bathed in late afternoon sunshine.

We work feverishly – on top of the waterfall, behind it, in the water, on the upturned slates that sit under the limestone – telling the geological history of the Dales. Five minutes before the sun vanishes behind the hill we finish the shot, and the main bulk of the film.

Fizzing with high spirits and adrenalin, we race down for our first post-shoot drink for a fortnight, and laugh at the appalling cloud still perched, for once, over someone else's hill.

In the meadow beyond the pub garden, the swifts are back, and – flitting low between the setting sun and the buttercups – swallows, dusted with gold.

A Walk Around the Block (1988)

It is becoming hard these days to justify the pleasures of simply 'going for a walk'. In a world of sponsored hikes and mass marathons, strolling smacks of introspection and an unhealthy lack of competitive drive. Ambling about with no badges of purposefulness (shell-suits and dogs are the favourites) you are looked on as a figure of fun or, worse, of danger. Children cross the road as you approach. Long-distance trekkers elbow you aside, a cissified obstacle not worthy of consideration. Even the physical act of walking is now being streamlined by the health industry. Going for a stroll, one of the most civilised of pleasures precisely because it can be indulged in purely for its own sake, is now expected to *do* something, either for you or the world.

Yet in a roundabout and less transcendental way this has always been one of the aims of casual walking. 'Just off to stretch the legs,' we say, meaning, as everybody understands, the less mentionable intention of stretching (or relaxing) the mind. Kim Taplin, in her book *The English Path*, recalls the old Latin proverb *solvitur ambulando*, which roughly translates as 'sort it out by walking'. She points out the various connotations of *solvitur* – finding out, working out, freeing, unknotting: all good strolling agendas. It is the combination of gentle physical activity and close contact with the natural world which seems to do the trick. Even the basic business of navigating, of confronting traffic, weather, pot-holes in the lane, seems to help. It may not always be calming, but it does bring you down to earth.

For Dr Johnson and George Borrow, both great wanderers in their time, making contact with the world took on a quite literal meaning during their walks. Both were dogged by recurrent bouts of depression, and to keep some kind of link with reality used to touch objects – trees especially – on their way. For William Hazlitt, solitary walking was a great aid to contemplation, particularly amongst familiar surroundings. 'I can saunter for hours,' he wrote, 'bending my eye forward, stopping and turning to look back, thinking to strike off into some less trodden path, yet hesitating to quit the one I am on, afraid to snap the brittle threads of memory.' Henry Thoreau also relished 'sauntering', and pondered the possible origins of the word in the phrase *sans terre*, 'without land or a home, which therefore, in the good sense, will mean, having no particular home but equally at home everywhere'. He found that he nearly always sauntered towards the south-west 'where the earth seems more unexhausted and richer'.

These ritual qualities and the sense of marking out a territory are an intrinsic part of strolling. We all have favourite times, occasions and directions for taking a walk, and favourite well-trodden paths, too. Even away from home, a quick turn around the town is always more than just a way of working up an appetite. It is a kind of first-footing, a way of confirming your arrival and getting your bearings. It can also be an act of geographical courtesy, like sampling the local beer, and can give you the same quick savour of a place. In after-dinner constitutionals round hotel grounds I have heard nightingales in Suffolk and found glow-worms in Sussex, edging an ornamental drive. Whenever I go to the Yorkshire Dales in late spring, the village hay meadows on that first evening stroll seem to have a burnished newness, a focus, that later, further-flung tramps can never quite recapture.

But dawdling on foreign territory is when you can look most conspicuously odd and out of place. One Easter in Suffolk, I broke a car journey to take an airing along a footpath that wound invitingly towards a copse in the middle of a barley field. It was an ancient track, banked and ditched, and I rather hoped there might be oxlips in flower in the wood. I left the path, climbed a gate, and sure enough there were. But soon there was also an outraged farmer who had trailed me up the track. I don't think it was my minor act of trespass that had upset him, nor my feeble waving of the Ordnance Survey map as an excuse, so much as the sheer casualness of my arrival. 'You've got a car,' he shouted, 'you could have come to the farm and asked.' It was a sharp reminder of the original purpose of fieldpaths that I haven't forgotten.

You are on surer ground on your home patch, and here the routes as well as the strolling habit can become ritualistic. There are maybe half a dozen walks near my home in the Chilterns that I take regularly, like doses of tonic. One, a mile out and back along a canal towpath, is really a walk of convenience, since it starts just a hundred yards from my door. Another, a short but sinuous tour of a famous wood of gnarled pollards called Frithsden Beeches, is a guaranteed cure for moodiness. Beechwoods are conventionally thought of as places for quiet meditation. Not this one. At all times and seasons it is a turmoil of gale-strewn trunks and fleeting patterns of light and shade.

But I suspect the reasons I am habituated to two other local walks are more complicated. Although one is a half-hour hilltop stroll just a short distance from my home, and the other a two-hour river valley circuit 10 miles away, they have a lot in common. Both are circular routes. Both repeatedly change their perspective, winding in and out of woods and round doglegs, and opening up sudden new views and hidden glades.

I began making the nearer walk when I was a teenager. I was in thrall to birds at the time, and this short lap was a condensed tour of all our best local habitats. For the first few hundred yards it followed a lane, past fields haunted by grey partridges and sometimes a barn owl. Then it struck off left into a thin strip of woodland where the first chiffchaffs usually appeared and where, if you were lucky, you might glimpse red-starts on migration in the spring. Here and there, through gaps in the trees, you could gaze down into the valley of a winterbourne.

Later my weekly (daily, sometimes) trudges round this circuit took on a more intense, contemplative character. I would follow not just the basic route, but my own previous footsteps: along the right-hand side of the lane, hugging close to the dense blackthorn hedge, cutting off the corner by the sentinel beech, turning for home along the field edge, *not* along the footpath just a few feet below. At one point I would always stop and gaze in something close to rapture at the vista that rolled away to the south-west: two miles of hills, copses, chalk scrub and green lanes, with the silver thread of the winterbourne knitting them all together.

In my adolescent years that walk became a bench mark, an arena in which I tested out experiences that seemed important to me. It was a path to take girlfriends along (and, nonsensically, to escape from them). I revised for exams along it, chanting the elements of the Periodic Table in time with my steps. Occasionally, when birdsong was over for the year, I would take a portable radio with me, to listen to the carols from King's College on Christmas Eve, and, in one absurdly romantic gesture, to a broadcast of Beethoven's 'Pastoral' Symphony on a high summer evening – a true promenade concert.

It says something about the character of this walk that it can still cast a healing spell over me, thirty years on. But when I fear that it is too domestic to work, or I want something on a grander scale, I opt for the further walk, down in the valley of the Chess. This is about as far as I would travel for just a stroll, yet, in contrast to my home patch, it has a distinctly southern feel. Bluebells bloom earlier and swallows arrive sooner.

My walk passes through a line of riverside water meadows, sudsy with blossom, where I once saw six cuckoos feeding together. Then it crosses the river, climbs a little and returns along the foot of a beech hanger. The beeches are regularly blown down and with each new gap (and new diversion in the footpaths) there are startling new views of the woodlands on the scarp to the north. They are beech and cherry woods, for the most part, cloaked with white blossom in April, and later ringed by it, when the petals fall and settle round their rims.

There is a flamboyant, southerly feel about the people here, too. It is a popular walk, strewn with picnickers and paraders whenever the weather is fine. One regular plods the circuit in climbing boots, carrying a small dog in his arms. Two others I have never glimpsed, but their polished champagne glasses are hidden high in the cruck of a riverside oak.

Can regular walking round a familiar beat influence one's thinking, become a kind of ingrained memory track that can be replayed at will? It can certainly affect the way one writes. Even a short walk can provide a writer with a ready-made narrative structure just as effectively as a Grand Tour. Yet what is intriguing is how often the *styles* of walking find their way directly into the styles of written accounts. One critic, for example, has suggested that W. H. Hudson's rambling prose 'perfectly echoed the long, slow, unhurried tramping of his feet as he roamed through the gentle southern counties each summer'. Hudson, though, was essentially a tourist, and for me his long-distance ramblings about England echo more with condescension than real curiosity.

Far better, and closer to catching the feel of everyday meandering, is Richard Jefferies, especially when he was producing a mass of effervescent journalism for the new urban audience. The essays in collections such as *Round About a Great Estate* (1880) are addressed directly to his audience: 'If you should happen to be walking . . .' many of them seem to begin. It is quite infectious. The reader is taken by the hand and *led*.

John Clare, by contrast, seems barely to consider his readers at all. He is caught up in the immediacy of the moment, or perhaps the remembered immediacy of his childhood; and his many poems which are based on favourite local walks conjure up the image of a boy darting with barely controllable excitement from one side of the road to the other:

> When jumping time away on old cross berry way
> And eating awes like sugar plumbs ere they had lost the may
> And skipping like a leveret before the peep of day
> On the rolly poly up and down of pleasant Swordy well . . .

There are others. John Cowper Powys' recollection of the 'sunken treasure' of his favourite field-path routes. John Bunyan's gossipy account of the Pilgrim's progress, which mirrors his own wandering about the Bedfordshire fields and up into the Chiltern heights.

The patron poet of strollers, though, is William Cowper. After his first mental breakdown in the 1760s, Cowper went to live with friends in the

Buckinghamshire parish of Olney. Like many before him he tried to keep his melancholy under control by busying himself in active, domestic routines – gardening, walking, looking after his pet hares – and in something close to communion with the physical details of his small universe. 'The very stones in the garden-walls are my intimate acquaintances,' he wrote in a letter of 1783.

All this is reflected in his Olney poems, which pay unfashionably vivid attention to the minute, living detail of the natural world. But it is the structure of his poetry, especially his masterwork, 'The Task', that breaks most graphically with the contemporary taste for carefully constructed landscape descriptions, and which owes most to his habit of walking. Much of 'The Task' is not ordered to any particular design but offers scenes, observation, reflections exactly as they might be encountered on a stroll. Scale and perspective are repeatedly changing, so that one moment a wild flower is in focus, the next a whole cycle of work in a distant field. One passage in 'The Task', where Cowper is playing games with his own shadow, is a perfect evocation of the state of mind of the habitual saunterer. It captures not only the idiosyncratic viewpoint of the stroller, but, with the lightest of wry humour, hints at one danger that may lurk on the path: the possibility that the rhythmic step and familiar route may become so hypnotic that far from escaping yourself, you become utterly absorbed in it:

> Mine [shadow], spindling into longitude immense,
> In spite of gravity and sage remark
> That I myself am but a fleeting shade,
> Provokes me to a smile. With eye askance
> I view the muscular proportion'd limb
> Transform'd to a lean shank. The shapeless pair,
> As they design'd to mock me, at my side
> Take step for step; and, as I near approach
> The cottage, walk along the plaster'd wall,
> Prepost'rous sight! the legs without the man.

A London Safari (1989)

It isn't the obvious setting for an outdoor break nor, for that matter, for nostalgically retracing old footsteps. London's green underground – a network of waste plots, canals, sidings and cemeteries that is permanently in the developers' eyes – can these days be a gauntlet of security company alsatians and unsavoury water. But twenty years ago, heady with Kenneth Allsop's explorations of the wildlife that haunted the last few east London bombsites, I got hooked on the sheer natural exuberance of this 'unofficial countryside', and especially by its infectious sense of incongruity. I once saw a gang of noisy pheasants crowding into a Hackney rubbish tip on the first day of the shooting season, and it seemed to me one of the most cheering things I have ever seen in London.

I took a long tramp around the city in the autumn, to see if some old stamping grounds had survived the new broom of aggressive prosperity. One of the ironies of the building boom is that it is swallowing up these wild corners just as the crucial importance of city green space is being recognised. I planned a roughly circular walk of about thirty miles, chiefly along that vulnerable ring of marginal land where the inner city frays into the residential and industrial belts.

I began in central London, in St James's Park. This is formal landscaping, and about as far from the urban wild as you can get. It is the haunt of bird-watching civil servants and of one of the biggest assortments of semi-tame water birds in the country. But it can still provide a basic lesson in urban ecology. Beyond their adaptations to the physical habitats (stone buildings used as cliffs are a favourite), city plants and animals fit with great panache into the human lifestyles of their chosen niches. In these Westminster pleasure grounds, they are quarrelsome, ingratiating and ostentatious supporters of the virtues of domesticity and the enterprise culture. There were, that day, pigeons and sparrows feeding *inside* one favoured man's parcel of scraps. A bird does what a bird has to do.

Out on the water there were a few wilder birds – great crested grebes, still in their raffish chestnut breeding plumage, and a scatter of late house martins skimming low over the surface. I followed them out into the sedate streets of Belgravia. There is almost nothing wild here. What is tolerated in the parks is most decidedly not acceptable in the residential areas of SW1. But the martins increased in numbers as I got closer to Hyde Park and to their celebrated nesting site on the French embassy.

House martins feed entirely on airborne insects, and they quit central London in the 1880s, when air pollution wiped out their food supply. They began trickling back twenty years ago, and now nest in half a dozen sites within a couple of miles of Trafalgar Square. This communal eyrie, 80 feet or so above Knightsbridge, must be one of the most strangely situated and safe colonies in the country.

I wondered how, amid the welter of residential possibilities in the city, they had lighted upon this well-nigh perfect site. But I have seen them prospecting the consulate and quango buildings in Belgrave Square, and sometimes swarming around the eaves of the Ministry of Defence, and like to think that they have a quick connoisseur's eye for secure properties. Half the country's estate agents now seem to use the bird as their symbol. They could have chosen worse. As I watched them flitting over the traffic to hunt for aphids above Hyde Park's trees, canny, adaptable, tolerant of human company without surrendering a jot of wildness, they seemed an ideal symbol of London's wildlife.

In Notting Hill Gate things began to loosen up. Wild plants here have eased their way back into the street. In Ladbroke Grove, wherever there is room for people to stop and chat, feed the pigeons, spill the shopping, the cracks in the pavement bristle with seedlings of sweet corn, wheat, millet, tomatoes and the occasional mung bean. Up by the jumble of gasworks and railway siding near the Harrow Road, herbaceous thickets shoot out of the gutters, and chimneys as well. How do they get there? Almost all these street flowers are foreign introductions that began as garden or crop plants, which proved to have an immense capacity to survive on their own in disturbed corners of English soil. Buddleia, the butterfly bush, came originally from scree slopes in the lower Himalayas. Michaelmas daisy is from the North American prairies. Both found the granite and grass of the railway system a perfectly good substitute, gained a beachhead, and have never looked back.

Ahead were the cryptic shrubberies of Kensal Green Cemetery: great fox country. I didn't spot one here that day, but one June, passing the cemetery in a slow train, I saw a vixen and three cubs basking on the embankment in the sunshine. Foxes live a largely unmolested but vagrant existence in London, sleeping rough and raiding dustbins rather than hen runs. But it doesn't guarantee them a carefree life. One vet who has done post-mortems on London foxes found that they share the food-based disorders of their unwitting hosts. Up in the prosperous north-west, many had hardening of the arteries; in the south-east, the first signs of rickets.

This basic urban survival tactic of making do was evident as I joined the Grand Union Canal, and set off eastwards. Even where it is bordered

by factories and lies under the swooping shadow of the Westway, the cut
serves as a makeshift river. Moorhens perch on floating tyres. The towpath
is edged with real riverside flowers – marsh woundwort, gipsywort,
angelica, skullcap, and great sheaves of sweet flag, its crinkly leaves
smelling of tangerine. There is orange balsam, too, a North American
plant that was first noted in this country by the philosopher John Stuart
Mill in 1822. Its seeds – hurled into the cut by pods which uncoil like
highly strung banana skins – are, like those of many of its neighbours,
water-borne, which is one reason why these artificial waterscapes are so
rapidly colonised.

It is uncanny how wildlife – plants especially – marks out the city's
social and cultural divisions so accurately. In Regent's Park the water
suddenly becomes as clear as a rural stream. Paddington's rowdy exotics
give way to dappled native shrubberies. There are spikes of purple loose-
strife, with which Millais fastidiously ornamented the edge of the stream
in his painting of Ophelia. Bullfinches, white rumps flashing, darted
between the hawthorns. I spotted a kestrel planing into an ash tree, and
would have spent a while watching it, if I hadn't become aware of a boy's
face peering at me out of the bushes, like a Jack-in-the-green. I've no idea
if he thought he was invisible, but it was one of the day's more intriguing
glimpses of feral behaviour.

By the zoo there were more anomalies – sparrows feeding nervelessly
in bird-of-prey cages, and local gulls wheeling disconsolately round with
exotic ibises in Snowdon's aviary. I ended the first day with the sun going
down over the bistros and craft shops of Camden Lock, sitting on the
edge of the lock and listening to New Age music wafting out of a narrow-
boat, where a New Age Bohemian sat drinking G & T on the deck. The
dark silhouette of a kestrel suddenly sheared out of the sunset and away
over the evening traffic jam in Camden High Street. City kestrels live
furtive, piratical lives, snatching sparrows from roof-tops: a quite different
existence from that of their soaring downland relatives.

Next morning I travelled out to Hackney, missing about three miles of
the circuit. Purists could do this stretch on foot, calling in at the Camley
Street nature reserve; having a peer at the little copse that survives as an
embattled woodland oasis just off Barnsbury Road; or, in winter, watching
those dazzling piebald ducks, smews, on Stoke Newington Reservoir.

At Lea Bridge you join the clutter of wharves, marshalling yards and
small factories that make up industrial London. It also used to be the site
of one of the city's prime bird habitats, a derelict Thames Water filter-
bed, haunt of kingfisher and snipe. Alas, redevelopment had started and
the place had been fenced up. So I took off instead over what was once
Hackney Marsh, and is now one of the biggest football pitches in the

world. But though it has been drained and manicured seemingly to the point of sterilisation, the spirit of the old swamp hasn't been entirely banished. A kestrel hunched on a pylon. Canada geese straggled in from Walthamstow reservoirs to the north. A heron loped by. Then, quite suddenly, the air was alive with swooping black and white birds. It was the house martins again. A flock of some two hundred, migrating casually south, had materialised from nowhere and begun hawking for flies over the field. A few – they are innately playful birds – began slaloming through the goalposts.

I took off south too, down the new Hackney Cut. This is an ordinary canal walk for the first few miles, and I had the company of big blue and black dragonflies, which seemed quite undeterred by the polystyrene flotsam. But by Stratford Marsh it had turned into a jungle track. Festoons of Russian vine half blocked the towpath. There were drifts of dwarf elder, still covered with rosettes of pink-tipped flowers, but already tinged blood-red in the stems. In English folklore it is believed to grow where the Danes were defeated in battle. There were scattered bushes, too, of one of London's botanical specialities, bladder senna, with its huge inflated seed-pods, which blue tits were ripping open for grubs.

I was by now beginning to feel more than a touch of claustrophobia. The towpath burrowed under huge rail bridges, and was only a couple of feet wide in places. I began to worry that I had missed the exit. But then, passing a bizarre breakers' yard, where rows of old telephone boxes lined the opposite bank, I heard the thin, metallic skirl of a black redstart, the bird I most wanted to see. Black redstarts, like dusky robins with rufous tails, haunt the lower reaches of mountains and stone-built villages throughout Europe, and began colonising the bombed-out moraine of inner London during the war. Since then they have nested in Woolwich Arsenal, Broad Street Station, the fireplaces of bombed buildings in the Temple, East End windowsills, and innumerable gasworks. I saw my first in 1975 in the derelict works at Beckton. But alas, this Stratford bird didn't show itself.

At the Tower I took the light railway down to the southern tip of the Isle of Dogs, and walked back up through Docklands. It's extraordinary to think that only ten years ago, Jonathan Raban described the scene here as like being 'on the frontier between Korea and Switzerland'. Now it is like being on the frontier between Dickens and Dan Dare. Yet though Docklands is being offered as a kind of Utopia-on-Thames, it has made barely a single gesture towards the kind of green space now regarded as a prerequisite of tolerable urban life everywhere else in the developed world. The piazzas between the luxury flats and finance complexes are made of exquisitely hand-moulded bricks, but not a blade of grass is permitted to deface them. The trees – shamefully, a rarity – have been planted in austere rows and geometric formations.

Even the water has been straightened up and hemmed in. I saw a grey wagtail, with its exquisite chrome yellow and slate plumage, bobbing on the edge of the Thames by the Shadwell watersports basin, but that is one of the very few places where one can catch even a glimpse of the capital's river. The Docklands Development Corporation seems to have given no thought to providing public access to the Thames, an asset which London's great nineteenth-century naturalist, Richard Jefferies, called morally the property of the greatest city in the world. But Shadwell still has a house martin colony, under the balconies of some 1930s flats on the very edge of the development.

I turned up Cable Street, where the East End fought Mosley's fascists. There were patches of so far undeveloped wasteland, thick with buddleia and bramble. A kestrel glided through a window of a derelict house, and I wondered how they would fare in this new part of the city. Kestrels are catholic in their choice of territory, and in the past few years have nested in the House of Lords, on gasometers in Poplar, the Savoy Hotel, Victoria Station, Broadcasting House, and an increasing number of tower-block window boxes.

Wasteland isn't necessarily the best model for city open space. But neither is the favoured alternative. The little churchyard in Scandrett Street was, the last time I saw it, a marvellous muddle of old tombs, long grass and wildflowers. Now it is thoroughly sanitised, the gravestones moved to the wall, the grass shorn and ringed with beds of funereal ivies.

But along Wapping High Street I at last saw a black redstart, darting around the remains of an old Port of London Authority building. Soon it was joined by a female, and the two dark-grey waifs flitted about the sooty stone, with that slight, evocative call echoing between the walls.

I was 3 miles short of St James's by the time dusk fell, but with the starling flocks that roost in the park flighting overhead, and yet more flocks of martins grabbing their last feed of the day just over the heads of Wapping's commuters, I felt the circuit was complete.

A Seaside Town in Winter (1989)

On a glum winter's afternoon on Great Yarmouth's vast and gusty prom, the red kiosk outside the old Empire Theatre looks like an oasis. 'Take the Health Ray', it urges, 'Check Your Vitality and Heartbeat', be reassured about 'How Old You Look'. No such luck. Like almost every other building on the front, the Health Ray is battened down against the weather, a tantalising Aladdin's cave whose inscrutable rejuvenations must stay under wraps until next spring. Meanwhile you stand out in the east wind, surrounded by empty amusement arcades and knowing all too well how old you look.

When Yarmouth first became a resort two centuries ago, people came principally for their health, to dose themselves with fashionably therapeutic sea water and bracing east winds, and the season stretched to all but the coldest months. Nowadays, the front in winter is less of a tonic. There are no cheering noggins to be had at Captain Flint's Bar, no rounds of novelty golf, not even one last rousing chorus of 'Agadoo' from Black Lace at the Marina Centre. It is a bleak prospect, and it would be verging on the perverse to be a willing off-season visitor to a place so thoroughly devoted to summer fun were it not for the fact that, with the illuminations switched off and the trippers gone, Yarmouth's other business with the sea starts to edge out of the shadows.

I have long been fascinated by shorelines, and the various spells they seem to cast; but the transmutation of this tract of melancholy marshland and fisheries into eastern England's favourite kiss-me-quick resort is surely one of their more remarkable stories.

I arrived in the town on a late November morning, by the road that runs along the front. Yarmouth's prom is one of seaside Britain's famous 'Golden Miles', and is so unnervingly straight and wide that, with barely another soul in sight, I felt in danger of losing my sense of direction. In a brief stab of panic I even wondered whether the whole town had shut down completely. But it is nothing so drastic. For six months, Yarmouth simply turns its back on the beach and, like a migrating salmon, retreats to home base. Old Yarmouth, seafaring rather than seasiding, lies about half a mile inland, clustered around the long harbour that has been formed from the estuaries of the rivers Yare, Bure and Waveney. It has always been a major port, gateway to the Norfolk Broads and once the foremost shipping town in Britain. Less than twenty years ago it was home to a huge herring fleet, and the quay was hectic with packing stations and market stalls. Now the herring is almost fished out, and Yarmouth has become a major European cargo terminal, not quite so amenable to those who simply wish to gaze at boats.

There is little visible evidence of the old fishing port. Yarmouth suffered terrible damage in both world wars, and most of the buildings are no more than thirty years old. It was one of the first towns to be hit during the Zeppelin raid of 1915, as the German airships made their way along the east coast, bound for Sandringham and, they thought, the King. During 1941, Yarmouth was on the receiving end of some of the most severe bombing of any small town in Britain, and by mid-November had been hit in seventy-two separate raids. What was left was bulldozed during the 1960s. Now, as you wander among the neon-fronted cocktail bars and chip shops, you come across little marooned remnants: a Customs house; an eighteenth-century Fishermen's Hospital; a score of chapels and meeting houses that are a testament to East Anglia's Nonconformist history. The fate of the town's spectacular medieval wall perfectly symbolises the changes. Built in 1261 to defend what was already a very wealthy town against land attack (there were iron chains strung out over the river to keep out hostile shipping), it has now become, rather like a redundant but favourite fence, something to lean other things against.

The wind will eventually drive you into Yarmouth's splendid little museums, and you will be able to make some sense of its various rises and falls as working town and resort. It began as nothing more than a scattering of huts on a bank of silt and sand which began to form across the Yare-mouth about a thousand years ago. Migratory fishermen from the Kent coast used to camp there during the herring season. The bank, as one contemporary historian put it, 'waxed in height and greatness'; the herring catch waxed, too, and Yarmouth grew into a large and prosperous mercantile centre.

A beautifully painted topographical map of 1570 shows housing development following the contours of the receding high-water mark. Another, two centuries later, notes a population of twelve thousand and shows the unique labyrinth of narrow alleys known as 'rows' which were built at right angles to the river – and, presumably, to the prevailing wind. A few survived the Blitz, and the Tolhouse museum has one of the slender, one-seat pony carts which were used for transport down them. All this happened at the harbour. The seafront was ignored until the fashion for seaside holidaying began around 1750. Within thirty years the first theatres and bowling greens had arrived, as well as a pastiche of the harbourside 'troll carts', in the form of a special lightweight carriage, drawn by two men, in which holidaying ladies were transported between the entertainment spots and the town. One of the earliest souvenirs has also found its way into the Tolhouse, a tiny labelled bag of the very stuff that has made Great Yarmouth famous:

> From Yarmouth, where the silv'ry sands
> Stretch as far as eye can reach
> Accept this little book of views
> And SAMPLE OF THE BEACH.

Yarmouth's sands are still a marvel, even under a dull winter sky, and I was amazed that I virtually had them to myself when I went for a stroll along them one morning. I then went to explore another patch of the littoral, the estuary and marshes from which, so to speak, Yarmouth was deposited. The curious thing about the landward side of the town is that it has a beach of a kind too, a transitional area of jumbled paddocks and allotment shacks before the creeks and waterscapes of the flood-plain begin. Breydon Water is virtually a tidal lake, and was formed after the estuary was sealed off by the sand-bar. It is surrounded by Halvergate marshes, an immense expanse of water meadows and grazing marshes, claimed out of the wetlands by centuries of drainage.

It looked, a few years back, as if drainage would go one stage further, and the whole area might be given over to cereals. But it has now been given a considerable degree of protection, and in winter is a paradise for wetland birds. That afternoon the first flocks of Scandinavian fieldfares were clacking from meadow to meadow. Flocks of golden plover flashed briefly in the distance. A heron flapped heavily in front of a derelict windmill.

Many of these birds fly to Breydon Water to roost, and later, in a brief glow of low sunshine, the low-tide mud was a vista of tens of thousands of gulls, dunlin and clamouring redshank, and an almost continuous stream of lapwing and curlew flying in from their feeding grounds on the nearby fields.

Back in the town that evening, after some while wandering the almost empty streets, I found what seemed to be Yarmouth's only fish restaurant, in a converted pub down among the quayside warehouses. Mr Kikis' whitebait and turbot, caught locally that day, were life-savers, the purest taste of the sea I had in all my stay. But they are getting hard to come by, Mr Kikis told me. Over-fishing and pollution (the Sandoz mercury trail had just about reached the Norfolk coast that day, I reckoned) had drastically reduced the catch; and what fish was available from the nearest port, Lowestoft, mostly went up to London to satisfy the huge new demand. But he had the adopted local son's pride in his own locality: 'The mange-touts are from Kenya, the potatoes from Italy, but the fish is *home grown*!'

There is talk in Yarmouth of a massive new development, a bunded deep-water haven stretching out from the harbour mouth. If it goes ahead, it will be the first time that the earnest commercial world at the town's heart has pushed so conspicuously into the pleasure zone. You will be able to see it from your deck-chair, and through the coin-operated binoculars on the piers. But it might be no bad thing. When Dickens set *David Copperfield* up here, it was the drama of shipping out at sea that brought the town's people down to the front in winter. One would earnestly pray for no more storms of the kind he described. But I have a feeling that the harbour development, and its dramatic views of those who have their business on great waters, might give Yarmouth's now deserted Winter Gardens a new life and a real meaning.

The Magnificent Severn (1989)

The Severn is not quite like other English rivers. You wouldn't think of lounging in a punt in it, or playing pooh sticks under the bridges. It is dramatic, unpredictable, rumbustious, as far from a willow-lined brook as you can imagine. It is an *epic* river, the longest in Britain, taking in two nations, half the West Country, and hundreds of square miles of hectic water.

Or rather part of it is. For three quarters of its 220 miles the Severn is a sedate mirror image of the Thames, meandering along the border country, through Upton upon Severn and Stourport on Severn and under the seventeenth-century bridge at Atcham, until it vanishes into its watersheds on Plynlimon – a river only really known to those who live near it. For the rest of us the Severn is synonymous with its estuary, an unruly snake of water that begins just below Gloucester and after one elegant ox-bow around Arlingham, surges out to the Atlantic on a front that is never less than a mile wide.

This is the stretch that gives its name to things other than quiet villages on the Marches. This is where Severn salmon still run against a ferocious tide-race and a gauntlet of wicker traps which are probably prehistoric in design; where there is a miniature island fortress (Steepholm) that has in its time been a medieval monastic herb farm and a Victorian gun battery; and where the biggest bridge in Britain stands so high above the water that traffic is regularly banned from it when the wind is up. It is the route, most memorably, of the Severn Bore, a wall of tidal water created by the river's sharply funnelled profile that sometimes charges upstream furiously enough for surfers to ride it all the way from Newnham to Gloucester. And in a nod of acknowledgement to the sluicing power of its tides, it supports a vast concentration of industrial development at Avonmouth, and no less than four nuclear power stations. It is teeming, diverse, energetic, and no one would dream of calling it Old Father Severn.

When I was at school and drawing the outline of Britain from memory was a regular chore, we were always told to imagine the Severn as the nation's mouth. Looking at a map now this seems more like a metaphor than a memory jog. The estuary is an immense rictus, already 12 miles wide at its notional entrance between Nash and Harlestone Points. By rights it ought to have become the national maw, luring in every adventurous colonist and trader and shifting our centre of economic gravity over to the west. That is one of our more tantalising historical 'what-ifs'. What if sassy, extrovert Bristol had become the capital of the UK? Or Cardiff, for that matter?

What stopped it was the Severn mud, which is as mobile and temperamental as its water. At low tide the river shrinks to a quarter of its full width, and the estuary becomes an outsized creek, with a sinister fretwork of dark rock shoals and sand spits.

During the spring high tides, when the water slaps up close to the rim of the flood defence banks, it can swing to the opposite extreme. My first glimpses of the estuary, like those of most visitors I suspect, were from way up on the Severn Bridge, and then glinting beyond the trees from the Forest of Dean. On both occasions it seemed too vast and distant to be a river. It had the feel of a delta system, or an inland sea. When I went bird-watching in Bridgwater Bay, where the estuary is nearly 20 miles wide, it became a geographical abstraction, an idea which lumped together a host of idiosyncratic local landscapes which had no connection other than their closeness to this mass of incoherent water.

Even when I had one of those concentrated but casual writer's intimacies with a Severn-side village in the mid-1980s, the estuary's image scarcely became any sharper. A cache of Victorian flower paintings had been discovered in the attic of the Clifford family's house in Frampton on Severn, and I'd been given the job of editing them into book form. The Cliffords have lived in Frampton since the days of William the Conqueror, and give or take a few floodings, minor court scandals and bouts of heirlessness, have had a long and harmonious relation with the estuary. Between 1837 and 1850 six of their sisters and aunts, mostly unmarried, painted a remarkable group portfolio of the wild flowers of the neighbourhood. Yet the estuary itself, which must have been the dominant feature of their home landscape, gets a mere half dozen species into the collection.

Down along these southern margins of the estuary it still seems as if the river is held at arm's length. Cattle follow medieval green lanes down to grasslands that owe at least part of their luxuriance to past flooding and silting. But that is about the only concession that is made to the river, and the fields are now drained and cultivated right up to the sea-walls. And though elvers – the young eels that migrate in astronomical numbers up the Severn in March and April – are still caught in cheese-cloth nets (and gobbled in competitions on Frampton Green), most of the harvests here are not from the river itself, but from the legacies it has laid down over the millennia. Gravel is quarried in the vale, coal and iron ore mined up in the Forest of Dean. A soapy blue clay that lies under parts of the river and in exposures in the cliffs, is still dug for bricks. The wall round the Victorian garden at Frampton Court is built from them, and weeps salt on hot days.

Now there is another crop on the horizon. The raw energy of the river, which was ultimately responsible for all these products, is itself being sized up as a possible harvest, and not for the first time in its history the Severn estuary is deeply immersed in a controversy about where we should draw the boundary between nature and culture.

There have been dreams of a barrage across the estuary since the 1930s, but the current scheme, supported by the Department of Energy, has got as far as a working model and feasibility and impact studies. It envisages a string of turbines 10 miles long between Lavernock Point on the Welsh side, and Brean Down on the English. The projected cost had already passed £6 billion by the end of 1988, and it is reckoned that the electricity it would produce would be notionally at least twice as expensive as that from coal-fired or nuclear power stations. Yet it remains a tempting vision, the harnessing of this great cauldron of natural, renewable energy, and the provision perhaps of a clean and safe alternative to what may become the estuary's *fifth* nuclear power station – the proposed PWR at Hinkley Point.

The barrage would close up and generate power only on the ebb tide, and would roughly halve the current tidal range between high and low water. So at low tide the estuary would be in much the same state as it presently is at mid-tide. There's little doubt that the project is viable, and that it could supply between 2.5 and 5 per cent of the power the nation needs. But its likely ecological and social impacts have still barely been charted. With the area of low-tide, food-rich mud reduced by a half, what would happen to the huge flocks of wading birds for which the estuary has been declared a Special Protection Area under the European Commission Bird Directive? Would the Bore become a ripple? Would spring salmon, having swum thousands of miles to reach their spawning grounds, be unable to get out to sea again? Worse, would the effluent from Avonmouth – already a potent cocktail of toxic metals and sewage – also be dammed in? Reducing the Severn estuary to a meek and rancid pond would be an ironic price to pay for our first large-scale project in alternative energy. For huge and diverse though it may be, it does have a character all of its own.

I had a belated taste of this during my sojourn at Frampton. It was a hot day in high summer, and Rollo and Janie Clifford, their four children and I decided to go for a picnic by the river. We set out on a bevy of ancient bicycles, along the flat lanes that etch the country south of the estuary. The air was hot and still between the high hedges and musky with meadowsweet and willow-herb, and we guzzled home-made elderflower cordial. We had the road to ourselves. We freewheeled and sang and spotted a pure white sparrow. It felt absurdly like a Famous Five expedition from the 1930s. But of the Severn there was not a sign. Then we swung into the field where we were to have our picnic, and suddenly there was the immense openness of the estuary not a hundred yards away, with what felt like a gale funnelling in from the Atlantic. We cowered on the cliff top, pegged the picnic down with stones, and watched the wind rattling the salmon weather vane on the top of Framilode church. Ten miles downstream we could see the grey bulk of Berkeley nuclear power station, and exactly opposite it, the Forest of Dean, with its Celtic temples and medieval mines. The two miles of white horses between them looked unnavigable, even under the baking July sun.

Then the tide went out and the river all but vanished. We clambered down the cliff and squelched our way through the claggy blue-grey mud. The children smothered themselves with muddy war-paint and the rest of us treasure-hunted under the cliffs. They were spongy and insubstantial, a precarious wreckage of landslips, fossils, washed-out trees and flotsam, and we kept a nervous eye on the state of the river even though the tide wasn't due for hours. Rollo told me that when the local fishermen wade out at low water to put up their salmon basket-traps, they always wear two watches, just in case one stops. Standing in the Severn's slippery foundations that afternoon it was not difficult to understand why Bristol declined as a port once its slave traffic had been outlawed. The muddy Avon Gorge that joins it to the Severn remained an obstacle to heavy shipping until it was circumvented by the new docks at Avonmouth.

The Severn is classic borderland. But it is nothing like the estuaries of East Anglia, say, where much of the territory is an unresolved no-man's-land between earth and water. Here, quite unequivocally, there is the river, and there is the land; and the plough ridges that stretch right up to the massive sea-defences show that things have gone about as far as they can in the business of turning one into the other.

What we glimpsed that afternoon on the cliff, a motif of cultivated landscapes cheek by jowl with wild water, is repeated with local variations all the way along the upper reaches of the estuary. To find Awre, the very first settlement on the north bank, you must burrow down through a network of hollow lanes with a ferny, almost Cornish luxuriance. The village itself is a cluster of houses around a soaring riverside church, and was the starting point for a ferry which used to run Dean charcoal over to Frampton. At Aust, you can sit under the flickering shadows of the evening rush hour on the Severn Bridge and watch the dunlin flocks (the estuary holds fifty thousand of this species in winter – nearly a fortieth of the world population) on their downstream fly-past to roost.

Between these two villages, along the southern side of the estuary, is a landscape of small fields and orchards and straggly hedges full of pollard ashes. It is one of the few places in England where pollards are still regularly cut for firewood about once every ten years, and the pale ends of the freshly lopped and stacked branches gleam behind the hedges.

Amidst these pastoral prospects you catch bizarre glimpses of the estuary's other human landscapes. A dip in the road and the hi-tech docks at Sharpness rear up momentarily between two barns. Oldbury nuclear power station is framed by garlands of pear-tree mistletoe.

Yet one is still never quite prepared for the first sight of Avonmouth. As you drive south from the Severn Bridge, the skyline begins to fill with cooling towers and gasholders, wreathed in pale orange smoke. This chemical metropolis now covers close on 10 square miles. Most of the big multinationals are there and the effluent that consequently pours into the Severn is one of the most concentrated mixtures of pollutants in any British estuary. I saw one of the discharge pipes when I was last there one February, spraying effluent straight onto bare low-tide mud. Yet with a contrariness that is typical of Severnside, as I was panning the binoculars away from the pipe onto the tussocky waste ground between Avonmouth and the river, a patch of brown detritus appeared to lift clear of the ground and float towards me. It was a short-eared owl, its huge tiger-yellow eyes glaring full ahead. It sheared off when it was about ten yards away, and I watched it circle over Severn Beach's caravan site, past the pub garden and the new holiday flats development, its plumage now a chequer of buff and chestnut in the evening sun.

Even at Slimbridge, where the Wildfowl's Trust famous reserve has an almost unseemly devotion to birds' comfort, these odd conjunctions continue. The shallow bay between Slimbridge village and the Severn is one of the last patches of real marshland on the estuary, and was a haven for waterbirds long before Sir Peter Scott rented it in 1946. Now it is probably the most civilised bird observatory in the world. There are hides sponsored by banks and binocular firms, admonitory and educational hides ('Remember, geese have ears'), double-storeyed, picture-windowed and centrally heated hides. From them you can gaze out over a teeming landscape in which it is difficult to separate the wild and the tame. Swarms of geese mill about in the lakes, the pinioned exotics tempting in the wild migrants. Bewick swans commute about between the wet meadows and the feeding pens. And on the extreme edge of the reserve, knot and dunlin flocks swirl about like a denser kind of smoke in front of the plumes rising up from the Welsh factories over the river.

This cheerfully promiscuous atmosphere is a powerful generator of confidence, in birds and humans alike. That February day there were coaches of children down from South Wales and the Midlands, and many and various were the sightings of Slimbridge's famous peregrines (wintering birds and occasional residents patrolling south from the Symonds Yat eyrie) recorded with shaky pencils in the hide log books: 'Falcon in bush'; 'Peregrine sitting in field near cow'. Some were no doubt wish-fulfilment falcons, but it is good that places exist where children from the Valleys can have such flights of the imagination.

Certainly the estuary looks a very different place from the Welsh side. England is barely visible through the spray when a Bore is brewing up. The decline of the coal and steel industries has left a ribbon of dereliction from Chepstow to Barry, a bleak landscape of corrugated iron fencing, gappy hedges, rusting factories and sour paddocks, in which the country-side seems as blighted as the towns. The elegant port office at Penarth is now a hostel for the homeless, and that splendid example of Severnside ingenuity, the Newport transporter bridge, seems to spend most of its time under repair. The bridge is an exquisitely engineered solution to the problem of getting cars over the River Usk at its junction with the Severn. It carries vehicles and passengers in a carriage slung under a moving trolley, cable-car fashion. Now, with no ships needing the headroom it was designed to provide, it has become an anachronism.

There are schemes to rejuvenate the Welsh side of the estuary, and the burgeoning leisure and technology parks do at least carry something of the optimism that transformed Swansea a decade ago. But the most ambitious scheme, to turn Cardiff Bay into a huge lake by means of a mile-long barrage, is a well-meaning but shortsighted attempt to create a Docklands-style development in a totally different context. Building the complex of offices, restaurants and marinas will provide thousands of short-term jobs in an area of severe unemployment, but it will mean the end for eight thousand wading birds that spend the winter in part of what is now internationally recognised as the Severn Special Protection Area. And in place of the decaying but distinctive character of old Cardiff, will come the anonymous glitz of International Maritime, the style of the times.

The Cardiff Bay scheme may provide a foretaste of the impact of the Severn Barrage itself, and be the first step in the transformation of the estuary into a giant *Howard's Way* set. It's a prospect which rather tickles the fancy of some of the villagers along the Gloucester shore, who foresee their property values soaring.

Barrages of all kinds are fashionable at present, but they are nothing new. Up in the Forest of Dean they have been fighting against attempts to level out the region's character and quirkiness for a thousand years. Dean, properly speaking, is not part of the estuary, but it has had a long symbiotic relationship with it, and Lydney was once an important port for off-loading coal, iron ore and timber from the Forest. But ever since the Normans declared Dean a royal hunting preserve, there have been attempts at expropriating its natural wealth by powerful outside interests. In the early sixteenth century it was big iron masters like Sir John de Winter; later that century the Navy. In 1831 the enclosure of the forest by the Commissioner of Woods and Forests led to a wholesale local uprising. In every one of these cases there were attempts to deprive the local people of their ancient and complex network of common rights. But in each case the commoners, Free Miners and 'ship badgers' (sheep keepers) fought back, and as a result Dean has retained a local distinctiveness that is probably unique in southern England.

The sixth-century temple that looks out over the estuary from just inside the Forest at Lydbrook is dedicated to Nodens, a god of healing who also took care of the river. The temple is decorated with fish and sea-monsters, and was almost certainly the work of Romanised Celts. So far the Severn Barrage, benign in intention but remorselessly authoritarian in its likely effects, is a very Roman-looking idea. What is needed now is some input from the Celtic tradition, with its love of ingenuity and ornamentation and its fierce tribal respect of the spirit of place.

The East Anglian Badlands (1991)

In 1668 the Norfolk village of Santon Downham was buried under a sandstorm, a blow-out from an inland dune system at Lakenheath Warren, a few miles to the south. It was, by any reasonable English standards, an outlandish occurrence. But this was the Breckland, 'a vast Arabian desert' straddling the Norfolk–Suffolk borders which had long been notorious with travellers. Many used to cross 'the horrible Brandon sands' in the dawn to avoid upsetting the horses, and there was a kind of wooden lighthouse to guide anyone unfortunate enough to be benighted. Seven years after the Santon storm the diarist John Evelyn noted that 'the Travelling Sands have so damaged the country, rolling from place to place, and quite overwhelmed some gentlemen's estates', and he urged them to plant 'tufts of firr' to stabilise the sand.

They didn't need much encouragement. As the fashion for improvement gathered pace during the late eighteenth and nineteenth centuries Breckland landowners went in for all manner of schemes to make their local wilderness bear fruit. They planted thickets for pheasants, turnips to enrich the soil and pine hedges to check the winds. Eventually – with more than a suggestion that poetic justice had been done – Santon Downham rose again as the local headquarters of the Forestry Commission, whose vast pine plantations had become the biggest single enterprise to keep the sand in its place. In the 1940s Lakenheath Warren vanished under the runways of an airfield (now the US base that despatched the Libyan strike force). During the last twenty years all the remaining open dunes have been tidily fenced off and labelled as nature reserves. Breckland has been very nearly brought to heel, and for the first time not everyone feels comfortable about this particular triumph of man over the waste.

For much of its recent history Breckland has been regarded as a classic piece of wasteland, somewhere to lose unpopular and land-hungry activities like battle-training and commercial forestry. There weren't many other obvious uses for an infertile plain which had the lowest rainfall in Britain, and which was almost devoid of the features usually regarded as making a picturesque landscape. I doubt if there is another comparable tract of rural England (it covers some 400 square miles, from Bury St Edmunds in the south to Swaffham in the north) that is so little known and so impatiently rushed through by travellers. When I first began exploring

East Anglia thirty years ago it felt like an occupied zone, an intimidating gauntlet of barricaded shooting estates and military bases.

Yet everywhere there were reminders of the old waste clinging on in the margins. You could pick up neolithic arrowheads in the fields. Species of wild flower grew on the road verges that didn't crop up again until you reached the East European steppes. Nightjars seemed to find echoes of their ancestral habitats in the new forestry clearings, and churred in ever increasing numbers through the summer dusks. I began to find modern Breckland a haunting and evocative place, a ghost of the old landscape of immense sandy heaths and stony scrubland, and when dust-devils were whirling across the carrot fields and through the stunted pine wind-breaks it didn't seem implausible that flocks of great bustard stalked the plains only a hundred and fifty years ago.

Given the seemingly run-down state of the place, it was a rather perverse fascination. But attitudes towards landscape change, and just as it seemed to be on its last legs, the Breckland has come into its own. It has even received the ultimate tribute of having a District Council named after it (though rather confusingly much of this lies outside the Breckland proper).

A better guide to its status may be the changing patterns of land-use, in which both the leisure industry and low-intensity farming are making strong showings. The annual tally of visitors to the Forestry Commission's Thetford Forest Park has passed the million mark. The Dutch firm Center Parcs have created one of their holiday villages in a pine plantation on the Iveaghs' estate at Elveden. And last year, in a move which challenged the assumptions underlying centuries of agricultural development, the government designated the region as one of the first Environmentally Sensitive Areas (ESAs) in which farmers are encouraged to return to methods which will conserve historic or locally distinctive landscapes.

The scheme is beginning to work quite well. But if some farmers are doubtful about taking part it isn't simply that they are unimpressed by the scale of grants and compensation. To *not* improve the land, to deliberately court infertility, goes against a whole tradition of husbanding instincts, and at a time when we are becoming sensitive to the consequences of deforestation and land degradation in the Third World, smacks of a peculiarly western brand of hypocrisy and indulgence. But the argument is nothing like as black and white as plenty versus barrenness, and the example of the Breckland may have something to teach us about a discriminating attitude towards fertility.

But there is no avoiding the fact that the Breckland is a prime home-grown example of what deforestation can lead to. Up to a couple of hundred years ago it was the nearest thing Britain had to a dust-bowl. In parts this may have been its natural state. The area is defined by deposits of sands and gravel that were washed here by glacial meltwaters, and there may have been areas of especially loose sand on exposed ridges that never sustained a permanent woodland cover. But most of the open areas were created or encouraged by human activity. The light soils made forest clearance relatively easy, and in prehistoric times it was one of the most densely populated areas of Britain. Grazing by semi-domesticated cattle would soon have converted what remained of the woodland to a mixture of wiry grass and heather. A large and sprawling network of trackways and drove roads connected the region with the Icknield Way and trading settlements on the East Anglian coast.

Amongst the most important items of trade ferried along these tracks were worked flints, for use in knives, weapons and farm implements. Flint is abundant throughout East Anglia, but Breckland had some of the best quality, and became a centre for flint-knapping skills. At Grimes Graves, just north of Brandon, there is a prehistoric flint-mine in which, to date, some 540 shafts have been uncovered. The strictures of Health and Safety regulations have rather dulled the experience of clambering down into these austere chambers in the chalk. But behind the grilles you can still see the scratch-marks made in the faces by deer-antler picks four thousand years ago.

Early farming itself was a less rewarding business. The thin soils soon began to lose their fertility, and at some unspecified date the system that eventually gave the region its name evolved. A field would be cultivated for a few years and then abandoned for as many as twenty to give it time to recover. These long-term fallow plots were named after an Old English term *brek*, meaning a tract of land broken up for cultivation and then allowed to revert. You can glimpse what these archaic stony plots were like in parts of Weeting and Thetford Heath National Nature Reserves.

Sheep-grazing was the most sensible use for both the grasslands and the brecks, and large flocks were roaming the region by Roman times. In the Middle Ages they were joined by rabbits, which were kept in enormous high-banked warrens. By the middle of the eighteenth century there were reckoned to be more than 15,000 acres of organised warren in the Brecks, and the traveller and agricultural reporter Arthur Young (1741–1820) quoted the figure of forty thousand rabbits as the production of just one warren.

At this time Breckland was probably as wild and inhospitable as it has ever been, with the areas of eroded sand growing as grazing pressure increased. This was the heyday of the exploration of Britain, and inquisitive travellers like Young, William Gilpin, the antiquarian Dr Stukeley and Charles Kidman all visited the region. Almost without exception they regarded it loathsome and treacherous. Only the duc de La Rochefoucauld, a waspish eighteen-year-old French nobleman who toured East Anglia in 1784, saw some merit in the place – in the rabbits if nothing else. Commenting on the landscape between Bury and Thetford, he wrote:

> The whole of the country through which the road runs for a distance of eight miles is covered with heather in every direction as far as the eye can see . . . no trees, no cultivation, everywhere sand, everywhere little clumps of reeds and bracken. A large portion of this arid country is full of rabbits, of which the numbers astonished me. We saw whole troops of them in broad daylight and we could almost touch some of them with our whips. I enquired the reason for this prodigious number and was told that there was an immense warren which brought in 200 guineas a year to the owner, being let to a farmer . . . In the eyes of the law, rabbits in a warren are as sacred a piece of property as the land itself, and to transgress the laws of property is a capital offence . . . The dry sand which pervades the district militates against improvements and I do not believe that it will ever be possible, in such an unfavourable soil, to put the twenty miles of country which we covered in the course of a day under cultivation.

In this he underestimated the ingenuity and ambition of the local squires. During the early years of the nineteenth century the farming systems of the Breckland were totally transformed. Between 1800 and 1820 forty-nine Parliamentary Enclosure Acts took in nearly 120,000 acres of grass and heathland. Common rights were extinguished and the rabbit warrens abolished. Pine wind-breaks – cut back like hedges to encourage lateral growth – made their appearance (and produced such distinctive rows of contorted trees that now, ironically, they are regarded as crucial elements in the 'landscape heritage'). Increasingly, the small farms were bought out by the large landowners, a process which accelerated once the great agricultural depression had set in in the 1870s. Breckland became a region of vast private estates – Elveden, Euston, Culford, West Stow, Stanford – many of them more than 10,000 acres in extent and able to turn the slump to their advantage by using their rough land for raising pheasants. Breckland became for a while the pheasant-shooting centre of England, and was the site of some terrible *battues*. The Maharajah Duleep Singh, who rebuilt Elveden into a passable imitation of a north Indian palace in 1870, once slaughtered 789 partridges in a single day. Tom de Grey, the sixth Lord Walsingham, used to go shooting dressed in a snakeskin waistcoat and a hat made from a whole hedgehog. On a winter's day in 1889, in the marshy heathland round Stanford, he bagged sixty-five coots, thirty-nine pheasants, twenty-three mallard, seven teal, six gadwall, four pochard, one goldeneye, three swans, three snipe, one woodcock, one pigeon, two herons, two moorhens, sixteen rabbits, nine hares, one otter, one pike (shot underwater) and a rat. Game shooting continues in the Brecks, and has left some unhappy local legacies, not least a rather cavalier attitude towards bird protection laws and an entrenched hostility towards public access.

But once farming became prosperous again after the war, landowners returned to the business of improving their cultivated areas. Now the sandy soils grow high quality carrots and asparagus, and much of the cultivation is sub-contracted out to specialist growers, who undertake the whole business from sowing to harvesting.

Bill Nickson, the Ministry of Agriculture Project Officer for the Breckland ESA, keeps a personal copy of the Ministry's journal for May 1952 (his birth month) as a benchmark against which to measure changing attitudes. It contains an exhortation from the then Minister, Thomas Dugdale, to produce more food from our own soil, and a book review of *The Elveden Enterprise* which described enthusiastically how a large part of this Breckland estate had been converted from the heath. 'They were responding to the needs of their time, just as they are now,' he reflects. The needs of the time now are seen in terms of the preservation of the heathland and the fallow 'brecks', and Bill is empowered to offer grants to farmers for various initiatives aimed at meeting these objectives. By the end of 1989 there were agreements for the conservation of 1300 hectares of heath and dry grassland, in which farmers agree to restrict their use of pesticides and fertiliser and manage the grass by grazing. There have also been agreements over some 300 hectares for the encouragement of rough flower-rich strips at the edges of arable fields. This is a small step towards an option which has sadly not yet been taken up at all, that is, allowing arable fields to revert to fully fledged brecks. Agreements have been entered into by both large and small landowners, but there are still vast tracts of the Breckland which are impervious to current ideas about conservation and access. Much of the land around Rushford, for instance, is in foreign ownership, and in the wake of the rabbit and pheasant there is now a third generation of Breckland sporting beast: the thoroughbred horse. The new stud farms, done up with neo-classical porticos and smart post-and-rail fences, stand out like South Forks in the tousled Breck prairieland.

But you get used to incongruous sights. I am up here in early summer, and the new unsprayed field-edges, full of mignonette and poppies, are also bristling with soldiers in camouflage. It is the middle of a big NATO exercise to simulate an aerial invasion of Britain, and I am rather lucky to get a guided trip round the Stanford Battle Area. Bob Berry from the Property Services Agency (PSA) which undertakes estate management for the army, is an expert and enthusiastic advocate of the MoD's new attitude towards conservation. He shows me hardwood plantings deliberately edged with scrub (equally good, eventually, for nesting birds and lurking tanks) and cleared pine plantations that they are attempting to return to a heather cover. The sheep that graze much of the 17,000 acres of land are worked according to the upland hefting system, in which small, clannish flocks graze their own patch of territory and need the minimum of shepherding.

The local birds seem ineffably unconcerned about the furious activity involved in the exercise. Swallows are commuting to nests in old pillboxes. Two curlews do a display flight around a low-flying helicopter. They have an ally in the camp commandant, who is also chairman of the Stanford conservation group. During the lambing and nesting season, he puts out radar traps to catch speeding tanks. War-games are not always played by such sentimental rules.

We drive up to the highest point in the Battle Area, Frog Hill. The view over miles of pale, stony grassland, studded with pine and scrub, is extraordinary, like nothing else in this country except perhaps the New Forest. You can just catch glimpses of Langford, Stanford and Tottington churches, all that remains of the villages that were appropriated to create the Battle Training Area during the war. As in many similar areas, the army promised that the villagers could return after the cease-fire. It never happened, and the only way the dwindling number of surviving inhabitants can return to their birthplace is to be buried there.

I ask Bob Berry whether there are any better prospects now of the general public being able to visit one of the outstanding wild open spaces in lowland England. But he is sceptical. Detente means that more troops are scheduled to return from Germany, and the MoD feels it needs more training areas, not less. Hopeful visitors must be satisfied with occasional marshalled coach trips in the summer.

Only on the Forestry Commission's land is one free to walk about at will in the Brecks. This was one of the first areas to be planted up by the Commission in its post-Great-War mission to increase the nation's strategic timber reserve. Now it is the largest single landowner in Breckland, with 21,000 hectares. Most of this is planted up with Corsican pines, which for decades put the countryside here under a forbidding and monotonous drape. But many of the early plantings are coming round for felling, and landscape is perceptibly more open. The FC is also now committed to promoting nature conservation and public enjoyment of its estates, and nowhere is this policy more evident than the Brecks. Les Simpson, their local officer, tells me that they are now paying almost a full tithe – dedicating eight per cent of their land purely for conservation purposes. There are nature trails and a red squirrel project, and the Forest Park, which includes a fair amount of the commercially worked area. On some sites the Commission is creating unusually large clear-fells of up to 30 hectares for reasons that have little to do with timber management. Beyond Emily's Wood, north of Brandon, the aim is to give travellers along the A1065 an idea of what the open prospects of Breckland might once have looked like, stretches of rough land clear to the tree belts on the horizon. Down in Wangford Warren there is an immense clearing specifically for the benefit of nightjars, woodlarks and hunting goshawks. (A while ago, with typical local opportunism, there was a sign outside the nearby farm which anounced 'Goshawks!' as lesser holdings do their honey and free-range eggs.)

Meandering between these forest clearings, watching the tree pipits doing their melodramatic free-fall song-flights, was the pleasantest part of my visit. And at night, with the vegetation underfoot smelling of fern and foxes, and the nightjars gliding out like ghostly kites against the silhouetted trees, there was a palpable sense of the old wilderness.

But much of the rest of Breckland seems to have become a cur-mudgeonly and inhospitable place. There is almost nowhere to walk. The network of ancient tracks that pass across the estates south of Elveden are all blocked off by curt Private signs. Even England's oldest road, the Icknield Way, summarily peters out once it leaves the FC's Kings Forest. Only the Roman Peddars Way, opened up after long and patient nego-tiation by Breckland local authorities, is an uninterrupted right of way, and on this I was turned back by a noxious cloud of smoke from a vast field-fire of rotting bean haulm. Feeling decidedly tetchy, I began to wonder if the time might not be approaching when, in the public interest, the whole of Breckland should be looked on – and administered – as a national asset. My private dream of the army leaving Stanford to become England's first American-style 'roadless area' will probably remain a fantasy. But public opinion is changing. More than a century ago, in his extraordinary description of the Dorset heathland in *The Return of the Native*, Thomas Hardy predicted that, 'The New Vale of Tempe may be a gaunt waste in Thule: human souls may find themselves in closer and closer harmony with external things wearing a sombreness distasteful to our race when it was young.' It would no longer seem out of place for the Breckland to become an Area of Outstanding Natural Beauty, or even a lowland National Park. Such possibilities are being whispered behind closed doors amongst those many conservation groups that currently keep an eye on the region's ecological health. They have noticed a worrying and widespread deterioration lately. Local specialities are declining. The heather is dying back. There is a growing belief that the place is probably over-grazed and over-manured, and that perhaps what is needed is a return to the old breck system itself – cultivation followed by a long fallow period. It is, ironically, a system that the much-abused Forestry Commission are already almost following. Their policy of short term rotations followed by large clearances is like a condensation of the prehistoric farming systems here. If they could be persuaded to allow longer periods before replanting they might produce a model for the Brecks, a landscape that, as Hardy put it, was 'impressive without showiness, emphatic in its admonitions, grand in its simplicity'. And, alternating forest with fallow, it would also be a salutary place for meditating upon the fact that fertility is not something which can be endlessly exploited without, so to speak, a break.

Gilbert White's House (1993)

Are houses always vital influences in their occupants' lives, shaping and registering what goes on inside? Sometimes, I think, they function as little more than rudimentary moorings. Gilbert White, eighteenth-century clergyman and author of the best-known natural history book in the English language, lived in the same house (the Wakes) in the Hampshire village of Selborne for all but the first eight of his seventy-three years, and used it as casually as an old coat. It was convenient, cosy, loved as a matter of habit, but in the end more or less taken for granted. Despite forty years of writing journals and letters which are remarkable for their acute sense of place, he scarcely acknowledges his home base. Yet much of the important business of his life was carried on inside the Wakes. Somewhere upstairs – perhaps overlooking the stable-yard with its nesting house martins, or looking out across the garden to the louring beechwoods – was the study where, for eighteen years, he conjured with the slow-growing manuscript of *The Natural History of Selborne*. Somewhere in the small T-shaped house were enough rooms to accommodate the vast numbers of relatives and friends that the bachelor curate entertained, and whose regular increase he logged contentedly among his gardening notes:

Mrs Edmund White brought to bed of a boy, who has encreased the number of my nephews & nieces to 56. One polyanth-stalk produced 47 pips or blossoms.

For all this industry and bustle, the impression White gives of the Wakes is not so much of a home as of an enthusiast's *pied à terre*. Sometimes it is an observatory or laboratory, sometimes a natural history curiosity in its own right, a *hybernaculum* (White's latinism for an animal's winter quarters) fascinating because of its responses to Selborne's turbulent weather. But mostly it was simply an anchor for a life lived somewhere else. Gilbert made no secret of where his heartland was. When he commissioned the Swiss artist Hieronymus Grimm to prepare illustrations for *The Natural History*, most were of the tangle of woods and tracks and sunken streams that made up the parish landscape. There were just two distant glimpses of the Wakes. They are nearly identical views, taken from the foot of the Hanger, the steep beechwood that rises to the west of the village. In the foreground are the Wakes' out-fields ('the Park') where the hay has just been cut and raked. Beyond the tall field-trees, the two-storey east wing of the Wakes is just visible, with White himself out in front, a tiny, self-effacing figure leaning on a stick.

One of the few heartfelt references he makes to the house in his writings is taken from a similar vantage point. When he was about twenty-five, and exiled on family business to the inhospitable flatlands of Cambridgeshire, he composed a nostalgic poem about his 'native spot' entitled 'The Invitation to Selborne'. The Wakes, glimpsed again from the Hanger, appears in the final stanza, a green refuge in a wooded vale:

> Now climb the steep, drop now your eye below;
> Where round the verdurous village orchards blow;
> There, like a picture, lies my lowly seat
> A rural, shelter'd, unobserv'd retreat.

Two centuries later, the Wakes still has an incidental, happenstance look, and has become something of a monument to the venerable architectural tradition of *extension*. What was a modest vernacular dwelling in the eighteenth century has been encrusted like a hermit crab with outgrowths and elaborations in half a dozen disparate styles. Seen from Gilbert's own viewpoint, from on top of the Hanger, it is hard to credit it is a single house.

To the left (or north-west) is the 'billiard room' wing, built in a rather severe Tudor revival style in 1903 by Andrew Pears (who also added downstairs bay windows at this end of the house, and a second storey). To its right is the library added by Professor Thomas Bell, Professor of Zoology at King's College London, and a White scholar, who lived in the house between 1844 and 1880. On the extreme right is the replacement dining, kitchen and servants' block put up soon after Gilbert's death by his brother Benjamin. Marooned in the middle of all these additions is the original cottage, a simple three-unit dwelling built from local malmstone sometime about 1500, and named after one of its early owners, a Mr Wake.

The house passed to the White family thanks to the foresight of Gilbert's grandfather (also Gilbert), who was vicar of Selborne from 1681 until his death in 1728. He bought the property as a security for his wife Rebekah, and when he died, she and her two unmarried daughters took up residence almost immediately – an easy move since the Wakes lies just a hundred yards across the street from the vicarage. The daughters were married the following year, and Rebekah, finding herself with an empty house, invited her son John and his growing family to move in.

Gilbert, then nine years old, was John's eldest child, and already had five brothers and sisters. By 1733 eleven people were crammed into the Wakes. It was probably a cheerful enough atmosphere, especially for the six youngest Whites, who were then all under eight. But Gilbert was five years older than his oldest brother, Thomas, and must have become used to spending time by himself, especially in the Wakes' grounds and the countryside beyond. His father, John, had begun to replan the garden, but he seems to have been a withdrawn and inadequate character, and can't have been much company or help in the household.

Gilbert went to school in Basingstoke, then to Oriel College, Oxford, to study theology, and was finally ordained in 1746. But because the living of Selborne was with Magdalen College, not Oriel, he was never able to become rector of the village to which he was so emotionally attached. With no great conviction he took up official posts at Oxford and a succession of temporary curacies in the Hampshire area. But his heart remained in Selborne, and increasingly his time was absorbed by a growing fascination with the natural world. The garden that his father had started became, in effect, his first field laboratory, and by 1751 he was recording his energetic work there in a journal he called the *Garden Kalendar*.

The garden he developed became a place which was both functional and floriferous. In borders underneath the dining-room windows he planted out crocuses and crown imperials, and wild plants transplanted from the Hanger. In the eastern half of the garden he built a south-facing fruit wall, and finished its coping with stones taken from Selborne's ruined medieval priory. (Parts of the wall still survive, and bear a plaque inscribed 'GW 1761'.) His orchard and kitchen garden took shape on a naturally raised mound known as Baker's Hill in the south-east of the garden, and were filled with more than forty different varieties of vegetable. He grew artichokes, white broccoli, marrowfat peas, scorzonera, skirret, squashes, and species like maize, wild rice and potatoes that had not long been introduced to this country.

But his greatest energy was reserved for what he referred to rather grandly as his 'melon ground'. Melons held a peculiar fascination for eighteenth-century growers, and in many ways seemed to symbolise contemporary attitudes towards the whole business of gardening. They were exotic, Gothic, and repaid technical ingenuity with huge productivity. Gilbert's hot-bed (also on Baker's Hill) was 45 feet long, and had some thirty cart-loads of dung applied to it annually. And each year, as he went through the rituals of preparing the ground and nursing these temperamental fruits through to harvest, Gilbert seemed to become locked in a personal struggle with the vagaries of the eighteenth-century climate. He built a thatched 'earth-house' to prepare and protect high quality mould for the fruits, devised ways of damping down the bed when it became over-heated, and built a sophisticated ventilation system for those melons that were in glass or oiled-paper frames.

There were more contrivances among the hedges and meadow grass of the park, where Gilbert had set down a series of follies and conceits: oil jars on 9-foot-tall pedestals, obelisks, an early bird-hide with a still-surviving brick walkway leading to it from the Wakes. In this he was following the fashion set by landscapers like William Kent. But some of his ornaments were so preposterous that they could well have been intended as landscaping parodies or puns. In May 1756 he cut a vista through the tall hedges in the out-fields, and ranged six gates so that they would be seen as receding images, terminating in a 12-foot-high figure of Hercules, painted on a board. Gilbert's life-long friend and correspondent, John Mulso, confessed that he was overwhelmed by the growing elaboration of Gilbert's estate, and caught exactly the right note of tongue-in-cheek appreciation:

> You see me with my hand over my Brows & retiring to the prescribed Distance, I wave my head about, & take them in with a critical Survey...

The serious point behind Gilbert's advanced gardening and landscape experiments is that they were all explorations of one of the central conundrums of the Age of Enlightenment: what was the proper relation between nature and humankind, and where should the line be drawn between productive wildness and disciplined culture?

In the end Gilbert, in his garden as in his writing, swept the whole notion of such a division aside – or at least underground. In 1761, the same year that he built the fruit-wall, he began work on the most significant architectural feature of the Wakes – the ha-ha between the garden and the park. He recorded the details meticulously in his journal:

> Jan 24: Long the mason finish'd the dry wall of the Haha in the new garden, which is built of blue rags, so massy, that it is supposed to contain double the Quantity of stone usual in such walls. Several stones reach into the bank 20 inches. The wall was intended to be 4 feet 7 & an half high: but the labourers in sinking the ditch on inclining ground mistook the level, especially at the angle: so that at that part to bring it to a level it is 5 feet 8 inch: high, & 4 feet 6 inch: at the ends: an excellent fence against the mead, & so well fast'ned into the clay bank, that it looks likely to stand a long while.

The ha-ha is an ingenious device consisting of a ditch and sunken wall between garden and outlying farmland or pasture. It was intended to act as a boundary and keep cattle out of the flower and vegetable beds without interrupting the view. Ideally, it provided a way of visually (and to some degree philosophically) merging the garden with the wilder countryside. For White it meant an uninterrupted vista sweeping all the way from his neat borders to the hillside beeches, those 'most lovely of all forest trees'. This prospect of the Hanger must have had a lasting influence on Gilbert's attitudes towards landscape. It is constantly in view, and rises steeply 300 feet above the village, reducing the daylight of those who live in its shadow by up to three hours. (In 1792, the year before his death, Gilbert rather poignantly notes the February day when he 'began to drink tea by day light'.) But it was also a wild wood, full of ferns and orchids, where swallows and martins hawked for insects in the late summer, and where he once watched 'near 40 ravens playing about . . . all day'. And rising like an intricate green parapet just a couple of hundred yards from the Wakes, it must have been a continual reminder that the vitality of nature lay in intimate detail and close-up, not in vague and grandiose vistas.

Despite all this outdoor enterprise, Gilbert undertook only one significant building project inside the Wakes. Inspired by his brother Harry's extensions in nearby Fyfield, he planned to create more space for visitors to the Wakes by building what he called his Great Parlour. Work began on 6 June 1777, and continued throughout the autumn. It was a considerable room, 23 feet long, 18 feet wide and 12 feet 3 inches high. Gilbert logged the progress of tiling, floor-laying and plastering in his *Naturalist's Journal* – and the times that work was held up by the weather. But by the New Year it was largely a matter of letting the room dry out, giving yet another opportunity for White the naturalist to take over from White the home improver. The plasterer, he believed, had skimped his work

> by improvidently mixing wood-ashes with the morter: because the alcaline salts of the wood will be very long before they will be dry at all; & will be apt to relax, & turn moist again when foggy damp weather returns.

On 28 January 1778 he notes:

> Frost comes in a doors . . . Little shining particles of ice appear on the ceiling, cornice, & walls of my great parlor: the vapor condensed on the plaster is frozen in spite of frequent fires in the chimney. I now set a chafing dish of clearburnt charcoal in the room on the floor.

Fortunately there were drying winds throughout February, and the room was soon well aired. As the days grew longer, Gilbert allowed himself some satisfaction at the alignment of the room, and noted that 'the sun at setting shines into the E: corner'. The fittings and furnishings chosen for the room were lavish. The chimney-piece was '23 foot 7 in. of superfishal [sic] white and veined Italian marble'; there was a large looking-glass (costing £9.19s) and the room was finished with a 'fine stout large Turkey carpet' and 'flock sattin' wallpaper in light brown with a coloured border (debited in G. W.'s accounts at £9.15s). That summer, Gilbert's favourite niece, Molly, declared the parlour 'one of the pleasantest rooms I ever was in'. It continued, as far as one can tell, to play that role until the end of Gilbert's life.

The most recent act in the history of the Wakes began when the last private owner died in 1953. The following year an appeal was launched in *The Times* for funds to enable the house and grounds to be endowed as a memorial to Gilbert White. Sadly the appeal failed to raise sufficient money, and the Wakes was saved only because of a link-up between the White appeal and relatives of the Antarctic explorer, Captain Lawrence Oates, who were seeking a home for the family's memorabilia. The result was the successful, albeit incongruous, purchase and endowment of the Wakes in 1955 as a museum and library jointly devoted to White and Oates. In the years that followed the White museum became a focal point for a good deal of active natural history work, which culminated in the establishment of an educational Field Studies Centre in the old stableyard.

But more recently, influenced by the current fashion for 'heritage' restoration, there have been moves to redecorate the interior of the Wakes in eighteenth-century style. White's old bedroom has been opened up and furnished with a facsimile eighteenth-century bed. The Great Parlour is being restored to its original dimensions by the use of curtains, and there has been much repainting in contemporary colours and general tidying-up. Eventually the Field Studies Centre will be moved elsewhere in the village so that nothing compromises the historic profile of the building. The result is a clean, elegant and, in academic terms, 'authentic' interior, but one which feels quite lifeless. It is certainly hard to detect any echo of the busy curate, naturalist, host and countryman whose life and example are the only reason the house is of any interest, and whose attitude towards house decoration is summed up by the occasion he used hair-clippings from his dog Rover in 'plaster for ceilings'. ('His coat weighed four ounces. The N:E: wind makes Rover shrink.')

There is only the Hanger, that 'vast hill' that dominates the view through almost every window, to remind one that the important thing about the Wakes was not its bricks and mortar, but its position, and its role in the continuing experiment which White made out of his daily life. This architecturally unexceptional building would have been a splendid site to challenge contemporary fads, and interpret conservation not as a kind of historical mime, but as a tribute to the guiding spirit of a place. The Wakes would then have become a naturalists' haven again, crammed as it was two centuries ago with books, plants, insects, and inquisitive children gazing at swallows over the Hanger and young house-crickets swarming about the hearth.

FOREIGN TRAVEL

Winter in the Camargue (1988)

It is only from the air that you can get a notion of just how thoroughly the Camargue is awash with water. For more than 60 miles along the Mediterranean seaboard, west of Marseilles, the Rhone delta frays into a fantastic labyrinth of marsh-fringed creeks and lagoons. The landing approach to Montpellier airport is low over this seaward edge, and from this angle the fingers of land seemed to be existing purely on sufferance. The autoroutes looked like lost causeways and Montpellier's runways about as secure as sinking aircraft carriers.

Then, just as we banked for landing, I glimpsed a scene that seemed to sum up the two faces of the Camargue. Between the sea and the lagoons were the jutting, pyramidal blocks of the new holiday complex at La Grande Motte, and, paddling in the choppy water in front of them, a hundred or so of the Camargue's most ancient and celebrated citizens, the flamingoes, glowing pale pink in the setting sun.

I had been looking for flamingoes when I was last here. It was high summer in the early sixties, before the French government hatched their scheme for the development of the Languedoc coast, and before La Grande Motte's architect had bragged that 'to start the resort a hard core was necessary to mark the countryside with its virile presence'. The Camargue then had seemed quite virile enough already. There were riotous bands of gypsies, black bulls raging through the streets in the non-lethal *course à la cocarde*, and the *gardians*, the Camargue cowboys, high-stepping through the marshes on their white horses. It was a hectic and colourful prospect, and I was glad I had hired a cine camera for the trip. It was unbeatable as virile shoulder accessory, but I did have one serious filmic ambition: to picture flamingoes wading amongst the samphire in what I couldn't help seeing as an exotic version of East Anglia. So one morning before it got too hot, kitted out with bottles of grape juice and feeling like real explorers, my friends and I slunk, then crawled across the blinding white salt pans where the flamingoes summered. We got within about 300 yards of a huge flock before they tired of our graceless progress and took to the air – an immense billowing surf of salmon and scarlet. I pressed the Bolex shutter until the film ran out.

Nature had rather more than the last laugh on this occasion. A few days later the camera was swamped by a monstrous wave as I was flaunting it at some starlets on a Riviera beach, all but ruining the mechanism and exhausting my holiday budget for the repairs. As for the flamingo footage, when I projected it back at home the distant birds were indistinguishable from the dust specks on the lens.

In winter, I reckoned, things would be different – especially twenty-odd years on. Unlike a good number of exotic Mediterranean birds, many of the flamingoes stayed on over the cold months, and I rather fancied seeing such fabulous creatures in a landscape stripped of all the machismo and forced picturesqueness of summer. But it proved hard to prise the Camargue entirely free of its theatrical aura. My two companions made wildlife documentaries, for a start. There was a Franco-American film crew staying at our hotel in Arles – here, mystifyingly, to make an episode for the TV series *William Tell*. Even the hotel manager had a winningly histrionic approach to his job. One morning at breakfast, he played out a tense one-acter about the time he was caught out in the street as the Allies were bombing the town's bridge across the Rhone in 1944. He had a photo taken from one of the bombers hanging ambiguously on his wall.

Arles straddles the Rhone, and is almost at the apex of 180,000 acres of marshland that have formed in its delta. It is, in consequence, on a major bird migration route. But it still surprised us that the first bird we saw on our first morning was a peregrine falcon, jinking amongst the muddled roofscape of the town centre, and causing consternation amongst its morose pigeons. It was only when we drove out of the shelter of the town that we realised the hapless falcon had been blown clean down the Rhone. The *mistral* had arrived, the cold wind which funnels down the river valley from the mountains, and which can blow for days on end.

As we drove south in the comfort of the car, it actually proved rather welcome, and lent a bit of briskness to the landscape. Much of the northern reaches of the Camargue has been drained, desalinated and irrigated, and given over to rice growing. It is flat and monotonous, but neither this nor the wind seemed to be the slightest deterrent to the birds. Buzzards floated over the rice stubble. Marsh harriers hawked along the thickets of tamarisk and giant reed that fringe the irrigation channels. And wherever there were bigger patches of reed and open water, there was always the chance of a little egret, its long, dazzling white plumage in disarray in the gale.

Further south were more traditional Camargue prospects of marshy pastures, with bulls and white horses and the first saline pools. The lagoons were covered with immense rafts of duck. A small group of flamingoes huddled together against the wind, into which they projected 4 feet further than the ducks.

Beating against it ourselves, we sympathised with them. This particular *mistral* did not seem to be especially cold or powerful (though they have been known to stop trains in their tracks). But it did have a persistent, nagging bitterness that eventually made us feel raddled and tetchy. But it could have been a lot worse. It was during a December *mistral* that Van Gogh, Arles' most famous inhabitant, cut off his ear.

Later in the afternoon the wind dropped a little, and we meandered further south, down amongst the salt settling pans, where brackish water is left to evaporate until the salt can be scraped away. Salt is the Camargue's major industry, and more than a million tons are produced every year. The pans make a bizarre landscape, too briny to support many birds in winter, but with an odd crystalline life of its own. The wind was whipping the salt liquor into foam along the edges of the pans, where it hung like unset meringue, glinting erratically in the low sun.

Even though it was early December, the air seemed to have a lustrous Mediterranean glow, and I think it must have gone to our heads. We set off to drive back to Arles, but kept finding the sun swinging hypnotically to our right hand. Every so often, as if part of a conspiracy, hand-painted noticeboards advertising 'Marc et Mireille's Café du Poissons' appeared always pointing enticingly to the left. We were among the natural lagoons now, on tracks that sometimes seemed to be below the level of the water. Soon we were driving on the precarious sandy edges of the lagoons themselves, and the germ of an island-dweller's ancestral dread began to surface, and refused to be calmed by knowledge that the Mediterranean is not tidal.

We reached Marc and Mireille's in the end. It was a converted caravan propped up on a beach. We were hopelessly lost, and put our predicament – and our maps – before a group of wind surfers camped out on the beach. They were vastly amused, but showed us the way back – and also several ways that would *not* get us out.

Our unintended diversion proved a happy accident in the end, because it gave us the best views of flamingoes of our whole stay. There was a large flock in a lagoon close to the shore, not much more than 50 yards from the bank. But as we moved closer they edged further away. I suppose they were simply wading, in their fastidious, slow-motion way. But they looked for all the world as if they were *gliding* over the water, like a fleet of dhows, or the swimmers in an elaborate Esther Williams routine. Flamingoes have such an extraordinary appearance that it is hard to see them as birds whilst they are grounded. But once they are in the air – in tight formations of startling black and scarlet wings, with their long, deep red legs held stiffly back to serve as tailplanes – they are breathtaking.

Each morning we would wake to a cloudless sky and walk up to the nearest square to see if the tops of the plane trees were still shaking in the wind. They usually were, but the *mistral* didn't restrict us that much. We visited the vast Etang de Vaccares, the heart of the National Reserve, where most of the flamingoes breed. At dusk we parked the car by the side of a road and watched more than fifty marsh harriers come swooping and toying in the wind as they returned to their communal roost in the surrounding reedbeds. We spent a few hours in the stony wastes of Le Crau, on the eastern edge of the marshes, but it was a Sunday, and the hunters were out in force. We made a brief visit to the ruined village of Les Baux, in the limestone hills known as Les Alpilles, north of the region, and would have explored it more, but that afternoon the *mistral* was at its fiercest. It sucked our map (marked up with various choice bird sites) right out of the car, and whisked it off in the direction of the artillery on Le Crau. We ended up cowering in the car park of what is reputedly one of the best restaurants in France, watching black redstarts and wall creepers and a blue rock thrush with plumage the texture of shot silk darting about the limestone crags.

The day before we were due to leave the *mistral* blew itself out, and we decided to go back to Les Alpilles, where there was a chance of seeing an eagle owl. The hills are only a few miles from Arles, and their low, jagged peaks form the background to Van Gogh's celebrated painting of the blue cart. On the way we passed the *William Tell* film crew rigging up lights on the roof of the Abbey of Montmajour, ready for a night shoot.

Our destination was a track at the foot of the hills. On one side were a few small olive groves, on the other stretches of aromatic Mediterranean scrub, sweeping up to two limestone crags with a wooded pass between them. We got out of the car and waited. It was an almost perfect evening, still and not too cold. A thin moon appeared over the peaks, and as the sky darkened over the tracts of evergreen oak and flowering rosemary it was hard to believe it was winter.

At about 5.30, the eagle owl called, a deep, croaking hoot, sounding as if it was uttered at the bottom of a barrel. I missed its first flight between the two crags, but picked it up perched on the top of a cliff, presumably watching us. Through the binoculars it looked like a dead log, standing on end. When it finally launched itself into the air, it was as if an immense gargoyle had broken free of the cliff. It sailed out against the now purple sky for nearly twenty seconds without flapping its wings, and vanished in the general direction of the Abbey of Montmajour. Eagle owls have a wing span of 5 feet and appetites to match. They have been known to eat dogs, sheep and small eagles, and I would not put a young lighting engineer past them. The French, with an untypical show of respect for a bird, call it 'le grand-duc'.

On our final day I looked in on the Museon Arletan. It was rather like an extended attic, with a series of rooms stuffed with furniture, folk-costume, bulls' heads, herbalists' potions, and even a fully mocked-up interior of a *gardian*'s cabin. But the first floor was more organised, and unfolded the fascinating economic and cultural history of the Camargue. There were displays on the use of reed and willow, on local boat- and house-building techniques, on the salt industry (with some exquisite salt-crusted curios made by dipping toys and models repeatedly in the salt pans), and a fearsome exhibit on bird-trapping, which showed a nineteenth-century marshman swatting small migrants with something resembling an enormous cricket bat.

What the museum demonstrated was that the Camargue has not been a true wilderness for a very long time. It has been intimately (but respectfully) exploited for at least two thousand years, and its wildlife has coexisted with this use, helped by the alchemy that occurs when sunshine and water mix. But these are difficult times for the marshes. Small-scale farming and pasturing are in retreat here as everywhere, and tourism and development growing in intensity. The saving grace for the Camargue may be that at last the French are beginning to become concerned about the conservation of their own wildlife and landscapes. Flying back over a *massif central* blanketed by snow I remembered the extraordinary story we had been told about the flamingo rescue operation mounted during the terrible freeze-up of January 1985. About half the region's twenty thousand flamingoes remained in France during the cold spell, and of these nearly three thousand died. Another thousand were found close to starvation. They were wrapped in blankets and taken off to be looked after in homes and schools right along the Camargue coast. They were fed on rice and dog food, and a further 20 tons of rice (equivalent to the annual consumption of a small town) was put down for the birds still sticking it out in the wild. When the freeze-up ended the birds were released. Not one of them had died, and the people of the Camargue had shown their affection for the real bird behind the tourist symbol.

Green Crete (1989)

The coastline of northern Crete is an embarrassing reminder of the fickle power of tourism. It is lined with rows of unfinished apartment blocks, identically framed in reinforced concrete, and already beginning to look like prefabricated antiquities. They were begun in a hopeful rush during Crete's tourist boom, and put on hold, maybe permanently, when the fashionable destinations moved east. They are just the latest in a long line of blights caused by culture contact. It is no consolation recalling that the Cretans were probably the first overseas visitors to the British Isles, and that we are, as it were, just returning the compliment. When the Minoans sailed into the newly opened English Channel nearly six thousand years ago, they set the mould for the evolution of the English landscape. It's them we have to thank for pastoral farming, the downs on the southern chalk hills, the first long-distance trackways, and perhaps for that persistent thread of nature-worship in our own culture. Summer season discos and a ravaged coastline seem a rather poor swap.

But flying out in the middle of April for the spring flowers and migrating birds, our little party had banished guilt under a sense of missionary purpose. We were, the brochures had assured us, amongst the pioneers of a new approach to tourism, which could turn it from a ruiner of landscapes to an economically powerful force for conservation.

The Cretan version of this idea had come from the Norfolk Naturalists Trust. Anne Cryer, who had been in thrall to the island since she first came here as a student, had begun to organise wildlife holidays for Trust members in 1986. The island has long been famous as a botanical paradise, a stronghold of wild bulbous species and hundreds of indigenous rarities. But Anne had also discovered another treasure – a string of lagoons on the north coast at Gouves, 16 kilometres east of Heraklion. For an arid island, perched on one of the trans-Mediterranean migration routes, these amounted to an oasis. Even on those early visits it became obvious that the lagoons had an exceptional tally of migrant birds. Flocks of three different species of heron called in, as did flamingoes, black-winged stilts and the piratical Eleonora's falcon, which haunts the seaways round the Mediterranean islands, picking off swallows and martins. In all, 168 species had been logged by 1989. Alas, there was one serious problem. Greece hadn't yet caught up with Europe's environmental awakening, and the lagoons, which are owned by the villagers of Gouves, were being used by them as a communal rubbish pit.

Anne returned to Crete with a plan to save the lagoons by promoting them as one of the key attractions of the area, flourishing the carrot of planeloads of green tourists. By a stroke of luck the lagoons lie right next to a commodious hotel, and there was no difficulty in getting the cooperation of the manager, who also happened to be a local politician. Things went well to begin with. The rubbish dumping was stopped, and the hotel agreed to a hide being built at the edge of its garden, over-looking the lagoons. The prospect of watching stilts within hailing distance of the poolside bar seemed a considerable bonus point for the jaunt.

The hide was clearly visible as the coach rolled up to the dazzling frontage – more Polynesian than Aegean – of the hotel. But the lagoons, strewn with hard core and not helped by the drought which had set in weeks earlier than usual, looked rather miserable. So did Anne. She had been biting her lip during the journey, and confessed that there had been some new developments. The Greek elections were only a few weeks away, and local political pressure had made the informal agreement over dumping go by the board. Nearly a third of the pools had been filled in. And now the villagers were putting Phase Two of their own development scheme into operation, and building a football pitch over the top.

Outside the hotel there were forbidding rows of coaches from Wuppertal and Dortmund. Inside, the open-plan lobby was full of brisk tracksuited couples and posters announcing tennis knock-outs and cycling races. The slightest flickers of disdain could be glimpsed on the British faces. It looked as if the scene were set for an old-style Athenian tournament, or maybe an Eistedfodd, with several ancient European tribes displaying their different ways of celebrating the land.

I was glad this hotel had been finished. My room had an extraordinary view, over the garden and swimming pool to the sea, which was no more than 50 metres away. When I drew back the shutters at about 6 a.m. the first round (Ritual Improvisation in Small Groups) was already under way. Out in the pool virile Wuppertalians in black wet suits were toiling through the water, pausing only for little bursts of aerobics on the side. Below my balcony a dozen or so Brits straggled back from the daily stroll to catch the dawn migrants, telescopes over their shoulders like retreating guerrillas. 'Anything about?' 'Not a lot. Eleonora's in from the sea. Flock of purple herons down on the lagoons.' A *flock* of purple herons! All I could manage were four night herons that clattered out of the willows next to my balcony, where they'd presumably been roosting. Down in the garden Sardinian warblers darted amongst the lawn-sprayers as nonchalantly as robins. Round one to the birds I reckoned for Economy of Performance.

Over breakfast I asked Doug Ireland, our West Country guide, about the herons, trying to disguise my chagrin at having missed them. There had been more than fifty, migrating north before the sun got up, and he reckoned they'd been disorientated by the low mist over the mountains. 'You have to get up early to see these things,' said Doug, in his off-duty sergeant's voice that we came to know and love.

I never did get my metabolism in a condition to cope with the dawn patrol, and had to endure these humiliating tallies every morning. But that first day the whole party – about thirty strong – had an introductory tour of what was left of the lagoons in the company of Doug, Ivan Loades, our botanist, and Chris Gibson, who worked for the Nature Conservancy Council and passed most of his holidays as a guide. There were still plenty of birds about. By the side of the river that fed the lagoon, tufts of giant reed and tamarisk rang with the croaks of great reed warblers ('You'll believe a frog can fly,' someone quipped) and the whiplash calls of Cetti's warblers. A little egret got up from the river, and wafted away like a windblown shawl. By midday the temperature was already approaching eighty degrees, and Chris Gibson spotted some terrapins basking on the muddy edges of the river, their shells tilted up to catch the sun.

But it was the plants that were most extraordinary. Down on the beach, amongst the debris blowing in from the rubbish-filled lagoons, were legions of wiry creepers and spreaders: a beautiful bi-coloured sea-lavender, naturalised mesembryanthemums from southern Africa, and the first of Crete's endemic species (there are 140-plus, almost a tenth of the entire flora), a dwarf chamomile with yellow button flowers. As we moved further up the beach into the scrub zone, the varieties of armour against heat and drought and browsing animals multiplied. There were waxy-leaved sea-hollies and a wild cucumber with exploding pods that sprayed would-be predators with a mixture of seeds and toxic juice. There was a shrubby burnet covered with a protective net of what looked exactly like chicken wire. Mostly though, the plants were spiny. The thyme was spiny. The saltwort was spiny. Even the local species of wild asparagus was spiny, and had an alarming resemblance to strands from a flagellant's whip.

That afternoon we walked onto the lower reaches of the steep rocky hill that rose behind the village. Everyone called this after the landmark on the top, two huge saucer-shaped US listening devices, pointed unambiguously at Libya, and christened 'the Mickey Mouse ears'. They were a favourite loafing site for griffon vultures, and several times we saw one of these feathered planks – 6 feet in wing span – soar out into the thermals. They are the most languid of birds, and when they have gorged themselves at a carcass they simply tip themselves off a rock ledge. I don't think I have ever seen one so much as flap a wing.

We were amongst olive groves here, and in a different kind of landscape. This was the *maquis*, the low scrub that covers much of the island. It is full of shrubs familiar in their garden versions – brooms, euphorbias, rue, lavender, myrtle – many of them aromatic from the oily coating that helps their leaves conserve moisture and repel browsing animals. But the strangest plant was the dragon arum, a relative of our cuckoo-pint whose 'flower' is a vast purple hood up to a metre long, sheathing a chocolate-brown spadix that smells of rotten meat. It grows quite promiscuously on roadsides, amongst the olives, at the edge of farmyards, sometimes out of cracks in the rock. Edward Lear, who travelled through the island in the spring of 1864, saw masses of the plant on the same mid-April date. He described it in his journals as 'brutal-filthy yet picturesque', which seemed a fair summing-up.

But the island as a whole he found far from picturesque. It was too rugged for his formal Claudian tastes, too much a place of muddled foreground detail, and he complained constantly about the lack of the kind of 'drawable' scenes he had found in earlier travels in Italy and the Near East. But he loved the birds, and his sightings for that day – orioles, hoopoes, bee-eaters – would have made him a star at the ritual into which we were initiated that evening. After dinner, as the fashion shows and talent contests reached clamorous heights round the bar, our contingent retired to a side room for the Calling of the Birds. The rules were simple but strict. Doug Ireland would intone the family names of Crete's 300-plus species, and members of the party would give details of their sightings that day. Precision was the thing. Our gleeful report of the languorous vultures, and the peregrine falcon that had streaked above us while we were rummaging in the *maquis*, was greeted with the phrase '*How many?*' – uttered in the tones of a man whose patience with the vagueness of his fellows was frequently tested, but inexhaustible.

The party – a mix largely of teachers, librarians, health workers, local government officers – were well able to hold their own in this kind of banter. It was the loosest possible kind of holiday, and over the next few days people could join in the organised activities as and when they wished. There were trips to Knossos, to the salt pans round the peninsula of Spinalonga, and down to the estuary at Agia Triada. But botanically it was not proving a good year, and the drought and unseasonally high temperatures meant that most of the spring flowers had already shrivelled up – at least on low-lying sites.

So with a friend I decided to take a private trip due south, over the hill country in the centre of the island and down to the coast. Away from the arid and over-developed coastal strip things looked decidedly brighter. The scrub got thicker and richer the further we drove inland, with dazzling shows of cistus and phlomis. The masses of exquisite white bells on the styrax bushes looked almost oriental amongst all this colour. Then, on the foothills, there were cyclamen and orchids scattered in the dappled shade of the evergreen oaks – including the delectable *Orchis papilionacea*, whose name for once exactly catches the flower's look of a cluster of folded purple butterflies. We found more Cretan endemics too: a woody goosegrass, whose sticky tendrils emerged from a solid trunk, like a cat-o'-nine-tails, and the island's most celebrated native, Cretan Ebony. This member of the pea family, with deep pink flowers and silver-haired leaves, grows in great clusters on the steep roadsides and white limestone cliffs, and from a distance has the look of a mass of heather lightly dusted with hoar frost.

We ate grilled chicken under an immense pollarded plane in Ano Viannos, and along with what seemed the entire village, watched the day's drama – a miniature bulldozer trying to create some kind of viaduct under the street. Pollarding was another sustainable technique probably invented by the Minoans, and it was surprising and depressing to find how little forest cover remained when we took off further south in the afternoon. As we began to tip downhill towards the coast, the landscape grew as brown and barren as North Africa. After an hour of hairpin bends on a worsening dirt track and nothing visible in front of us except miles of bare mountains, the first tremors of panic began, at the possibility that we might have somehow got off the road system altogether. The pot-holes became bigger and the space between track and cliff narrower. Then, quite sickeningly, we were motoring along what seemed to be a ridge, with sheer drops on both sides of us. The mountain had simply been dynamited apart. We'd strayed into an agrobusiness version of terrace cultivation – not for grapes or maize, but for what we could now see spreading out below us – a vast honeycombed metropolis of polythene greenhouses. Not a soul was about but through rips in the brown plastic we could see that the houses were stuffed with two of Crete's principal exports – carnations and bananas. Like most cash crops, they didn't seem to have benefited the locals much. When we finally arrived at a village it was like something from a Steinbeck novel – a sad collection of shacks and run-down bars, with piece-workers leaning listlessly against the walls.

Crete's landscape and economy have been buffeted by centuries of occupation and over-grazing, and now have to endure the mixed blessings of the Common Agricultural Policy. But the treelessness of the south and the whole coastal belt has just as much to do with the intense heat and summer drought (the Libyan Desert is only 400 miles to the south). To see how lush Crete can still be you have only to travel to the west of the island. The hills south of Rethymnon have something of the look of the Lake District. There are woods of plane and the native cypress in the ravines, and meadows of orchids and turban buttercups.

This is also gorge country. There are more than a hundred gorges in the island, mostly ranging north-south and ending up at the sea. Driving down one afternoon to Plakias (where there is a small colony of the island's strangest endemic, the stumpy and wistful Cretan palm) we passed through the gorge of Kotsiphou. It is only a little wider than the road at its northern end, and alpine swifts and crag martins flickered about the cliff faces high above. Further south the gorge widened out, and we stopped to watch the birds of prey gliding in the thermals. There were kestrels, buzzards, a brief glimpse of a peregrine, and two gorgeous golden eagles, soaring at such an obliging angle to the sun that I could see the pale patches on their rumps and wings.

Then, watching a group of griffons idling above the furthest ridge, I saw a different bird join the circle. It had the jizz of an immense falcon more than a vulture, with narrow scimitar wings and an extraordinary diamond-shaped tail. I was sure, though I had never seen one before, that it was Crete's supreme bird, and Europe's largest and rarest vulture, the fabled lammergeier. Lammergeiers haunt the most remote mountainous reaches, and have the unique habit of dropping bones from a height onto rocks to split them open for the marrow. Watching this one circling with its cousins, a dark, ominous crossbow, outstretched wings held dead level, it seemed like a mythic bird, something half-remembered from another age. I remembered John Fowles' account of resting while mountain-climbing not far from here, and suddenly finding a lammergeier hanging 20 feet above his head, 'its great wings feathering and flexed to the wind current, a savage hooked beak tilted down towards me. I lay as still as a stone, like Sinbad under the roc. For some ten seconds the great bird and I were transfixed, in a kind of silent dialogue.' I wondered what kind of reception my more distant encounter would get from the House Meeting that evening.

It got, needless to say, a steely inquisition from Doug Ireland. Lammergeiers were one of the most longed-for species, and ever since one had been spotted, stuffed and mounted over the bar in a mountain taverna, sightings had been greeted with scepticism. I still do not know if my record was accepted. But after nearly a week everyone was willing to have a go at bird-log banter, sure enough of their own skills – and Doug's – to risk spoof sightings and irreverent quips.

'Any shearwaters?'

'Corys. Lots of them. Over the sea.'

'*How many*, Janet?'

Janet, the librarian, who had been gently ribbed all week for her disorganised vagueness over the red-throated pipit populations, replied quick as a flash, 'Two thousand five hundred, if I heard you correctly this morning.' Peter the planning officer, a master of one-liners, logged a swan he had spotted in the Knossos murals. 'Almost certainly mute.' Richard, who had made something of a cabaret act out of his sightings of sparrows, received huge applause for rising to the new challenge of greenfinches. 'How many?' '*Four.* Outside the taverna. *Before* lunch.'

In the bar, Wuppertal was demolishing the small Dutch contingent in a ballroom-dancing competition. I wondered if our evening routine, a cross between Bingo and ornithological Mastermind, was just a more decorous British version of holiday sports. Or worse, a kind of ecological colonialism. I can only hope that it was making some small contribution to the logging of the biological resources of what is still only a patchily known island.

On our last day we went out to the plain of Lassithi, and had a glimpse of the direction Cretan land-use is currently taking. Lassithi is a high plateau, perhaps the dried-out remains of a prehistoric lake, and is an oasis of rich soil amongst the mountains. We were due to walk straight across, a comparatively easy tramp of about seven kilometres on the flat. But it was blazing hot, the wind was blowing up sandstorms, no one was quite sure of the right path, and we ended up straggling for hours amongst the parched fields. All over the plain were the remains of hundreds of small windmills, once used for irrigation. Now the water is pumped electrically. But the soil was still desperately dry, and the crops looked in a dejected state. Tractors and mules passed each other, harrowing adjacent strips. Cretan men, lounging under trees, urged their wives on to greater efforts with the hoes, and seemed unsurprised by the sight of this gaggle of mad English people hiking across the prairie in the afternoon sun.

A scarce swallowtail butterfly took a shine to one of our number's blue anorak, and we heard a quail giving its persistent, knife-whetting call out in the fields. But there was precious little natural life about and a stench of pesticide in the air. We thought we glimpsed a man broadcasting seed, but he was strewing fertiliser pellets, by hand. It was an image which seemed to sum up this place, caught – as Crete itself now is, in a way – between two different attitudes towards nature and the land.

The Lubéron (1990)

The Montagne du Lubéron, a flower-decked limestone bastion 15 miles north of Aix-en-Provence, has been a favourite retreat of the French middle classes since the last century. Full of stone-built hillside villages and poised between the airy woods of the *massif* and the warm south, it is a kind of Mediterranean Cotswolds, picturesque and pastoral but rapidly losing its indigenous inhabitants. In 1977 the government designated the whole region as a Parc Régional Naturel, in the hope of reviving its rural communities and achieving a *modus vivendi* between tourism and the traditional economy. Since then the Parc has become a showpiece for changing French attitudes towards conservation. It has a reputation for magnificent wild flowers and *aspects naturels* and seemed a place where it was worth chancing an early spring visit.

We were based in Les Baux at an elegantly converted farmhouse. Les Baux itself is a medieval fortress town and one-time troglodytes colony, perched on a sheer spur of rock at the western end of the limestone ridge. From the hotel garden we could just make out what would be our terrain for the next few days, a pale swell of hills looking rather worryingly distant and austere.

But our base was too comfortable to make us bothered about the daily haul into the Parc. And Les Baux itself is a salutary reminder of the cavalier way that history and climate can treat settlements in wild country-side. In medieval times it was best known as a centre of the troubadour tradition. But it was also a stronghold of troublesome Protestant warlords, and in 1632 Cardinal Richelieu ordered that its castle and ramparts be destroyed. When the surrounding marshlands were subsequently drained and cultivated most of the remaining population moved down onto the plain. Les Baux became little more than a ghost town. When we arrived it was under siege by *mistral*-driven rainstorms, and busloads of French schoolchildren were doing passable imitations of troglodytes sheltering in the decaying archways and rock-gouged dwelling spaces.

Next day the *mistral* was still gusting, and the billboards trumpeting 'La Route du Soleil' along the road from Les Baux to the Lubéron looked absurdly optimistic. But in summer it is clearly a different story. There were forest conservation posters beside the roads, too, nailed up above blackened pine stumps and ground seared down to the bare rock, evidence of what an inflammable brew sun and holidaymakers can be. '*Pensez à la forêt*' and '*La forêt embellit la vie*' they read, a sign perhaps that two summers of rampant forest fires were having the same effect on French tree-consciousness as two hurricanes have had on ours.

But the climate has also made the southern foothills of the Lubéron perfect for fruit-growing. To the south of the hills the Durance valley is full of orchards of cherries, pears and peaches, trained and pruned in every conceivable way. There were cordons, espaliers, *double* espaliers. In the village squares even the plane trees were pleached.

We left the valley near Mérindol and climbed up towards the ridge, through tiers of pine-sheltered holiday villas. Then they thinned out, and we were in the *garigue*, the tangle of aromatic shrubs and herbs that covers much of the hill country of the Mediterranean. On cue the sun came out, and as if a wand had been waved over them, clouds of butterflies wafted into the air – swallowtails, clouded yellows, adonis blues. Buzzards and black kites materialised in the thermals, and we found early spider orchids lurking amongst the juniper and thyme. After our somewhat gloomy first glimpses from the hotel, the Lubéron began to look like the natural paradise it was reputed to be. But these high plateaux seemed to have been virtually abandoned by agriculture. The surviving farmhouses had been expensively converted, and livid patches of swimming-pool blue shimmered incongruously in a landscape of withering vines and burgeoning Mediterranean scrub.

Further on the wildwood was making even more impressive advances. Stretching along the Lubéron's western ridge is a cedar forest, which the Parc authorities are taking steps to protect. The day we were there the through road had been closed specifically for the benefit of the wildlife and vegetation. All this was carefully and courteously explained on notice-boards, along with the story of the cedar trees. Although they are no longer native to Provence, they had apparently grown here twenty thousand years ago. These new specimens had arrived here ('*par eaux*' the board said mysteriously) from the Atlas Mountains in Morocco in the 1860s. Presumably they were planted, but they are already sizeable enough to be setting their own seedlings and nourishing a host of fungi. Visitors were welcome to pick these, the notices advised, provided it was done '*avec mesure*'.

On the damper north-facing slopes, the cedar forest merges with homely oakwoods. To the south it dissolves in a haze of rosemary, box and cistus scrub studded with grape-hyacinths and jonquils. Much of the current vegetation of Provence is the result of the deforestation and over-exploitation of poor soils. So the return of woodland cover is generally welcomed, especially now that cultivation itself is retreating even further down the hill. The old crops of silkworms and lavender and even olives have largely vanished. So have the communities that grew them. The hilltop villages look dramatically beautiful clinging to the steep limestone terraces, but have the feel of open-air museums.

Bonnieux, where the medieval ramparts still survive, is full of art galleries and up-market estate agents. Menerbes, 10 kilometres to the west, is an eyrie of a village, and once a strategic fortress during the conflicts between Catholic and Protestants that raged violently in the Lubéron in the sixteenth century. The most stunning of the villages is Roussillon, which stands on a rare outcrop of red sandstone. The buildings are almost entirely constructed out of this local rock, which comes in something like twenty different shades of ochre and gives the village the sense of being a piece of rare confectionery. But there was no one in the restaurants, and the tourists in the streets walked in slow, reverential motion.

We found a more cheerful refuge in Lacoste and sat outside a hillside bar, eating omelettes a foot long and watching the returning swallows coasting up the valley. The village, where the Marquis de Sade had his estate in the late eighteenth century, had a distinctly bohemian feel and there was a boisterous group of expatriate English artists and teachers at the bar. With them was a prime specimen of an increasingly common species in the wilder areas of rural Europe: the off-the-tracks know-all. He happened, on this occasion, to be English and visiting a daughter, and was dressed in a telling combination of viyella shirt and bare feet. Any turn in the conversation would be capped by him with a story more exotic, more knowing, more homespun. He had a Catalan joke, a Palestinian joke, a fresh-minted Latvian nationalist joke. When his *pommes frites* arrived, he had a first-hand Harry Ramsden's Fish and Chip Shop yarn. His recently acquired London bus-pass seemed capable of magically whisking him to his weekend house in Bruges. He collected culture bites like lesser mortals amassed car stickers.

He would, I suspect, have felt completely at home in the august museum of *bories* at Gordes. The *bories* are a feature of local vernacular architecture, and are shelters built – usually in the rough shape of igloos – from layered limestone slabs, much as dry-stone walls are constructed. They were normally used as sheep-pens or barns, but the earliest date from the Iron Age and probably served as dwelling places. In accordance with upwardly mobile Lubéron trends, a group of the best have been spruced up, gentrified and preserved in an outdoor museum. We got a more vivid sense of them by prowling around the patchwork of orchid-strewn scrub and pastures near the villages, where many still have a working role as outhouses.

On our penultimate day it was perceptibly warmer, and we opted to explore a south-west facing hillside that looked – from the map at least

– as if it might squeeze the most from the sunshine. It was better than we could ever have imagined. Just a few yards from where we parked, the *garigue* was thick with tiny jonquils, rock-roses and budding wild pinks. A few hundred yards further up the narrow hill road, the irises began. They were *Iris chamaeiris*, very short-stemmed but with big blowsy blossoms, in a huge variety of mauves and blues. Some, coloured with striations of deep Tyrian purple, had a bouquet like that of Florentine irises. There was another extraordinary scent experience a little higher up. Amid sheets of stubby, dark blue grape-hyacinths and pink valerian, so thick that in places they obscured the powdery white rock below, were spikes of the buttercup *Ranunculus gramineus*, with the clear, penetrating scent of jasmine. And at the top, up to our knees in wild thyme and looking out across billows of snowy mespilus on the crags, we realised that we were standing amongst clumps of star-flowered yellow tulips, arranged as exquisitely about the limestone terraces as if they had been in a rock-garden. I doubt that we had covered much more than a mile through the scrub, yet had strolled amongst galleries and bowers of flowers the like of which I have seen nowhere else.

We had a celebratory feast that evening, on the kind of *haut paysan* cuisine in which our Mas specialised: tangy aperitifs distilled from local herbs and flowers, a lasagne made with langoustines, home-made brawn, *lotte* and rice from the Camargue (only 10 miles to the south), rabbit, and sheep and goat cheeses.

When we got up the next morning, departure day, we found the weather had leaped straight into summer. Alpine swift packs were hurtling round the fortifications of Les Baux against a clear blue sky, and nightingales and hoopoes were singing in the valley. It was Mediterranean weather, tourist weather, but maybe not the weather for that wild alpine garden on the Lubéron slopes, that we had probably seen on its best day of the season.

The Burren (1991)

Landscapes are supposed to be cut down to size on second visits, to lose their sense of holding something back. Not so the Burren in County Clare, which, for me at least, has swelled to sublime proportions over the years. I first visited this 400 square kilometres of shattered limestone in the mid-seventies. There were four of us on the trip, all mad for flowers, and we spent that June week in a kind of myopic ecstasy, riveted by the magic and sheer Irishness of every incongruous bloom and crevice. Down on the shores of Galway Bay, we scraped sea-salt crystals from the beds of spongy, lichen-blacked limestone that dip down into the Atlantic. In Lisdoonvarna, a town of shrines and spas, we lounged under palm trees in the languid air and watched the nuns parade past. But mostly we just peered in amazement at the flowers at our feet, at their brilliant profusion and contempt for botanical protocol. Spring gentians grew next to sea-pinks; mountain avens – tufts of pure-white petals and twisted, silky seed-plumes – were more luxuriant than the grass; and there were centuries-old trees, rooted in the deep fissures in the rock, that had never reached above ground level. I remember wearing through a brand new pair of fashionable Kickers hopping about the razorbacked crags – an achievement which sums up rather well my naive passion for the place. I saw all the bejewelled fragments, but barely noticed the immense geological story written in the rocks, or the evidence of at least four thousand years of human occupation.

When I returned to the Burren, fifteen years older and not quite so single-minded, it seemed impossibly vast. As so often in this place of incongruity and optical illusion, serendipity played a part in broadening my outlook. I had been driving down from Shannon airport, through miles of that archetypal Celtic fieldscape of straggly blackthorn hedges and rushy pastures dotted with little round haycocks. Then, somewhere north of Lisdoonvarna, I got tangled up with a herd of homebound cattle on a steep downhill road. We spiralled through the narrow S-bends together at a graceful, glacial pace – and through the mêlée of Friesian necks and roadside trees I caught my first glimpse of the Moneen hills rotating gently the other way – as white as bleached bone, and like a bright new island rising out of the green valley-lands.

I had the same view, only closer, from my hotel in Gragan. It was a classic Burren vista: a series of hunched limestone ridges, receding into the distance. That evening I sat by my window and watched the rocks pick up first the golds, then the pinks of the sunset; and then, as the light faded, show every glaciated shelf and terrace in silhouette.

The Burren is named from the Celtic *boirrean*, a stony place. There are tracts of sour shale and moorland, but it is exposed limestone that dominates the landscape and gives it character and liveliness. Limestone has a stark and austere feel only in distant profile, and in every other way seems disarmingly open and adaptable. It wears its history on its sleeve – or maybe like lines on a face. In his strange, audacious poem 'In Praise of Limestone', W. H. Auden called it 'a stone that responds', an ice-sculpted, weatherworn rock that is marked out 'because it dissolves in water'. Almost all the typical features of the Burren landscape – the scree-strewn scars, the flattened terraces, the grooved 'pavements' – depend on this fact.

The Burren was even born this way, laid down under shallow seas 300 million years ago from the slow, skeletal rain of myriads of dead sea creatures. Later, earth movements raised and buckled the hills and sent searing splits through the rock layers, most of them running roughly north-south. (The splits are known as 'grikes' and the flat rock slabs between them as 'clints'.) Thousands of years of weathering scraped out the rough pattern of valleys, hills and terraces that are visible today. Finally, about twenty thousand years ago, the glaciers of the last Ice Age rounded off the slopes, scoured the limestone bare in some places and dumped drifts of clay and gravel in others.

Seven thousand years ago the Burren almost certainly developed a scattered cover of open, deciduous woodland. Then, about 3,500 BC, the first farmers (probably from the Mediterranean) arrived with their crops and cattle. They found the light woodland, loosely rooted on soft rock, easy to clear, and grazing animals, heavy rainfall and soil erosion ensured that it didn't grow back. For the last few hundred years the Burren has been as open as it probably was soon after the retreat of the last glaciers.

Has the landscape helped shape the inhabitants, as well as being shaped by them? Auden reckoned these intricate regions of 'short distances and definite places' bred hedonistic, capricious characters. Certainly the Burren's history seems full of paradox and impulsiveness. It looks barren at first sight, but, well-drained and warmed by the Gulf Stream, stays green enough through winter for the local farmers to operate a system that is a converse of the continental tradition of transhumance. The stock is taken up into the hills in late autumn and down into the valley pastures in summer.

Yet despite this year-round fertility, occupation in the Burren seems to have been a transient and hard-won affair. The area is littered with the shells of dwellings and monuments from almost every period of history since the Bronze Age – all now tumbling back to rock. Even its basic ecology is baffling, an aggregation of plants that occur together nowhere else in Europe – Mediterranean and Arctic, mountain and seashore, woodland and field species sometimes growing in the same few square yards. How did they get here? Or is it more a question of why none of them was driven away? Ten thousand years ago, before the climax forest was fully established, plants we now think of as confined to specialised habitats probably grew side by side throughout the dry part of Britain. The weather was benign, the ground open and unshaded and there was no great competition for space. Then – in eastern and northern Britain, at least – came climate change, the great shading by the wildwood, and the arrival of agriculture. Each one of these developments acted to drive the more sensitive species into marginal refuges.

But these traumatic changes were much less marked in the Burren. It has remained a congenial place, free of frost and flood and of dense woodland cover, and its remarkable flora may be an authentic relic of that post-glacial Eden.

Limestone seems to exert a congenial influence on me, too. For a whole day I ranged about the hills between Ballyvaughan and Kilnaboy, stopping the car at any likely crag or pavement and rock-hopping away. The bright – barefaced, you could say – intricacy of the rock seems to pull you up and along, niche-hunting like a migrant plant yourself.

At the foot of the hills the rock is usually tangled with low blackthorn scrub, drapes of bloody crane's-bill (in full magenta flower in early July) and burnet roses, whose cream-coloured flowers fill the breeze with scent. You climb up, and every lip and crack of rock seems to be different – bevelled, rounded, honeycombed, leached by water, sometimes redeposited as stone worm-casts or imitation fossils: 'definite places' indeed. You spot a glossy hartstongue fern in a deep grike, grown enormously long in its search for the light; feathery sprays of meadow-rue; an ancient ash tree, extending horizontally along a crevice, and another topiaried by grazing animals into an almost perfect hemisphere.

Every so often the rocky hillsides flatten into plateaux, or into true limestone pavements which have been scoured of most of their turf. This is where the great mats of spring flowers grow, often on thin platforms of humus that have built up on the clints. It is also a very sonorous landscape. Desiccated lichens and rose-leaves crisped in the July sun scrunch under foot; loose clints sway and clatter, a bony, ringing, almost tonic note. In the distance I hear a few words floating from the Tannoy of a sightseeing coach – 'four hundred years ago, the Burren . . .' I never hear the rest. The past here seems insubstantial, rock-dust, not much older than the seed heads of the gentians and orchids that drench these plateaux blue, white and purple in May. The landscape seems fresh-minted, and in the glaring sun reflected off the white rock, has the look of an emerging image on a photographic plate. I am tugged this way and that by things just at the edge of vision: a pool of distant yellow which turns into a prostrate gold-leaved holly; a *trompe-l'oeil* wedge-tomb 6 inches high, which some walker has propped up on a slab. I need to make a conscious effort to stop and perch on a boulder. Even then the landscape still seems to be on the move. Flakes of mica-thin rock, limestone *mille-feuille*, flutter down the terraces. The breeze ruffles a thin puddle of water on top of a slab – a 'tadpole runnel' that will eventually dissolve its way through the rock.

I look down over miles of terraces below me, and find it hard to believe that there was ever anything as monumental as a forest here. How long could a tree have lasted (even without human interference) with its roots twisted round this friable rock? Was the primeval woodland here not only full of glades and gaps, but feet deep in fallen timber?

But what has survived are the hazel woods. They were the natural pioneer woodland here and their nuts must have been a valuable food source for the Stone Age settlers. They may even be advancing again as grazing animals drop off in numbers. The Burren hazel woods come in all sizes. Some are so dense that you must crawl about them on your hands and knees. Others are growing in minimal soil or grazed hard back so that you can experience, like Gulliver, the bizarre sensation of wandering through a forest that comes up no higher than your chest. It is in these stunted woodlets on the barest rocks that you can also have the disorientating experience of seeing alpine flowers – gentian and mountain avens especially – growing under the trees.

I shoulder my way into one of the taller hazel groves, on the site of an Iron Age fort at Cathair Mhor. It is humid and oddly hushed inside, and the floor is strewn with boulders and fallen branches, and swathed in a blanket of moss up to 8 inches thick in places. I creep about as softly as I can, but the moss still shows deep, accusing pits where my feet have been. For a moment I have a mad fancy that I may be the first person to have been in this particular corner of the wood since the Iron Age. It is, I suppose, more of a bower than a wood, and though it has primroses, bluebells and orchids, they are not growing in masses as in woods where the ground is less tenanted, but in ones and twos wherever the moss is compact enough. And in the dappled shade at the edge of the woodlet I find my first specimen of the Irish spotted orchid, a pure white spike so distinctive to this part of the world that it has an Irish Latin name –

Dactylorchis fuchsii ssp. *okellyi* – after the Ballyvaughan nurseryman who discovered it.

The next day was what the Irish euphemistically call 'soft'. There was scudding low cloud and a threat of rain, and I decided to curb my puppyish scampering about the rocks and go on a more purposeful journey. I armed myself with T. D. Robinson's lyrical map of the Burren, which eschews contour lines in favour of outlines of the geological forms of terraces and cliffs (what he calls 'the grain of the land') and which is densely covered with the sites of cairns, ring-forts, tombs and turloughs. It is a map – understandably, among these history-cheating rocks – organised around the sense of vision, not time.

In the hamlet of Turlough itself, just east of Ballyvaughan, I found a huge example of those mysterious pools, which during wet weather fill with water bubbling up through subterranean channels in the limestone, and drain the same way, sometimes in a matter of hours. This one was nearly half a mile across and maybe 10 feet deep in places – only it was almost devoid of water. Cattle were grazing the flush of grass which follows flooding, and which makes the summer turloughs an important part of the Burren farming system.

I drove on south, and during a squall of rain stopped the car near a derelict farmhouse close to Poulbaun. Up on the hills to the west I could see the slivers of stone, like crosses and hands, which have been jammed upright in the crags above the crumbling remains of ancient, curving enclosures. Even under louring skies they didn't seem like emblems of melancholy or hardship so much as, in Robinson's words, 'memorials to the tedium of the herdsman's life'.

A few miles on, just north of Kilnaboy, the relics of the triple cliff fort, Cathair Chomain, c. AD 1,000, looked scarcely more durable. The hazel woods were creeping up the hill towards it and the stone fortifications slowly collapsing into the scree. Just below it, precisely the same thing was happening to the shell of a lurid farm bungalow, built with blue and pink bricks c. 1958. And a few hundred yards further on, I saw the garden of a roadside cottage which, despite a shrine to Mary near the pergola, was being slowly reclaimed by the vast natural rockery outside.

Why has occupation been so casual and ephemeral here? What has repeatedly made people settle in numbers and then just walk away? There was famine, of course, during the nineteenth century, and a continual leakage of people since. But the visible remains of settlement in the Burren go back at least three thousand years. There are sixty-six megalithic tombs dating from between 2,000 and 1,400 BC; nearly five hundred ring forts (cathairs) and similar enclosures, from between 200 BC and the late medieval period; and many hundreds of farms, hovels and goat huts abandoned since then.

I sat by one of the neolithic gallery graves at Creevagh and pondered this almost nomadic history. These communal tombs, made out of limestone rocks and topped with three giant slabs in the shape of a wedge, are the most enduring features of the landscape. Yet there is not the slightest air of melancholy or Gothickness clinging to them. The tomb at Creevagh had wild flowers on its huge topping slab, and turf that may have been there since it was first raised. Inside the wedge it looked friendly enough to sleep in. I wondered if animals ever bedded down there in bad weather, as the last Irish bears had in Ailwee cave, near Ballyvaughan. The early human settlers were apparently more claustrophobic: no evidence of human residence has been found in any of the local caves. Even then this ringing landscape seemed to be saying the same thing to its visitors: stay on top, hang loose, move on.

A freewheeling spirit certainly infuses the few settlements that have survived in the Burren. I spent my last day, a Saturday, meandering round them – and rapidly wished I'd been based in one, instead of out in the backlands. In Kilfenora, there is a Burren visitors' centre, owned and run by the people of the village and showing videos and displays of the region's history and ecology. Doolin, away on the west coast above the Cliffs of Moher, is a small but rumbustious village, a centre of local craftspeople and of Irish music. O'Connor's bar was a furious place at lunchtime, full of old hippies, fishermen, travellers of the more adventurous sort, and ad hoc musicians. I supped a stew and watched the place start jigging to a solo penny whistler who just happened to start up between pints. Musical tastes here are very eclectic: the Dutchman pounding his glass of Guinness on the table next to me was wearing a Pogues T-shirt, and in Lisdoonvarna, the live music that was advertised in every bar on every day of the week ranged from show band and country and western to unaccompanied Celtic ballads.

Lisdoonvarna is the eccentric capital of the Burren, and the place to take its human pulse. It is a spa town, a place of festivals and reunions. On the walls of the bars there are countless pictures of one-time regulars, news clippings about emigrants, mottos and snippets of crackerbarrel philosophy. In the autumn, after harvest, there is a celebrated 'match-making week' here, when bachelor farmers of a certain age come in the hope of finding wives. In 1990 they rounded the season off by holding the World Barbecue Championship here. Any moment you expect the travelling medicine show to ride into town.

I remembered the opening words of the Kilfenora Centre's introductory video about the Burren: 'Here on the farthest western edge of the Old World . . .' and realised that the whole region feels at times like frontier country. But it is no badlands, and deserves (and is most usually given) deep respect. Down in the extreme south-east of the Burren is Mullagh-more, one of the most hauntingly beautiful places in Europe. It is dominated by a dramatically buckled limestone hill, whose bowed layers of rock glow soft pink and grey behind a pure blue lough. You can walk for hours in its foothills, through drifts of orchids and thickets of yellow-flowered shrubby cinquefoil, crossing streams and fingers of water on natural stepping stones scratched by otters, and smell again the warm honey and cream of the burnet roses. The whole enchanted scene is visible five miles away. It is Ireland's Ayers Rock, as close to being a sacred place as is possible in the sceptical West. Yet as I write it is threatened by a development scheme of scarcely credible barbarousness. It is here (rather than in one of the already developed villages) that the Irish Office of Public Works have decided to deposit a new Interpretation Centre, along with 30 acres of car park, roads and 'landscaped walkways'. One can only hope that if the project comes to fruition it will be subject to the same trial by rock as every other human claim staked out in this exuberant, flirtatious landscape.

Extremadura (1991)

For its first twenty or so miles out of Madrid, the Badajoz road frays into a ribbon of hypermarkets and prefab factories. There are no olive groves, no parched hills, no bristling stretches of *maquis*. The only signs that you are in the Mediterranean high plains country rather than suburban Kent are the glimpses of tobacco plantations between the blocks. Even on a late winter's day warm enough for short sleeves and precocious swallows, it hardly pumps up one's spirits as the threshold to one of the last wild places in lowland Europe.

I'd first read about Extremadura in Norman Lewis' travel books. He called it 'a landscape of antiquity restored by the banishment of humans' – a mouthwatering description for anyone living in the UK's over-manicured countryside. Then venturesome friends began returning with tales of what sounded like a wildlife El Dorado. In summer the evergreen oak groves shimmered with colour and song as golden orioles, rollers, bee-eaters and hoopoes flickered over carpets of wild gladioli and asphodel. In winter it was home to fifty thousand cranes, something like a third of the entire north European population, which come here to fatten up on acorns before the epic mass return flights that mark the beginning of the Scandi-navian spring. From the grey and enervating depths of an English winter it sounded irresistible, and a group of us began dreaming of a winter trip – or better still, one which caught the best of Extremadura's two high seasons: the last of the cranes and the first of the orchids, so to speak. Luckily, we'd chanced on an organisation called WILD SPAIN, which arranged expeditions as well as campaigning on conservation issues, and its English-born founder Damian Martin reminded us gently that the break between winter and spring there is quite abrupt. He suggested that we could see a Mediterranean spring almost anywhere (and probably had), but the vision of cranes nibbling acorns in the morning mist . . . well, need he say more?

So it was that six of us, packed into a 4×4, were bowling down the road to Extremadura on a glass-clear, late January morning, feeling a little forlorn about the seemingly endless built-up zone that surrounded us, but full of anticipation at what lay ahead – and at the first hints of a vein of wry theatricality in our guide. The suburban hinterland gave out with a flourish at Talavera, the town that supplies most of the world's kitchen tiles, and a few miles later we caught our first glimpse of the snowcapped peaks of the Sierra de Gredos to the north. Damian, a natural-born ringmaster, swung abruptly off the road and we bumped over a track between huge spreads of arable and savannah grassland. In the distance we could pick out hunched flocks of pin-tailed sandgrouse and little bustard. But there was the chance of better things, and Damian warned us that birds here often appeared unexpectedly, and that we must be prepared to fall out of the vehicle on command. Five minutes later, driving back towards the road, we had a full alert. A flock of great bustards – as big as turkeys, and patched with a desert camouflage of chestnut, black and white – put up about thirty yards away. We piled out of the car and watched spellbound as they circled round us. They flew against the dazzling snowclad backcloth of the Sierra, then put down again and slipped into their courtship display, ruffling up their underfeathers like petticoats.

It was a dramatic introduction to Extremadura's refractory landscapes, where wild things seem repeatedly to arrive like rabbits out of a hat, or to metamorphose into something (or somewhere) else. But on this first day there were even more remarkable manifestations. Thirty miles on the landscape began to change again. There were scatters of dumpy holm and cork oaks on the skyline, then whole pastures full of them. Soon we were in an open evergreen forest, stippled with mossy boulders and cistus bushes. This was our first sight of the *dehesa*, a habitat which stretches most of the way to Portugal in the west and Andalucia in the south, and which is unlike anywhere else in Europe.

It proved to be white stork country, too. My lifetime first had been soaring above the bustards, as unmistakable but incomprehensible in flight as an archaeopteryx. The further we drove into Extremadura the more we saw their bulky tenements on municipal buildings, farm chimneys, tree stumps, even electricity pylons. And everywhere the sun had nudged them into breeding mood, repairing nests (and pair-bonds) amid much bill-clattering and ritual stick-shifting. At the end of that first afternoon Damian, with another of those implicit, silent tugs by the hand, led us up to a café roof in the village of El Gordo, where we found ourselves eye to eye with a huge colony on a church roof. We sipped black coffee while having what felt like a Close Encounter. Barely 20 feet away one of these village familiars pulled a piece of flannel from its nest and waved it in the air, as if it were a flag, or a carpet that needed beating. Through my binoculars I could see right into its dark, tear-shaped eyes, which seemed to have unplumbably benign depths, and I understood why, for all the clutter they make, storks are seen as signs of good luck and fertility throughout Europe.

Storks haunted us through the night, too. We were staying at Trujillo, the medieval hilltop town where Francisco Pizarro, the conqueror of Peru, was born c. 1475. His statue stands in the Plaza Mayor, which is as full of different levels, stages and grand flights of steps as an opera set. We had supper there, an immense meal of tortillas and dark *jamon* from Extremaduran pigs. Then we ambled round the plaza, past its baroque arcades and loggias and the palaces built in the sixteenth century from the spoils of the returning conquistadors. Bells clanked from towers hidden in the darkness, and as we squinted up at them, we could just make out the ghostly outlines of storks, perched like gargoyles on their nests. In summer they would be joined by packs of swifts, lesser kestrels, common and red-rumped swallows, and even hoopoes, flying like vast ginger-striped butterflies from their nests under the pantiles. Trujillo is a town of birds as much as of people, and a token of the easy, close relationship that exists between people and wildlife in Extremadura.

But glimpses of spring and dreams of summer dissolved the next day. The Spanish plain's proverbial element had returned. It rained for a few hours every succeeding day, not buckets but a thin, insidious drizzle that found its way through even the waterproof sheet which was supposed to protect our cases on the luggage rack. The odd thing was that after an hour it barely mattered. In that time we had driven into some serious *dehesa*, and into a feast of birds that made the dry confines of the car just too inhibiting. There were black-winged kites hovering over the road like enormous kestrels and glimpses of cranes through the trees. The prospect before us seemed barely European at all. Gnarled cork and holm oaks stood in sparse clumps in pools of rainwater. Close to, spotless starlings swarmed in the branches with garrulous flocks of azure-winged magpies, smaller cousins of our much-demonised bird, with sky-blue wings and tails and pinkish bodies. They are extravagant, gregarious, restless birds, given to fanning swoops into the trees that show off the best of their exotic plumage. In the middle distance great grey shrikes bristled on telegraph wires and storks padded across the grass, stabbing for frogs with their red dagger beaks. Egrets waded more decorously in the pools and along the edges of streams.

The *dehesa* thrives on winter rain, but is currently having a troublesome time with water. The area we were exploring is the flood-plain of two big rivers, the Tietar and the Tajo. The gradual collapse of self-sufficient farming and the resultant leaching of the rural population have encouraged the Spanish authorities to view it as wasteland, and much of it has been deliberately flooded to make enormous reservoirs. A little further south in the Guadiana valley is the region of Cijara, known as the Siberia of Extremadura. When Norman Lewis first travelled here at the end of the seventies, he found that the whole area, 60 kilometres across, held a sprawling complex of artificial lakes, but only four villages and a total population of less than 2,500. New lakes and water engineering schemes are still appearing (currently, for instance, to dam the Tietar at Monteagudo) and many of them would benefit mobile birds of prey and mammals – wolves especially. The price is that they inevitably drown great swathes of unique *dehesa*, and the human and other communities that live in a kind of symbiotic relationship with it.

We soon became infatuated with this landscape, with its dappled ever-green shade and subtly changing glades. Most days we would amble about some part of it, nibbling the sweet acorns of Iberian holm oaks, admiring family values in cranes (they go around in parties of three or four), searching for bits of cork-bark and wild boar tracks, learning to swig wine from goatskin *botas*. For some reason the *dehesa* got us into the habit of strolling with our hands behind our backs – something I can only explain by the way it echoed an English parkland gone wild, and for that matter archetypal forest-with-clearing landscapes across the planet. We thought a lot about how deep that motif is in our imaginations, and I recalled that the American biologist E. O. Wilson regards it as the kind of habitat in which most human evolution happened. In *Biophilia* he argues that 'whenever people are given a free choice, they move to tree-studded land on prominences overlooking water'.

On a Sunday we got the chance to see at close quarters how the economy of the *dehesa* works. We'd spent a balmy, rain-free morning pottering amongst the cork oaks. There were nine of us in two vehicles now, as we'd been joined by three redoubtable Spanish wildlife photographers, all dab hands with the *bota*. At what we regarded as a late lunchtime we had taken off on a long sortie into the hinterland, on rough tracks through endless miles of *dehesa*. Damian kept mum about our destination and likely time of arrival, despite whimpers of complaint from those of us who hadn't yet adjusted to the lateness of local meal-times. But it was worth the wait. We pitched up at a remote farmhouse belonging to the Flores family, a refuge of satellite dishes and self-sufficient agri-culture that seemed perfectly to express the spirit of modern Extremadura. We ate lunch with the whole family, grandmother included, at three tables packed into the kitchen. And everything we ate had been grown or raised on the farm, from the chickpeas at the top of the cauldron to the cryptic lumps of smoked meat that lurked at the bottom. We passed round our hip-flasks of malt whisky after the meal, which were countered by recycled sauce bottles full of an evocative purple liqueur. We debated its identity knowingly with our hosts in a combination of botanical Latin and dog Spanish, and were amazed when it turned out to be none other than a local version of that northern winter warmer, sloe gin.

Then it was time for the guided tour outside. It had begun to rain whilst we were eating, which gave the panoply of animals outside a rather bedraggled, prehistoric appearance. There were herds of multicoloured goats, Merino sheep, long-horned retinto cattle and multitudes of pigs and piglets, some ginger like Tamworths, some dark brown *cerdo ibericos*, which are close to wild boars in ancestry. The pigs feed on the same sweet acorns as the cranes. The oaks are lopped every eight or so years to stimulate acorn production, and the cut wood is converted into charcoal for export to the north European barbecue market. The cork is also stripped from the trunks on an eight to ten year cycle, though this does reduce the life of the cork oaks to about 150 years. The ground under the lopped trees is grazed by sheep and cattle, and some of it ploughed up for arable crops every fourth year.

The whole system is the exact opposite of industrial farming. It is hugely diverse in output and very low in input, and close to the 'forest farming' of parts of Amazonia, where naturally occurring woodland is not so much harvested as simply nibbled at in a sustainable way.

Later that afternoon, decidedly merry, we took off on a hallucinatory cross-country drive through the *dehesa*. As it got dark we bucked across flooded fields, past surprised barn owls perched on fences and pools whirring with toads. What seemed like hours later we had reached the edge of a reservoir where the cranes fly to roost, the Embalse de Navalcan, and squatted with what little composure we could muster under the trees. We'd seen five thousand cranes fly out from another reservoir the previous dawn, an immense, gathering stream of birds that had filled the still dark sky with flickering wings and legs, and a wild, rhapsodic piping. At Navalcan we watched them come back, clearer but more nervous silhouettes this time, all too aware of our awkward crouchings below.

The rainy afternoons often produced our most exciting moments. After another morning spent strolling in the *dehesa* we'd called for lunch in a small hut in the woods. It was stone built, with the roof held up by a single manna ash trunk. There was an open fire at one side of the scatter of tables, and a bar with a corrugated iron roof, festooned with strings of home-cured sausages, on the other. As we were finishing our meal, a group of men by the fire began to sing, almost imperceptibly. Damian explained that they were local piece-work woodmen and gypsies, and within a few moments their singing had turned into the goosefleshing tones of real, unaccompanied flamenco. It was improvised and musically awesome. They would turn fierce single notes into poignant quarter-tone tremolos, utter gasps of pain and exultation, sound Moorish and Irish all at once. Each one tried in his different style to outdo the previous singer with more outrageously boastful lyrics, or more elaborate rococo curls and twists in his delivery. Yet though it was a competitive performance, a kind of musical duel, each singer cheered, clapped, even hugged his rivals during especially triumphant flourishes. Damian did his best to translate the words, and at one point casually reported that they were wondering why the English visitors weren't singing. A few moments later, paling slightly, he said they had issued a direct challenge. Our consternation escalated as we realised the full paucity of our vocal skills by the side of these half-dozen working men. I can't begin to understand why we decided to sing 'Greensleeves' for them. But, led by the thin but brave soprano voices of the two women in our party, we launched into this sixteenth-century courtly serenade. It was like a confrontation over Offa's Dyke, we nervous and inhibited Saxons one side, these hugely talented Celts standing bemusedly on the other. They had the grace to clap us at the end and to buy us cider. Then they tried to sell us horses, whereupon Damian felt that it was prudent to say our farewells.

We never discovered whether this whole episode was another of his prearranged *coups de théâtre*. It hardly mattered because the image and sound of that singing was unforgettable. In that afternoon's drizzle we saw many extraordinary sights – the antlers of an enormous herd of red deer below the skyline, a family of wild boar, facing us off in the scrub, and yet another Extremaduran cartoon, a Spanish Imperial eagle perched on top of an electricity pylon. Yet it was the memory of those men, singing each other up, arm in arm, that seemed the more telling symbol of this land where humans work *with* the grain of the wild.

POLITICS IN THE LANDSCAPE

Landscape: The Real Stuff (1993)

What is landscape? Is it, as Adam Nicolson has suggested, not a real thing at all but 'an aesthetic category'? Not mountain ranges and water meadows but the emotional patterns we make with these in our minds? Edward Thomas had one kind of answer. When Thomas enlisted in the Artists' Rifles in 1915, Eleanor Farjeon asked what he thought he was fighting for. 'Literally for this,' he replied, picking up a handful of unimpeachably English earth. With hindsight it seems a naive and theatrical gesture. But one knows what he was getting at. The soil – *the* landscape – has always been looked to as a cultural bedrock in times of trouble, a repository of history and a source of inspiration as well as subsistence. It is that strained word 'literally' which sounds so disingenuous, by the side of Thomas' transparently symbolic gesture.

But then landscapes, for all their intricate, living detail, are forever being squeezed down to abstractions and generalities. They are distilled for essences, bottled as heritage and then offered up as 'literal' patches of the real world. The landscapes themselves, not to mention the cultures they support, are made poorer and more vulnerable in the process.

The real stuff of landscape can't be pinned down so easily. Not far from the Hampshire chalk hills prowled over by Thomas is another celebrated landscape – the long stretch of wooded shoreline between Lyme Regis and Axmouth, known universally as the Undercliff. It is a wild and Romantic place of ivy-draped rocks and wind-bent ash trees, and the auras left by generations of visiting writers and artists. Jane Austen must have glimpsed it on her visits to Lyme. Tennyson (who once celebrated a more domestic English landscape as the 'haunt of ancient peace ... all things in order stored') rambled amongst its dark pools and bushy chasms. Most famously it figured as a powerful, liberating backcloth – almost a supporting character in its own right – in John Fowles' novel *The French Lieutenant's Woman*. It is turbulent, as is the way of the Devon coast, but seemingly timeless, and elsewhere Fowles has written of it: 'It looks almost as the world might have been if man had not evolved, so pure, so unspoilt, so untouched it is scarcely credible.'

In William Dawson's 1840 painting, however, it has an almost pastoral look. Inside the amphitheatre formed by the crumbling chalk cliffs is a wheatfield. Reapers are working through it, and people are picnicking and talking in groups around the edge. A Union Jack is being hoisted above them. It is a rustic scene and unquestionably 'old England'.

Its real history is rather different. The events that formed the Undercliff and lay behind Dawson's *View of the Great Chasm of the Axmouth Landslip* are a long way removed from the mythology of a changeless, immemorial landscape. Two centuries ago this was an unexceptional West Country coastline. It was haunted by religious dissenters and the occasional smuggler, and supported a scatter of cultivated fields on top of the cliffs. Then, one night late in 1839, it literally fell apart.

In one sense this was nothing new, as the cliffs along this coast have always been unstable. But the landslip of 1839 was a more cataclysmic affair. A huge chalk floe, 6 hectares in extent, slid off towards the sea, leaving a chasm into which the next section of cliff collapsed. On top was a sizeable wheatfield, already carrying its crop. It fell more or less intact, the right way up, and on 25 August the following year it was ceremonially reaped. The whole event became a source of wonder and foreboding in the district, and more than ten thousand people came to watch the harvest. The reapers were led by young women, who had been given silver brooches in the form of sickles as souvenirs.

More landslips followed and within a few decades the present landscape of the Undercliff began to evolve – a secret wild garden, benignly Gothic on the surface, but underneath an impenetrable and precarious wilderness. Every year the local rescue services are called out for someone who is lost, or has fallen down one of the covered crevices.

The history of the Undercliff is a dramatic one, but is really just an extreme example of the way that change and tradition, natural forces and human labour intertwine in real landscapes. Any country parish will understand that harvest ceremony of 1840 and the ambivalence that seems to hang over it – the shock giving way to curiosity, the insistence on things going on as usual despite the chaos. These are the traditional rules of human survival in the landscape. Get the upper hand again, if only for a season. Make the best of things. Celebrate the inevitable. Life goes on. Landscapes have always been looked on to bridge the gap between two opposed sets of human needs: for a haven of continuity on one hand, and for the vitality of nature on the other; for a familiar environment, fashioned by human hands, and then again for something that transcends the man-made and the artificial.

Myths have abounded in this gap, feeding on its unresolved tensions, and nurtured by ideology and taste. One of the most powerful has been the idea of a national landscape, *the* landscape – some spirit or essence underlying and unifying actual landscapes, which symbolises the British (or more usually English) character. It is of course a rural landscape, despite our having been principally an industrial and urban nation since the late nineteenth century. It was not only Edward Thomas who saw this essential England as being what the First World War was fought for. Rupert Brooke recoiled at the prospect of 'English soil' being desecrated, not long before he became a misplaced piece of it himself, interred, as he had prophesied, in the corner of a foreign field. The wheelwright's son and social historian George Sturt thought the 'Prussian armies' were 'outraging England in her . . . pleasant cornfields and country lanes'. In letters from the trenches and recruiting propaganda in the home villages, the notion of what was being defended was repeatedly reduced to a small cluster of familiar rural images: the Downs; stooks glowing in a field at sunset; the call of rooks flying home to a vicarage copse; wild roses in the hedges . . . a country wholly identified with its countryside.

Similar feelings surfaced in the Second World War, and were tapped by the Ministry of Information in their campaigns to boost morale. 'Your Britain. Fight for it now' runs the caption over a celebrated Frank New-bould watercolour of what is unmistakably the South Downs. The view is from the top of a hill looking down. In the foreground a shepherd is leading his flock over the open hills, back to a village in the valley. A big, double-chimneyed manor house nestles in a billowing crescent of oak trees. In the distance there are more soaring downs, a lighthouse and, just glimpsed between the hills, the English Channel, the last ditch between us and the enemy. The picture captures the character of the English landscape of popular mythology, and implies that this was part of all the people's heritage. But in what sense was this true? What exactly did that phrase 'Your Britain' mean? Not the privilege of ownership, of course. Nor that we had a right of access. Nor, for the majority of British town dwellers whose landscapes were being destroyed nightly in the Blitz, was it any part of their ordinary, direct experience. The poster's heart of course was in the right place in suggesting that landscape transcends land as property, and does indeed 'belong' to the people, as do the cultural qualities it expresses – fertility, stewardship of the land, peace, space and continuity. But, as on every occasion when this generalised appeal has been made, the intricate fibre of real landscapes and the lives they encompassed was glossed over.

Fifty years on, during which time the character and working life of the Downs had changed dramatically, Newbould's picture was used again, in a campaign by the Council for the Protection of Rural England. The slogan was the same – 'Your Britain. Fight for it now', but this time the enemy, as everyone understood, was closer to home.

What gives a particular landscape its identity? Over the centuries local patterns of farming and vegetation on these famous downland slopes have been repeatedly transformed. The hills were covered with trees six thousand years ago and almost devoid of them in the seventeenth century. Settlements built in times of plenty have vanished during plagues and recessions – or if they happened to spoil the view from the Big House. In prehistoric times small arable fields would have been cleared straight from the wildwood, especially near the foot of the hills. In the medieval periods, sheep took over many of the hills, and their grazing produced a classic, flower-rich, short-turfed pasture. During the Agricultural Revolution of the eighteenth and early nineteenth centuries, much of this was ploughed up for turnips and then wheat – only to revert back to grassland, and then scrub and wood, during the long agricultural depression of the Victorian era. This century the Downs have been cleared and ploughed again, for barley, kale and oil-seed rape. The view from the top of the hill has stayed much the same. But each one of those shifts in the balance between wood, grass, arable crop and human settlement meant dramatic changes in the local ecology and social life; and doubtless every one of them was mourned at the time as spelling the end of the old order. Which stage represents the 'true' landscape of the Downs? Who decides?

But if evolving landscapes are often viewed as immemorial, so there are ancestral habitats which are seen as ephemeral human constructs. Next to the South Downs, for example, is the densely wooded region known as the Weald. An abundance of archaeological and ecological evidence has confirmed that there has been a more or less continuous woodland cover here since the end of the last Ice Age, and that many individual woods are direct and unplanted (albeit greatly modified) descendants of the wildwood. Yet the myth persists here, as throughout the wooded areas of Britain, that woods derive from, and can only be sustained by, the planting of trees by humans.

What links these two seemingly contradictory myths, I believe, is their common denial of any independence to the natural landscape. It is either appropriated for an abstract, generalised idea of 'heritage' or claimed as the product of benign human stewardship.

Landscape is an old idea but a comparatively new word, and part of the confusion it causes is a consequence of not having a comfortably settled meaning. The term came originally from the Dutch *landschap*, meaning a region or province, plain and simple. It entered the English language (as 'landskip' originally) in the seventeenth century as a piece of fashionable artistic jargon, and, despite three hundred years of currency in the turbulent world of rural affairs, it has never quite lost that slightly precious air of the salon. Landscape may imply more than the view, but in one kind of usage it is always *out there*, remote and painterly, exterior design on a grand scale. The same could be said of the putative landscape 'designer', who is perhaps seen as a benevolent landowner, perhaps God, or just occasionally nature itself, as an equally remote force. What is barely even conceived of is landscape as a vernacular production, made in a rather haphazard way by *us*, nature and the weather.

Yet there is another, more anciently rooted sense of place which has no satisfactory English word to describe it. This is landscape as the home ground, the native patch which becomes familiar by being experienced from ground level, landscape as something you look out *from*, not at. This is the way we look at the outside world when we are children, and it can turn ordinary waste patches and favourite trees into whole kingdoms. The poet John Clare wrote unaffectedly of what he called 'pleasant places', and though, for him, they were intensely personal and local, they make a list with universal appeal:

> Old stone pits with veined ivy overhung
> Wild crooked brooks o'er which was rudely flung
> A rail and plank that bends beneath the tread
> Old narrow lanes where trees meet overhead

Yet all such intimate, interior landscapes are set in objective environments of rock, vegetation and climate that change enormously from one corner of Britain to another. Many of these physical features are entirely natural, and seem to permeate the character of different regions however much they have been overlaid or modified by human activity: the stark angles of granite country, for instance, and the softer swells of chalk and limestone; stiff red earth in the Welsh border country, blown sand in the East Anglian Breckland. Over these regional languages, the intimate local details are inscribed like dialects, and only become intelligible (and often visible) close-to.

Hedges, often regarded as the most defining of all our native landscape features, are a case in point. From a distance they have no identity beyond their functional role as boundaries: they are the grid lines that divide up the fabled English 'chequerboard'. Yet they are hugely varied in age and character: the turf and stone banks – 'reaves' – that separate the narrow Bronze Age fields of Dartmoor; the beech hedges round the windswept edges of Exmoor, and the even taller ones rooted like mangroves along the banked lanes of Somerset's Blackdown Hills; the hedgerow hollies planted – or simply tolerated – as ploughing guideposts in East Anglia; the tall, double shelter belts of the Sussex Weald known as 'shaws'; the hedges that are all that is left of whole woods, and which are evocatively known as 'woodland ghosts'.

Boundary features like this are conventionally attributed to deliberate plantings during the heyday of Parliamentary Enclosure in the late eighteenth and nineteenth centuries. In fact most of them are vastly older. Less than a fifth of England was enclosed by Parliamentary Award, and the majority of our hedges are the result of piecemeal enclosures going back as far as the Bronze Age. Many were never planted at all. They began life as strips of natural woodland which were left after a field had been cut out of the forest. Others were the result of shrubs naturally colonising the lines of staked, 'dead' hedges that were features of the landscape even before the Normans arrived. In fact most hedges are a kind of community that the strict hierarchies of landscape mythology don't care to admit – a symbiosis, a partnership between humans and nature.

So are heathlands, but here the mythology is of a primeval, naturally formed wilderness, which because it hasn't apparently been 'reclaimed' by human work is 'wasteland'. Even Thomas Hardy, whose landscape history was usually impeccable, took this view. His description of Egdon Heath in the opening chapter of *The Return of the Native* – 'A Face on Which Time Makes But Little Impression' – is one of the most evocative passages of landscape writing in the language, yet it still paints Egdon as literally, as well as emotionally, primordial:

> Civilisation was its enemy; and ever since the beginning of vegetation its soil had worn the same antique brown dress, the natural and invariable garment of the particular formation . . .
>
> To recline on a stump of thorn in the central valley of Egdon, between afternoon and night, as now, where the eye could reach nothing of the world outside the summits and shoulders of heathland which filled the whole circumference of its glance, and to know that everything around and underneath had been from prehistoric times as unaltered as the stars overhead, gave ballast to the mind adrift on change, and harassed by the irrepressible New.

Heathland, characterised by sweeps of heather, fine grasses and small shrubs such as gorse and broom, is created by the clearance of woodland on poor soils. And it can only be maintained as heath if the cutting, burning or grazing, be it natural or deliberate, is continued. Otherwise it will eventually revert to woodland, as is happening at the moment to many of the unmanaged heaths of southern England. But variations in climate, soil and natural vegetation across Britain mean that this simple regime produces immensely different kinds of heathland: the dry commons of Surrey and Hampshire, and rain-drenched moors of upland Britain; the cliff-top stands of wind-pruned, sun-burned heather on the Lizard peninsula that may be entirely natural, and the fenny heaths of west Norfolk, so pocked with small-scale diggings and glacial scourings that it is futile to draw any line between which are natural and which man-made. Heathlands, as one modern writer put it, 'represent nature's response' to various human activities. But they are also vulnerable to human activity. The south Dorset heaths that Hardy immortalised as Egdon have been largely destroyed by enclosure and ploughing.

The myth of Parliamentary Enclosure as a creative process, concerned solely with the hedging of the open fields, has been astonishingly persistent. In fact, as well as the Acts which led to the enclosure of four and a half million acres of open field and pasture, there were another 1,893 Acts relating to the clearing and cultivation of more than two million acres of commonland. In almost all instances enclosure involved path-stopping, road-straightening, drainage, the clearance of wood and heath, and a wholesale reorganisation of the geography and economy of the parish.

In this respect Parliamentary Enclosure (despite its strictly local impact) symbolised the processes of centralisation and modernisation that had been gathering pace in the countryside during the 'Age of Improvement'. This is often called the era of 'planned countryside', as distinct from 'ancient' and more organically moulded landscapes. Ancient countryside evolved out of centuries of do-it-yourself enterprise, often involving the whole community. It is asymmetrical and small-scale, and typified by sinuous boundary banks, old trees, oddly shaped copses and tapering commons and greens, whose arrangement reflects the natural contours and vegetation. Planned countryside, by contrast, was set out – on a drawing board as often as not – without much sensitivity towards the natural features of the land or the people who lived and worked there. It is uniform and geometric, a tidy patchwork of rectangular fields, symmetrical plantations, straight roads and low hawthorn hedges. As a landscape style it looks much the same in Dorset as in Durham, and everywhere lacks that human scale and quirkiness which makes ancient countryside so appealing.

Planned countryside in this sense is still created, most conspicuously by insensitive tree-planting programmes. The *imposition* of trees on a landscape, often regardless of the character of the place and the species of tree, is still widely regarded as a conservation panacea. The flowering cherries which adorn suburban streets across the land are now being set down in increasing numbers in deep countryside. Hybrid Italian poplars and weeping willows are planted along wild river banks, and ornamental American oaks on medieval Chiltern commons. Indigenous trees (that help give local landscapes their distinctive character) are often bulldozed to make way for them, just as they are in commercial plantations.

Even in the Age of Improvement itself, though, there were contrary views. In *A Description of the Scenery of the Lakes*, William Wordsworth takes issue both with the idea of a timeless, changeless landscape, and with the lofty presumptions of the landscape engineers. And his ecologically precise account of the way natural woodland colonises a Lakeland fell demonstrates his belief that natural landscapes expressed social as well as aesthetic ideals:

> From low and sheltered places, vegetation travels upward to the more exposed; and the young plants are protected, and to a certain degree fashioned, by those that have preceded them. The continuous mass of foliage which would be thus produced is broken by rocks, or by glades or open places, where the browsing of animals has prevented the growth of wood. As vegetation ascends, the winds begin also to bear their part in moulding the forms of trees; but, thus mutually protected, trees, though not of the hardiest kind, are enabled to climb high up the mountains. Gradually however, by the quality of the ground, and by increasing exposure, a stop is put to their ascent; the hardy trees only are left; those also, by little and little, give way – and a wild and irregular boundary is established, graceful in its outline, and never contemplated without some feeling, more or less distinct, of the powers of Nature by which it is imposed.
>
> Contrast the liberty that encourages, and the law that limits, this joint work of Nature and time, with the disheartening necessities, restrictions and disadvantages, under which the artificial planter must proceed, even he whom long observation and fine feeling have best qualified for his task.

Wordsworth was in no way hostile to humans shaping the landscape. Yet the point he was making about the vitality and particularity of nature, and the contribution that this makes to the continuing evolution of landscapes, has been all but dismissed in recent years. The current 'heritage' view of the rural landscape assumes that historical evolution is *over*, that what we now hold, however precariously, is a landscape fully realised.

And yet there is a perceptible new exuberance in many of our native landscapes. In the south, for instance, there has been a remarkable and unpredictable regeneration in the woodlands devastated by the hurricanes of 1987 and 1990. In northern England, lime-rich tips outside derelict chemical factories are turning spontaneously into facsimile chalk downs, covered with sweeps of wild orchids. (The Cumbrian poet Norman Nicholson celebrated similar makeshift landscapes around the worked-out haematite mines near his home, and even saw mining as an essentially rural industry like the 'harvesting of a root-crop'.)

We are back with John Clare's 'pleasant places' here, those small-scale, distinctive, familiar refuges which perhaps form the best basis for a common language and understanding of landscape. The view from the hill – appropriative, generalised, reducing humans (and most other living things) to inanimate props – has always missed the details of both destruction and growth. The view from the hedge may be more restricted, but it does register the real stuff of landscapes, and the fact that fossilisation is every bit as deathly as obliteration.

Living in the Past (1978)

In 1976 the television producer John Percival persuaded the BBC to finance a project in which a group of volunteers would live for a year under Iron Age conditions, and be filmed going about their daily business. He outlined the terms of the project exactly in a fine, underrated and honest book:* 'What we set out to do – and this has been much misunderstood – was to see if a group of quite ordinary young people, most of them born and brought up in towns, could learn to live successfully within the limits of an Iron Age technology. It was clearly impossible to recapture the beliefs and superstitions, the skills and experience, the basic social attitudes of prehistoric people, and this was never our intention.'

The fourteen episodes of Living in the Past that came out of the experiment became one of the most obsessively debated series ever put out by the BBC. In general, public response was lukewarm, not to say cynical. Critics found fault with the villagers' youthfulness and middle-class backgrounds (fair comment, though this was what most of the volunteers were), and their lack of manual skills. And though the project's terms of reference were continually restated, viewers took offence whenever the volunteers strayed 'out of period', or took the smallest archaeological liberties. Most of all they objected to the slights cast upon civilisation by the volunteers muffing a seemingly crude prehistoric task, or seeming positively to enjoy their state of wretchedness.

I suspect that these ill-tempered reactions said more about the spectators than the participants. As a friend of John Percival, I had been fortunate in being involved with the project from its outset. I'd met the volunteers before they moved in, helped in a small way with their training and with the selection of the site, and eventually had the special privilege of staying at the camp for a few days. Never once did the project seem to me feeble or amateur, and my stay there made me wish I had volunteered myself. I am grateful that Vole gave me the opportunity of recapturing what remain the few most sensually vivid days of my life.

In the aerial shot that opens each episode of Living in the Past, the settlement has the look of a raft or an ark, an incarcerated colony adrift in the woods. You can make out the prow and bridge, and the walls,

* Living in the Past, BBC Publications, 1980.

built for a long journey. They are familiar shapes if you walk about the southern chalk hills, where the earthworks of past occupations have much the same look of forlorn hopefulness.

So I was hardly prepared for the thrill of my first glimpse of the camp. I had just turned a corner along a woodland track when the thatched roof of the great hut swam suddenly into view, ringed with wisps of smoke and glinting where new straw caught the winter sunlight. Something that I had only ever seen in drawings or dreamed about, that had been always insubstantial and fanciful, had quite literally come to life, and I had my first real experience of culture shock.

Inside the stockade first impressions came so fast and unexpectedly that I can only remember them in disconnected detail, like a mass of snatched snapshots. Cows' trotters strung up from a pole. A row of wattle and daub beehives. The smell of hides and untreated fleeces hanging in the air like a sharp smoke. People pottering incessantly, even whilst they were talking to you – querning, shelling peas, basket-making, spinning. It was only later, when the assault on the senses had quietened a little, that I realised that, whatever it was to the BBC, to the ten volunteers this makeshift ancient monument was *home*.

A second visit, on a bright, early spring day. There are other guests about. One, an anthropologist, is showing the volunteers different aboriginal techniques for creating fire, a skill they have so far failed to master. Once they know the tricks (it helps to have two pairs of hands, working in relay, to keep up the speed of the drilling rod) they have a fire going in half an hour. It goes down on film, and the villagers go back to their own concerns. They have kept their own fire going continuously for twelve months and at this stage they are more interested in what the prehistorian being filmed on the other side of the camp is saying about them. He believes the experiment to be archaeologically devalued because the community did not adopt a hierarchical structure. The volunteers are resentful that he will not argue out this point with them on film. They believe that they could never have coped temperamentally with such a structure. Neither they nor producer John Percival have ever seen the project as an exercise in impersonation or method-acting. You cannot shed twentieth-century consciousness just by wearing animal skins for a year. What is important is the interplay between the two cultures, the new perspectives that emerge when modern people are obliged to use a primitive technology. All of them see the project as an *exploration* of another culture rather than an imitation.

The visitors leave and the farm gets back to business. The goats have to be milked, work on the cart resumed and Sarah's birthday celebrated.

The preoccupations of people living on their own wits and resources have not changed much in two thousand years. They must survive, create wealth against the bad times, and enjoy themselves when they can.

It is the ineluctable power of darkness that strikes you most sharply when you come here from a culture dependent on electricity. The pattern of life is governed absolutely by the hours of daylight. You move indoors with the dusk, get up with the dawn. In the long winter nights the team often used to stay in bed for fourteen hours. Inside the hut itself, with its two low entrances, it is permanently twilight. The central fire lights up a circle a few yards wide, but it takes minutes for your eyes to adjust and take in the complex architecture in the far recesses.

The hut is over 50 feet wide and everything from store-chambers to bread ovens has been crammed in. The layout has a logic, when you can see it plainly. The looms are near the doorway so that the weavers can work in the dry but also in natural light. The odd-shaped cuts of meat, strung about the roof like macabre Christmas decorations, are there to catch the smoke. The little wattled cubicles – one for each couple – that lie against the perimeter walls also make sense, though true Ancient Brits may have been less concerned about privacy. The volunteers all missed this greatly, and as the communal hut took three months longer to complete than they had expected, they were grateful for the small oases of quiet their cells eventually provided.

Yet the fire draws them together. It has burned out a lot of tensions in the group, and forges a peculiar kind of temporary intimacy. It is remark-able how living in a circular space with the light source in the centre can shape your relationships with your cohabitants. You face in, towards each other. It is always the nearsides of things and people that are lit up. It is surprising, too, what you can do in a circle round a fire if you have to. You can have a bath, mend a shoe, even eat a soft-boiled egg without a plate – if you have practised enough. And that scene, I suppose, sums up the image which many critics have of the experiment. It is a banal party game: holding the ring; charades; a kind of musical chairs in which it is not you that revolves precariously around, but the world – a cup, a loaf, an argument, a whole reconstructed version of history. And so it can seem, until it is your forfeit. Clumsy at the best of times, and hopeless in the dark, I spilt the drink and dropped my egg. Worst of all I upset the salt, which is a scarce product they have to trade for, and as I shamefacedly tried to shovel it back from the earth floor, I had a sharp lesson in value scales.

Using the BBC as a middleman the members of the team have incorpor-ated trade with the outside world into their economic system. They bartered the surplus of young animals they had in the summer for salt and extra honey. When they heard about the bread strike in the winter, they went into mass production of their loaves – stoneground to a fault – and got venison in return from the locals. With more common sense than some of their critics, they have seen that these occasional indulgences in twentieth-century foods do not compromise the spirit of the project one jot. So, with bed and board to trade for, and a birthday to celebrate, I had taken in a good supply of alcohol to add to their own potently sharp mead, and we stayed up very late.

Helped by the community of the fire, they talked about their year. They still remember the early months with bitterness, the bad advice they had been given, the claustrophobic rain, most of all the back-breaking hay harvest. It had taken them six weeks on their knees, working with small hand sickles, to cut the 3 acres of grass and carry it back half a mile to camp. There was a good deal of disillusionment at this time. No one objected to hard work, but was that really all there was? In Programme 3, Sharon – hair tied neatly back in a way that said a good deal about her disenchantment with barbarianism – spoke for them all. They had hoped to be 'Iron Agers' and had turned into builders' labourers. Any lingering fantasies that donning a hand-woven shift would be like taking a trip – the gateway to an instant expansion of historical consciousness – were rapidly lost. But was it too much to hope that they might have time to use their imaginations a little? If they could not, the experiment would indeed be nothing more than a meaningless re-enactment, a kind of historical mime.

I realise now that I was not wholly immune from the 'changed consciousness' fallacy myself. I think I had expected (and half hoped for) a more complete rout of modernism – a surrender to mysticism or primeval terrors, perhaps, or the evolution of a private language, at least something *different* about them. Well, there was. They were surer, sharper, more relaxed than when I had met them before the experiment. Whatever illusions they had had about the experiment had dissolved, and they were beginning to enjoy the challenge of making a going concern of a pre-industrial technology. The chat round the fire that night was more like that in a senior common room than a charged encounter group. They talked about the habits of owls, the merits of pair-bonding, and the more arcane reaches of prehistoric scholarship. I was struck especially by how openly they would talk amongst themselves about others in the group who could hear what they were saying.

The temptation to opt out had stayed with each one of them since those first hard months, and on this particular evening they were still concerned with the last successfully suppressed 'escape'. (There had been a few temporary disappearances that the press, thankfully, had not found out about.) John, a keen bird-watcher, had been visited by friends with news of a rare bird (a wallcreeper) wintering in Cheddar Gorge. It was a once-in-a-lifetime chance and only a short car journey away. There were long heart-searching talks. No one wanted John to go, and though it was a last-minute decision, he stayed at home. In the end they are quite clear about their loyalties to each other, and about what constitutes 'cheating'. An indulgent day out in a car is very different from a celebratory bowl of light ale.

The counterpart of the frankness that has resulted from living and working in close contact is the very great care they take of each other. They were trying, this evening, to work out a way of recompensing John for his disappointment, and were thinking about all taking him to see the wallcreeper on the day the farm closed down.

My own contribution was about as accomplished as my handling of the salt, and I realised how far they had progressed in the art of speaking one's mind without rancour. I was offered a spare cell for the night, but did not think I could face my confusions in the pitch black, and curled up by the fire for company, wrapped in a sheepskin.

A short while later there was a curious episode that confirmed their cohesion as a group, and exposed still more of my preconceptions. I couldn't sleep in these unfamiliar surroundings and at about one in the morning noticed that the villagers were coming out of their cells, talking earnestly by the fire and going out of the hut in relays. For a moment, I must confess, I presumed this to be the signs of the sexual liberality I'd also expected. But when I got up to investigate I found that Brian hadn't 'come in yet'. Inspired by the mead, no doubt, he'd wandered off to gaze at the stars, and with touching maternal concern the villagers were worried in case he'd fallen down a ditch or tripped over an animal, and were scouring the site for him. He turned up eventually, and everyone settled back to their private attachments.

Morning starts slowly, but decisively. Everyone knows their job and when to begin it. The pair who are responsible for the food that day are up first, have the fire stoked, and breakfast – a standard dish of boiled wheat, honey and goat's milk, not far removed from frumenty – simmering in the cauldron before anyone else is awake. Today the cooks are Martin and Helen. For the rest of the day they will have complete responsibility for gathering firewood, butchering meat, preparing vegetables, and providing three meals for the community. But the responsibilities of the cooking-pair are more complex than the simple provision of food. In a sense they are stewards for the day. They must keep the fire going and manage one of the community's most precious resources – continuously boiling water. There is only one large iron pot in which water can be boiled for any period (their clay pots tend to break up) and anything less important than cooking – and this includes washing-up, bathing and dying wool – normally has to make do with momentarily hot water, produced by plunging red-hot lumps of iron into bowls.

After breakfast everyone gets on with their chosen (or allotted) task with the minimum of fuss. Jill and Sharon go out to plough with the two Dexter cows and a single-bladed wooden share. They finish sixty furrows that morning. Martin begins to butcher the rabbits they caught yesterday, Helen to make dumplings out of flour and pig lard. I go out with Kate, Sarah and the two Johns to forage. I am thinking the first wild vegetables may be showing their shoots and take a basket, but they bring Sirius, the farm's sparky little lurcher, whose reputation as a hunter-gatherer does not rest on her botanical skills. She tears off through the woods at regular intervals after invisible quarry. I am uneasy and the girls are delighted. They have overcome their qualms about hunting and now positively relish it. They know what Sirius is chasing by the calls she makes.

In the end we go back with a basket of hedge garlic for the rabbit stew and an exhausted but unfulfilled dog. It is a curious scene at the camp, the women returning from the fields and the hunt, the men working in the kitchen and the yard. The blurring of sexual roles (which owes as much to twentieth-century liberalism as Celtic sociology) runs right through the pattern of life on the farm. Everyone, regardless of sex, has done their share of the hard graft of building, ploughing and reaping. Everyone querns three bowls of flour a day. It is only in their relationships with animals that any significant division seems to have evolved: the men kill the bigger animals and the women milk them. How much this is due to purely physical factors – the men also do the other heavy axe work, for instance – and how much to the symbolic meaning of these acts, is difficult to tell.

Apart from the extraordinary achievement of living successfully together, most of the villagers regard their relationships with animals as the experience which has affected them most deeply. It is not hard to appreciate this. Nowhere in the farm are you removed from close physical contact with animals, in varying stages of life and death. Goats roam about outside the stockade, and chickens and polecats inside. You wake up to the undeniable summons of a cockerel *inside* the hut, go to bed in skins that are still sticky with lanolin. You cannot sit down for long without a dog or calf touching you, or avert your gaze from the hard visual evidence of slaughter. Flayed heads and hides hang from the trees, entirely functionally, but grim totems to a novitiate like myself who has not been through the rites of killing.

This constant intimacy has helped them through the painful conflicts of killing animals they had come to know and love. Like others before them they have found, paradoxically, that it is easier to kill, for food, an animal you have held and nourished yourself. Except for the vegetarian Ainsworths (who left the experiment before Christmas) they have become progressively more enthusiastic carnivores, encouraged no doubt by a surfeit of Celtic beans. The men became such adept butchers that they once killed and decapitated a ram for the cameras before the focus could be changed. That they then went into a slapstick routine of trying to stick the head back on for a re-take is typical of the odd mixture of affection and matter-of-factness they show towards their animals. They joke a good deal about killing – especially Martin, who, as the village's qualified doctor, is well aware of the role of operating-theatre humour. They would not hurt a hair of the mice that live in the goat-hut; they even have pet names for them. But when rats invaded their grain store and haystacks – the harvest they had nearly broken their backs getting in – they went for them in a bloodcurdling orgy of vengeance. They killed the lot, babies included, and ate the biggest in a stew.

It is an afternoon in early March. There are only three weeks to go. Most of the housework has been done and the villagers are about their private schemes. Kate and Sarah are lounging against the haystack playing with the polecats and spinning desultorily. Pete, John and Brian are working on the cart, their biggest piece of wooden technology yet. Brian is turning pegs on a pole lathe and Pete is shaping a solid 3-foot-diameter wheel with axe blows of deadly accuracy. Shaggy Maggie, a nanny goat with ineffably gentle manners and a passion for carpentry, nibbles away the rough edges. It is an idyll a pre-Raphaelite would have been proud of. Their skills and sense of ease are unrecognisable when compared with the awkward fumbling of their early months. Although their admiration of real Iron Agers increases with each new experiment, they have created a perfectly viable economy of their own. They are producing new resources faster than they are using them up. They understand the annual cycle of work better now, and that the months of numbing summer labour are rewarded with months of leisure. That is what they are enjoying enormously now, and what has seemed the ultimate effrontery to some viewers.

The moments they will remember most have almost all been embellishments above the call of duty, as they probably are with all cultures: the clay hair-washes; the contoured wood loo seat; the 20-foot-tall wicker man they burned for the festival of Samhain; the lyre strung with stretched sheepgut; the fat trouser legs woven on tubular looms; the day they went tobogganing with the pigs whilst the rest of the West Country was para-lysed under snow (they helped with car rescue, too); and another, warmer day when, desperate for wind, they climbed the hill and winnowed on the crest of the downs, a vision for the passers-by; and their 'trifles' – vast follies of cake and mead and fruit they cook on birthdays to make up for their yearning for sweets.

It's true that they might not have been so relaxed if they had had to prepare for another year; that they have not had the economic drain of child-rearing. Yet the skill with which they can now work as a secondary activity suggests that they would have coped very well with a growing population.

All of which proves nothing. Iron Age culture was obviously viable, otherwise we wouldn't be here now. The strength of *Living in the Past* seems to me that it happened in the *present*, that it was a celebration of perennial hardiness as much as a proof of ancient skills. Whether the experiment was archaeologically authentic is largely academic. It was a compromise from the outset, set up to provide material for a television series, and should be judged as a story, not as history. As such it seems to me to have a touch of the stuff out of which myths are made. Not the story of 'Iron Age Man', particularly; certainly not the myth of the 'Noble Savage' (the villagers are neither). It is closer to the ageless story of the peasants, who for some thousands of years lived (and still live in many parts of the world) lives of ingenuity, endurance and independence without ripping the planet to bits. *Living in the Past* is a reworking – a reliving, you might say – of this story through modern imaginations. To me its greatest contribution is yet another counter to the belief, desperately clung to by highly industrial civilisations, that life under earlier technologies was inexorably nasty, brutish, short and joyless.

In a few weeks the camp will be demolished and the villagers will pick up the threads of their previous lives. Since it is the business of myths to provide inspiration, I rather hope they think of a name for the settlement before then, for it would be good for us to be able to go on telling stories about them – the group of young people in Wessex who worked out their own version of a very old parable about man and the earth.

The Promised Landscape (1981)

It's hard to have original fantasies these days. The dreamtime is fuelled by great communal longings, and is full of converging Arcadian visions – green, pleasant, pacific and handwoven. You may regret these collectivist tendencies or rejoice in them, but there's no getting away from the fact: Eden is commonland.

My favourite Utopia was set down as long ago as the fourteenth century by the writer of that wonderful alliterative poem, 'Piers Plowman'. William Langland fell asleep on a hilltop in the Malverns ('In a somer season whan soft was the sonne' – he was fantasising before he began) and had a vision of the whole kingdom of England as

> A faire feld ful of folke . . .
> Of alle manner of men, the mene and the riche
> Worchyng and wandryng as the world asketh

A modern, Alternative Service-style version has rendered down this last line as 'moving busily about their worldly affairs', which is hardly the stuff that dreams are made of. But looking back, as one often does when imagining forward, I can remember a time when the countryside was indeed full of people 'worchyng and wandryng', and am happy to report that these activities had nothing whatever to do with mundane industriousness.

It has become fashionable to lament the overcrowding of the countryside, as if the fields were at this very moment being choked by some kind of human pollutant. But this is not the impression you get if you stray just a little way from the roads. Here you will see not an overpopulated landscape, but one being drained of figures just as surely as it is losing its colour and variety.

When I was a child, twenty-five years ago, I can remember the woods and fields brimming with other children, climbing trees, building camps, cooking, trading, tramping about the footpaths in little packs reciting rude limericks, and disappearing into the bushes for private experiments. The older ones would sometimes wander off in pairs, and we would catch enthralling, ethereal glimpses of them in pink tangles under the hedges, or glowing palely under the moon in harvest fields. Now the only loving couples you see are wedged into the back seats of parked cars.

I enjoy solitude as much as anyone, but I do not relish barrenness, and I view fields fleeced of folk as unnatural, unjust and full of foreboding. I have a persistent vision of them reclaimed by people up to all possible versions, authorised or not, of worchyng and wandryng.

I hope no one misunderstands this. I don't wish any blight upon our farmers and landowners. But I don't think I am alone in hoping that they might soon begin to take their social obligations as seriously as their economic, and play the role of stewards that, as they frequently tell us, is theirs by dint of profession. I wish them continued good fortune in escaping the axe applied to every other sphere of public subsidy, but I confess that I do still dream of the day when there is more reciprocity in our relationships, and farmers say a small thank you to the taxpayers for keeping them in business (and free of planning controls) by allowing them to enjoy their investments a little more . . .

The day is Rogation Sunday to be precise, the traditional date for the beating of the bounds, and the day appointed for the annual celebration of the new access rights. The processions follow the routes not just of the parish boundaries before local government reorganisation, but of all ancient footpaths and tracks. Here and there the assembly halts for a small bonfire, on which is thrown any illegal fencing and the odd 'Private' notice which has not found its way into a rural museum. These bonfires apparently commemorate the martyrdom of St Ubble, who was burned to death in one of the great conflagrations of the old farming order, somewhere near the sacrificial site known as M4. (These ceremonial fires occasionally used to be encouraged to spread to plantations of Scandinavian conifers. But there aren't many of these left now, and the practice has been discouraged out of courtesy to the Swedes who are, by custom, honoured guests on each parish procession. Sweden has always had a Right of Common Access – *allmänsrätt* – over virtually its whole land surface, and Swedish advisers were present on all the early processions. The custom stuck.)

But it is at harvest-time that the differences between the old farming landscape and the new are most conspicuous. The arable prairies of East Anglia, for instance, are now the most extraordinary chequerboards of colour, a mosaic of vegetable patches in every stage of leaf, flower and fruit. The change happened quite quickly. Landowners, faced with prohibitive prices for fuel and fertiliser, realised that the most logical and economical extension of 'Pay-and-pick' crops was 'Pay-and-grow', and began leasing out their land in strips along lines that were scarcely distinguishable from the medieval open field system. The most eager tenants were health food enthusiasts from north London and the Stour Valley, many of whom gave up the dole to tend their vast new allotments. As a result, the vegetable fields of central Norfolk, garlanded with the flowers of Jerusalem artichokes, asparagus-peas and pumpkins, have become as great a tourist attraction in blossom-time as the fruit orchards of Kent.

In those areas where cereal crops are still raised intensively the ancient practice of gleaning has been revived, and many families find they are able to gather enough grain for their Moulinex blenders to keep them in wholemeal flour for the winter.

Orchards are as busy and beautiful as they were before the days of Golden Delicious, but are enormously increased in number now that every parish has its own communal fruit garden. Even towns and cities have municipal orchards, since planners realised that their traditional objection to planting fruiting as well as flowering cherries – 'But the public may *pick* them' – was ludicrous. The widespread enthusiasm for farming has also resulted in some fascinating experiments in vertical cropping, and vines can be seen trained hundreds of feet above pavement level on the walls of office blocks.

Now that the countryside is more accessible (and the people, incidentally, much healthier) the British winter is no longer something to be reviled and hidden from. There has been a resurgence of informal winter sports and frolics and some ingenious new inventions. Now there's no need to produce butter mountains to satisfy the whims of EEC economists, many hills have been given over for public enjoyment, and mud-tobogganing has become a national craze.

In London the chic event of winter is no longer the New Beaujolais race but what has become known as 'First Faggot'. The ancient trees in Epping Forest are lopped for firewood every winter, just as they were in the nineteenth century (the forest is so light and airy as a result that primroses have returned to bloom), and on the first day of the cutting season, teams race to cut and cart the first bundle to the wood-burning stove in El Vino's.

Meanwhile, in front of wood fires all round the country, parents tell their children tales about the time when the land and the things that grew on it were regarded as exclusively private property. The children treat it as a wonderful tall story, and have invented an energetic new game called 'Farmers, keepers'.

A Dorset Fable (1986)

It was meant to be an uncomplicated break with an old friend, something we try to take once a year for a spell of none-too-serious bird-watching. We chose Dorset this time because we had not been there together before, and because in the shrivelling cold of May the Wessex coast seemed the last best chance of sniffing a spring breeze, and maybe glimpsing a swallow.

Dorset also has a famously diverse landscape, and we planned to work the county over in three or four days, shuttling between puffin-haunted cliffs and nightingale copses, between the great chalk scarp and what remains of the heathland, and a coast that, when the wind is right, can positively bristle with rare migrants.

At least that was the idea. My companion was, by now, wise about the curious habits of writers, tolerant of my brown studies and constitutional inability to shut down the scribbler in the head. Holidays mean new copy as well as fresh fields.

We arrived down on the south-west coast, Dorset's rock bottom, in weather rather worse than we had left behind in the Chilterns. A fierce wind was blowing in cold air from central Europe (and, as it later transpired, a new load of Chernobyl dust). Chesil Beach, rolling into the distance under a sky the colour of pewter, looked like something the tide had washed in. Its 7 miles of sullen shingle wall off the longest string of tidal lagoons in Britain, and we had hoped for a panorama of exotic wading birds. But the water level was high, and the surface so choppy that even Abbotsbury's famous swans had taken to skulking in the reeds.

The swarms of newly arrived swifts and martins were hunting for insects, bizarrely, over a mass of white horses, but as the wind began whipping sheets of freezing drizzle into our faces, we watched them more out of a sense of duty than gratitude, and soon retreated for shelter.

We sat shivering behind a breakwater and discussed why the pebbles of Chesil Beach grew larger as you moved east. Perhaps the wind was *always* like this, and we were sitting at the gritty end of the line. It was a miserable debate for a mid-May afternoon, and it reminded me uncomfortably of how I had been frustrated by this place for nearly twenty years.

Dorset has always been my soft spot, or perhaps I should say, my Achilles heel. It is the one area of Britain that in my mind's eye quite obliterates all my historical understanding and first-hand experience, and sends me slipping away down that long, glowing tunnel towards what Housman called 'the land of lost content'.

The Dorset of my imagination, fashioned by Thomas Hardy, Kenneth Allsop and Geoffrey Household's *Rogue Male*, is a cryptic, intricate, ancient landscape, locked behind great bulwarks of chalk, and dwarfing the humans that inhabit it. It is always either late March, with rooks tossing over a leafless ash copse in a deep combe; or midsummer on the vast sweep of Eggardon Hill, with Vaughan Williams' 'Lark Ascending' playing somewhere in the distance. I only have to read the village names on the map – Mappowder, Melbury Bubb, Winterborne Whitechurch, Melcombe, Sydling, Hazelbury Bryan – strung out like old almanack entries along the yellow by-roads and I am back buried in those fifties children's television serials that seemed always to be set in south country rectories.

I really ought to know better by now. Dorset in the flesh was almost always just like this day on Chesil: unromantic, reticent, a collection of weatherbeaten parishes losing their amenities like every other rural area. Yet I still keep going back, and every trip becomes, for me, an attempt to exorcise my own myth – or perhaps, just perhaps, find one place where it holds true.

For the next couple of days we stalked through a Dorset as thoroughly distorted as it was in my fantasy. A dense fog lay over the whole coastal strip. The great network of barrows and Celtic field systems above Compton Valence were no more than a thickening of the mist. The downland that should have surged dramatically around the trackways was reduced to thin smidgeons of livid, over-fertilised grass under barbed wire fences.

On Powerstock Common, once a medieval Royal Forest, the air among the Forestry Commission plantations was about as invigorating as water-logged felt. But at least here the fog lifted a little. We heard a few desultory bursts of warbler song, glimpsed buzzards and a sparrowhawk. But only after hours of tramping among the conifers did we light on the last remnant of the original forest – a tract of gnarled, fern-draped, elfin oaks, where we saw a lone willow warbler (our first of the spring) singing over a carpet of primroses and marsh marigolds.

And that was how the pattern continued: brief patches of brightness amid the gloom. It was as if we were trapped in some seasonable fable, and being visited by ghosts of Dorset Past and Yet to Come. A strange meadow of late-flowering wild daffodils in Marshwood Vale, and miles of invisible hills. A countryside almost stripped of birds and a muddle of reedbeds and pools at Radipole, slap in the middle of Weymouth's new housing estates, alive with warblers.

Radipole proved our undoing. We heard talk of a bee-eater down on Portland Bill, and despite disbelief that the flamboyant Mediterranean bird could have allowed itself to be blown on to this clammy promontory, sped down among the grim prison and naval base blocks.

Darkness closed over us (about 4 p.m.) as we drifted aimlessly amongst a ghostly landscape of wet radio masts, looking for a sub-tropical vagrant to the sound of foghorns. If Dorset was trying to tell us something about the arrogance of tourists and townie journalists, hoping they could catch a *genius loci* on the wing, so to speak, it was doing a good job. On the way back to the hotel I amused myself imagining how Hardy might have described the hapless Country Writer: 'He was sure and quick of step, yet his face wore an expression of agitation, as of a messenger who has lost his way.'

Our final morning is best passed over quickly. The fog lifted, but was replaced by a gale. Poole Harbour and the Arne heathlands – the last remnants of Hardy's Egdon – were shorn of birds. We tried to walk east along the cliffs at Kimmeridge, hoping for puffins and guillemots, but were driven back by showers of razor-sharp shales being torn off the cliff face and blown vertically upwards, into our faces.

The day had an oppressive, charged feel about it. In a pub on the ridge above Lulworth Cove, where the cottages have barracks numbers, we ate lunch nervously among a large gang of young soldiers getting drunk for the Cup Final.

Thinking that things could not really get any worse, we decided on an impulse to go down into the Ministry of Defence ranges at Tyneham, which were open to the public that day. We drove down the switchback road into the valley for a couple of miles, and suddenly we were face to face with the Dorset that had eluded us for days. Around us was an extraordinary vista of soaring downland, derelict tanks and vast clumps of flowering gorse. Sheep grazed on the still visible medieval field systems, up to their knees in cowslips and shell cases, and in some of the scrubby craters and combes, nightingales were singing exultantly into the teeth of the gale.

The ironies of this forced marriage of discipline and wildness were a bit too much to stomach in places, especially in the melancholy shell of Tyneham itself, which has been washed and brushed up and generally restored as a classic example of an historic Dorset hamlet – except that nobody lives there.

The villagers were moved out to make way for a training range at the height of the last war, with a promise that they would be able to return when it was all over. They left a note pinned to the church door saying: 'Please look after our village while we are away.'

They never were allowed back, of course, and four decades of argument about whether resettlement and access and land rights can be measured against the national interest are faithfully reflected in the visitors' book which the Army thoughtfully provided in Tyneham's little museum. The Army argue that their presence has conserved both landscape and wildlife, which would otherwise have been obliterated by post-war intensive farming. They are probably right, though it is a sad comment on our political will, if we need armed occupation to preserve our countryside. The immediate locals largely support them, for the employment and privacy they guarantee. Further afield, feelings seem to be very mixed. Some visitors want the village resettled, some simply find the whole paradox deeply offensive.

But for venom, nothing matched the comments of those locals who were protesting against a recent brief invasion of 'plastic cottages' on the site. They proved to be props for a forthcoming feature film on the Tolpuddle Martyrs, the group of Dorset farmworkers who were transported for having the temerity to start a trade union during the great agricultural depression of the 1830s, when the whole countryside looked as heart-tuggingly beautiful as Tyneham. Now, the only glimpse of ancient Dorset that was authentic enough for the film-makers was fossilised inside a battle-training area. It was hard to tell whether the indignation was felt most fiercely against the plastic, or against the intrusion of uncomfortable reminders of what life in an idyllic landscape had really been like. Either way, it made the point that there is no 'getting away from it all', no imagined island of tranquillity and content in the countryside. Our own fogbound explorations had started with a frivolous search for spring migrants, and ended in the midst of a political debate that is as old as the hills.

I rather think all parishes should have a visitors' book. It might help to remind both curmudgeonly locals and glib outsiders that the land is far too complex to be appropriated by, or contained within, one-sided definitions.

Anatomy of a Village (1988)

Newton Regis, on the advancing edge of Midlands commuter country, has, like all villages, the essential ingredients that make gripping drama: plot, characters and a limited number of sets. The stories about it tend to be wry and ambivalent, like this one from last summer.

Not long after Newton Regis is chosen as the Best Kept Village in North Warwickshire, a car draws up outside Alan and Maggie Hall's sixteenth-century cottage on the main street, and a family disembark to take a photo of its nostalgic mix of thatched roof and whitewashed, timber-framed walls. There is nothing odd about this. The cottage, tucked up next to the pub and duck pond among billowing foxglove borders, is one of the village showpieces. But this family, more venturesome than most, come right over the fence and into the garden, and – to the amazement of the Halls, watching from inside – pose against the climbing roses. Then, changing their minds, they go back to the car, rummage about in the boot and return with a spade. They pose again, this time with the spade firmly planted in one of the beds. The snap is taken, and the satisfied family drive off with their instant comic postcard. It is a story which expresses more than just familiar rural complaints about townee boorishness. It catches other fears – about, for instance, the dangers of village life and experience becoming a museum piece, or just an effortlessly collectable commodity.

We all share these worries because the rural village is, for better or worse, a central symbol in our culture. For at least a century and a half it has been a model of the most desirable kind of community, a tranquil, timeless ideal where lives are played out in harmony with the soil and the seasons, and contained within a contented social order that is in marked contrast to the madcap unneighbourliness of the town. But more recently a less comforting story has begun to surface, of villages becoming little more than retreats for the rich and mobile middle classes. The old, the sick and the poor have either been exiled altogether by soaring house prices, or shifted to outdated council estates, where they have become trapped and isolated with a paucity of services that would be intolerable to a city dweller.

Common sense insists that both these images are over-simplifications. Yet the rural village must have adapted to have survived so successfully. What is its character today? Is the pattern of life still based on the immemorial rhythms of the agricultural year? If not, what is a village, beyond being just something rather smaller than a town? Does it still have any role or meaning for that major part of the nation that lives beyond the village boundaries?

Every village would give different answers, and there is no sense in which Newton Regis could be seen as 'typical' without insult both to its own and every other village's human complexity. But it is not an exceptional village either. It lies more or less in the centre of England, in bland farming countryside, uncomplicated by hills or woods or wasteland. Very few of its five hundred strong population work on the land, yet it has kept the form of the classic Midlands agricultural settlement, with church, pub, pond and farms compactly clustered round the single street.

To Dave Atkin of North Warwickshire Borough Council's Planning Department in Atherstone, developments in Newton typify changes that are occurring all over southern England. The imaginary line between 'the north' and the prosperous south, he reckons, has now moved some way north of Birmingham. The boundary between town and country was shifting, too, not just from village-edge development, but because it was increasingly a division between working and home life. In Newton Regis it was some time since more than a handful of inhabitants earned their livelihood inside the village. Even thirty years ago the Leicester coalfield had been a more important employer than the local farms. Now villagers travelled to work in a brickworks five miles away, or to small industries in Tamworth. The crunch year for the village had been 1986, when the first section of the Birmingham–Nottingham motorway was opened less than half a mile from the village. Newton suddenly became a short, fast drive from the whole expanding nexus of Midlands enterprise: Wolverhampton, Warwick, Stratford, the National Exhibition Centre, Birmingham Airport. The resulting inflow of commuters might have led to a rash of new high-price housing, but for the fact that the ancient core of the village had been designated a conservation area, and the whole of the parish a minimum-growth zone in the structure plan. But housing, consequently, was at a premium, which meant the undermining of one of the cornerstones of village mythology – the sense of family lineages inhabiting the same parish, and sometimes the same house, for generations. Dave Atkin told me of other long-running threats to the old order: the prospective opening of a commercial clay pigeon range, the proposed closing of the village school.

But there was one oddity in this story of seemingly relentless modernisation. Newton was – at least in terms of real estate – still a manorial village. Both the farms, several of the houses, the school and much of the land were owned by the Inge-Innes-Lillingstons, who lived at Thorpe, just north of the village.

As I was going to leave Dave mapped out a route to the village that would give me the best picture of the surrounding landscape. 'I call it the spire country,' he beamed, the planner vanishing for a moment behind the more familiar English figure of the village enthusiast.

Driving up to Newton again later that winter, I could see what he meant. All round Newton the skyline is punctured by church spires. They soar up from Appleby, Orton-on-the-Hill, Seckington, Thorpe, smudged with soot from the Black Country factories to the west, and standing out against a gently swelling, wide open landscape that reminded me of Suffolk. In Newton itself the church, looking a little the worse for wear and swathed in scaffolding, soared above a cluster of allotments, cottages and school buildings.

I had an appointment in the Queen's Head, which by one o'clock was full of customers, many from outside the village. The landlord, Ron Starr, is a slight man in his sixties, with a quiet, mischievous energy. He had come here from a roadhouse just outside Tamworth sixteen years before. It was meant to be a partial retirement, a busman's holiday in 'a pub in the country'. Now, with two bars and masses of passing trade, he is busier than he ever was in the town. Ron took me on a quick tour of the pub, down to see his spick and span cellar and the letters of commendation from the brewery, and outside to see his 'chimney garden' which was slowly taking shape at the back of the pub. The whole thing had been a last-minute scheme, he told me, beginning with 'the fastest potato harvest known to man. I had them in one week, out the next, and the whole plot sown with chimneys by the end of the month.' His collection of pots and pipes, stuffed with bulbs and geraniums, had the surreal look of an unfinished sculpture park as they waited for the sun to bring them to life. Many of the pieces had come from the local brickworks, donated by friends and customers.

In the bar there were more signs of informal barter. Eggs were going one way, seedlings the other. One disabled man who had to make regular trips to hospital was using the pub as the pick-up point for his lift. Chatting with the regulars I asked what the public services were like. Were the newly deregulated buses reliable? Did the fact that the nearest medical practice (at Polesworth) was 3 miles away cause any problems? No one seemed to know. The question didn't seem to have arisen. There was no shortage of cars in the village, and those few inhabitants who didn't drive never had a problem getting lifts. Was it different in other places?

Newton, I soon discovered, was a prime example of how the car has stretched the village as well as emptying it. There were the usual bingo evenings and pub quiz leagues held locally, but the villagers' sense of where they *lived*, rather than just resided, wasn't limited by the parish boundaries. They did their chores, went shopping, got their entertainment in a larger catchment area that they saw as a kind of extended village. Although the days when goods and services were delivered to the door were missed here, as everywhere, no one I talked to regarded the lack of facilities on the doorstep as seriously reducing the quality of their lives.

Over the street from the pub, Jack Rutherford, one-time farm worker and Chairman of the Parish Council, expressed stout approval of this self-help philosophy. Jack, a widower and no longer very mobile, has lived in the village much of his life, most of it in this dark Grade III cottage. '*They* tell me I must preserve the roof. But can I get *them* to pay for it . . . ?' He makes no secret of his strict Tory view of village fortunes. Newton, he believed, was a *good* village. The Lillingstons looked after the fabric and the villagers looked after themselves. The local playing field and pavilion were good examples of the fruits of such partnership. The Lillingstons had donated the land, the Parish Council had levied a penny rate to raise funds for building. Much of the work had been done by the villagers, and one of the farms had lent a tractor for the mowing. Charity, hard work, service, paying your dues – these were what had made the village survive and prosper. He thinks well of the newcomers, and there is no hostility in his nickname of 021s for Brummies (after the city's STD code). They join in. They take his dog for walks. He just wishes that they would be a little less pushy in their efforts to keep the village school open, and would make their children sandwiches for lunch instead of relying on school-dinner handouts. But he is sure that no one in the village wants any new developments, either of housing or light industry and certainly none of the suburban frippery of restaurants and shops. These were the things people moved to Newton to get away from.

Talk of work puts him in a wistful mood. 'There were three tailors in the village once, just to serve the Big House. All that livery!' His house is crammed with family and village mementoes, kept close to hand to save his legs. He showed me a rushlight holder, his late wife's books on herbalism, a pint barrel his father had used to take beer into the fields, reminders of a more spartan life. But it wasn't the working village he missed so much as that immemorial, well-oiled hierarchy of duties and responsibilities he believed were still hanging on by a thread in Newton. Then he fishes out his *coup de grâce*, a glimpse of Jack the Lad: a photo showing him, younger and more worldly, shaking hands with a local Labour politician.

But it wasn't the village's own radical representative. Surprisingly, perhaps, for such an upwardly-mobile community, Newton and its neighbour, No Mans Heath, had elected a Labour member to the Borough Council. Steve Norman is a sales rep for an industrial plastics firm, and lives in a cottage buried deep among the fields and plantations on the northern edge of the parish. He agreed with Jack Rutherford's view of a harmonious village, but laughed at Jack's appropriation of this for his own political side. It is one of Labour's periodic weeks of self-immolation, and he is careful what he says. He sees no real party issues here. There is some unemployment in the area, but it is not a village problem. The lack of cheap housing may become one, but at present there are only five names on the waiting list for council houses, and the conflict between old and new villagers – which was partly a class conflict – was barely noticeable.

What concerned people here was more parochial, he reckoned. The provision of street lights, winning the Best Kept Village award, keeping the school open, and now, above all, the looming threat of the gun club. An outsider from Uttoxeter, who owned a parcel of land on the edge of the village, had applied for permission to open a commercial clay pigeon range. Free enterprise had, for once, confronted the new rural culture's other aspirations, for peace, privacy and security, and hadn't stood a chance. Nothing had so completely united the village, from council house to mansion, since the threat to the school.

From their different standpoints both Jack and Steve nominated the new rector, Stan Marriott, as one of the important unifying influences in the village. Stan, in his early sixties, had only been in the parish for eighteen months, but had already earned himself the affectionate nickname of the White Tornado, for his energy in getting things done. He and his wife Joan came here from a nearby mining village. They were convinced that the mutual caring that is evident here is a common and necessary trait in this part of the Midlands, and that it had survived the transition from rural and industrial village to commuter settlement. Stan is a generous and respected man, with a huge sense of humour that has already helped him to minister to those dark moments that afflict all small communities. He told me how last year an uncanny series of tragedies had struck every member of the bell-ringing team, and that what had helped begin the healing process was a blackly comic hearse race to the cemetery.

He filled in more details of the crisis that had recently faced the village school, when the roll fell into the low twenties and closure had seemed imminent. The village had rallied round and campaigned to save it. But what clinched the outcome was an influx of travellers' children from the permanent site at Alvecote, a few miles west of the village. The roll rose above forty, and the school looked safe – for the time being anyway.

Stan regards the travellers as part of his parish, and visits them regularly. He believes their children have integrated well with local youngsters. He is more concerned about the fate of children generally in the area. They haven't the same mobility as adults, and the image of a carefree country childhood is now a dangerous delusion. The recent spate of child murders in the Midlands had given grim confirmation to what most parents have begun to take for granted – that children are no longer safe playing by themselves in woods and fields. 'They have changed people's perception of country life,' Stan acknowledges philosophically. Now when he is visiting parishioners in the evenings he always phones first, and agrees a coded number of rings on the doorbell.

Spring in Newton arrives more conspicuously in the village than in the countryside beyond. Ron Starr's chimneys begin to bloom and stir hopes that Newton might scoop the Best Kept Village award for a third time. There are signs of a new broom in the village store, where Rob Hilditch, a redundant welder, and his wife Linda are taking over the reins and have plans for extending its stocks and services. The first broods of ducklings from the pond are beginning to make mad forays across the street into the yard of Manor Farm.

This is the larger of the two farms and the tenancy has been in the Wilson family for generations. It is a medium-sized unit of 400 acres on good soil, with a mixture of grazing, cereal and potatoes. The current tenant, Stewart Wilson, a single man in his late thirties, sees no problem in juggling the proportions of crops to meet any changes in Common Agricultural Policy quotas for milk or cereal. Nor does he think the current talk of taking farmland out of production will drive him into trying fashionable crops like flax or evening primrose, or into Pick-Your-Own. Mind you, there was a time when the farm was host to all manner of visitors. Up until a few years ago they had an annual summer dance and barbecue for 1,500 people, twice the number that lived in the village. There are, as yet, no signs of the 'Shire Wars' disturbances that have been disrupting other rural areas, but gatherings of that size were out of the question now. Instead Stewart is looking forward to hosting a more modest gathering of the breed society for his new French dairy cattle. The only problem he can see in the future is that there is no obvious successor to take over the farm after him.

The problem of succession is more critical at the smaller of the two holdings, Newton Farm. Clifford and Nancy Rowe are nearing retirement and there is no one in the family to carry on the work. They will have to leave the farm when the time comes, and perhaps the village too, with house prices being what they are. As for the farm itself, there is a real chance of it going the way of Old Hall Farm, with the land being broken up and sold off, and the farm buildings converted into dwelling units.

But for the moment, life goes on. It is late in the lambing season, and I walk across the yard with Cliff and his part-time stockman to a pen where a ewe is having a difficult delivery. There is no vet present, but Cliff is accustomed to this kind of situation. He buries his arm deep inside the ewe, and after minutes of intense straining and twisting, pulls out the lamb, feet first. It looks dead to me, but Cliff wipes it down, whirls it round, shakes it like a wet blanket, and suddenly, as if it had been given an electric shock, it jerks into life. A short while later it is nosing blearily towards its mother's teats. Newton Street, locked in mid-morning quiet just a few yards away, and the flat fields beyond, stretching out towards the M42, seem part of another world.

It is 14 May, Rogation Sunday. Jack Rutherford has successfully lobbied for revival of the ceremony of Beating the Bounds, and at 2.30 p.m. in the afternoon about fifty of us gather by the lych gate of St Mary's Church to circumnavigate the parish. The plan is to be back in time for tea. In Selborne, I recall, it used to take three whole days to parade around just 18 miles of boundary.

The weather is ominous for a ceremony that began as a pagan fertility rite before being Christianised in the fifth century. The Chilterns were being lashed by thunderstorms when I left, and up here a sickly haze hangs over the whole landscape. Steve Norman has wisely donned his Pennine walking boots, but most of the company's clothes would be more appropriate for a stroll down to the Queen's Head. Our guide is Bill Tunnicliff, retired hedger and woodman and walking archive. He leads us out of the village at a furious pace, treating anyone who can keep up with him to a continuous commentary.

It's a pleasant, garrulous assembly, of all ages and from all sections of the village. For many of them this is the first time they have ever explored Newton's home countryside. The problem is that much of the old field pattern – and the parish bounds it incorporated – has vanished. The old hedges have been grubbed up, and footpaths obliterated by cereal crops on which the sour-sweet smell of pesticide still hangs. We pick our way – straggling already – along trackways that as often as not come to a dead end in an unnavigable drainage ditch. Some of the children fall, with relish, into the mud. Bill cuts his hand climbing over a new fence, but does his best to make sense of this transfigured landscape. He waves towards where the bounds had once been (or perhaps still are, if only we could reach them) and intones the old field names: 'Old Moor, Sandy Spinney, The Common. C'mon.' He has rehearsed his jokes well.

Every so often, in correct Rogation style, we stop for a hymn and a prayer. Gina Cooke, in a red outfit that is the brightest thing in the landscape, plays guitar for the children to sing:

> *The tall trees in the greenwood, the meadows for our play,*
> *The rushes by the water, to gather every day.*

Alas, there is not much greenwood left in Newton, and no flowery meadows for playing or picking. For a brief, ungracious moment I feel disgruntled with this village for being so content with its bland, fenced-off countryside, and pine for the Chilterns. I could imagine what the beechwoods would be like in this tempestuous weather – turned into rainforests, full of flayed, whirling leaves, and green mists rising off the bluebells . . .

Just before we reach the old sewage works, the haze turns the colour of fading oil-seed rape. Jack Rutherford, driven here by a friend, peers from a field gate like a soothsayer. 'God's sun shines on the righteous,' he proclaims. 'What does that make us Jack?' a voice shouts back. I recall what the seventeenth-century parson George Herbert had written about the virtues of the Perambulation. It promoted 'Charitie, in living walking and neighbourly accompanying one another, with reconciling differences, if there be any . . .' Around me, this is exactly what people are doing. Newton isn't a village of walkers, and this isn't walking countryside. What occupies them is not their surroundings but 'neighbourly accompanying' – chatting about gardens and holidays and what the children are doing at school. Telling stories, too: 'We had a day out in London. On a coach. Only it broke down and we had to get a bus. Well, everybody was asking everybody else how they felt and would they be worried back at home, when the conductor comes round. Good Lord, he says, what's the matter? Nobody's talked on this route since the war.'

My brief fit of pique is soon banished by the general high spirits and I join in the gossip. I meet a couple who had to leave Newton after the birth of their first child, for a bigger but more economical house in Tamworth, but who are so fond of the village that they come back for a day out whenever they can. The Smedleys moved the other way, decamping to Newton to raise their family. Their children are with them, enjoying the stroll but more intent on collecting snails than noting land-marks. Caroline Smedley is a leading light in the WI, and doing research on parish history (a sparse field, she admits, once you have gone beyond living memory) and Michael is director of a fine art firm in Lichfield, 10 miles to the west. They are all deeply fond of the village and would not have it any different. They recognise that it is liable to lose a whole generation from lack of moderately priced housing, but point out that this happens anyway to twenty-year-olds in most communities. Michael, especially, enjoys the sense of refuge the village provides when he comes home from work. There was no local protest when the M42 was built, and most Newtonians regard it as a blessing – an easy route out to work and urban pleasures, and an even more welcome lifeline back to family and home, *village* pleasures.

Remarkably, we are straggling back along the outskirts of the recreation ground as teatime approaches, our abbreviated circuit complete. Stan Marriott's peroration near a little covert called Newton Gorse is a masterpiece, as much Bunyan as Herbert. He stretches his arms wide and asks for blessings on an immense cornucopia of living things that might just possibly be within their compass: rabbits, squirrels, oak trees, cuckoos, the staff of life ... a vision of a vague but encircling green fulsomeness that I suspect exactly catches the way Newtonians feel about their parish.

A few weeks later I travelled back to Warwickshire to talk to George Lillingston, whose seat, Thorpe Hall, is a couple of miles north-west of Newton. It was real spring weather at last, and swarms of house martins were busy at the nests around the Hall. For a while I was lost in the labyrinth of outbuildings and estate offices, but we eventually found each other, and, once settled in the drawing-room, I passed on my concern about the state of the local footpaths. He agreed there was a problem. The local network wasn't as comprehensive or as diligently maintained as it might be. On the other hand he hadn't noticed much local pressure for access – particularly along those paths that originated as field-workers' short cuts. Perhaps people up here were more reconciled to agriculture leading the way than they were in the more environmentally anxious south? It wasn't, I could see from his wry smile, an entirely rhetorical question.

He was well aware of what lay behind some of my queries, and rejected any suggestion that Newton's air of placidity results in part from being under a benevolent squirearchy. 'It would be hard enough being any kind of interventionist squire in the 1980s, even if I lived in the village. Three miles away – *and* in a different county – it's downright impossible.'

But he did lay a modest claim to having set in motion the transformation of the village that led to its present social mix. We had moved into a quiet room at the centre of Thorpe Hall, away from the din of the estate lawnmowers. 'When I came here in the 1950s, Newton was still a Victorian village. There were one-up, one-down cottages with outside lavatories. It

needed a boost to its self-respect, an injection of new blood with aspirations for themselves and the village. So we built four semi-detached
three-up, three-down cottages in Hames Lane, and then demolished
Newton House Farm – an ugly place that spoilt the view of the church –
to make room for bungalows.'

He toyed with the phrase 'social engineering' to describe what he did,
but it sounds too harsh and grandiose for a scheme which, after all,
simply reflected the mood of the times. He was well aware that the lack
of first-time housing was likely to cause problems in the future, and
said that he was already examining the viability of housing association
schemes.

Summer comes, a few well-loved names enter the Register of Deaths, and
a Mr Present Lee joins the list of marriage witnesses after a particularly
high-spirited travellers' wedding. Down in the school the children are
helping to put together their contribution to the St Mary's Flower Festival.

That afternoon I had been out with a group of seven to nine-year-olds
on a nature walk to Newton Gorse, which the Lillingstons have given to
the County Wildlife Trust as a reserve. They fizzed about like fireworks,
bright and inquisitive, with the kind of pent-up energy you normally
associate with inner-city children let out for a day.

Later, their head-teacher, Margaret Fulleylove, confirms the Marriotts'
view that village children no longer have the freedom to explore their
own countryside. But the school is doing well, and she believes it can
survive. The roll is now just past 50 and still expanding. Her main
preoccupation is working out the implications of the Education Reform
Act. The budget for the school will now be the responsibility of the Board
of Governors – an especially complex body in Newton's case, given St
Mary's hybrid status as an assisted church school in a privately owned
building. The budgeting is bound to be tight; Margaret is banking on the
management and financial skills of newcomer parents on the Board.

In the meantime there are always the travellers to keep the school on
its toes. They are fiercely protective of their children (during a recent
meningitis scare they would not bring them to school) but are beginning
to involve themselves in the Parent Teacher Association. I heard no scur-
rilous or even mildly hostile tales about the travellers during my whole
six months of visiting Newton. The village is fond of storytelling, but
seems to have little use for outright gossip. There are occasional good-
humoured nudges about certain individuals' fondness for the bottle, but
nothing scandalous or unkind. Into this vacuum pour the mischievous
spoofs invented by Bob Lane. Bob leads a packed life as garage owner,
folk music enthusiast, parish councillor, smallholder and general entre-

preneur. He also runs the only bed-and-breakfast establishment in the village, in the commodious setting of Newton House, and every so often starts a rumour about an impending 'change of use'. It has been destined to become the venue for an open-air rock festival, the headquarters of an extreme religious sect and a dubious foreign consulate. The village, for its part, pretends to believe these tales, as if it needs a continuing shadowy threat from outside, however improbable.

But on those topics that preoccupy village watchers – housing and employment especially – Newtonians are largely silent, even unconcerned. John Bird runs a community work programme in Tamworth, where there are currently 3,600 unemployed and only eighty job vacancies. But he believes the problem is less pressing in the countryside. There is more scope in a village economy for multiple employment, do-it-yourself, part-time work. He took me to see his greenhouse where he had built a brilliant device for providing controlled watering, converted from a flushing lavatory cistern.

It is a kind of ingenuity that is echoed throughout the village. A pair of young men have set themselves up with a chain-saw as a mobile logging team. The man who is repainting the Queen's Head doubles as a carpet layer. Rob and Linda Hilditch have already expanded their business at the village store to provide a video loan service and an off-licence. They are currently working eighteen hours a day. Rob sorts the mail first thing, runs the shop in the daytime and fits in deliveries to pensioners whenever he can find a spare moment. Linda drives to market for supplies before going off to her second job as a computer operator. It is way past six o'clock on a Friday evening, and customers are still popping into the shop for bottles of shampoo, soft drinks (quaffed on the spot), a couple of onions, bits and pieces overlooked in the weekend shopping. Rob and Linda have noticed a pattern in the villagers' buying habits. People from the council estate spend more, on better quality goods, west-end Newtonians use the shop for things they have forgotten to buy in the town. The Hilditches are grateful for their custom, but hope everyone realises that village shop economies are always precarious and that if the shop goes so will the post office.

The next day, Flower Festival Saturday, is mercifully bathed in sunshine. Newton's countryside looks as green and bosky as anywhere in England on a fine June day, and inside the village the farm tractors have been out tidying up the verges until the street is as smartly shorn as a municipal park. Bill Tunnicliff has heard a rumour that Newton is favourite to walk off with the Best Kept Village award again, and is fretting over some barely visible weeds in the graveyard grass. I tease him that if I was a judge I would disqualify the entire village for over-fussiness.

But it is hard not to be wooed by the displays in the church. This year the theme is country crafts, and the stands are decorated with mixtures of flowers and handmade goods. Some are modern – loaves, lacework, home-made wine; some are mementoes, and one of the displays is set off against a 1919 peace celebration tablecloth, washed spotless for the occasion. Way above us hangs another odd conjunction: one of the church bells carries a seventeenth-century inscription written backwards, to ward off evil spirits. I sit chatting with the village women, with swallows dipping in and out of the church porch, and realise that Newton is getting pleasantly under my skin. One young woman is here to visit her parents for the weekend and confesses that, like me, she prefers wild country, and moved to the Dales to escape Newton's 'claustrophobia'. But I am beginning to understand what keeps the rest here. It hasn't much to do with the usual preconceptions of village life. Newton isn't rustic or quaint or arty. It has more or less divorced itself from agriculture, from fossilised notions of 'heritage', even from its own landscape. And though it is too prosperous to be typical in this respect, it has given robust answers to the conventional belief that villages automatically decline when they become non-working dormitories or are missing a generation. Most Newtonians want something more limited but quite specific from their village. It is an oasis, a bubble in the green, a home base, a hibernaculum, and the villagers regard their neighbours as their chief amenity. There are plenty of natural models for using the environment as a protection rather than a resource; but given the importance of the church in what must, like the rest of England, be at heart a secular community, perhaps it would be simpler to see this village as a place of sanctuary.

The Great Storm (1987)

Out of the welter of images left in the wake of the hurricane that ransacked south-east England on 16 October [1987], two will stick in my mind. The first was a group of Londoners who made an heroic expedition at the height of the storm to lash down a rocking neighbourhood tree with guy-ropes. The second was more personal, and glimpsed during a tramp through a rather orderly Chiltern wood the following afternoon.

There was surprisingly little evidence of the turmoil, just a quarter of an acre of devastation surrounded by trees that had barely lost a leaf. About fifteen large beeches, cherries and hornbeams had been completely uprooted and lay in a heap. From a distance it looked as if an immense hedge had been forcibly driven through the wood. But it was the *smell* that stopped me in my tracks. One of the beech trunks had split from end to end, and the air was full of that warm, sawmill odour of resin and raw wood. A few shafts of sunlight had penetrated this unfamiliar land-scape – perhaps the first for decades – and as they flickered over the flints in the root-holes, across the ash and maple seedlings given an unexpectedly early place in the sun, and on to this rank, awesome tangle of still-living wood, I felt, I must confess, an extraordinary pulse of excitement – that this is what a real forest must be like.

Both these responses were extreme, in their different ways, but under-standable. The hurricane has exposed, like no other single event, the strength of our national passion for trees, and yet also the extent to which they are mysterious, maddeningly unpredictable beings whose social status is something we are still hopelessly muddled about. We somehow contrive to view them both as deities and domestic retainers, offering veneration one moment (there was talk of a memorial service 'for the fallen' at Kew) and dismissing them as lumber the second they fall out of line. August authorities have been talking of 'irreplaceable' losses, and then proceeding to give precise details of their replacement plans. In a state that I suppose was close to collective grief at the sudden departure of so many old friends, the one thing that has been forgivably overlooked is that trees are living organisms for which injury, death – and regeneration – are entirely natural parts of their life-cycles.

The damage in my part of the Chilterns was no worse than that from an average March gale, and it was hard to believe the stories that were coming from only thirty miles further south. But there was no mistaking the sense of shock and bewilderment in the voices of the people from the Woodland Trust and the NCC that I called, or of the normally imperturbable Suffolk botanist who could barely bring herself to describe the scene around her house. The most unsettling thing, she said, was that you could pick out the shapes of the huge oaks toppling, but could not hear them above the din of the storm. From Essex, Ronald Blythe told me of a Day-of-Judgement scene in his local churchyard. The yews had been blown out of the ground, and underneath was the bleached glint of human bones ...

A couple of days later I drove south to look at the battle zone for myself. It began almost imperceptibly, the way snow cover does when you travel north: at first just a few limbs and the odd roadside beech down; then sudden tongues of flattened trees at the edges of woods. Windsor Forest was badly hit, and yet the ancient, squat oaks in the Great Park had escaped with no more than the loss of a few branches. Looking at them with, so to speak, a weather eye, I realised that they weren't simple pollards, but had had their tops blown off at some time in the past, and had been saved this time by their low centres of gravity.

But in most places the storm seemed to have struck at random. It had broken, twisted and uprooted without discrimination or mercy. It had taken venerable giants and young saplings, hardwoods and conifers, deep and shallow rooters alike, and to blame the damage, as some observers have, on 'the decrepit, overmature' condition of our tree populations is as misguided as blaming it on poor weather-forecasting. Indeed, half-dead and diseased trees that were without their usual complement of leaves were among the most frequently spared.

The further south and east I travelled, the worse the damage became. I saw a 20-acre Scots-pine plantation with every single tree snapped off 12 feet from the ground, and the surrounding hardwoods barely touched. Yet not half a mile away huge beeches had been torn out of waterlogged root-holes the size of ponds.

In some of the worst hit areas every other tree was down, and I edged the car along by-roads carpeted with green leaves, dodging lianas of fallen power and telephone cables and fresh-sawn butts that were only inches from the window.

It was the patchiness of the damage that was the strangest thing. There would be miles where the leaves were not even scorched, then one of these zones of intense devastation; woods with their perimeters intact but their hearts torn out. Time and again I heard people attempting to account for this – and for twisted crowns and trees not just uprooted but turned upside down – by saying that the wind had 'swooped down'; and I am sure that there must have been swarms of tornadoes up in the front of the hurricane, just as there were in the Great Storm of 1703 and in Scotland in 1968.

Yet though the localised damage is awe-inspiring, there is no sense in which the landscape of southern England could be described as 'irrevocably changed' – the phrase used by some commentators just after the storm. The woods – even where they have lost more than half their timber trees – are still indisputably woods. The dense Wealden double hedges are thin and ragged in places, but still follow the same boundaries as they did before. Overall, the landscape looks as if it has been raked through rather than destroyed, and it has probably lost no more trees in total than went during the massive clear-fellings of the First World War.

But it is easy to take a calm and long-term view when you come to a calamity from the outside. The odd few plane trees blown down in the London squares seemed of no account to me, but I know their falling shocked many people who lived close to them and saw them as some kind of fixed landmarks in an unstable world. Down in the south-east and East Anglia there are towns and villages that have not just lost a handful of trees but have had the familiar geography of their home patch transformed overnight. The National Trust has seen landscape parks and gardens which have been maturing for two centuries taken back to base again. The Woodland Trust was especially badly hit. Sixty-eight of its 200-odd woods were damaged, and Stour Wood in Essex has probably lost more than half of all its trees. National nature reserves at Ham Street and Blean in Kent have been wrecked.

And there may be more to come – not just from winter gales, but from the gangs of cowboy contractors currently roaming the south-east with newly purchased chain-saws, and opportunist nurseries trying to offload their stock of cramp-rooted flowering cherries. There is already news of 'preventative felling' of surviving trees, and the chilling prospect that a minority of land-owners may use storm-damage as an excuse for bull-dozing burdensome woods.

It is no real wonder that there has been an almost universal call for massive, urgent replanting. It is a heartening sign of public concern, this desire to make some kind of physical reparation. But now, just as in calmer times, replanting may not be the most appropriate or helpful first response. In many places it may not even be necessary. The priority must surely be for all of us to muster what faith we can in nature and history, and make an act of *acceptance*.

The hurricane was, for better or worse, an entirely natural catastrophe, an integral part of the workings of the environment, not some alien force.

Similar storms have probably torn across England's woods twenty times since they first became established, and yet they still managed to survive. Even inside our own experience we ought to remember that much of what we admire as 'character' in old trees – the blasted tops and gnarled branches of Sherwood's and Windsor's ancient oaks for instance – is the consequence of past storm damage, mellowed by time and the trees' own healing processes. Trees do not lose this character even when they are uprooted.

One of the saddest aspects of the current disaster is the readiness with which supposedly historic trees are being written off simply because they have assumed a horizontal posture. I know I am not the only one who can remember vast reclining trees – 'fallow' trees as Francis Kilvert called them – from my childhood just as well as standing specimens. They were landmarks, meeting places, climbing frames and camp-sites, and they lasted with all their fantastic array of knots, burrs and rot-holes intact for decades. I hope that, once the valuable timber has been extracted, we can leave some of the great fallen trees where they are, as memorials to the storm, as natural sculptures (or carved ones, for that matter) or just to crumble gently back into the soil. Dead and rotting wood is, after all, a natural component of living woodlands. In the last remnants of Europe's primeval forests in Poland, it is reckoned that half of all the timber is fallen or fallow.

And large numbers of apparently damaged or displaced trees may not even be dead. During the 1968 hurricane that devastated south-west Scotland, many of the oaks in the famous Loch Lomond woods were, to all intents and purposes, uprooted. Yet they survived, and are now flourishing, twenty years later, as an extraordinary colony of diagonal trees. It is good to hear that the Woodland Trust, in spite of the terrible damage its woods have sustained, will be trying every possible ruse to save trees, before writing them off and replanting: coppicing and pollarding damaged trunks, pushing roots back in holes, taking cuttings and collecting native seed, encouraging natural regeneration.

There will have to be replanting, of course. There is no other way of restoring the tree-cover in towns and gardens and historic parks. Commercial plantations will need to be restocked, too. Yet though the economic losses must be enormous, the most remarkable – and heartening – aspect of this whole drama is the extent to which it has been almost universally perceived and reported as a communal loss, not as the destruction of private property. And it ought, wherever it is possible, to be up to communities to decide how to go about the business of restoration.

Many, I suspect, will not want to reproduce exactly the old landscape, but to achieve a line of continuity with it which chimes with their present needs and feelings – and the last thing they will want is planting plans and instant saplings from a hundred miles away. A few may have the courage just to step back and see what nature will do to remake a naturally ravaged landscape.

And, next spring, there will be small miracles to cheer them on. Spectacular displays of spring flowers will bloom in the new sunlit gaps. Sappy logs, abandoned in the wet ground, will sprout roots and shoots. So will windthrown branches, speared into the ground by the wind – just as they do in American woods after hurricanes. And throughout south-east England, the crop of acorns and beechmast – so conveniently immense that you could believe Gaia's hand was behind it – will cover every open patch of ground with myriads of seedling trees, the true descendants of the 'fallen'.

The Battle of the Bogs (1987)

What came to be known as the Battle of the Bogs in 1987 was a border conflict with an almost Byzantine complexity of layers. At its heart was the Flow Country, 1,500 square miles of wild peatland in Caithness and Sutherland, home to tens of thousands of wading birds and a scattered community of crofters. Ranged against them were the forces of commercial forestry, attracted here, as to many upland areas, by the expectation of cheap and apparently useless land, and hoping to create what would be the biggest single forestry estate in Britain.

It was the latest chapter in a familiar and long-simmering squabble about afforestation. But the Flow Country had provided some extra and highly combustible ingredients. Distinguished conservationists were arguing that it was a wilderness of international importance, on a par with Serengeti and Amazonia, and there were counter charges from landed Scottish interests that the whole landscape was 'a foul, bankrupt land . . . a denuded wilderness through man's intrusion'. There were accusations of absentee landlordism and bureaucratic English meddling in Scottish affairs, whiffs of tax-avoidance loopholes and dreams of a job bonanza. When the press discovered that there were celebrities involved as well, that show business figures such as Terry Wogan and Cliff Richard owned blocks of 'investment forest' in the Flows, the argument became a hotly debated national issue.

It was a bemusing confrontation, on a scale more usual in land feuds a continent or two away than in our small and already intensively settled islands. But to some onlookers (and some of the participants) the Flows *were* as foreign as Brazil or Antarctica, a sodden, midge-infested quagmire whose cultural and biological values were mystifying.

When I flew up in late July it was unknown territory for me, too, the furthest north I had been in the British Isles, and I wondered if it would overcome a long-standing distaste for bleak uplands. I was based in Golspie, a pleasant little golfing and fishing resort on the east coast. It was full of cafés, boutiques and estate agents, and when I explored it on my first evening, with the swifts racing between the chic cottage conversions, it was hard to believe that this was the gateway to an expanse of primeval bogland the size of Lancashire.

Yet the region was no stranger to land battles. On a ridge overlooking the town is a statue of the first Duke of Sutherland, clad in an imperious red sandstone robe. Early in the last century the English-born Duke had been responsible for the notorious Sutherland Clearances. Between 1814 and 1820 he evicted a third of the entire population of the county from their homes (by burning them down in most cases) to make way for sheep ranching and shooting, and to provide cheap labour for his factories on the coast.

His agent's defence of the purge has an ironic ring in the current circumstances. Their intention, he said, was 'to render this mountainous district contributory as far as possible to the general wealth and industry of the country, and in the manner most suitable to its situation and peculiar circumstances'. The Clearances are an ineradicable part of Highland folk memory, a symbol of all misappropriations of the land, and it was a measure of how deep feelings were running here that each side was accusing the other of initiating 'the New Clearances'.

I went back to my hotel and tried to make some sense of the tangled history of the affair. There did at least seem to be a ground base of scientific facts. What was at stake was the world's largest remaining concentration of blanket bog, a series of rain-drenched plateaux and pools with one of the richest collections of breeding birds in Europe: waders such as greenshank, dunlin, golden plover; loch haunters like red-throated divers – birds whose survival depended on expanses of remote, wet wasteland.

'Blanket bog' is a remarkable enough thing in itself. It is a living skin of sphagnum mosses, a vast, intricate carpet of plants, unrooted except for their own mutual entanglements. Sphagnum is honeycombed with capillary tubes and twice as absorbent as cotton wool. In the very high rainfall of the region it becomes permanently waterlogged and swells sufficiently to blanket areas of moss that are dying back. This moribund sphagnum becomes part of the underlying layers of peat, and the live and dead moss form a permanently moist ground base for other plants.

Yet the Flows has never been an uninhabited wilderness. For thousands of years it has also been the habitat of marginal farmers, who have grazed cattle, cut peat on the bogs, and raised crops in the valleys in ways that are entirely compatible with the bird life. Since the Clearances they have borne the brunt of land-use changes.

Trees, until recently, played no significant part in the crofting life. The unrelenting winds and high rainfall made it all but impossible to grow them, except in sheltered valleys. The Forestry Commission, as a result, was a latecomer to the region, and most private forestry companies would not touch it. But in 1979 the Perth-based Fountain Forestry noticed a happy coincidence of business opportunity and technological know-how. Land prices were low (as little as £100 a hectare in some places), government planting grants were favourable, and machines were at last available that could work in even the most intractable bogs. Fountain began buying up estates in the Flows and selling them off to investors (mostly southerners: 72 of the 76 listed in the Scottish land register that year had English addresses). By the beginning of 1987 it had acquired 40,000 hectares and had earned its investors more than £12 million in grants and tax exemptions.

Fountain's expansion into the Flows coincided with an upsurge of interest in the cultural and biological interest of so-called wastelands. Since the early eighties, the Nature Conservancy Council (NCC) and the Royal Society for the Protection of Birds (RSPB) had been noticing drastic changes in the ecology of the afforested areas of the peatland, whose most conspicuous effect was a plunge in the breeding populations of wading birds. The NCC, as the government's statutory advisers on conservation, obtained an agreement that from February 1987 the Forestry Commission must refer to it all requests for planting grants in the Flows.

Things had come to a head a couple of weeks before when the NCC published a report giving its scientific evidence on the threat to bird life, and making a plea for a moratorium on further planting over all the remaining 400,000 hectares of peatland. The report was met with almost universal hostility from the Scottish establishment. The Highlands and Islands Development Board said that it had been drawn up 'without consultation or regard for the delicate economic and social fabric of the northern Highlands'; Robert McClennan, the SDP MP for Caithness and Sutherland, had described its scientific conclusions as 'preposterous' and predicted its proposals would lead to the loss of '2,000 jobs in the long term'.

The forestry lobby accused the conservationists of valuing birds above people and of meddling in affairs beyond the NCC remit. Conservationists retorted that it was not them but the alien conifers that were driving out – at public expense – both indigenous crofters and new tourists. Each side (it is the shadow of the Clearances again) has accused the other of 'sterilising' the Flows, showing, to anyone who needed convincing, what a flexible and subjective concept 'productivity' is when it comes to land.

It was not just the scale and venom of the quarrel that were exceptional. Beyond the revelation of show business stars' investment portfolios and the intricacies of government forestry policy, it was stirring ancient and unresolved questions about what we value land for. Was economic usefulness the only indicator? Did wasteland invariably mean wasted land? How could its value as a global asset be compared with its worth as a national raw material?

Later that evening there was music in the hotel bar. It was advertised as a Ceilidh, but it was really a local talent contest for the tourists, an anodyne mixture of country and western and Kenneth McKellar. I recalled another musically tinged evening years before in Fort William, the frontier town between Highlands and Lowlands. That night I had watched two pipers in full regalia sitting in the corner of a bar, playing laments whilst tears rolled down their cheeks, and their wives, done up in stilettos and blue-rinsed hair, sipping gin by their side.

The Flows felt like frontier country too, and with all the feuds, prospectors and bounty hunters it didn't seem too extravagant to view the galloping advance of 'the forestry' as a Great Timber Rush.

Next day I drove out into the Flow Country with my guide, Lesley Crenna, local officer for the NCC. Two features of the unplanted peat strike you when you drive in from the hillier land to the south. One is the sense of immense space, of a gently undulating flatness in which there are no straight lines, no harsh colours and, unless you looked for them, very few foregrounds. In clear weather you can often see the peaks of Sky Fea and Genie Fea in the Orkneys, 40 miles to the north.

The other is what I can only describe as a kind of plasticity. The swell of the peat hummocks, the honey-coloured tussocks of sedge, the dark pools all seem, if you stare at them long enough, actually to be moving. Perhaps they are. The whole system is full of mobile water, which regularly seems to overload the sphagnum 'sponge' and spill out to form pools – the dubh lochans. There are many thousands of these, ranged in places like ladders, elsewhere in concentric arcs. From above they have the look of pool clusters on a saltmarsh at low tide, or the pitting in limestone rocks. Against this curving, tremulous landscape the severe stripes and rectilinear furrows of the new plantings seemed misplaced and bizarre enough to have been created by extraterrestrials.

The Flows are really a kind of tundra. During the short, intense subarctic summers they buzz with life, with myriads of insects and wading birds. Four thousand pairs of dunlin (35 per cent of the European population) nest close to the pools, where they winkle out insects with their toothpick bills. So do the same number of golden plovers, and smaller numbers of greenshank, sandpipers and snipe. There are huge populations of meadow pipits and skylarks and, feeding on these and the abundant voles, are hen harriers and merlin, and peregrines and eagles hunting out of the high ground adjacent to the bog.

I talked to Roy Dennis, director of RSPB operations in the Highlands and a crofter himself, and he admitted that the richness of the birdlife is only just being appreciated, after years of survey work. It might have saved a good deal of misunderstanding if this information had been available earlier, but the remoteness and sheer extent of the land had made surveying a slow, laborious business, and no match for the speed of the new machines. Roy pointed at a map on the wall and said wistfully: 'The land is so flat you could start a bulldozer in Wick and drive it straight to Bettyhill.'

And that, more or less, is what had happened. Out of 65,000 hectares owned by Fountain and the Forestry Commission, roughly half had already been drilled into order with a gusto that would have done credit to the seventeenth-century Dutch fen drainers. Giant excavators had dragged out drainage ditches in the peat, 8 feet deep in places, and raised cultivation ridges for the rows of spruce and lodgepole pine seedlings. There were aerial spraying programmes of fertiliser and pesticide, and hundreds of miles of deer fencing had been strung across the moors. Extraction roads had been built whose width was often double that of the local highways.

But as the trade association Timber Growers UK assured me, there was a plan behind it all. The original intention was to create an integrated forest, big enough to be economically self-sustaining and to support at least two new sawmills. One of the keys was the Lairg–Wick–Thurso railway. The new plantations had been sited as close as possible to this line, to minimise transport costs when felling came round. This, TGUK stressed, was why the industry was so anxious to continue its planting programme up to the original target of about 100,000 hectares. Only then could the planned economies of scale be realised.

Looking at the map I could see some logic in this. The railway meandered past many of the plantations – the older blocks round Loch Shin; Strathy Forest, where a sizeable chunk of a National Nature Reserve had been accidentally ploughed up; Wogan's woods near Broubster. But the line was economically precarious, the sawmills still a figment of an economist's imagination, and the whole enterprise looked less like an unfolding plan than an exercise in opportunism.

Even scientific fact had come to be regarded as negotiable currency up here. The most frequent demand I heard from Scottish authorities was for a 'court of appeal' against the hated, English-based NCC. Not just against its proposals (which are only recommendations) but against its evidence, which it was felt should be open to compromise. It was a relief that nobody had any illusions about ecology being an exact science, but disturbing that the age of a tree, say, or the nesting territory of a bird should be regarded as open to something like plea bargaining.

The debate about bird populations was rife with such nimble legalistic footwork. It was still being argued, for example, that plantations *increased* the number and diversity of breeding birds – which, of course, they do, though only of those species that are abundant in woods and gardens throughout Britain, and, temporarily, a few birds of prey. The specialist birds of the wet peatland are completely unable to adapt. But, the foresters argued, surely they could be more sociable, 'bunch up a bit' in the gaps between the new plantations. As Michael Ashmole, Director of Fountain, said of the greenshank, the Flows' third commonest but still somewhat expansive wader: 'If a bird cannot survive on 650 acres, then it doesn't bloody well deserve to survive.'

A decade of intensive research had shown that the greenshanks do try to bunch up for a year or so. Then the stresses of competition and over-population start to show. The birds lose weight, lay sterile eggs, lose chicks by drowning in the drainage ditches or to crows patrolling out of the new plantations, and the inexorable decline into local extinction begins.

Just as serious was the persistence of the argument that commercial forestry was simply restoring a landscape destroyed by earlier farmers. Although some of the region's prehistory is still obscure, fossil pollen and stump fragments show that the last time native woodland (chiefly birch, rowan, hazel and Scots pine) grew on the open plateaux was 4,000 years ago. A decisive wettening of the climate after that meant that young tree growth could not compete with the expansion of the moss on the peat, and woodland survived only in the better drained valleys.

This is not to say that there hasn't been some glamorisation of history on the conservationist side. Lesley Crenna, a Highlander herself, told me that many locals were distressed to hear their homeland repeatedly described as 'the last wilderness' and compared with the Russian Steppes or Alaska. Up here this wasn't seen as a compliment, but as an insult to the work they and their ancestors had put into the land. It made them feel 'like savages'. Sometimes, Lesley told me, crofters burned off patches of the grass – not because it made much difference to the grazing, but to say 'I live here too'.

Even remote corners of the Flows showed the marks of hard, subsistence farming. Lonely homesteads, a few small plots of barley and oats, thin channels cut in the peat to provide fresh water. These were difficult times for crofters, and a few had already sold out to Fountain. But what was alarming the Crofters Union more was a move towards speculative trading in crofting land. The holdings in this part of the Highlands were much bigger than those in the west, often several thousand acres in extent. Some had been purchased by outsiders, and there had been attempts to amalgamate and appropriate the common grazing so that this could be sold off for forestry. This was within the law of the 1976 Crofting Act, giving crofters the right to buy their holdings from the landlord for 15 times their annual rental, but quite against its spirit.

We drove to Andrew Cumming's holding by the dubh lochs of Shielton, along roads lined with narrow peat diggings, each with a handwritten sign giving the owner's name. Andrew gave us a cheerful elevenses, but was gloomy about afforestation, which he likened quite explicitly to the Clearances. 'They burned us then, now they are blanketing us' was his curt verdict.

Close to his homestead, now a feed store, men were fencing a new winter stock-pen. Nearby was a more ancient stockade, knitted together out of waste metal and old farm machinery – a frugal way of recycling rubbish that no one would ever bother to collect this far out. But beyond the farm on the bog itself, the marks of humans and nature were less easily distinguished. It was too late for most of the breeding waders. But the dark crossbow shapes of Arctic skuas skimmed across the swaying plumes of cotton grass, adding to that persistent impression that the entire landscape was shifting.

Walking about in the oppressive humidity was a queasily disorientating experience. The sodden sphagnum rocked underfoot. It had an insubstantial, blubbery feel, like a jelly. Every square yard of it was different, a constantly reshuffled mix of stag's horn lichens, sedges, and a dozen different species of sphagnum, speckled with the sticky scarlet jaws of insectivorous sundews. The pools were different too, encrusted with moss, full of bogbean, or edged with the golden stars of bog asphodel. Thin sheets of rain swirled in from the north-west blotting out first Sky Fea, and then the high Sutherland peaks to the west, until I hadn't the slightest idea in which direction I was facing. Several times that afternoon I had waves of inexplicable anxiety – something I'd often read of American writers experiencing in wild places, but hadn't expected only 50 miles from Inverness. The bog was criss-crossed by cryptic trails and thin ribbons of seepage water, as if the sphagnum had cracked. They may have been natural, but the bog's skin is so fragile that it can show traces of damage for years. One was the track of an otter, a darting, decisive run that plunged into the pool, parted the bogbean and slithered out through the sedges on the far side.

But another that Lesley showed me was a human trackway, the old mail route that was until quite recently the postman's path across the bog. She told me a story that showed better than any abstract definition where the Flows lay on the scale between wilderness and wildness.

A few years ago a group of crofters were walking home along this trail in winter and became benighted. When they eventually reached a croft one of them was suffering badly from exposure. The others attempted to revive him by pressing hot stones against his feet, but overdid it, and succeeded in burning his feet as well. In the end he had to be carried off the bog on a stretcher – out along the post road.

Time and again that day we saw what afforestation had done to this 'delicate economic and social fabric'. Croftlands had been flooded as a result of the diversion of water down drainage ditches. Silt from deep ploughing had been washed into salmon-spawning areas. Pesticide and fertiliser run-off was polluting watercourses and streams.

Even the economics of the operation began to look shaky, especially when you have, in addition, to consider the damage from windthrow on this exposed plateau, and the ravages of the pine beauty moth, an endemic pest which chews alien pines (but not natives) to ribbons. Some of the trees were growing better than had been painted by conservationists, but only because of the forestry equivalent of intensive care. The National Audit Office, costing out the business the previous year, was scathing in its criticism. The real increase in the value of the trees was little more than one per cent, which hardly justified the public subsidies being lavished upon them.

The *principle* that tree planting should be eligible for public money is obviously a commendable one. It means for instance that local authorities can establish and support native woodlands as amenities for their rate-payers. But from any political point of view it is a preposterous waste of public money as no public good accrues.

Scanning the list of names and figures on the land register I wondered what conservation benefit had been seen in Fountain's operation by Timothy Colman, an ex-member of the Countryside Commission and an NCC advisory committee in his 790 acres of afforested bog. Or whether Lady Porter, founder of the Westminster Against Reckless Spending campaign, felt there should be any cap on the £500,000 she was then legally entitled to in planting grants and tax relief.

Even the generation of jobs in the forestry sector looked like part of a prospector's dream. Fountain employed some 60 people in Caithness and Sutherland. The much-publicised figure of 2,000 jobs turned out to be a projection for 40 or 50 years hence, when the first trees would be due for felling and processing. Over the whole of the Highland region only 1,500 people were employed in the forestry and sawmilling industries, and a good deal of the work was done by outside contract labour, sometimes from as far afield as Germany.

Yet there were already models of a different kind of development here which respected the wildlife and crofting traditions of the peat plateau, but encouraged alternative agriculture and new small industries in the valleys. At Berriedale, north of Helmsdale, for example, there was a flourishing native woodland of birch, oak and rowan, a spring water bottling plant, and an experimental wind generator (the local authorities wanted this to be painted conifer green, but it remained a defiant airy cream above the open moors).

I travelled home from Sutherland the long way, and out of the train window I kept catching glimpses of the North Sea, itself under siege from over-fishing and pollution, and a reminder that the exploitation of wild places is no local problem. Between pages I dipped into Barry Lopez's wonderful celebration of northern landscapes, *Arctic Dreams*, to try and get a wider perspective on the Flows issue. 'Confronted by an unknown landscape,' he had written, 'what happens to our sense of wealth? What does it mean to grow rich?' I hoped we were becoming wise enough as a people not to regard land as waste or sterile just because it had no over-riding economic use. The Flow Country was already rich beyond accounting. Perhaps only a lucky few would see its wading birds, as they flew down to Africa. But its sub-arctic wastes, teeming with birds on the long summer evenings, were one of the great landscapes of the imagination, an engine of life for the whole northern hemisphere.

If the foresters were sceptical about this it would do them no harm to wait a decade or two till the arguments had settled. The peatlands had no such choice. They were the product of thousands of years of evolution and could never be recreated in our time.

The Roots of Civilisation (1988)

Every Ascension Day, the children from the village school tramp across the fields to our little parish wood for a service among the bluebells. Surrounded by vaulted beech trees, hung with freshly opened leaves, they sing hymns to new life and crops and the mysteries of transubstantiation. The adults on the sidelines, lumps in throats, gaze heavenwards too, and give quiet thanks that the canopy is opening again, undamaged.

It is a touching ceremony, pious and pagan and ecological all at once, whose springtime precursors were held as fertility rites thousands of years before Christ. And every year the question it raises becomes more insistent: if such numinous feelings about trees are so anciently universal and so easily tapped, why are the world's forests – cradles of most life forms and regulators of the atmosphere – in such a state of crisis?

In the hour or so we are in the wood another 10 square kilometres of tropical forest will have been obliterated, burnt along with all its orchids and birds of paradise to make way for quick-profit ranching and mining. By the end of the year another 100,000 square kilometres will have been irreversibly damaged or destroyed, and the pall of greenhouse gases made a little denser.

How can this be? In the clarity of a Chiltern wood in May, it is hard not to feel unchristian rage at those who haven't yet seen the light.

Yet we are in no position to be self-righteous. Our wood is run as a kind of community plot, and a few months later we are back there, knocking over trees ourselves. It is all quite proper, we assure ourselves, just thinning and good management, making space for new growth, producing a crop for local use. But there is no hiding the exhilaration that can grip you when you start working with trees, the satisfaction of a clean fell, the tang and feel of fresh-cut wood. I have seen our helpers – friends of the forest to a soul – saw and strip a tree down with the single-mindedness of jungle ants reducing a dead animal to a skeleton.

Trees are a *challenge*. Their immensity and longevity and sheer stubborn rootedness spark off all manner of agitated responses. To a puritan a wildwood is a barbarous offence, something not yet in a state of grace; to a farmer a waste of tillable land; to a capitalist a resource well past its cashing-in date.

Woods challenge ecologists, too, to crack their codes, and we are apt to defend the opening-out of our Chiltern patch as helping to speed the wood's natural development – enlightening it, so to speak. But underneath I fear that apostles of the New Woodmanship and Malaysian log barons share the same presumptuous belief: that *our* plans for the forest are better than its own.

These contradictory feelings have coexisted since the beginnings of civilisation. In pagan cultures trees could be both symbols of creativity and the refuge of evil spirits, and placatory rituals were necessary when they were cut down. In Europe there was a kind of secular equivalent of these rites of arbitration in the techniques of coppicing and pollarding (developed at least five thousand years ago, and still relevant today), which took a continuous crop from trees without killing them. What was common to most pre-agricultural societies was a respect for trees, and a thread of common meaning about their significance.

Set against that there has been the overwhelming image of the forest as the enemy – or at least the converse – of civilisation. The deliberate clearance of the European wildwood was one of the most extensive acts of geographical engineering in the history of the world. It was an absolutely necessary prelude to the establishment of Western-style cities and agri-culture. In all periods and places since, it has been not so much the sensible use and harvesting of forests that has destroyed them as the desire to turn them into other kinds of land.

In the developed world, perhaps in an act of contrition, trees have become synonymous with Green thinking, and planting them is seen as a kind of environmental panacea. Yet that ancient ambivalence is still thri-ving, to judge by the symbols they provide: olive branches and hearts of oak; the tree of knowledge and Newton's apple; family trees, Christmas trees, the crown of thorns ... And whenever they cease to behave in the ways we expect we have the vocabulary of human domination to fall back on: 'dereliction', 'overmaturity', 'scrub' – as if trees, the most suc-cessful and durable of plants, were incapable of living correctly without supervision.

There may be less of a gap than we like to imagine between our own mixed feelings about trees and the pillaging of the rain forests. It was certainly an exported version of the European creed of 'improvement' which provided the model and the rhetoric for most large-scale forest clearance.

When the Plymouth Brethren landed in North America they found 'a hideous and desolate wilderness ... the whole country is full of woods and thickets'; and they set about civilising it with chilling thoroughness. Within two centuries their descendants had obliterated seven-eighths of the continent's natural woodland (and whole species like the passenger pigeon) in massacres whose arrogance and violence rival those in modern Amazonia.

Back in England in 1712, John Morton summed up the prevailing attitude when he proclaimed: 'In a country full of civilised inhabitants timber could not be suffered to grow. It must give way to fields and pastures, which are of more immediate use and concern to life.' The same argument is still being used in Brazil, where successive governments have condoned the conversion of a forest millions of years in the making to short-lived grazing, with the facile slogan 'Land without men for the men without land' – a policy which has impoverished both the men and the land.

In the developed world the philosophical conflict between the need for timber and the mistrust of forests was resolved by making trees submit to the disciplines of cultivation, putting them, in many senses, in their place. Some conservation organisations now believe that the best chance of saving what remains of the tropical forests is to repeat this formula, albeit for superficially different reasons. The realistic alternative to rampant plundering, they argue, is not the establishment of pristine forest reserves, which would take no account of the economic plight of the human inhabitants of the forest, but controlled exploitation.

Yet the history of 'controlled' exploitation in Europe and North America – which has been predominantly a centralised and narrowly commercial business with precious little concern about its social and ecological side-effects – hardly inspires confidence in this as a solution for the tropics. It may not be the best vehicle either for accommodating our dawning understanding of the central role of trees in the economy of nature.

It is worth spelling this out in some detail. Put aside for the moment all the ingenious uses which humans have for trees and tree substances: rayons and cellophanes (made directly from wood cellulose); wood alcohol and forest bark mulch; brazil nuts and drugs still to be discovered; windbreaks and flood control; a huge range of chemicals (even more if you were to include those we take from the fossils of an earlier generation of trees). Put aside, too, the vast assemblages of animals, insects and plants (maybe thirty million species) that don't just inhabit the forest but *comprise* it, and whose breathtakingly intricate relationships it is our species' unique privilege to be able to glimpse.

Think simply of the role that trees themselves play in the natural scheme of things. They are the architectural climax of evolution, scaffolding for the rest of terrestrial life, the enduring idea of rock expressed in plant tissue. Collectively they make up an immense bank of the chemicals necessary for life, and above the thin soils of the rain forests, the sole such bank. Collectively they contain two million-million tonnes of carbon – four hundred times the amount released each year by the burning of fossil fuels.

If one had to design from scratch the primary vegetation for the planet, to house and feed the other organisms, to regulate the water and nutrient cycles, it would be hard to improve on trees. Even their present depleted ranks still provide the planet's greatest engine for fixing the sun's energy, which they do by converting carbon dioxide and water into living tissue. In one day a large deciduous tree can pump and transpire thousands of litres of water and take up as much as twenty grams of carbon dioxide. In one year the earth's trees make twelve billion tonnes of new wood in this way.

It is a wonderful process of transmutation which helps control the composition of the atmosphere and its suitability for life. Its reversal – the burning of the tropical forests, which both releases carbon dioxide and depletes the major agency for absorbing it – is one of the factors contributing to the now infamous 'greenhouse effect'.

Trees have played crucial roles in the evolution and support of the variety of natural life. They provide food and shelter. Their spatial complexity rivals that of their chemical structures. They are vast elaborations in three dimensions, not just of ever more intricate branching, but of knots, burrs, bark reticulations, rot-holes, layers of moss and lichen. It is impossible to measure the area of a tree's surfaces exactly. It is what is known as a 'fractal' quantity – one which increases indefinitely the closer you examine it.

Finally, they accommodate the passage of time more comprehensively than other organisms. This is part of the biological function of woodiness, to provide a bulwark against transience and death. And as a tree lives and accrues, sometimes for several thousand years, all its experience – of storms and droughts, human lopping and animal browsing – is incorporated, ingrained, as it were, in its physical structure. No wonder that old trees have so often become landmarks and totems for human communities.

Perhaps this is why generalised campaigns to increase tree cover, regardless of place or the feelings of local people, have rarely been happy or even successful. They touch too many of the ancient contradictions between forests as danger, as wasteland, as ancestral havens. As Sue Clifford has written:

> We have given ourselves a conundrum, without answer. The very notion of creating new forests flies in the face of all we know, and much of what we practise. We know their great age, in the geological sense and domestically. We carved ourselves out of the forest in Britain ... and in our elsewhere

lifetimes. And ever since, we have spent our lives in clearings, on farms, in gardens, in parks, by the wayside, even on buildings, trying to stop trees growing. In parallel we have developed a working relationship with trees which has given us great cultural knowledge, affection and wisdom.

Perhaps our newest knowledge of the nature of that relationship may solve the conundrum at last and restore trees to their proper cultural role, as a commonwealth, as far beyond property as the atmosphere itself. Their most important function, we now understand, is simply to stand there, reminding us of the continuity of life, full of cryptic activity, and *breathing*.

I treasure the memory of a four-year-old in our wood one spring, hugging the trunk of an ash tree and whispering softly into the bark. It seemed then and seems now the best possible way of using another living thing.

Dungeness: The Terminal Beach (1990)

On a grey day Dungeness Point can look as if it deserves everything that has been visited on it, giant leeches included. The great shingle headland tails off into the Channel like a collapsed scree slope. It is a harsh, windswept, infertile place, and like most 'wastelands' has become a gathering ground for all kinds of flotsam that isn't welcome inland. Two nuclear power stations squat next to a shanty town of holiday shacks and bungalows. Small arms fire from MoD ranges echoes through an ancient, stunted holly wood. Underneath it all the shingle bedrock seems quite impassive, but in fact is being shifted remorselessly eastwards by the sea. The whole promontory is like one of those cryptic, unsettling landscapes in J. G. Ballard's novels, England's terminal beach.

Environmental problems have flourished in this volatile atmosphere. In the sixties there was the construction of Dungeness B, which limped forward in such chaos that even the Central Electricity Generating Board (CEGB) admits to 'straightforward engineering idiocy'. But in those days it was not ecological catastrophe that nagged at liberal sensibilities so much as eyesores (especially along our symbolically potent coastline), and Dungeness was chiefly notorious as a supreme example of the sprawl and industrial blight that were everywhere edging the urban fringe deeper into the countryside. I still have the roll of snaps I took there on my first field-trip as a would-be writer in 1966. They are full of strikingly banal contrasts: pylons and skeins of cables dwarfing the Bird Observatory's mist nets; grubby children playing amongst the plotland bungalows. What is odd – and a sign of the times – is that I didn't seem to take the slightest interest in what was being obscured by all this unaesthetic clutter. It was simply a matter of cosmetics – the Sceptr'd Isle's Ravaged Face, Britain versus the Beast.

Twenty years on it is harder, thankfully, to take such a superficial view, not least because this time it is the actual fabric of the headland that is under siege. Dungeness has some of the largest expanses of shingle and gravel in the world, and they have been exploited in one way or another for centuries. In the Dungeness Countryside Plan the local authorities have categorised it as an ongoing 'strategic reserve'. And recently the needs of the massive construction works in and around the Channel Tunnel, just twenty miles to the east, have put a new premium on its very accessible supplies. The Tunnel alone is hoping for more than half a million tonnes from Dungeness, and gravel companies are energetically reactivating old extraction licences and applying for new ones. As a spokesman for Amey Roadstone stresses, everyone wants houses and roads and the gravel has to come from somewhere. Many might feel that it is better taken from this bleak headland than from fresh gougings in the rural shires. And isn't shingle still just shingle, even with its top layers scraped away?

This is a view which smarts deeply with Pat Doody, coastal ecologist with the Nature Conservancy Council (NCC), and Brian Ferry of Royal Holloway College, who have done much to show that Dungeness is far more than just a mass of undifferentiated pebbles and a stop-off point for migrant birds. I am down here with them on a dustily hot day in early May, and have to try and control my excitement at the sight of migrant black terns wafting over the tropical blue water which fills the old diggings. As Pat Doody points out, almost any patch of coastal fresh water would do for them. What he and Dr Ferry want to show me is something altogether more special. They are particular about the route we should take, ushering me along a low path by the edge of a pit, past the conveyor belt which carries wet gravel non-stop to the grading machine, and then up over a steep ridge. I imagine we are being considerate to the birds, but it proves to be a canny piece of stage management. At the top of the ridge, a huge view suddenly opens out, not of a flat block of shingle but of long ridges, topped with vegetation and curving gently away towards the point of the Ness for nearly a mile. This is what makes Dungeness unique. For the past five thousand years sea currents have torn shingle out of beaches to the west, and deposited it on the far side of this tooth-like promontory. And for reasons buried deep in long-term tidal patterns and the physics of pebble movement, the sea doesn't dump the shingle at a steady rate, but rhythmically, as ridges. A ridge reaches its maximum height and breadth after about ten to fifteen years, and once it is stable, wave action starts building the next. There are more than four hundred in the Dungeness system, which makes it one of the most extensive and exquisitely formed in the world. I can see why Brian and Pat find it so austerely beautiful, and why an aerial picture of the headland reminded me of the annual rings on an immense tree stump.

The vegetation of the ridges has its own pattern of succession, beginning with isolated clumps of sea-kale on the newest ridges, and maturing as dense, heathy mixtures of stagshorn lichens, mosses, and unusual flowering plants like Nottingham catchfly and prostrate broom. And it has an insect population to match, with an extraordinary profusion of bumble-bees, moths and beetles, and a whole miniature pastoral society of lichen-grazers.

What is odd is that, against all the rules, this succession doesn't usually end up as woodland. There are patches of blackthorn and elder, and deep inside the MoD ranges at Holmstone (that is, 'holly-stone') Beach an extraordinary assemblage of ancient, prostrate hollies that is the only community of its type in the world, and which was first recorded on an eleventh-century charter. But over the bulk of the shingle either conditions are too frugal for the development of trees, or the life of the ridges is too short. Already the oldest are being eaten away by the same tidal movements that created them, and being redeposited to the east of the Ness.

We make slow but sonorous progress, crunching on lichen dried to a crisp by the drought, and clattering on the pebbles. Locals used to travel on a kind of wooden ski, which was kinder to the ridges as well as to their calf-muscles. Every stray shell and passing vehicle leaves an ineradicable dent on the surface. Even footfalls irreversibly disturb lichen-crusted stones that may have been in the same position for thousands of years. Brian, who has been coming here since the fifties, is uneasily aware that many of the dim footprints here are his. 'It is', he says, 'like walking on the surface of the moon.'

But Dungeness has natural pits, too, formed like eddies in the waves of shingle. They used to be full of marshy vegetation (and a good population of medicinal leeches) but are now inexorably drying out, a process which reflects the exploitation of Dungeness' other great natural resource – an immense freshwater aquifer held not far under the shingle. It is formed direct from rainwater and since it can be used with almost no treatment, has always been an important drinking water source. But since 1950, the volume extracted has risen five-fold, and the impact on the aquifer been still further multiplied by the increase in gravel digging over the same period. Every excavation which goes below the water table increases the area of open water subject to evaporation. And as the freshwater-table drops, so sea-water can begin to seep in. Salt contamination has occurred several times since 1984. Without stricter controls the stage is set for a collision between the needs for two of the prosperous south-east's most precious materials – a reminder that crises in natural systems almost always prefigure trouble for humans, too.

Looting of resources has always been worse in so-called 'wastelands'. Their apparent infertility and uselessness were an affront to Enlightenment 'improvers' and Victorian moralists alike, who both seemed to resent the fact that they had a teeming life of their own. One nineteenth-century surveyor summed up the attitude when he said of southern England's wasteland: '[it] strongly indicates the want of means, or inclination, to improve it, and often reminds the traveller of uncivilised nations, where nature pursues her own course, without the assistance of human art.'

The attitude has stuck, and after the beginnings of large-scale gravel extraction in the 1880s and military training during the wars, the nuclear industry arrived in the 1960s. It has proved to be a costly piece of siting. Every year 20,000 tonnes of gravel, carried east by the tide, have to be ferried back by lorry to shore up the western beach foundations of the power station. And when a seismic survey of the area was done prior to the building of the now abandoned Dungeness C, the site was found to sit above a fault-line.

The CEGB seems fatally attracted to follies. In 1987, they fulfilled a promise made at the 1958 public inquiry to replace some moth-hunters' 'sugaring' posts. Unfortunately they seemed to believe that these posts were part of the moths' habitat rather than mere trapping devices, and dug in a long, straight row of some three hundred railway sleepers just outside the power station perimeter, crushing some of the best shingle vegetation in the process. It looks like the remains of some forbidding wartime fortification, and by comparison, the interwar bungalows, converted from prefabs and old railway carriages, and ornamented with shells and driftwood half-timbering (and in one instance a range of miniature henges built out of upturned pebbles), seem a delightful and natural addition to the landscape.

We take a last walk down to the beach west of the power station. Pat, who is currently much concerned about the effects of global warming on sea-levels, is worried about what might have happened after the storm-surges earlier in the year. He is aghast by what he sees. A 50-yard swath has been bulldozed clean across a series of ridges more than two thousand years old, to make a rough, and almost certainly futile, new sea-wall. It is ironic as well as sad, as the whole ridge system has, ingrained within it, centuries of invaluable data about how the sea behaved during past eras of unstable weather. Pat is convinced that the NCC should redouble its efforts to have as much as possible of the headland scheduled as a National Nature Reserve before it is too late.

If it happens it could be a salutary example. It would be the first such reserve with mobile boundaries – a reminder (to some conservationists, amongst others) that nature is not a fixed, specialised commodity, a rare moth stuck to a post, but a *living* heritage. It would point up the facile injustice of that word 'wasteland' too. Gravel could always be won, given the political will, in bland deposits offshore or under surplus farmland. But natural systems like Dungeness are irreplaceable *cultural* as well as scientific resources, immense memory banks of the ways in which our thin skin of inhabitable earth goes on evolving.

Filthy Images (1991)

No one could have anticipated the power of those first images of the Gulf oil-slicks on 26 January [1991]. After ten days in which the reality of the war had blurred into a bland series of firework displays and ambiguous statistics, this terrible, seeping collision between life and matter was like the surfacing of a suppressed nightmare. It won't be easy to forget the bewildered eyes of those stricken cormorants; nor the lapping of waves on the shoreline – once the oldest, brightest sound on earth – muffled to the dull beat of a funeral drum. Even ministers of state and hardened war correspondents, skilled in giving blandishments about human tragedies, found themselves choking over the pictures.

Perhaps it is not so surprising. In a far-off war, fought by computers, sanitised by censors and the guardians of media taste, cormorants dying are about the only casualties we have been allowed to see.

But I believe there is more to it than that. Animals have always become symbols at moments of human crisis, and it would be hard to imagine a more pointed metaphor for this war than a cormorant drowning in oil. A native of the open seas, feathered and tarred, forced into the final humiliation of trying to crawl onto the concrete highways to escape. A bird, smothered by ancient waste products that the earth wisely seals up beneath its skin.

Animals caught up in human conflicts are true neutrals. Their suffering hasn't been chosen or voted for. It is not given for the sake of aggrandisement or abstract values. It is stripped of propaganda, obfuscation, religious cant and political hedging. It is the starkest mirror of what war means to us as fellow living creatures, which is why we are so shamed by the sight of it.

For Edward Thomas, in the First World War, the chastening came from an English owl. He heard it in Hampshire one cold February night in 1915, two months before he left for France:

> No merry note, nor cause of merriment,
> But one telling me plain what I escaped
> And others could not, that night, as in I went . . .
> Speaking for all who lay under the stars,
> Soldiers and poor, unable to rejoice.

Time and again, animals seem able to focus and clarify the complicated and fuzzy entanglements of human affairs. Remember the cranes returning to Vietnam in 1986, the first signs of the healing of a landscape ravaged by ten years of war? Or the release of the two grey whales trapped in the Alaska ice in 1988? This frantic, inspiring rescue mission by Eskimo, Soviet and American teams was watched with bated breath around the world, and seemed to presage not just the thawing of the Cold War, but a new phase in our respect for other species.

I don't believe that finding moral or metaphorical meanings in animals has anything to do with sentimentalising them or imbuing them with human characteristics. Mostly it is exactly the opposite, a momentary glimpse of their one inalienable and unarguable right, to be themselves, or simply to *be*. It is not always a reassuring vision. No one who watched *The Trials of Life*, for instance, with its harrowing sequences of killer whale and chimpanzee hunting sprees can harbour any illusion about gratuitous violence (or so it appears) being confined to the human species.

Yet, perhaps, like military strategists, we have been duped by a surfeit of unconsidered information. We know about tactics for ambushing prey, about territorial defence and group bonding, and persuade ourselves that we therefore 'understand' animals. We do not, of course, and the labyrinth of their inner lives remains a mystery to us.

In the late thirties, Colette wrote an extraordinary essay, inspired by her horror of zoos, in which she argued that we had intruded too far into animals' 'real' lives:

> We are no longer free even to remain ignorant of how a boa constrictor chokes a gazelle, or how a panther . . . rips open the throat of a goat which – since the combat must be spiced and the cinema has no use for passive victims – has a kid to defend. It is high time we said good-bye to reality . . . I shall dream, far from these wild creatures, that we could do without them, that we could leave them to live where they were born. We should forget their true shapes then, and our imagination would flourish again. Our great-nephews would once more invent an indestructible fauna, which they would describe as they beheld it in their dreams with dazzling intrepidity, as our forefathers used to do.

Colette was not arguing that humans and nature should be separate, but that animals can be imprisoned, *limited* by literalness and scientific presumption as well as by cages. In other essays – on listening to her dog's heart, on watching the motion of a python ('it liquefies, flows along the branch and on the other side, becomes rigid – it is creating a tension within itself, presaging some emergence I cannot guess at') – she identified precisely what common ground and what fellow feeling lie between us. We share universal, irreducible needs for space, freedom, nourishment, affection and the flow of the seasons. But as humans, we also have a unique (and grossly abused) imaginative insight into the whole intertwined variety of creation, in which individual creatures – the returning swallow, the oiled seabird – have meanings for us as well as flesh and blood existence.

I do not know what new horrors will have occurred by the time you read this. But I doubt if there will be a more chastening image of this war, and the current condition of humanity, than the accusing glare in a cormorant's eye, and that vision through the wrong end of history's telescope, of the glint of life slipping back into the slime.

James Lovelock (1991)

Halfway along the overgrown road that links James Lovelock's Devon mill-house with the outside world is a meticulously printed sign: 'Experimental Station. Please Shut the Gate.' There is something beguiling about this mixture of rustic civility and slight scientific menace, lapped by ferns and standing apparently in the middle of nowhere. But it is an apt entrance to the world of a man who is something of a paradox himself: one-time NASA advisor and champion of 'small science'; visiting Professor of Cybernetics at Reading University and enthusiast for nineteenth-century farming; and now internationally known as the originator of a unifying theory of global ecology which welds together a commitment to scientific advance and a belief that nature knows best: the Gaia hypothesis.

Lovelock has been an independent and maverick scientist ever since the post-war years, when he used to piece together his apparatus from war-surplus gear bought in Soho. It was an invention to measure minute concentrations of gases that led to his theory, which states that the geology, atmosphere and living systems of the earth are linked in a self-regulating system, called Gaia after the Greek name for the Earth Goddess. The system is coherent enough, Lovelock believes, for the living skin of the planet to be regarded as a super-organism in its own right. His theory goes beyond conventional ecology in suggesting that the living systems of the planet, far from being at the mercy of the physical environment, collectively manipulate it to keep conditions supportive of life. Gaia will (automatically and unconsciously, of course) put this objective above the survival of any individual species – humans included.

Since it was launched in 1977 (in *Gaia: A New Look at Life on Earth*) the theory has taken on the stature of a myth. For many readers it has underlined the interconnectedness of life, validated holism, put man in his place. New Age pagans, normally contemptuous of science, have taken it as 'proof' of the existence of an Earth Goddess. More rationally-minded Greens have found it sketching in some of the long chains of cause and effect through which human activities influence the planet.

But the theory has attracted notoriety, too. The Left (suspicious of Lovelock anyway for his attacks on the politicisation of ecology) deplore the theory as fatalistic and anti-human. Conventional science has accused it of being experimentally unfounded and verging on the mystical. Perhaps it is no wonder that its inventor (or, as he prefers to describe himself, rediscoverer) has retreated to this secluded valley, a mile from the nearest house, and cut off all telephone communications except the fax machine.

Lovelock is far from being a recluse, though. He lives here with his second wife Sandy and son John, a colony of peacocks and a battery of computers, and does *not* grow his own organic vegetables. He has a small laboratory in the house, and with the support of the Hewlett-Packard Corporation, continues to refine his analysing equipment. One of the old barns houses a sophisticated dilution chamber, in which he can work on precisely measured low concentrations of gases like CFCs. 'It wouldn't work in a city or university lab,' he explains. 'One person with an aerosol can of deodorant at the end of the corridor could throw the measurement.'

He is in great demand as a speaker and sage, especially from those who believe that an understanding of the earth's self-regulatory systems may help us avoid pushing it towards final ecological collapse. I am here on a similar quest myself, seeking his opinion on the dramatic case histories of pollution that the *Sunday Times* have been featuring over the past six months. Are the palls of industrial toxins that hang over Cracow and the open refuse dumps of Mexico City of more than local significance? Does the sewage in the Ganges threaten the world's oceans as well as the health of tens of millions of Indians? Does Gaia have a prescription for car exhaust pollution in Athens – or for that matter in Plymouth, just 20 miles away? Are they really cases of 'planet abuse', which amount, incrementally, to a threat to world ecology, or just parochial blights like urban crime and homelessness?

We are talking in the summer, at the end of what has been a hectic month for Lovelock. He has just been honoured by the Dutch Academy of Science, and featured in Channel 4's 'Visionaries' series. In a couple of weeks' time he is to be the local guest in a West Country edition of *Any Questions*. What he hasn't seen is the contents of a virulent, full-page attack on him in the *Guardian* by an Oxford ecologist, which rails against the growing 'irrationalism and dogma of ... popular ecology', and points the finger at Lovelock as 'pre-eminent amongst the causes of this shift', which will eventually lead to the arrival of 'the Thought Police'. He reads my copy with increasing amusement, and it is obvious that he relishes being a stirrer of hornets' nests. And as we talk it also becomes clear that the precepts of the Gaia theory and the views Lovelock has of the procedures and profession of science are intimately connected. The mill-house is neither an ark nor a hermit's cell, but it does reflect some of the principles of intimacy and localness that he sees operating in Gaia.

'I've always thought that science was something to be done at home, like writing or painting, a kind of cottage industry if you like.' When he delivered the Schumacher Lecture in 1988 he made this point even more explicitly. 'I take the advice to think globally by acting locally most seriously. I practise global science as a family business ... not as some vast, remote and potentially dangerous activity.' There is something almost wilful in his determination to stay clear of institutional pigeon-holes, and though he is one of the Greens' heroes, he repeatedly upbraids them when they take up 'inappropriate' issues, or mount arguments based on flawed evidence or 'political' preconceptions. He is sanguine about nuclear energy ('an entirely natural process') and the burning of PCBs. ('No one makes them any more and they need to be destroyed.') Indeed there aren't many examples of what is conventionally regarded as pollution that he considers to be ecologically important – but not because he underestimates the threat they pose to the quality of human lives. He repeatedly makes the distinction between the degradation of human social life and damage to the biosphere, what he describes as 'people problems' and 'planet problems'. They don't always coincide, and wishful holistic thinking to the contrary is just another example of the difficulty we have in seeing things in other than human-centred ways.

The death of the Aral Sea, for example, probably has little global significance. But Lovelock acknowledges that the destruction of the environment of thirty million Central Asians by a mixture of bureaucratic folly and ignorant agriculture is a human tragedy without precedent. He is constantly bemused by the fact that a nation which occupies a fifth of the world's land space is not even able to feed its own people. Nor does he see much hope for improvement in the short term. 'The sums the Russians are asking for in aid from the West are chicken-feed. They will not even begin to solve their problems.'

But the issue that he puts at the top of the list is clearance of the tropical rain-forests for agriculture – though not for the usual reasons of loss of potentially useful plant species and rare animals (a typical 'people problem', ironically).

'The tropical climate is ideal for trees, but this isn't a given state of the earth. The conditions are maintained by the trees themselves.' The rain-forest is a microcosm of Gaia. The trees keep their climate just the way they like it by the shade of their canopies and by the evaporation of vast volumes of water through their leaves. This water vapour forms a cloud cover which eventually falls back on the trees. The trees and rain form a single system; there can't be one without the other. If the trees are cleared, the rain they produce ceases, the cloud cover disappears, and in the direct heat of the sun the ground can rapidly turn to desert.

There is still enough rain-forest for its cloud cover to have a considerable effect on global climate, especially in reflecting sunlight back to space. Every acre that is cleared adds a tiny increment to the earth's warming.

'I've recently had a go at costing out what the rain-forests are worth in terms of their cooling effect. You can do this by estimating what it would cost to refrigerate the same area artificially. The forest cloud cover reduces the heat reaching the canopy by about ten per cent. To get the same cooling effect you would need a refrigerator with a power of eighty-four kilowatts per acre, which would cost about £30,000 per annum. After they have been cleared for cattle the yield rarely gets above £100 an acre. These figures mean that the climatic value of the remaining forest in Amazonia alone is £450 trillion.'

Typically, he adds an example of the wrong way of looking at the problem: 'The Brazilians had a go at costing their forests, too, but they made the mistake of trying to value them as the major producers and exporters of oxygen. It was an interesting idea, but the net output of oxygen in a forest is almost zero. The local animals and micro-organisms use up most of it themselves.'

The transactions between the atmosphere and the various inhabitants of the earth have always fascinated Lovelock. In the fifties he perfected the electron capture detector, a refinement of the gas chromatograph which was able to detect substances at very low concentrations. It is so sensitive that if a drum of a particular fluorocarbon was allowed to evaporate in Japan, the gas would be detectable in Britain a few days later. It was this instrument that enabled scientists in the sixties to grasp the extent to which pesticides were persisting and spreading throughout the globe. It picked up DDT in Antarctic penguins, and Dieldrin in the milk of nursing mothers in Finland, and provided the data with which Rachel Carson was able to write *Silent Spring*, the book that turned into the first text of the burgeoning green movement.

In the sixties NASA invited Lovelock to help devise ways of assessing whether there was life on Mars. His talent for lateral thinking led to him to suggest what he calls 'a top-down view of the whole planet' instead of the more conventional idea of a search at the landing point. This would involve analysing the composition of the red planet's atmosphere. If Mars was lifeless, its atmosphere would be determined by physical and chemical processes alone, and would probably have reached some sort of chemical equilibrium. But if it carried life – at least in some quantity – then its organisms would almost certainly need to use the atmosphere as a source of food and energy and a depository for waste matter, and these would register in its composition. The much-lived-in atmosphere on earth could be used as a bench mark.

In the end it proved possible to do the measurements from earth by infra-red astronomy. The results showed an astonishing divergence between the atmospheres of the two planets. The atmosphere of Mars was dominated by carbon dioxide, and was close to chemical equilibrium. By contrast the envelope of gases surrounding the earth contained only traces of carbon dioxide, and was exceptionally unstable in composition, like a slow-burning fuse just waiting for a spark. (Lovelock, fond of using cars as metaphors, likens earth's atmosphere to the combustible mixture of gases entering a carburettor, and Mars' to those leaving the exhaust pipe.) The coexistence, over aeons of time, of stable concentrations of active gases like oxygen and methane was a chemical impossibility without some intervening agency to top up their levels. Oxygen in particular ought to have reacted with almost everything until it was virtually exhausted (levels on lifeless Mars are just 0.13 per cent). Instead levels have stayed constant at around twenty-one per cent for some hundreds of millions of years. A few per cent lower and complex life forms could not survive; a few higher and all surface plant life would become dangerously combustible.

The average air temperature of the earth has also remained surprisingly steady. Despite a twenty-five per cent increase in the amount of solar energy reaching us since life began three and a half billion years ago, the mean atmospheric temperature has oscillated between the narrow limits of ten and twenty degrees Celsius. Again, a shift much beyond either of these limits would have meant the eventual elimination of life.

Lovelock became convinced that the long reign of these improbable and unstable circumstances could only have come about if the life-systems of the planet had evolved mechanisms for regulating their environmental conditions. And the more he looked into the chemistry of the earth's skin, the more examples of this there seemed to be. There was, for example, the puzzlingly low concentration of carbon dioxide in the air. Most scientists agree that CO_2 levels were high at the start of life, as a result of volcanic eruption, and if the atmosphere was simply an inert sink, there is no reason why it should have declined to its current status as a trace gas. But it was essential that this should have happened, because even when it originates 'naturally', carbon dioxide acts as a greenhouse gas, preventing radiated and reflected heat from leaving the earth, and high levels could have maintained temperatures too high for most life.

Although land-bound plants take up carbon dioxide, it is unlikely that they act as regulators, as they release the gas again as soon as they die and decay. But plants and bacteria weather alkaline rocks so that they can chemically take up CO_2 more rapidly. There are also hosts of small organisms in the sea that either directly, or as elements in the food chain, use dissolved carbon dioxide to form calcium carbonate for shells and skeletons. As they die, their remains rain slowly down to the sea bottom to form chalk and limestone rocks, taking the carbon out of the cycle for very long periods. Since the numbers of these marine organisms increase with the raised temperatures associated with high CO_2 levels, they could form a natural thermostat.

They may also play a part in regulating the salinity of the sea. So much sodium chloride is washed out of the land by rain and rivers that the oceans would all be as saturated and sterile as the Dead Sea if there were not some mechanism for constantly removing it. Organisms which incorporate sodium (as a silicate) in their skeletal parts might be one such agency, especially in estuaries and over the continental shelves, where marine life is most abundant. Lovelock has even speculated that the growth of coral reefs (which form lagoons and hasten the evaporation of water and deposition of salt) might be a Gaian mechanism. Satellite photographs have shown that wave patterns in the vicinity of reefs are unusual, given the prevailing sea and wind conditions. What seems to happen is that coral organisms secrete an oil which forms a layer one molecule thick over the ocean surface, altering its surface tension and damping down waves. Has coral evolved this mechanism, Lovelock wonders, as a protection against wave damage?

The mechanisms that may be involved in these self-regulating cycles are remarkable but far from mysterious. They can all be explained by conventional theories of natural selection. An organism which has evolved the ability to regulate its own environment has obviously improved its chances of survival over one that hasn't. Similarly, an organism which is able to improve the survival potential of those species it uses as food or associates with, also has an edge.

If the kind of homeostatic mechanisms that Lovelock proposes do exist, are they robust enough to withstand the stresses to which we are currently subjecting the planet? Might we see the evolution of estuarine micro-organisms which were able to remove heavy metals like mercury and cadmium from the system, as well as carbon? Might the organic sulphides which are emitted by some marine algae and which encourage the formation of clouds, increase enough with temperature to cause a cloud-blanket effect and help counteract atmospheric warming?

The problem is that the regulatory mechanisms evolved over many millions of years and may not be able to cope with the sheer pace of change at present. On balance Lovelock thinks that Gaia probably will be able to manage, but not necessarily in ways that will guarantee the survival of higher forms of life. Our ability to weather the storms to come depends, he believes, as much on our willingness to work *within* the rules of Gaia as on sheer scientific cleverness.

For him, this has meant a personal rather than a political response. The temperament that made him pursue his career as an independent scientist makes him look for small-scale solutions: 'If you take a Gaian view, things always start off from the action of an individual organism, an individual gene. It doesn't have to be a very big change to make a big difference in the long term.'

His own initiative was the move to Devon, and the gradual purchase of more than 30 acres of rough farmland around the mill. With the help of grants he has planted this up with twenty thousand trees, and is leaving much of the rest to go wild. We walk round it, and with buzzards wheeling overhead and the overgrown hedges ringing with warblers' song, it is like a vision of the bittersweet days of Victorian farming. He has an ambivalent attitude towards farming, respecting the contract with the land that traditional agricultural systems represented, but regarding modern intensive farming (and cattle-rearing especially) as one of the worst blights on the earth. He points angrily to some fields on a neighbouring farm, stripped recently of their hedges, and already drying out so much that the few remaining trees are showing their roots.

He hopes his own trees will serve a double purpose. Trees 'buy time', tying up carbon dioxide for a few centuries at least. But he also sees them restoring some of the 'natural seemliness, free from any taint of the city' that he remembers from the countryside of his boyhood. I ask if he will harvest them for fuel, but he wants to let them grow as they wish. There is more than enough firewood brought down the river during its winter spate. But he is no enthusiast for wood-burning stoves, and prefers what he regards as the more efficient and cleaner power supply of the national grid. He parades very few of the tokens and paraphernalia that are usually associated with ecologically minded households. There are no solar panels and no private recycling arrangements. The public are not allowed to walk even on the outskirts of his property. Lovelock sees more value in his preserving a small stretch of wild land than in gestures which are essentially designed to make human life more tolerable.

Nor will he be drawn into suggesting neat panaceas for global ecological crises while our understanding of how the planet works under normal conditions is so poor. When his stint on *Any Questions* came up, the home audience was audibly disappointed by his restrained response ('cut down on cars and plant trees') to a wide-ranging question about 'what we could do', and his support for Mrs Thatcher's environmental platform (to which he gives marks for conservatism as much as Toryism, I suspect).

His distaste for environmental politicking may seem disingenuous in the light of this. But it is consistent with his philosophy, and with a favourite aphorism: 'There are no prescriptions in Gaia; only consequences.' To the extent that he has a policy for the future it is to wait, watch and think. When the crisis arrives – and he thinks it is inevitable – what we should do will be much clearer. He likens our position now to that of Britain in 1936: 'People knew that a war was coming. They chatted about what they would do. But it wasn't until it started that they began to take sensible measures to cope.' Inside the cautious scientist there is something of an old-style Roundhead, an English Revolutionary (an echo of a youth spent as an agnostic Quaker perhaps) who thinks that a good crisis might do a lot to concentrate our minds. In his address to the 1989 conference of Friends of the Earth he said: 'I believe that soon the prospect of large and daunting changes will be seen. Then we shall become aware of a larger need and science will cease its pettifogging and come together as it did under the lesser stress of war. It might even evolve to become like the science of 1940, a shining vocation, lean and fit and tough in mind and heart.' That is about as close as he will go to giving comfort to an increasingly anxious humanity. The disturbances that will be precipitated by global warming will be surprising and probably nasty. There will be turbulent weather and unpredictable social and political consequences. He thinks that, to give the greener parts of the earth time to adapt and recover, humans should withdraw as much as possible to the cities (though he still believes that 'city life reinforces the heresy of humanism, that narcissistic devotion to human interests alone').

But he is far from fatalistic. He thinks we should try as much as we can – within our present knowledge – to press more lightly on Gaia's mechanisms, but not presume to put them into intensive care. He is full of examples of well-meaning but ill-thought-out 'solutions' whose consequences have been decidedly double-edged. Biodegradable plastic, for instance, which seems irreproachably Green, but whose increasing popularity will rob us of one of the more effective means of tying up lethal carbon dioxide: the *non*-biodegradable plastic. Or the tragedy that befell Lapland in the wake of the Chernobyl nuclear disaster, about which he has written: 'Thousands of reindeer, the food prey of the Lapps, were destroyed because it was thought they were too radioactive to eat. Was it justifiable to inflict this brutal treatment for mild radioactive poisoning on a fragile culture and its dependent ecosystem?' Lovelock is on the reindeer's side, and more particularly on the side of the earth's bacteria and micro-organisms and lower plants, for whom he has nominated himself 'shop steward'. It is these that make the world go round and make up the heart of Gaia, not the essentially free-loading higher animals.

And it is in their heartlands – in the soil and rain-forests and continental shelves especially – that the fate of planetary ecology may be decided.

If the Left dislike his view of humanity as just 'one member of a very democratic planetary community' many middle-of-the-road biologists abhor his disregard for the niceties of scientific etiquette and peer review. Prominent amongst his critics are what he styles 'the Oxford neo-Darwinists' centred around Richard Dawkins. Lovelock calls himself a classical Darwinist, but still admires Dawkins' celebrated 'selfish gene' theory, and his initiative in modelling evolutionary pathways on a computer. But he cannot understand the sheer vitriol of the attacks that come from some Dawkinsians (like Dr John Horsfall's *Guardian* piece). He is perplexed by their charges that the Gaia hypothesis is unscientific because it cannot be falsified, and that it presupposes that altruism can exist in non-thinking systems.

Some of Lovelock's proposed cycles are currently undergoing experimental tests, and so far the marine algae/sulphur loop has shown little evidence of being a potential cooling mechanism (though the critics are right in stating that the disproving of any single hypothetical mechanism could never falsify the whole theory).

But neo-Darwinists of all people ought to have a care before accusing others of creating untestable hypotheses. The whole framework of evolutionary theory is untestable, since it refers to particular, unrepeatable events in the past. No one can ever check out the mechanism of the evolution of red blood cells, let alone of a whole order like the dinosaurs. The theory of evolution stands (as the Gaia hypothesis will stand or fall eventually) on a considerable weight of circumstantial evidence, not rigorous scientific proof.

Nor is it right to suggest that Gaia assumes the existence of 'altruism' in lower orders of life. In Lovelock's view its mechanisms are all entirely automatic, worked out over aeons of trial and error and mutual adjustment. Each new species on the earth evolved not on a *tabula rasa* but in the atmospheric and environmental conditions set by its predecessors; we breathe in the air that plants breathe out. Each increase in biological diversity extends the resilience and flexibility of the system in response to change. Collectively the system cannot *but* be interactive.

Gaia could be seen as the solution to an immense number of simultaneous equations, each one of which describes the relationship of a given species with its environment. Or, as Lovelock's close colleague Lynn Margulis has put it: 'Each species to a greater or lesser degree modifies its environment to optimise its reproduction rate. Gaia follows from this by being the sum total of all these individual modifications and by the fact that all species are connected, for the production of gases, food and waste removal, however circuitously, to all others.'

I ask Lovelock whether he ever wishes he had opted for a low-profile definition like this rather than going on to describe the earth as an organism in its own right. He retorts that even conventional biologists are now prepared to use the phrase 'super-organism' about complexes like beehives and termite mounds. So why not about the earth? But he admits that, yes, he was being deliberately provocative: 'I wanted to stir them into thinking about the whole planet.' He is coming round to the view that it doesn't matter whether the full Gaian theory is true or not, provided that we learn to take a 'top-down view of the earth' and to think in terms of 'planetary physiology'.

My own view is that the theory may turn out to be a kind of high-level tautology, that the biosphere simply could not exist in any other way. We do, for instance, now regard as self-evident the notion that all animals are perfectly constructed for what they are and where they live, although this was an heretical idea in the human-centred view of the eighteenth century.

Or perhaps Gaia is not so much a single organism as a tightly knit group, rather like a remarkable species of weevil recently discovered in New Guinea. *Symbiopholus* lives with dozens of plants growing in the cracks in its shell and rooted in its flesh, and is 'gardened' by a whole ecosystem of insects and bacteria. It is 3 centimetres long, and lives a long life, untroubled by predators.

Either way I suspect that it will be Gaia's power as a metaphor that turns out to be its most enduring feature (though this may please neither Lovelock nor his critics). Although Lovelock is right to emphasise that individual organisms are important in Gaia, what shines out most strongly from the theory is the idea of mutuality, of the interdependence of all organisms and their environments. Humans, quite properly, will always want to play their part in this, to help out, have their place in the sun (and in the countryside), use their unique biological gifts of intelligence and creativity.

Jim and I are both admirers of the American biologist and writer Lewis Thomas, and I remind him of the passage in Thomas' *Lives of a Cell* (1974), where he describes a future for the human species as 'handyman to the earth' ('I would much prefer this useful role . . . to the essentially unearthly creature we seem otherwise on the way to becoming'). Lovelock smiles, gives the phrase the slightest twist and says 'Employed *by* the earth. Yes, I like that!' He is already beginning to take a more benevolent view of an actively engaged humanity himself. He has always recognised that the Gaia can survive without humans, but not vice versa, and is currently working on a new book, a 'textbook of planetary medicine' – what we might be able to do, without making things worse, to help alleviate acid rain, famines, global warming, etc. Despite his hostility towards 'big science' it will discuss the contributions which might be made by private, corporate 'planetary physicians' (Shell's scheme for burning power-station coal in pure oxygen and liquefying the carbon dioxide, for instance; or producing more purely synthetic food to take the pressure off the land).

But mostly it will be medicine of the barefoot, preventative, and minimum intervention kind. Gaian fundamentalists see humans at best as shamans – interpreting and conjuring nature but never really presuming to intervene in it. It will be fascinating to see how far Lovelock himself has moved towards viewing us as altogether more actively involved, and perhaps in the role that he seems to fit most closely himself: the quirky, eclectic, not always consistent but resolutely wise General Practitioner.

Lairds of Creation (1991)

There is a sad inevitability about the battles which wage continuously over the future of the wilder uplands of Scotland. Wherever there are vast reserves of empty land there are people eager to appropriate and exploit them. In the Highlands the process has been all the more hurtful because the usurpers have so often been outsiders with grandiose ambitions. In the seventeenth and eighteenth centuries, the native pinewoods – one of the last extensive remnants of the north European forests – were looted for the English navy. In the nineteenth century it was the native inhabitants' turn, and the Highlands suffered the terrible injury of the Clearances. In Sutherland alone one third of the population were evicted (by burning down their homes in most cases) to make way for sheep-ranching and game-shooting. The massive increase in sheep and deer ensured in turn that the pine forests would be unlikely to regenerate.

In the twentieth century much of this open country has been put under another alien regime – huge shrouds of conifers that for much of the 1980s gave tax relief to absentee entrepreneurs and speculators. Now power and ownership have drifted even further offshore, and walkers and birdwatchers just up for the day from Clydeside can find themselves fenced out of the moor by the multinational grouse-shooting and deer-stalking syndicates.

But recently the Highland bubble has looked like bursting. Forestry companies no longer granted tax concessions have been trying to offload their holdings. Big corporate estates, pressed by the recession, have been put on the market. From the Cairngorms, through the Spey valley pine-woods round Abernethy and Rothiemurchus, out to Wester Ross and even the inner isles, so much wild country is changing hands – or at least changing status – that it has begun to look as if Scotland might at last be able to possess a tract of untroubled land, a sanctuary free of commercial pressures and of what the poet Thomas Gray called 'the pomp of power', where native wildlife could flourish and humans meditate upon their species' past follies and arrogance. In fact, a kind of wilderness. I use the word with hesitation, since in these days of global tourism and ubiquitous pollution it is, to say the least, a somewhat relative term. It is also a contentious one that riles both landworkers and ecologists, devaluing the presence of humans in remote areas and over-valuing their contribution elsewhere. Yet in a country where even nature conservationists often seem bent on taming every last acre, I think that the time may be ripe for bringing the word – and the kind of land it refers to – back into currency. And the Scottish Highlands may be the only remaining region where we can find it.

But up on the estates, even the dismembered ones, old limbs are still twitching with archaic reflexes. The sanctity of traditional ownership and lineage are hoisted like clannish standards. The 'stewardship' and 'caretaking' of nature are spoken of as if they were self-evidently desirable aims in a wild place. And a host of urgent, practical problems are clouded by old border feuds and special pleadings. Even in these great spaces we seem unwilling to let go of the reins.

The case of Mar Lodge has been the most publicised, because of its somewhat tawdry recent history. This 77,000-acre estate has been described as 'the jewel of the Cairngorms', but it has been passed around recently like a shop-soiled Rolls Royce. It was owned for years by a Swiss businessman, who installed ski-lifts where there was never any snow and scarred the hills with new tracks. He sold it in 1989 to an American multi-millionaire, John Kluge, whose wife fancied living next to Balmoral. It was their divorce in 1990 that led to the estate going on the market. Yet Mar Lodge remains a remote and beautiful place, and full of superb examples of almost all the classic Highland habitats, from the flood-plain terraces of the River Dee to the montane grasslands of Ben MacDui, the second highest peak in Scotland. It has golden eagles and wildcats, and a fabulous alpine flora on the high crags. It also has probably the finest and most ancient native pines in Scotland, venerable trees whose gnarled, weatherbeaten habit has more in common with old oaks than with the conifers we are used to seeing.

The problem is that there are very few young trees to succeed them. As in other remnants of the Great Wood of Caledon, pine seedlings (abundant enough to begin with) are mostly browsed away by red deer. Deer numbers have been climbing steadily ever since the animals became a valuable resource for owners of stalking rights, and in many areas of the Highlands are now at levels which the land cannot easily support. What to do about them is one of the biggest practical obstacles to the creation of truly wild reserves in Scotland. The most obvious and frequently canvassed solution is regular, heavy culls. The distinguished Scots ecologist Adam Watson believes that the native pinewoods cannot even survive without a great initial reduction in deer numbers followed by a regular programme of culling. Dr Watson has worked in and watched the region for forty years and his opinions carry great weight. So I hope it isn't just sentimentality that makes me baulk at his drastic solution. There is, after all, more than a mite of sentimentality behind his cautionary picture of what is likely to happen if there is no great cull: 'Nature will produce her own solution with mass starvation. I have seen hundreds of dead adults and calves in woods and treeless glens after a snowy winter. They were emaciated, with their ribs sticking out, and in summer their decomposing carcasses made the glens stink.' It is a dismal and discomfiting picture, but it is a 'natural' one. This is the way that wild animals do die in times of hardship, and perhaps we need sometimes to see, on our doorsteps, the consequences of our past ignorant and selfish plunderings of nature.

But I am more bothered by the implications of losing what may be the last chance of an indigenous refuge free from ongoing human interference. The alternative currently being offered – where the population of the largest mammal is planned by humans, and its desirable genetic character-istics chosen by stalkers, where as a result the whole environment is a delicate and discreet piece of stage management – is not, for me, a wilderness at all.

Over in Wester Ross the deer are just part of what is seen as the larger problem of who is in charge, and who makes decisions about wild places. West of Loch Maree, the Countryside Commission for Scotland (CCS) is considering the possibility of creating a National Park on the English model, to include at its core the wild and remote montane tracts of Strathnasheallah, Letterewe and Fisherfield forests, collectively reckoned to be the largest 'roadless' area in Britain. The local landowners and crofters have countered with an alternative proposal for a Wester Ross Wilderness Area. It is an acute and intelligently framed plan, which sug-gests that encouragement of, or even provision for, large-scale recreation in these remote heartlands is quite inappropriate, that pressure needs to be taken off, not increased. It also argues with some force against the human-centredness, the 'anthropocentrism' of the CCS scheme, and that in these places the interests of wildlife and ecology should be given absolute priority, even above human 'spiritual replenishment'. It reads at first sight like a selfless Magna Carta for the wild – until you begin to glimpse (as in that ancient charter) the barons' hidden agenda. The Wester Ross Wilderness proposal, it appears, only objects to the centredness of certain kinds of humans (mountain bikers, Monro-baggers, etc.) and it urges the CCS to recognise the crucial role of the local landowners as 'good stewards' of this region, to acknowledge how 'well-run' the wilder-ness has been (and presumably would be under the same regime in future) and how adept their bailiffs and stalkers have been at pursuing 'a careful policy of highly selective culling, a scientific approach to hind and calf management'. If such a carefully managed site is a wilderness then it is one where the word has radically changed its meaning.

Of course no definition of wilderness these days can aspire to an absolute absence of human influence. There is now nowhere on the earth which is free of man-made changes in the atmosphere or radioactive fall-out; only a few remaining places where no humans have trod; and in our own islands only a handful of inaccessible sites which have escaped some deliberate interference with their ecology. Nor can any reconstructed, facsimile wilderness ever approach the condition of nature as it was before human influence became dominant. Even in the most jealously guarded 'non-intervention zones' the absence of big predators makes them a shadow of what they were in the past.

Yet surely the word becomes nonsensical once we begin to talk of a 'well-run' wilderness. We may argue about the importance of a site's past history, and the relevance of purely accidental human influence (the 'fall-out' effect). But the idea of wilderness becomes meaningless unless it implies a state of affairs in which, over some quite large tracts of land, deliberate human control has been removed. A wilderness is a place of contrast, where our own rules and values for living can be challenged, where we can learn something about humility and the inventive resilience of unmanaged nature.

In his seminal study *Wilderness and the American Mind* (1967) Roderick Nash made the point that 'wilderness was a state of mind – a perceived rather than an actual condition of the environment'. One child he spoke to saw wilderness as 'the dark space under my bed'. To Wordsworth, who wrote some of the earliest and stoutest defence of the concept (including a damning comparison between plantations and naturally sprung woods in the Lake District), it was a condition of the spirit as well as of the land. His much-quoted phrase 'a wilderness is rich with liberty' occurs in a poem on the release into the liberating wastes of a pool in the pleasure-ground of Mount Rydal of two goldfish from a bowl:

> . . . No sea
> Swells like the bosom of a man set free;
> A wilderness is rich with liberty.
> Roll on, ye spouting whales, who die or keep
> Your independence in the fathomless Deep! . . .
> If unreproved the ambitious eagle mount
> Sunward to seek the daylight in its fount,
> Bays, gulfs, and ocean's Indian width, shall be
> Till the world perishes, a field for thee!

To those who framed the US National Wilderness Preservation System a wilderness was an area which '*appears* to have been primarily affected by the forces of nature . . . where man himself is a visitor who does not remain'. Indeed, the permanent absence of humans has rarely been cited as a condition.

Wester Ross and Mar Lodge, could, I fancy, fit most definitions of a wilderness – if all humans entered them as equals, and on the same terms as their animal inhabitants, on foot and unarmed. 'Calf and hind management', pest control, special tree planting or 'encouragement' schemes are entirely acceptable procedures in nature reserves with clearly defined goals, but not in a wilderness. A wilderness must allow the possibility of things turning out quite differently from expectations, of disaster, catastrophe and maybe even degradation as well as creative surprise.

But can we really afford to take such risks with our limited space and natural resources in Britain? Shouldn't the over-riding aim of conservation be the saving of natural species, regardless of how much unnatural management this may entail? In his best-selling book *The End of Nature* (1990), the American writer Bill McKibben argues that nature holds other crucial, non-material values for us, and that with the onset of man-made global warming and the spread of genetic engineering, 'our sense of nature as eternal and separate will be washed away'. He continues:

> Before any redwoods had been cloned or genetically improved, one could understand clearly what the fight against such tinkering was about. It was about the idea that a redwood was somehow sacred, that its fundamental identity should remain beyond our control. But once that barrier has been broken, what is the fight about then? It's not like opposing nuclear reactors or toxic waste dumps, each one of which poses new risks to new areas. This damage is to an idea, the idea of nature, and all that descends from it.

He attacks, too, the idea of becoming stewards of a managed world, 'custodians' of life: 'For that job security we will trade the mystery of the natural world, the pungent mystery of our own lives and a world bursting with exuberant creation?'

McKibben is writing about a global crisis. But his defence of an independent natural creation seems to me to apply just as powerfully to our home acres. Yet, unlike America, the idea of unmanaged wild places is almost universally rejected in Britain. Of course our landscapes are mostly small-scale, and have been fashioned by centuries of human work, and there is a strong argument that the conservation of species (*not* of wildness) is best achieved by conserving 'traditional' patterns of management. Yet the case is rarely put as calmly and pragmatically as this. It is tinged sometimes with a blinkered nostalgia, a belief that there really was a Golden Age in the countryside when humans and nature were in harmony; at others with a more ugly neo-colonialism, a conviction that wildernesses are all right for the Third World, but not for us civilised folk.

When the idea of set-aside was first mooted a few years ago, the hostility reached almost hysterical proportions. In the *Observer*, a normally wise and balanced political commentator outlined a vision of what the English countryside might become if abandoned to nature that was like something out of a Dark Ages bestiary, a nightmarish waste of swamp and scrub, thick with rats, disease and the remains of derelict farm machinery.

Nature conservationists and farmers (who both know what really does happen to abandoned land) should know better, but in the past few years seem to have become possessed by the same fear of some dark and profuse genie escaping from the bottle. Of course, heaths, downland, coppice all need management if they and their customary inhabitants are to survive (though we seem to have conveniently forgotten that though these habitats are manicured, they are not man-invented, and all have prototypes in the wild created by fire, storm, flood and wild grazing animals). But conservation orthodoxy is beginning to resemble the credo of a business studies course. *Everything* must be managed. After the 1987 hurricane the Tree Council went as far as to say that 'unless positive encouragement is given to owners to restore these woods . . . they will revert to scrub and never recover'. So much for several million years of woodland evolution.

Do we really want nature to be so comprehensively at our beck and call? Do species have to be maintained as uniformly and tidily, as predictably, as if they were part of a genetic card index? Don't we all want revelation, surprise, inspiration from the wild? Those unbidden spurts of protean growth or sheer defiance that can scupper scientific smugness and fashionable pessimism alike?

It is wilderness that gives the best chance for such events. One of the classic cases in Britain is Lady Park Wood, an ancient and very mixed coppice in the Wye valley, which has been conserved as an unmanaged reserve for nearly half a century. Up to the 1970s it was presumed to be proceeding towards the beech high forest which ecologists believed was the stable climax on limestone. Then came elm disease, followed smartly by the drought of 1976, which killed off many of the beeches. Gales and hard winters followed, including one severe ice-storm freeze-up which welded coppiced small-leaved lime branches to the ground – where they promptly took root. Lady Park is now dominated by survivors, especially ash and bizarre lime trees, and has become an exciting, vital wood which has transcended ecologists' rather narrow predictions for it.

Yet even scientific curiosity in such places is minute in this country, and I fear that our national outlook is still tainted by that Anglo-Saxon authoritarianism that the first English settlers took with them to the New

World. Fortunately North America pulled back from total destruction before all the wild land was gone, and that sense of a still existent frontier in nature is reflected in their writing. To match our quiet, domestic landscape, we have the intimate, closely observed writing of Gilbert White, Richard Jefferies and Edward Thomas. In contrast, North America has the vast scope and imaginative daring of Thoreau, Loren Eiseley, Edward Hoagland and Annie Dillard.

I hope I won't be misunderstood here. I adore the British countryside, though I think we all sometimes deceive ourselves about its imagined idyllic past. I accept that downs and heaths and the like need management if they are to survive. I even admit, with sad reluctance, that red deer may need to be reduced in parts of Scotland. But I find it hard to accept that all our land should be so buttoned up, and that we should continue to allow ourselves the arrogant and indulgent belief – against, I should add, every lesson of history – that we can run things better than nature.

My first published piece of nature writing was about the pinewoods in Abernethy. I had gone up to visit the RSPB's osprey reserve at Loch Garten, and had been struck by the symbolism of that site, where the birds flew free and the humans were, in effect, in a cage. That, of course, was a classic piece of management legerdemain. But I don't think my long walk through the forest in an April dawn was. It remains one of the most vivid and magical memories of my life. For hours I strolled through the birch and Scots pinewoods with herds of roe deer only yards in front of me. Crossbills and red squirrels showered stripped pinecones around me, and I saw my first crested tits, trapezing in the canopy. Turning a corner along a narrow track, I came face to face with a blustering capercaillie, as big as a turkey. And echoing across Loch Garten I heard the last wintering whooper swans and the trills of common sandpipers. It was like a vision of Scotland before the Fall.

I don't think it was an illusion, a clever deceit produced by scientific culling and stringent access modelling. But the odd thing was that it didn't fill me with the slightest sense of humility or feelings about the separateness and 'otherness' of nature, but with sheer joy at sharing that old world on a new morning with my wild Scots kinfolk.

The Nature of Local Distinctiveness (1993)

Our sense of locality, I suspect, is rooted as deeply in territorial feelings as in topography. We become imprinted by places, and become familiar with them just as a cat or fox does. We plod out private routes, touch trees and mark (in our imaginations, at least) our special spots – a bend in a road, a gate to lean on, a face glimpsed in a trunk. Loyalty to these marking posts can be fierce and personal, and given without the slightest regard for what is locally distinctive.

Certainly the first place that I got to know and love when I was growing up as a rather gypsyish boy in the Chilterns didn't have a trace of local identity. It was the remains of a landed estate at the back of our road. The big house had been demolished in the 1920s, the landscaped grounds were reverting to wilderness, and we neighbourhood kids (and a good many adults, too) treated it as the local common. We stalked it like aborigines, marking out a cryptic network of landmarks, totems, for-bidden zones and hideouts. But its random mix of brick piles, bramble patches and parkland cedar trees could have been anywhere from Surrey to Galloway. What was important – and distinctive – to us were the meanings we had given them.

It was not until my late teens that I recognised, with something of a shock, that places could also have an objective character. I was on a first trip to the Norfolk coast (which proved to have its own tangy sense of place), and on the way passed through that vast and mysterious inland sand-bowl called the Breckland. The sandstorms and great bustards had vanished long before, but not the bizarre wind-breaks that had been created in the eighteenth century from lopped and layered Scots pines. These stunted trees, rising from the sandy fields beyond the sinister US bomber base at Lakenheath, were like no other landscape I had seen. It was a desert, an English badlands.

These pine-belts still give me goose-flesh when I am driving east, and it is good to learn that they now have official recognition as a unique and defining element of the Breckland scene. But they are also full of irony and incongruity. For a start, they are a more or less alien tree which hasn't grown naturally in eastern England for six thousand years. They also played a crucial role in the process of Parliamentary Enclosure in East Anglia, which helped both to drive indigenous commoners off the

land and to obliterate the open heaths and mobile sands that had pre-
viously contributed to the Breckland's local distinctiveness.

A further irony is that more than a century later, in the 1920s, Breckland
became the site of one of the earliest and largest Forestry Commission
plantations. Scots and other pines were again planted out in rows in the
sand, but this time in vast, dour blankets that were to become a symbol
of the homogenisation of the countryside, and of a process that was
making immense tracts of Britain from Inverness to Norfolk indistinguishable.

The contribution of nature to local character is often like this – ambivalent, mutable, as likely to be some new, accommodating growth that fits
the rhythms and continuity of the place as an ancient presence or heritage
cliché. My home town of Berkhamsted is probably named after the birch
trees that grow on the acid plateau above the settlement. They still thrive
there, but I find I simply cannot think of my home country as 'the place
of the birches'. If the trees do figure in my sense of my own patch, they
have become an unconscious backcloth, a kind of second nature yet to
be put to the loyalty test.

Natural features were often obvious or important enough to provide
names for places, but the names usually outlive them. There are no lime
trees left in Linwood or Lyndhurst in the New Forest. The ravens have
long gone from Ravensden on the outskirts of industrial Bedford. And
despite the annual neo-Celtic festival in Glastonbury, I doubt that woad
is any longer a significant local crop (*glasto* is woad in Old Celt). Even
when naming features survive, they can seem as remote and cryptic as
Latin family mottos on village war memorials. The weed fat-hen is still
common enough amongst the sugar-beet fields of mid-Suffolk. It was
called *melde* in Old English, eaten as an important staple vegetable in
prehistoric and even medieval East Anglia, and probably gave its name
to the village of Milden, near Sudbury. A few present-day inhabitants
certainly believe so, and about fifteen years ago put up a cast-iron statue
of the weed on the edge of the village. It is one of the most unusual and
distinctive parish boundary signs in the country, but I wonder what most
of the rest of this still predominantly farming community make of it,
having spent the last few centuries trying to wipe out plants like this from
the fields?

Features as arcane as this may be too bookish or ghostly to contribute
to a real sense of locality. Yet those that are striking and persistent can
become communal motifs, sources of pride and maybe even passion,
something which can join locals and outsiders in a common sense of
place. The wild daffodils that have given the country between Dymock
and Ledbury the nickname of the Golden Triangle are a good example.

A few centuries ago many parts of Britain could have offered the sight of whole copses and meadows lapped with yellow under the March sunshine. Now, it is only a few oases like this stretch of the border country that have the plant in any quantities. It was already becoming a speciality of this region in the 1930s, when the Great Western Railway used to run 'Daffodil Specials' here, and local farmers and fruit growers threw open their fields to pickers. After the last war, the local colonies were reduced still further by agricultural changes, and local daffodil consciousness declined. But there are signs it is picking up again. There are local daffodil festivals, and a remarkable cooperative effort by landowners, local authorities and local people has created a 10-mile walk through woods, meadows and churchyards that is never out of the sight of the 'dancing host'.

Similarly, limestone in the Yorkshire Dales is recognised by native and tourist alike as one of the defining features of the place. It isn't quite like limestone anywhere else in Britain – in Derbyshire or the Mendips or the Brecon Beacons, say. The difference is not just a matter of natural geological features, of limestone pavements and scree slopes, but of what local people have done with the stone: the way dry-stone walling follows the patterns of layering in the bare terraces; the 'found stones' and vernacular gargoyles that adorn so many cottage walls and roofs.

This is a landscape where the human presence has been sympathetic towards local quirks and savours. These days most human manipulation of natural features involves a deliberate ironing-out of local identity and diversity for the sake of commercial convenience. Forestry plantations, CAP cash-crop fields and new golf courses, are as characterless as international airports. Off-the-peg ornamental trees – Japanese double-flowering cherries, robinias, black alders – are giving a uniform, garden festival look to towns across the land that maybe once sported indigenous willows and whitebeams. Even conservation policies, with the very best of intentions, can lead to a levelling out. Britain's hedges, for instance, a wonderfully diverse legacy, are declining and disappearing, and it is good that there are government-backed schemes to regenerate them. But the hedgerow revival has been accompanied by an indiscriminate zeal for management for its own sake, and tall Exmoor beech wind-breaks, Suffolk ancient wood remnants and thick Dorset double-rows are all being beaten down to the level and scale of Midland quicksets.

But maybe I am being a killjoy. Isn't a regimented living hedge better than a vanished local speciality? Aren't street robinias brighter and more resilient than pollarded willows? Mightn't a commitment to local distinctiveness be difficult to disentangle from high-handed puritanism, or isolation, or even an unpleasant xenophobia (as in the recent pogrom against escaped American ruddy ducks)?

Earlier this year I was driving back from Shropshire on the first warm day of March, and all the way through the Long Mynd hills pairs of buzzards were spiralling in courtship displays on the thermals. As soon as I was down on the Midland plain, they were gone. I marvelled at what an extraordinary thing the buzzard line is, stretching as it does from Dorset through the Cotswolds and the eastern Lakes, even dividing lowland Scotland in two; and how entering buzzard country, and seeing those meditative, soaring shapes above the hills, is a sure sign of having crossed into the west. Then I remembered that this is an entirely unnatural state for the bird, which a century and a half ago, before persecution by the game lobby, had been common throughout Britain. Its current restricted distribution, as flavoursome a westerly thing as cider or chapels, is, like that of the wild daffodil, an indication of unnatural depletion as much as local distinctiveness.

And as Dutch elm disease got a grip again this spring, I thought about its victims, whose story is another salutary if ambivalent parable. Elms are one of the most locally diverse of all our native trees. Different types, reproducing largely by suckers, have evolved in different parts of Britain: stiff, fastigiate kinds, twiggy kinds, varieties with an almost black bark, and an all but infinite variety of leaf shapes to match; and some, like the Boxworth elm of the country round Huntingdon, more or less resistant to the disease. The great elm specialist Professor R. H. Richens found that there was a distinctive elm type in almost every East Anglian valley. The local trees, isolated genetically from those in the next valley, were the source of the cuttings and suckers used to make the local hedges, which after a while formed a treescape subtly different from that in the next village. Ironically, the human inhabitants were probably quite unaware of these botanical differences; and though the genetic variety of the nation's elms is part of the species' insurance policy, the cloning of local varieties means that if any one tree in a village catches the disease all will likely go under. Local distinctiveness in terms of natural resources, pursued too narrowly, can represent a dead end, a state of siege as much as an oasis.

The fenlands of East Anglia are an extreme example of a distinctive locality which has become an impoverished landscape for all its life forms. It is still a place with a powerful aura, determined by the huge imperatives of sky, wind and water. Yet most of its old liveliness has been drained and sprayed into oblivion, and it has become a place of sad paradoxes. I have seen scores of black-dressed women hunched over the potato crop like a vision of the worst times of the nineteenth-century agricultural depression. And a few hundred yards away, signs warning passers-by to stay off the fields because of the 'deadly poisons'.

People living on the edge of the Fens have an inexhaustible supply of slanderous stories about the inhabitants of this drained swamp, inland from the Wash. They are, the myths go, insular, inbred and violent – 'Fen Tigers'. They work their children as slave labour in the fields. They are so greedy that they plough up to the very edge of the drainage dykes, and are forever falling off their tractors and drowning themselves. The Fens are eastern England's Balkans. Every stereotype that has been glimpsed in, or fabricated about, the rural population at large has been magnified and dumped on this vast plain of fertile peat. Even the landscape itself, a grid of featureless flat rectangles clear to the horizon, can seem like a bleak caricature of the modern farmscape.

The unusual thing is that the local people themselves don't dispute many of these images. They are acutely aware of the brutalising effects of centuries of isolation, of the ceaseless battle against flooding, and of the corrosive influence of modern agriculture. In the nineteenth century, rheumatism and 'the ague' were endemic, and opium use was common well into the 1920s. Today it is depression and drink, and 'fen syndrome', described by psychiatrists as a kind of 'cultural retardation', is a matter of medical record in the region.

But people have loved and still love this place. The poet John Clare did, even after the first stages of its enforced enclosure and modernisation had helped drive him mad. It is a measure of just how vital locality is to us that we cling to, and can get comfort from, the slightest shadows and echoes of the old spirit of a place. The challenge, in a world where the differences between native and stranger are fading, is to discover veins of local character which are distinctive without being insular and withdrawn.

Flora Britannica (1992)

Most summers a curious tale of misanthropy leaks out of one of Britain's high security nature reserves. The scene of the action is often different, but the story the same. Wardens, fearful that some of the last surviving colonies of rare orchids may be dug up by piratical collectors, hack off the flower spikes as soon as they are in bud to make the plants less conspicuous. The plants survive – but only as emasculated, joyless, botanical specimens.

True, or a kind of modern myth, the story does catch something of the vein of puritanism that bedevils our official attitudes towards wild flowers. We don't publicly *relish* them in the way we do birds. They have a fey, marginal image. Television largely ignores them because of their inconsiderate lack of movement, or anatomises them as biological wonders. They are distanced, as rarities, scientific specimens, or props in a nostalgic, Edwardian afterglow.

Yet down in the parish, the vernacular relationship with our flora is flourishing. We still kiss under the mistletoe (though without much clue as to why), thread daisy chains, make solemn black-lists of weeds, fight to save landmark trees, munch blackberries, put heather in the car radiator (and keep May out of the house) for good luck. And every November, in a remarkable survival of ancient plant symbolism, we wear poppies – a symbol of blood and new life ever since the Egyptians – for remembrance.

At the grass roots we still have a half-instinctive, almost aboriginal respect for wild plants. They chart the seasons for us, from primrose to holly time, colour our place-names, increasingly invade our houses as herbal medicines, natural dyes and handmade furniture. Above all, they help shape the character of the places where we live. It would be hard to think of chalk country, for example, shorn of the white plumes of old-man's beard in the hedges, or moorland without heather.

These are all dynamic relationships, which are constantly adapting to change and picking up new meanings, and they are the channels, I suspect, through which most people come to plants. When I was a fervid teenage naturalist myself, I had time only for the dash and romance of birds, especially those that marked special moments of the year or favourite spots, like swifts and barn owls. A decade later it was the same sense of a meeting ground between the human and natural worlds that began to fascinate me about plants.

I'd begun haunting the north Norfolk coastal marshland, still on the trail of birds, and had stumbled on a surviving local custom for eating wild vegetables. Samphire was the most popular and also the strangest. The bright green shoots – half seaweed, half maritime cactus – were sold from fishmongers and cottages all along the coast, and were cooked and eaten rather like asparagus. There was a strict local lore about picking. The shoots were best after midsummer day, and should only be gathered where they were 'washed by every tide'. There were stories of fabulous saltings where samphire grew like a lawn for acres, and of the monster specimen that had sprung up near a local sewage outfall after the floods of 1953. It was six feet tall and thick as a leek at the base. It was carried back to Blakeney on the crossbar of a bike and later hung above the bar in a local pub, like a prize eel.

Soon I had progressed to sea-spinach and sea-kale, to the feathery sprays of fennel (introduced to this country by the Romans as a medicinal herb for indigestion, but also wonderful cooked with fresh mackerel), and another Roman pot-herb, the angelica-scented Alexanders, whose early sprouting, bright-green leaf sprays are naturalised on most coastal banks and lanes.

That process of 'naturalisation', by which a foreign plant escapes to become settled and self-perpetuating in the wild, is analogous at many levels to the way in which plants settle into a human, cultural substrate. Sometimes the two processes proceed in parallel. But they can be intensely local, parochial almost, to such a degree that they haven't yet become part of popular knowledge. Japanese knotweed (a throwout from Victorian gardens) has become established as our most aggressive and uncompromising shrubby weed. But has this begun to generate local nicknames? Were any of the bizarre coinings volunteered during a House of Lords debate on weeds in 1989 really in current usage? Is anyone eating the young shoots, as they do in the Far East and the United States?

And what is the street-level opinion of another vast and vigorous weed, the giant hogweed (from the Caucasus mountains, circa 1893, again via Victorian gardens)? This was christened 'the triffid' by the popular press back in 1970, when it was realised the sap caused rashes of blisters on skin exposed to the sun. Children, no doubt fascinated by the plant's gothic appearance, had been making pea-shooters out of its hollow stems. Have *they* given it any more expressive names, or worked out any ingenious ways of using the stems safely?

Newcomers they may be, but these alien weeds can sometimes create a real *genius loci*. Along the River Don in Sheffield there is an extraordinary population of fig trees, dense enough in one place to form a small wood. They are all about seventy years old, and it looks as if their concentration in this incongruous spot may be intimately linked with Sheffield's eco-nomic history. The source of the seeds was most probably sewage (though just possibly refuse from sauce and pickle factories) but these Mediter-ranean plants almost certainly have the steel industry to thank for their successful establishment in the 1920s. At that time river water was used in the factories for cooling, and the outfalls kept the downstream reaches of the Don at a steady twenty degrees Celsius – sufficient for the germi-nation of the seeds. Following the decline of the steel industry, the river temperature returned more or less to normal, and no new trees have been able to sprout. Dr Oliver Gilbert, who unravelled the figs' history, says 'they are as much a part of Sheffield's industrial heritage as Bessemer converters, steam hammers and crucible steel'.

There are botanical floral landmarks like this all over Britain. Some are ancient and possibly ecclesiastical, like the snakeshead fritillaries that turn Oxford's Magdalen Meadow purple in late April; or literary, like Wordsworth's host of daffodils, which still nod on the edges of Ullswater. Some are obstinate living monuments, which mark out the ground of old settlements: skeletal (but reviving) elms, along the closes and boundary banks of vanished East Anglian villages; herbs such as birthwort (once used in midwifery, and probably as an abortifacient) amongst the ruins of nunneries in Godstow, Norwich and Cambridge.

It is trees which make the biggest contribution to a sense of place – though sometimes they are only fully appreciated when they are threatened. The story of the fall – and rise – of Selborne's churchyard yew is a striking example. This 1,500-year-old Hampshire tree, immortal-ised and measured by Gilbert White and William Cobbett, was blown down in the January 1990 gale, but was stood back on its feet after heroic efforts by local forestry students. Days after the replanting, a water main burst under the roots and gave them thirty-six hours of bountiful drenching. And when the tree was relieved of its massive top branches and foliage to give its damaged roots a better chance to thrive, the feel of the village green and churchyard was transformed, and they looked suddenly airy and *right*. Since then it has come more sharply into parish consciousness than ever before. Old Selborne inhabitants have come long distances to buy souvenir slivers of the tree under which they used to meet and court and have lunch, and larger pieces have been made into all kinds of woodware, including a concert lute for the church.

Often whole constellations of trees form a background so familiar that it is barely remarked on – even when the tree is as striking and local as the native black poplar, beloved of Constable and figuring (though often misidentified) in many of his paintings. In the 1970s it was believed there were only a thousand specimens left. But a long and exhaustive survey has turned up populations throughout England and Wales, especially on the Welsh borders and in East Anglia and Gloucestershire. It is a dramatically handsome tree. The trunk is massive and fissured, covered with bosses and burrs, and often developing a decided lean in middle age. The branches turn down towards their ends, then sweep up again into twigs which, once the voluptuous crimson catkins have fallen, carry dense switches of shiny, beech-shaped leaves. In the Vale of Aylesbury it is the commonest tree, a stunning sight as the amber buds and straw-yellow flower stalks shine in the spring sunshine.

Colonies of plants like this are an integral part of our sense of locality and season, part of what makes one place different from another. They are the most steadfast living things in the community, and will have an increasing significance as political and economic change tends to make all places homogeneous.

The aim of the *Flora Britannica* project is to raise our consciousness about local vegetation and its part in our lives, to record, before it is too late, the vernacular names of plants that are still current, the games that children play, the great surviving botanical landmarks – and the more modest but much loved parish clumps, and the continual reinvention of meaning for our national flora.

Geoffrey Grigson, author of a pioneering if more historical book in a similar mould, *The Englishman's Flora* (1955), railed against our tendency to reduce the natural world to compartments – sentimental, scientific, exotic, tamed. We hope that *Flora Britannica* may encourage a more unified experience of plants, and of how those that have found places in our lives help to blur that bothersome distinction between the 'natural' and the 'man-made'. Nothing illustrates this better in early spring than the fortunes – and the mysteries – of the true wild daffodil. It is one of the best known but most local of our native lilies, and its present distribution is a paradox. It is doggedly persistent and remarkably unfussy in its favoured localities (south Devon, for example), thriving on roadside verges and in paddocks, and even at the edges of conifer plantations. But it is curiously absent over large areas of seemingly suitable habitat, and has plainly declined drastically since John Gerard described it in 1597 as 'growing almost everiewhere through England'. Are these gaps simply a result of unsuitable soils or climate? Or have local customs and attitudes towards the plant influenced its distribution too? Has there been transplanting, or an unusual degree of protectiveness in some of its traditional sites – or conversely, over-picking where it has vanished? Is there anywhere the flowers are still regarded as an economic crop, offered on a pay-at-the-gate and pick-your-own basis, as they were in the 1930s in the 'Golden Triangle' in Gloucestershire? The Great Western Railway used to run weekend 'Daffodil Specials' down to this stretch of country between Dymock and Newent, which provided a strong financial incentive to local landowners to look after their flowery meadows and orchards.

Now, by one of those ironies of history, the 'Lent lily's' fortunes may be changing. The fashion for wild gardens has made it a popular species in cultivation, and there are already signs that it is escaping back into the wild from these cosseted colonies. It is a perfect symbol of the versatility and resilience of nature, and of the ancient relationship between plants and ourselves.

ART AND ECOLOGY

Art and Ecology (1991)

Goethe's artist Young Werther, in one of his less tragic moods, believed that it might be possible to understand the mysteries of existence if only he could lose himself in nature, at its literal grass roots:

> When I lie in the tall grass and, closer thus to the earth, become conscious of the thousand varieties of little plants; when I feel the swarming of all that diminutive world among the blades . . . when I feel these closer to my heart, and feel the presence of the Almighty who created us in His image . . . then how often, longingly, do I say to myself: 'Ah! if you could but express, if you could but bring to life again on paper, the feeling that pulses so richly, so warmly within you, so that it might become the mirror of your soul . . .'

Seeking heaven – or at least revelation – in a wild flower, hoping to comprehend or portray the universe through its 'minute particulars', has been one of the fundamental impulses of green-tinged art and philosophy. Behind it is a belief that there is some kind of unity in nature, and that the complicated patterns and associations of the whole are echoed, or crystallised, in its smallest fragments.

This assumption has been the gathering ground for all kinds of disparate holistic creeds, from the toughly political to florid New Age paganism. Yet increasingly they have science on their side. Modern biology is more and more inclined to see organisms and their environments as whole entities. One does not have to be a hardline Gaian nowadays to accept that all living things are linked through the great commonweals of air and water. Or that evolution might have proceeded not just by the repeated outstripping of the poorly adapted by the fit and flexible, but by all kinds of marriages of convenience, symbioses and combinations. Even our own cells can no longer be appropriated as our private property. We are, as the American biologist Lewis Thomas has said, 'shared, rented, occupied'. The interior of our cells is a cooperative of minute, independent creatures that swam together for mutual convenience aeons ago, and stayed that way. The picture of the cell community increasingly resembles one of those hybrid, mythological chimeras – the griffin, sphinx, centaur, and the like – with which the world's bestiaries are full, and which seem to represent an intuitive understanding that the evolution of life on earth has been a matter of cooperation as well as competition.

Modern biology is full to bursting with artistic resonance and mythic power, yet it seems barely to have shown its head in the ongoing debate about the relationship between science and art. The arguments have been preoccupied with the teachings of modern physics and the psychology of perception, and have had an arid, reductionist feel about them. Both sides seem, paradoxically, to be locked into an antiquely dualistic world. There is Art and there is Nature. There is an Artist and an Art Object and a Viewer, having – though more often it sounds like *consuming* – Aesthetic Experiences, shaped by either deep neural structures or human experience.

But is this the end of it? Can't artistic transactions also be untidy, diffuse, mutable? Aren't they often expressions of instinctive outrage or passages of pure play as much as divinations of structural beauty? And isn't one of the clearest analogies of artistic activity the protean business of biological evolution itself?

Any art which is open to these kinds of ideas is already beginning to be biologically sensitive. Ecology is a more complicated matrix, as it has, in popular understanding at least, a moral as well as a descriptive component. Art informed by ecology would have to reflect holistic views and consciously try to harmonise its own processes with those of the natural world. The flow of images and ideas between the disciplines would also be two-way, with the art helping to illuminate and criticise the science, to highlight its ethical dilemmas and insights, every bit as much as the reverse.

The vision of a harmonious creation has been one of the universal grails of art. Young Werther's dream itself had been perfectly, if pedantically, realised two and a half centuries earlier by his fellow countryman Dürer. In *Large Tuft of Herbs*, Dürer created an exquisitely detailed portrait of a single square foot of grassland, in which the remarkable features are not just the liveliness and accuracy of the individual plants but the fact that they are patently contributing to each other's lives. The dandelions and plantains are flowering, bending, propping each other up, finding their niches, fading and seeding, living in both time and space.

Today the picture has the look of a vivid and accomplished botanical illustration, ecological with a small 'e'. But in 1503 it presupposed a view of nature as an autonomous, complex and mutually supportive creation that was two hundred years ahead of its time.

Landscape painting has had a long fascination with holism since at least the fourteenth century, when the early Italian calendar studies por-trayed whole environments at precise moments of the year, complete with their proper crops and working peasants. Visions of an interdependent nature crop up in the most surprising places, in surrealism and magic realism for instance. Henri Rousseau's invented jungles, for all their fantastic plastic blossoms and neatly pruned trees, have a compelling sense of rightness and mutuality. They *work*. And even the bleakest of Paul Nash's wartime landscapes (*Totes Meer*, for instance, with the wrecked planes metamorphosing into sand-dunes) seem to offer the possibility of a resilient, Gaian regrowth out of chaos.

But though these works catch glimpses of a holistic world, one huge unanswered question stands out from all of them. Where do *we*, as humans, stand in relation to these scenes, to the exterior world of nature? Where, more specifically, does the artist stand? It is one thing to make connections out of chaos, to fabricate unified landscapes, to create surface worlds in which the shortcomings of nature and the destructiveness of man have been flushed out. (Some would say that this is precisely what art is *for*.) But the evidence of the works in this tradition – finished, immutable, fixed in their frames – is unequivocal. They are monuments to a relationship in which the artist is in absolute control of nature. However artistically satisfying they may be on their own terms they do not even address ecology's central ethical conundrum – how we may reconcile our special, distinguishing abilities as a uniquely creative kind of animal with democratic membership of the planetary community; how to be simultaneously the self-conscious artist and the aggregated amoeba.

Lewis Thomas has explored the ramifications of this paradox as eloquently as anyone, and in his celebrated essay 'Natural Man' he has described how we have been through at least two revolutions in thought about our relationship to nature. The oldest and most comfortable idea was that the earth was man's personal property, to be ordered, tamed, consumed as we wished. Then came the Ecological Enlightenment, when there was a recognition that we were part of the system, as dependent on the health of the rest as trees or tadpoles. Now, whilst still believing in this new wisdom, we have come back to the realisation that, like it or not, we are in charge. He could very well be writing about the history of art in the late modern period:

It is a despairing prospect. Here we are, practically speaking twenty-first-century mankind, filled to exuberance with our new understanding of kinship to all the family of life, and here we are, still nineteenth-century man, walking boot-shod over the open face of nature, subjugating and civilising it. And we cannot stop this controlling, unless we vanish under the hill ourselves . . . The truth is we have become more deeply involved than we ever dreamed. The fact that we sit around as we do, worrying seriously about how best to preserve the life of the earth, is itself the sharpest measure of our involvement. It is not human arrogance that has taken us in this direction, but the most natural of natural events. We developed this way, we grew this way, we are this kind of species . . . Perhaps, in the best of all possible worlds, functioning as a kind of nervous system for the whole being. (*The Lives of a Cell*, 1974)

But this existential balancing act is one that we haven't mastered yet, and the reluctance of artists to grapple with it is a reflection of its difficulty. Only the group that, for want of a better label, are called 'land artists' – Richard Long, Michael Fairfax, Andy Goldsworthy, David Nash, John Maine, *et al.* – who are working directly with living materials, often *in situ*, seem to be exploring different energy flows and power structures in the relationship between humans and nature, which is echoed in that between artist and subject.

Land art's long and eclectic range of influences lies in craftsmanship and writing as much as in the fine arts. In landscape painting a movement towards less anthropocentric work was characterised by closer and more equitable engagements with the subject. First the move down from the elevated, literally superior, viewpoint of the classic Claudian prospect; then an increasing emphasis on dense, detailed foregrounds as against formal but vague distances. Some of John Sell Cotman's extraordinary Yorkshire watercolours (1805–7) in which the larger, *knowing* view is wilfully obstructed by teeming foreground vegetation, are as far along this line of development as it was possible to go without abandoning the canvas altogether.

The writing of the Romantics forms another important strand, exploring as it does the idea that humans may experience *themselves* as nature, as objects as well as subjects. Thomas Gray's celebrated account from the 1760s of a visit to Gordale Scar at Malham, in which he shudders for 'a full quarter of an hour' under the waterfall and the 'loose stones . . . which hang in the air, and threaten visibly', was an early if gushing example of this change in sensibility.

This sense that the observer can himself be the canvas was taken much further by Coleridge half a century later. His account of becoming stuck on a ledge during a hair-raising climb up Eskdale in 1802 is a crucial text:

my whole Limbs [were] in a *Tremble* . . . I lay upon my Back to rest myself, & was beginning according to my Custom to laugh at myself for a Madman, when the sight of the Crags above me on each side, & the impetuous Clouds just over them, posting so luridly & so rapidly northward, overawed me/ I lay in a state of almost prophetic Trance & Delight – & blessed God aloud, for the powers of Reason & the Will . . . I arose, & looking down saw at the

bottom a heap of Stones – which had fallen abroad – and rendered the narrow
Ledge on which they had been piled doubly dangerous/ at the bottom of the
third Rock that I dropt from, I met a dead Sheep quite rotten – This heap of
Stones, I guessed, & have since found that I guessed aright, had been piled
up by the Shepherd to enable him to climb up & free the poor creature whom
he had observed to be crag-fast – but seeing nothing but rock over rock, he
had desisted & gone for help – & in the mean time the poor creature had
fallen down & killed itself. – As I was looking at these I glanced my eye to
my left, & observed that the Rock was rent from top to bottom – I measured
the breadth of the Rent, and found that there was no danger of my being
wedged in/ so I put my Knap-sack round to my side, & slipped down as
between two walls, without any danger or difficulty . . . so I began to descend/
when I felt an odd sensation across my whole Breast . . . and on looking saw
the whole of my Breast from my Neck to my Navel – & exactly all that my
Kamell-hair Breast-shield covers, filled with great red heat-bumps, so thick
that no hair could lie between them . . . startling proof to me of the violent
exertions which I had made.

There are foretastes of all kinds of later preoccupations here: signs and
portents in the landscape; the journey as an emotional record (the letter
could easily be hung in a modern gallery as 'A Vertical Walk in the
Lakes'); nature acting apparently benignly towards humans. Later that
year Coleridge wrote: 'Everything has a Life of its own . . . we are all *one
Life*.'

Another root is in the craftsmen who carved the decorative, naturalistic
foliage that adorns many Gothic cathedrals (notably in this country at
Southwell Minster). In their delight in ornamentation, in taking natural
forms (the fingered leaf is their favourite motif) and making them pro-
liferate, join, evolve, play and mutate, they reached a harmonious
marriage between human and natural invention. Perhaps the one misunderstanding in John Ruskin and Peter Fuller's love of Gothic was seeing
only its austere, reverential aspect, the product of spiritual devotion and
hard work. Yet Gothic was also satirical, impish, exuberant, thoroughly
immersed in *aesthesis* as well as *theoria*. And to this extent it more
truthfully reflected the natural processes which inspired it.

It is dangerous to take value descriptions too literally when talking
about the natural world. But there is no doubt that for every aspect of
natural creation that is brusquely functional there are others that are
capricious, prolific, almost whimsical. The idea that nature is frugal and
sternly purposeful, abhorring waste and pointlessness, is a product of
puritanism and the work ethic more than of biology. More often it is
profligate and experimental. The point about natural selection is not that

it always picks the high-fliers, the most perfectly adapted, the winners, but simply that it excludes the unworkable.

As a result (and accepting the absence of intention) the objective business of natural evolution is barely distinguishable from the business of artistic decoration. They are both part of that instinctive creativity that goes with being a living creature, of Dylan Thomas' 'force that through the green fuse . . .'; both inventive explorations of matter and possibility, not of meaning. Function and concept follow, they do not precede, natural creativity. Leaves fray at the edge, split into pairs, join up, multiply, change colour, drop off. Feathers are washed with iridescence and tonal change beyond any useful purpose. Feet grow supports, spikes and joints, with all the abandon of an animated cartoon, and it is only later that these accoutrements may come in useful for gripping branches, balancing upright on the ground, running, kicking. And provided they don't actually disadvantage an organism these inventions persist, as pure embellishment. This kind of extravagant diversity is, in the global scale of things, nature's great defence against extinction and entropy. To that extent artistic ornamentation for its own sake has the highest sanction from nature, and, perhaps, something of the sacramental about it.

Land artists may feel that their inspiration comes chiefly from the Romantics, but the way they work seems to me to belong to the Gothic tradition. Like the Gothics they are celebrating natural forms more than human feelings. And much of their work follows a standard pattern, beginning with a natural object, adding a 'human quickening' and then allowing nature to decide the final form or fate of the work. What evolves is neither strictly man-made nor natural, but is again a hybrid, an exploration of that artistically and politically crucial hinterland between two types of creativity.

Andy Goldsworthy is the most accessible and prolific of this group. Much of his work is a challenge to the idea of the immutable art object, and celebrates transience, natural weathering and decay, the slow dissolution of one form into another. Even whilst they are still intact, his ice bridges and monumental sand-castles are mercurial, changing with every declension of light and weather. Other works explore the qualities and potentialities of plants, probing their boundaries in time and space. A snowball, kept until midsummer, melts to disgorge a winter's cargo of fir cones, daffodils, stones and debris. Chestnut and plane leaves are sewn together by pine needles or thorns, into the forms of boxes, horns, pyramids. They have a bewildering lightness and resilience that seems beyond the qualities of either leaves or boxes. They are *evolved* forms. Andy

Goldsworthy's relationship with his material is like that of a rogue twist of DNA or a benign virus with its host cell. He worms his way into a bunch of twigs or a leaf, and sparks off new developments and mutations, new possibilities. What the subject provides, or how it responds, is as important as the distinctive style of invention that Goldsworthy brings to it.

Richard Long, by contrast, brings almost nothing of himself to his works:

> [it] is simple and practical ... I like the idea of using the land without possessing it ... My work has become a simple metaphor of life. A figure walking down his road, making his mark. It is an affirmation of my human scale and senses: how far I walk, what stones I pick up, my particular experiences. Nature has more common means: walking, placing, stones, sticks, water, circles, lines, days, nights, roads.

This sounds ecologically impeccable, a prescription for an art that 'treads lightly on the earth', and it has produced some poignant works, especially the ephemeral 'water drawings'. Yet I wonder if it has any place in a gallery. What Long describes is the commonplace, vernacular art of the outdoors, the universal habit of arranging twigs, skimming stones, recounting journeys in the pub at the end of the day. To elevate and frame this as fine art-work, is to make a very unecological appropriation of common cultural property.

Ironically, Long's insistence on minimal intervention, also undervalues *human* creativity – the quality that both Coleridge (who 'blessed God ... for the powers of Reason & the Will') and Lewis Thomas recognise as essential for any harmonious resolution of our clouded relationships with nature.

In the end David Nash impresses as having most successfully married a powerful personal vision to a respect for the independent life of nature. He works almost exclusively in wood, which he sees as 'a weaving of earth and light'. The results are muscular explorations of the nature of wood and the way it warps, cracks and weathers, that at times almost transcend its inherent woodiness. Nash's elephant's trunk *Ubus* (titled after playwright Jarry's caricatures of royalty) are even able to joke at the occasional inelegance of tree growth. His *Ash Dome* incorporates still-growing material (a hemisphere of trained ash saplings) into the work. His *Comet Ball* is a large, aboriginal, almost comic-book cone, with the rough-carved head charred in a bonfire, and is such a stunning, elemental image that you feel it has come from a time when the natural world – wood, fire and fantasy – was all of a piece. And like the exhilarating series of *Running Tables* it comes close to that ancient, benevolent myth – symbol of a cooperative evolution and of the artistic process – the mixed life-form, the hybrid, the optimistic chimera.

Christo (1991)

What a wonderful caper to have a show based chiefly on 'Projects Not Realised'! The idea could catch on. We could have recitals of fugues that never got beyond their subjects; anthologies (I have a promisingly thick file myself) of authors' aborted synopses. But with Christo, of course, it matters less if the work is finally complete, since so much of the power lies at a purely conceptual level, in the sheer, grandiloquent impertinence of his ideas.

He started modestly enough, with simple *Wrapped Objects* in 1958. It was when he had the vision of putting something as substantial as a whole building or a geological formation in wraps that he became a public figure, and grist to every kind of cultural theorist. His work was the apotheosis of consumerism; a satire on it; he was a Marxist, exploring the 'objectification' of the physical world, or just a conjuror with rather large silk handkerchiefs.

One of the 'unrealised' projects is a good example of the ambivalence of his work, and how it scarcely needs to be finished to make its point. In 1968 he had a scheme for packing the Allied Chemical Tower in Times Square. The scale model is a delicious dig at this austere cathedral of the science business, and bundles it roughly up in polythene and twine like a delivery from the garden centre. Some, though, may see it as a homage to the building, or a comment on the secret mysteries of chemical structure, or a sexually political statement on the arrogance of capitalism's masculine spires. Christo's work is, in McLuhan's terms, decidedly 'soft'. The one incontestable element is a good deal of benign fun at other people's expense. Confronting a Christo is always like waking up in Gotham and finding City Hall cloaked in pink satin. Is it really the Riddler, or just the Joker?

But the works in progress are more problematic. Taking shape on a huge scale in the real world, their indiscriminateness and lack of decisive purpose can turn into political naivety or social affront. No one but a killjoy could object to the Umbrellas Project, in which, for three weeks this October [1991], 3,100 coloured parasols will sprout like cocktail decorations simultaneously in valleys in California and eastern Japan. But I'm relieved 'Wrapped Trees, Project for the Champs Elysées' never saw the light of day, even temporarily. The rows of muffled limes and planes have, in the sketches at least, a miserly, municipal look, like a bureaucrat's way of keeping bird droppings off the parked Citroëns.

Events in the real world quite properly affect the meanings of public art. Christo's scheme for wrapping the Reichstag – 'a physical encounter of two values of life and human existence' – was first mooted in 1972. The recent tumultuous events in Eastern Europe have given new significance to what Christo regards as an indomitable 'symbol of Democracy'. Even his proposed materials seem serendipitously to prophesy the raising of the Iron Curtain, and make one look forward to the fourteen days this September when the work will be in place: 'The shiny light-coloured fabric will enlarge the size of the structure, it will be almost 30 per cent more voluminous, the folds of the fabric will take the force and direction of the wind and will make the building strangely and constantly breathing.'

But history has been less kind to 'The Mastaba of Abu Dhabi'. Since the Gulf War this plan for a giant pyramidal anthem to oil has come to seem in thoroughly bad taste. Constructions from barrels have been one of Christo's preoccupations, and back in 1962 they had another (ironic, now) meaning, when he built an *Iron Curtain-Wall of Oil Barrels* to block the Rue Visconti in Paris. Currently he is stacking 390,500 oil barrels for the Abu Dhabi project: 'Nothing comparable has ever existed in any other country. Hundreds of bright colours, as enchanting as the Islamic mosaics, will give a constantly changing visual experience according to the time of the day and the quality of the light.' Its intention, he says, is to be 'the symbol of civilisation of oil throughout the world' – a vision which certainly puts Mrs Thatcher's rhapsodies over 'the great car economy' in their place.

What this kind of declamatory art needs, I reckon, is not fewer public associations but more. One of the best aspects of Christo's works is the huge degree of popular involvement in their actual construction. The Mayles brothers' ebullient documentaries have caught this well, especially the joyous, communal raising of the famous *Running Fence* in California – 2 million square feet of nylon stretching over 24 miles. These events put Christo in a long tradition of outdoor vernacular art that includes England's chalk-hill carvings – which were scraped out by vast armies of workers, and in an atmosphere probably rather similar.

But it is worth remembering that public participation didn't end there, and that locals went on tinkering and scouring for centuries. It now looks, for instance, that the famously vast penis of the Cerne Abbas Giant was once a more modest organ, joined up with his navel by nineteenth-century Dorset rowdies bent on scandalising the local clergy. Demystifying Abu Dhabi's 'symbol of civilisation of oil' would be a more perilous business, but in a fine and ancient tradition.

Don McCullin, *Open Skies* (1989)

When he was five years old, Don McCullin, doyen of war photographers, was evacuated to Somerset, and imprinted with a memory of a pastoral England drowsy with blossom and Arthurian echoes. Half a century later and spiritually exhausted by the sight of human corpses and bomb-wrecked land, he has been stalking the fields round Glastonbury again, searching for that lost domain. His solace, he explains, 'lies in recording what remains of the beautiful landscape of Somerset and its metallic dark skies'. *Open Skies* is his photographic elegy to those remains.

But McCullin is a haunted man. Images of starving Biafrans and shell-shocked GIs still 'ferment in my darker self' and cast a shadow over his landscape pictures. This collection is full of elemental Somerset scenes – distant swans in the empty Levels, the sweeps of dairy country below the Tors and Roman temples, tangled ditches, flooded cart-tracks. But they are dark, depopulated, trapped in winter. Far from reflecting the 'open skies' of the title, they cower under oppressive cloud. Louring cumuli seep like bloodstains above the horizon of 'The real English countryside, Somerset, 1988'; the Dorset borderlands seem to tilt under the force of a hailstorm.

This is a faithful, albeit relentless, view of a kind of countryside not often admitted in the tourist brochures. But as John Fowles suggests in his introduction, it is less a view of East Somerset than of a state of mind, 'the subjective reflection of an uneasy spirit'. And Fowles stresses another undercurrent of meaning in these bleak prospects. McCullin has not really given up war photography at all, but is now recording that 'most terrible and senseless conflict . . . between man and his own environment'.

This is a weighty project for photography to bear. Symbolism can easily collapse into contrivance or melodrama. (I hope 'Peaceful fields under threat of development' – in which a checkerboard Somerset lies beneath a cloud of such fearful symmetry that all it lacks is a few avenging angels – is intended as a joke.) Realism can fade into ambivalence from, ironically, its sheer immediacy, its lack of history and context. In 'Burnham-on-Sea, with the dreaded Hinkley Point Power Station in background', the dreaded pile, lit up by a shaft of sunlight in the distance, looks as innocent as a standing stone. In 'The unacceptable face of bad land management', the fertiliser bags and debris strewn around a dyke have, in the leaden light, the look of huge windblown leaves.

In all this gloom it is impossible not to be reminded of John Ruskin's spiritual crisis in the 1870s, when he became convinced he could detect a black storm-cloud stationed over the country. He described its effects as 'Blanched sun – blighted grass – blinded man', and said he felt 'disconsolate . . . as if it was no use fighting for a world any more in which there could be no sunrise'. This was the despair of a man who had lost his faith not just in a human reconciliation with nature, but in nature itself.

There is something of the same hopelessness in McCullin's Somerset photographs. It is not that they are monotonous or morbid – indeed there is a compelling, almost runic fascination about them – but that they are indiscriminate. In the end, their obsessive, dark motif dominates and levels out the vitality of nature almost as surely as the forces it is directed against. But one conspicuous exception is 'Wintry morning sun', a fieldscape much of whose foreground is occupied by a bramble patch. It is hunched and bristly, like a Green Man or an ancient sea-urchin that is about to be warmed back into life by the rising sun. It is an oddly cheering picture, and it may be no coincidence that it is the only one to have a close and sympathetically observed detail rather than generalised background scenery – just the kind of feature that gives even the most harrowing of McCullin's war photographs their sense of hope and humanity.

Tony Evans (1992)

A couple of months ago I was browsing over a dilapidated map of the Cotswolds when I noticed a scatter of faintly pencilled plant names between the mud stains. 'Alkanet' and 'Dames violet' hovered above the villages between Barton and Lower Slaughter. 'May' was ringed in thick circles over half a square mile of hillside near Winchcombe. I suddenly realised it was the map Tony Evans and I had shared on one of our plant-hunting expeditions, marked up with sites for Tony to visit later with his camera. And in a trice I could remember every detail of that spring foray – the drifts of escaped alkanet dotting the village lanesides; the one perfect clump we found against a dry-stone wall, with its clear blue flowers caught up in lacy nets of fading cow parsley; and the hill called Belas Knapp, from which we scanned the billowing rows of hawthorn blossom – H. E. Bates' 'risen cream of May-time' – marking out the contour lines and field boundaries.

Tony died of cancer in the spring of 1992, having almost single-handedly rescued plant photography from the dark ages. I knew him as a dear friend, and we spent six summers on the road together, working on our cultural history of wild plants, *The Flowering of Britain* (1980). It was a transforming experience for me – a voyage of discovery of my home country, a first taste of the joys of fieldwork, and above all a process of learning and exchange about different ways of looking at the natural world.

We met exactly twenty years ago. I was a tyro writer, fresh from *Food For Free*, and Tony, a few years older than me, was already one of the most distinguished figures in commercial photography, famous for his meticulousness, his weakness for gadgets, his immense expenses bills and anarchic sense of humour. His *Radio Times* cover photo for the Royal Variety Performance – a corgi emerging from a top hat – is still one of the best photographic jokes. But he was restless, and longed to do more meaningful and intellectually rewarding work.

It was the editor of *Nova* magazine, Gillian Cooke, who brought us together, to collaborate on a feature on the troubled fortunes of our wild flowers. Tony came over with his wife, Caroline, to discuss the project with me in the early spring. We hit it off from the outset, and by the end of the day I was confiding to him my dream of a book that would go beyond the *Nova* feature, and celebrate in words and pictures the role which wild plants had played in our human and physical landscape.

Within a couple of weeks Tony had been on a trip to the wild daffodil country round Dymock in Gloucestershire, and brought back an astonishing portfolio of pictures. They were unlike any wild flower photographs I had seen before. The daffodils rippled in deep focus over the floor of an ancient oak coppice, buoyed up the walls of a medieval church, jostled along trackways and boundary banks. It was as if Tony's film was sensitive not just to light, but to all the historical and ecological resonances of a place. And in one study, that troubled me initially because of its unashamed revelling in the sheer *look* of the plants, he had filled the frame with a whole troop, animated, glowing, all facing the same way – Wordsworth's golden host to a T.

I was confident that we could do the book together, yet I think I initially envied the initiative and insight that had helped him find the core of the daffodil's character so quickly. (I had never even *seen* one at this time.) I rationalised the feeling as a worry that he might be too much in awe of pure composition. He doubtless found my over-intellectual view as to what constituted a 'good' plant picture equally worrying, not to say impertinent.

That slight tension between our respective ways of looking at the natural world came to the surface on our first field trip together a few weeks later. We'd travelled to the Bradfield Woods in Suffolk, to try for oxlips. But the auguries weren't good. The oxlips were past their best and thinner on the ground than usual. I was embarrassssed at getting the dates wrong, and made all kinds of excuses for myself, for the plant, for the whole philosophy of the book. When we did find a clump big and fresh enough to warrant a picture, I was hugely relieved, and considered that my contribution to the process was finished. I was all for moving on and finding something else, a wild pear tree or herb paris, perhaps. With a head full of romantic ideas about plants as symbols and indicators, the mere presence of the oxlips seemed sufficient for me.

But not for Tony. He insisted that I sat still and explained to him what we *needed* from this plant. And as we talked, he began to assemble his own vision of this oxlip, not just as a member of a species with an ecological history, but as a unique and particular individual, with its own character and its own relations with the light, the weather, its neighbours and this moment in the wood. It was a perspective which sowed in me a new awareness of the immediacy and vitality of plants, and which shines through in Tony's finished oxlip picture. A clump of more than a dozen flower spikes rises like a sheaf, ungardened and luxuriant, in the left foreground. It is tangled up with dead twigs, young meadowsweet leaves and the flaying stalks of tussock grass. Behind it, caught by a wide-angle lens, the ancient coppice shears away towards the sky. The oxlips aren't just in the wood, they are *of* it.

We spent the next six springs and summers exploring places like this, always trying to discover scenes that showed plants in their ecological and cultural contexts. In the flat reaches of the Norfolk Broads we stalked fenland species from a boat, trying to catch the weaving and windiness of the lush vegetation. In the highlands of western Argyll we failed dismally to reach any true alpines but found mountain plants growing at sea level on the balmy west coast, on a day so hot that we both spent much of the time under Tony's pink photographic parasol. We pored over Suffolk estate maps tracing Saxon boundaries that were still marked by pollard elms and poplars. And in Westmorland we walked gingerly over the sun-baked and glacier-scoured limestone pavements of Underbarrow Scar, marvelling at plants that seemed to be growing out of bare rock. We seemed to be blessed by perpetual sunshine in those mid-seventies summers, and I remember resting between the dwarf junipers and bloody cranesbills on that north-western trip to eat wild strawberries which had been turned into melting beads of sweetness by the heat.

During the height of the flowering season we lived like a couple of botanical gypsies. We travelled and worked from Tony's dormobile, which was stocked not just with dozens of aluminium cases of equipment and a comprehensive botanical library, but hoards of the kinds of gadgets Tony found irresistible: an altimeter to tell when it was worth searching for alpines, ski-stick ends to support tripod legs on boggy ground, his famous custom-built portable wind-tents, electronic (and quite useless) mosquito repellents. One summer evening in Sussex we chanced on some glow-worms near our hotel. Tony stayed up late taking time exposure portraits of them, having found that their diminutive lamps registered on his specialist Weston lightmeter.

Fortuitousness of this kind was a feature of our trips. There were tip-offs in pubs; unexpected vistas glimpsed in the driving mirror. In Oxford we found Oxford ragwort growing in a bottle-strewn waste patch in front of a line of posters advertising the arrival of the circus in Oxford. (And only Tony had the charm to explain to an increasingly resentful band of local denizens and winos why his camera was pointed towards the gents' convenience all day.)

Yet if there was serendipity, there was also a routine of a kind. Joe Cocker tapes to keep Tony awake when he was at the wheel. Long picnic lunches, with cheap white wine (river-cooled, if we were lucky) over which we would hold Socratic debates about the progress of the project and the rest of the day's work. I think that after a couple of years we had learned a good deal from each other. I had started to come out of my archival shell where plants were chiefly signs and landmarks, and begun to revel a bit more sensuously in the wild thyme. Tony, for his part, was absorbing the idea that plants had landscape and historical contexts, and beginning to express this in the most subtle of ways. His portrait of five marsh marigold flowers peeping between the gnarled roots of an ancient tree stump is strangely evocative of a great ecological crisis six millennia ago, when the climate chilled and wettened and the great forests began to decline, but is a long way from being a dull lecture slide.

Yet even when we were working most closely, I like to think that we found and respected the limits of our different skills: writing, an organised, narrative, essentially abstract business that hopefully reaches out towards the specific; and photography, rooted in moment and particularity, but striving towards general statements.

It is easy to forget what plant photography was like in the sixties. There were landscape pictures and – always separate – there were close-ups, usually flash-lit or taken against contrast screens. They had the look of plants in glass cases, devoid of growth and setting and atmosphere. Tony never used a flash in his wild flower photography, and barely ever arranged his subject for a 'better' shot. Instead he would spend hours – days sometimes – looking for an example that would, *in itself*, say everything that we both wanted to convey. He used trees as backcloths to isolate a single bloom from a mass (as in his bluebell picture from Dorset). He relied on the complications of leaves in hedgebanks and woods to provide the depth and shading in his pictures – exactly as they did in an ecosystem. His field poppy – probably the best known of all his pictures – is a brilliant example of the use of focus to convey time. I had rather hoped to have poppies glowing amongst golden corn, but Tony had glimpsed something much less clichéd – that the whole cycle and texture of a poppy's life could be contained in a single picture. In sharp focus are the fully open flowers and seed-heads (one entwined by black bindweed). In the foreground engorged buds droop, while at the rear, out-of-focus flowers – floppy, translucent, like 'painted glass' as Ruskin suggested – merge into a dappled mist of green stalks.

His patience and persistence were extraordinary. His portrait of the historic pollard elms in the village of Knapwell, Cambridgeshire took a week of customised weather forecasts and at least four day trips to the site. Tony wanted (and eventually got) a thin, early morning mist, a natural gauze filter, that would emphasise the elms' monumental quality and hint at both their antiquity and their uncertain future. The unplanned feature was the white horse that posed with almost Arthurian resonance amongst the trees.

We did not always get such good results. We were in the Derbyshire Dales in 1974, just nosing around. It was another baking day, and climbing up towards Lathkill Dale Tony suddenly stopped, pulled the scissors out of his immense rucksack of equipment and said, 'Cut my legs off, Rich.' Later we found an extraordinary colony of columbines, both blue and white, growing on a steep slope, and Tony, now wearing nothing but his newly beshortened jeans, set to work on them under the fierce sun. He stayed in the same spot for the next six hours, and I watched him with increasing anxiety, as he rotated slowly round the columbines like a sundial's shadow (or maybe like heliotrope: I always felt at times like this that Tony *became* the plant). But the picture didn't work. The columbines looked gangly and parched, sticking to the short grass on the hill. I understand why now, since they are really woodland plants, and as Tony always insisted, you cannot photograph what is not there.

But we had our best times among limestone plants and landscapes. They had a frankness and vivacity that suited us both. Near Shap, not really knowing what we were looking for, we tracked down bird's-eye primroses on the very dome of the fells, in grassland shining honey and silvery under the late June sun. And in the Burren in County Clare, during our long stay in 1977, Tony took perhaps his most evocative picture, of burnet roses around a flat limestone rock. In the rock is a puddle, like a tiny turlough, and on its dead-calm surface a reflection of the sun is surrounded by white rose petals. It is a picture of the whole Burren in miniature.

When Tony died I was going through a bad patch of my own, regretting a life that seemed too small and solitary. Grieving for him forced me to remember those times we had together, the unique experiences we shared and I hope communicated to others, and most of all the exhilaration of knowing him as a friend and as an apostle for the living. His last words to me, when I enquired anxiously about his health just weeks before his death were, '*Today*, I am very well.' Now, whenever I sense cynicism or over-intellectualism stealing up, I recall Tony's sheer delight at a single dandelion flower in a plain green field. This June in the Burren [1993] I think I found the exact spot where he took his burnet rose picture. It was as hauntingly beautiful as ever, but needless to say, totally different from Tony's picture – which remains a triumphant record of a unique, unrepeatable moment that no one can take away.

The Painter as Naturalist (1994)

The painter of nature, as distinct from the painter of, say, landscapes or vegetable still lifes, has a never-ending tussle with the subject's intransigence. Nature, by definition, simply refuses to 'sit'. It escapes, wilts, metamorphoses, dies, and quite often turns on the hapless portrayer. Even demure botanical draughtsmen aren't exempt. Sydney Parkinson, son of a Quaker brewer, was the artist on Cook and Banks' historic expedition to Australia in *The Endeavour*. In Tahiti he sat on a beach and tried to paint in a cloud of flies so thick they not only covered his paper but ate the paint off it. In the 1750s, Georg Ehret collapsed whilst trying to draw the highly toxic and 'effluvious' hemlock water-dropwort in a closed room.

All these alien and generally uncooperative traits in organic creation have nurtured a common fascination with technicalities among natural history artists (these days seen most graphically in the obsession of documentary film-makers with the mechanics of slow-motion and extreme close-up). It is as if there was a 'fix' or frame which could catch the essential, obdurate life of wild things; or a conviction that they only really exist for humans as form or function. Ruskin despised attempts to reach an artistic understanding of the way nature *worked*, and made a famously snide comment about the worthlessness of seeing leaves as 'gasometers'. But his own view, that the art of nature should be concerned 'only with appearances', seems scarcely any different. Both attitudes sidestep an assumption that is almost automatic in other fields of 'naturalistic' art: that representation should also be concerned with meaning, with the feelings of the artist about the subject, and – to the extent that it can be intuited in a non-human – with the *subject's* feelings also.

Of course, it can hardly fail to do so accidentally, as Madeleine Pinault's sumptuous anthology demonstrates. But *The Painter as Naturalist* is historiography rather than analysis or criticism, exhaustive on such matters as patrons and collections and the evolution of techniques, and the author skates over questions about the relationship between artist and subject. But then, in the period on which she has chosen to concentrate (roughly 1400 to 1840) so did the majority of artists themselves. By the mid-fifteenth century the dark ages of nature painting were more or less over. The straitjackets of both formal religion and pagan superstition were being loosened, artists no longer slavishly copied from each other or adhered to fables in classical texts, and for the first time, the mythological creatures of the bestiaries were being challenged by clear-eyed, real-life observations. Accuracy and faithfulness to the subject became the norm, but the artists of the Enlightenment had few doubts about their role in the hierarchy of creation. They were there to glorify God and his works, of which the greatest was Man, God's steward, the explorer, revealer and discipliner of the remainder of unruly nature.

Leonardo da Vinci's drawings set the pattern for the period, and in a way for the structure of Pinault's book. For Leonardo, drawing was not so much an end in itself as a means of scientific investigation, an anatomisation of nature. In his *Dissection of a Bear's Foot* (c. 1500) the long rapier claws are splayed and flattened, cut down to size. They have the look of a rake, or an abandoned set of scissors; much of the documentary nature painting done prior to the mid-nineteenth century similarly contains or subdues or anthropomorphically frames its subjects.

Madeleine Pinault uses some of the more formal devices and contexts as her chapter divisions. She uncovers a tradition of *trompe l'oeil*, and shows how Benjamin Smith Barton's watercolour *Dissection of a Rattle-snake* (1796) uses the split skin – pulled apart and pinned down – almost like a parchment screen to display the snake's organs. Later she cites a bizarre Georg Hoefnagel study of a *Mussel and Flower* (1596), in which the flower is painted as if it had been taped to the page, like an herbarium specimen. Shells were popular subjects, especially during the eighteenth and early nineteenth centuries, and Pinault suggests that of all nature's creations, they 'most fascinated painters by the beauty of their forms, colours and marking, their evocation of voyages, distant seas and exotica, their symbolism and mystery'. Perhaps just as pertinent was the fact that they didn't move, and that their sculpted, china-like forms resembled human artefacts more than most natural structures. They also made elegant ornaments for the 'cabinet' portraits which were a hybrid between the nature painting proper and the still life. Leroy de Barde's *Collection of Foreign Birds in Boxes* (1810) is little more than a minutely detailed record of a case of taxidermist's specimens (including sixteen individually stuffed partridge chicks), but at least the birds seem more animated than in Landseer's necrophiliac studies.

From the late seventeenth century the circular field of view of the microscope became another 'found setting' for fragments of skin, plant tissue, insects' legs. Franz Bauer, Kew Garden's first official painter-in-residence, prepared several collections of microscopical studies. The distinguished botanist James Bateman described his unpublished sketches of a grain of wheat in all its stages of growth as 'a national boon' whose publication ought to be undertaken and financed by the government. But

Bauer's *Illustrations of Orchidaceous Plants* (1830–8) was published, and in it Bauer worked close to the available limits of magnification (× 200 at times). His drawings of an orchid's sexual apparatus have a strange and occasionally grotesque beauty that confirmed contemporary belief that order reigned in even the smallest details of the plant world. And a cross-section of a *Bletia* orchid stalk, reconstructed to appear as if it were being viewed from an angle, has the oddly comforting appearance of a knot garden.

Gardens themselves were used as settings (theatres almost) for plant and landscape paintings. They provided an excuse for introducing humans into the picture, in their role as planters, tenders and organisers of the natural world. They were also centres where artists could make contact with scientists and explorers, and with the swelling cargoes of exotic and often bizarre plants which these were bringing back from around the world. Travel ought to have broadened the outlook of nature painters; but more often the harvests it yielded were simply warped and processed until they fitted into the prevailing ideology about nature. (Sometimes this was literally true, and that stretched, dachshund look of so many animal drawings of the eighteenth century was a consequence of their being drawn from skins desiccated after months of travel.) Even Sydney Parkinson, the most open-minded and unsentimental of artists, could not take an unedited view of Australian forest. His first sighting of the new continent, he noted in his journal, reminded him of the English shires: 'The country looked very pleasant and fertile; and the trees, quite free from underwood, appeared like plantations in a gentleman's park.'

But alongside all this reassuring, restraining portrayal, there was painting which took a more respectful and sympathetic view of nature. While Hans Holbein's *Bat* (c. 1530) was drawn as if it were crucified – 'an impure animal,' Pinault explains, 'associated with the devil and hell [and] the murky world of alchemy' – Marie-Thérèse Vien, two centuries later, could paint *Two Pigeons* as if they were truly communicating. Their beaks interlock, the breeze ruffles their neck feathers. They are comprehensible, fellow creatures.

Sometimes a simple shift in point of view made a dramatic difference. Dürer's famous and precocious *Large Tuft of Herbs* (1503) is observed from ground level, which gives each blade of grass and dandelion flower a startling significance. In Jacopo Ligozzi's towering study of an *Archangel angelica* plant (late sixteenth century), the artist has positioned himself directly under the huge umbels of seeds, which radiate against a cream sky. They are transformed by this insect eye's view, becoming awesome and cryptic, like some Byzantine astrolabe.

The most fascinating of these more sympathetic painters is Maria

Sybilla-Merian, whose extraordinary life seems to inform all her pictures. Born in Germany in 1647 into a family of artists and engravers, she showed an early talent for drawing plants and insects, and at the age of thirty-two published the first of three volumes on European insects. In 1685, after seventeen years of married life, she converted to a radical religious sect (the Labadists), left her husband and reverted to her maiden name. In 1698 she set sail with her daughter Dorothea for South America and spent two years travelling and painting in the barely explored forests of Surinam. The result was the magnificent *Metamorphosis Insectorum Surinamensium*. She was, as Pinault points out, especially fascinated by the phenomenon of metamorphosis, and in one of her works she traces the entire life cycle of a frog. The various stages – spawn, tadpoles, froglets – are lively, animated amphibians, their movement round the page guided by a sinuous aquatic plant, which suggests the flow of water. One endearing adolescent frog looks straight out at the viewer, and, in a nicely humorous moment, the full-grown animal is about to gulp one of Maria's favourite insects.

Perhaps Maria could be seen as a proto-Romantic. But Romanticism proper made nothing like the impact on natural history painting that it did on the art of landscape. A few botanical artists made Romantic flourishes – notably Marianne North, whose sumptuous, primitive, tropical flowerscapes, hung collectively as she intended at Kew, are a fantastic celebratory mural of a kind of floral Eden. But such an approach would collapse into melodrama or mawkishness if attempted for animals. Empathy with other creatures can be explored in literature, but seems to lose credibility when imaginatively pictured. Ironically, it is in animal photography that the naturalist and Romantic artist have most successfully come together, because of the *mana* of authenticity carried by the photograph.

Maurice Cockrill (1994)

Maurice Cockrill has been tuned in to cycles of regeneration and decay for most of his life. His own 'fragments of autobiography' repeatedly pick out – albeit with hindsight – moments of awakening and growth amongst ruins. In 1940, aged four, he was staying with relations in Hartlepool when his infant school was destroyed by night bombing. The next day he 'joined in the looting of thousands of coloured chalks and battered exercise books to draw on the jetty'. Five years later the family moved to the North Wales industrial belt, and Maurice, enthralled by his father's tales of the origins of pottery, dug raw clay out of a bank with his bare hands and made a rough pot. In 1961, as a mature art student in Wrexham, he lived out on the Welsh mountains, 'making a sketchbook of drawings, with Sutherland in mind, of the carcasses and skeletons of thousands of rabbits ravaged by myxomatosis' – a harrowing glimpse of one of our early, self-inflicted environmental wounds.

Cockrill is fifty-eight this year [1994] and has come to an acute awareness of the layers of meaning in the idea of 'generation'. He sees himself, without any self-pity, as approaching a state of degeneration, on the downside of the ageing curve. He has two adult sons, aged thirty-five and thirty-one, who are in the middle of that curve, and four years ago, had an unexpected bonus in the shape of a new son. William, he thinks, has helped to close the circle, and provided him with not just a new generation but, by proxy at least, a new beginning. He was also the young witness of an exploration which helped focus the theme of this collection. Cockrill has an ash tree in his south London garden, and the ground underneath it is littered with twigs raked out by pigeons. One day in the summer of 1993, moved by the same atavistic urge he had felt nearly fifty years before when his father told him stories of pot-makers, he scooped out handfuls of raw Lambeth clay from beneath the tree and began to mould them. He made archetypal landscapes, miniature hills quarried with pits and cliffs, and embedded with flints as nodes of growth. And into the clay he planted the ash twigs, cut and spliced roughly with the help of a kitchen knife (an echo, as it happens, of the ancient use of split ash trees to cure ruptured children – the child being passed through the split, which was then bound up). These aboriginal constructions figured the entire motif for the *Generation* sequence – earth, wound, healing, and new growth.

It would be hard to overestimate the importance of Cockrill's father – and of the whole idea of lineage and continuity – to his work. Cockrill senior – ex-bookie, ex-carpenter, nomadic construction site engineer, hard man and heavy drinker – died in 1970, before Maurice had truly got to know him. But Maurice calls him 'the maker' and still regards him as a hero. 'Sometimes I feel as if I have his wrists,' he says, holding his arms out like a boxer waiting for his gloves.

He is, in the fullest sense, a maker himself, not a conduit or channel or representer of another's creations. He revels in the physicality and exactness of paint, and in the heroic tradition of Titian, Rubens and van Gogh, and his ambition as a painter, though disarmingly simple, is aptly Promethean: 'I paint these pictures because I want to see them exist in the world.'

But the way Cockrill makes his pictures isn't really as straightforward as that. If there is a single stylistic thread running through his work, it is the urgency and energy he brings to the business of painting, which in his hands takes on some of the qualities of organic growth. He once called his approach 'plastic automatism'. Yet he is a long way from being an instinctive action man. He takes pleasure in language, for instance, playing with the verbal associations of colour and coining ambivalent titles for his pieces. He talks with a rare willingness and intelligence about his paintings, and about their relationship with literature and philosophy. He has always been an avid reader – existentialism when he was a student, the Romantic poets and, recently, American nature writers like Edward O. Wilson and Annie Dillard.

Just how these different perspectives could counterpoint each other became clear from his early work. In the early 1980s, he produced two powerful sequences of mythological characters (including *Venus and Mars*, partly stimulated by Rubens' *Horrors of War*) set in wild, disquieting landscapes. And in 1992, he painted *Four Seasons*, landscapes without any figures at all – except that they are full of relics and echoes of human activity. Imagination and the land are impacted in them. They surge with life, and, closer-to, with more subtle poetic and ecological reference. In *Summer* (1990), enormous fruits, like strawberries (or vegetable hearts), float above hills of poppy-red and corn-yellow, which themselves confront an impenetrable wall of green. What looks like a field system is surrounded by hedgy tangles, and its grid of ploughlines echoes the icy, hard-edged crystalline forms which seem to grow and elaborate through the whole quartet. The colours are fierce and earthy, but wonderfully diverse. In *Winter*, a pewter snowstorm breaks out over a dark skein of spines. The dissociations, the compressions of time and place, the suggestiveness of forms (there are shells, leaves, seeds, and trees which transpire directly into clouds and then into an intense rain, as radiant as a beam of light in a Renaissance fresco) have a topographical logic of their own. They are expressionist, documentary, romantic, argumentative and symbolic all at once – exactly like one's experiences of the exterior landscape. They are a kind of subjective map. Cockrill is fond of David Sylvester's quote on Bomberg, that 'In the best landscapes we are fascinated by the mysterious shiftiness of the scene under our eyes . . . it has its own weird anima, and to our wide-eyed perception it changes like a living animal under our gaze.'

The new paintings carry this creative process one stage further. If the *Four Seasons* were metamorphosed landscape, the pictures in *Generation* go back to the roots, to the raw stuff of nature itself. Structurally, and in the way in which they evolve, they have some links with *Entrances*, the 1991 series which Cockrill produced by gashing cheap, mass-produced doors, and building up restorative layers of paint around the wounds.

The *Generation* series also have a dark centre, a kind of quarrying, in which a brighter nucleus begins to energise the growth of new forms out beyond the shadows. Above them, tiers of hook-like, runic forms seem to be pulling the growth, the regeneration, up towards the sky – except that, unlike most of his earlier paintings, there *is* no sky. Nor is there anything suggestive of the land or even a horizon. As whole pictures they are highly abstracted, and though they are full of zoomorphic forms, they don't have the voluptuous, sympathetic comfort of *Four Seasons*. These are unsettling and alien life forms, from deep under the sea or far back in the past, and sometimes, it seems, from the dissecting room. Yet the pictures' intricacy and flux give them an undeniable sense of life. When one of Maurice's older sons saw the series, he felt that Maurice had stepped back from landscape, and was painting whole metaphorical worlds. My first reaction was exactly the opposite, that he had gone into microscopic close-up, to focus on the painterly equivalent of primitive life: on bacteria and the living cell itself. Then I remembered the biologist Lewis Thomas' meditation on the revelation that, seen from space, planet earth did look like a cell:

> Viewed from the distance of the moon, the astonishing thing about the Earth, catching the breath, is that it is alive. The photographs show the dry pounded surface of the moon in the foreground, dead as an old bone. Aloft, floating free beneath the moist gleaming membrane of bright blue sky, is the rising earth, the only exuberant thing in this part of the cosmos . . . It has the organised, self-contained look of a live creature, full of information, marvellously skilled in handling the sun. (*The Lives of a Cell*, 1974)

Cockrill had begun the *Generation* sequence by experimenting in black and white, to highlight the structure he was seeking. But the results were lifeless, and at times the starkly formal motifs became too literal. The images with which he had been imprinted during his childhood in industrial Wales – slag heaps, crucibles of molten metal, quarry scars – entered some of the early roughs barely modified. His ascension hieroglyphs became, for a while, very obvious grapples, butchers'-hooks, crane gantries, hoists, even scrapyard magnets. The colour had to come back to broaden the frame of reference. He decided to use a different monochrome ground for each of the nine pictures, much as a composer might choose different key signatures and tempi to give varying moods to the movements in a work.

But they were also chosen for their affinities and associations. *Porphyry* is painted on a searing yellow ground (actually cinnabar green) inspired by the ancient volcanic rocks in the Massif des Maures region of southern France. The last of the nine pictures to be completed is entitled *Beyond*, which partially, and punningly, translates its ultra-marine setting and the brooding, bathyspheric shape which glides through it.

Cockrill is relaxed about the resemblances and allusions that are invariably sensed in his work. He sees them himself (and has one more to contend with after I admitted to glimpsing *One Foot in the Grave*'s mating turtles in *Virulence*). But they are neither wholly calculated nor wholly fortuitous. They emerge from the kind of person Cockrill is, and the way that he works. He absorbs influences, ideas and affinities much as a tree records its experience of weather in its grain. When, for example, he admits both Cézanne and Jackson Pollock as influences, he is not describing aspects of his painting but aspects of *himself*. Similarly, the philosophical sub-texts of his pictures are light years away from the substitution of words and explanatory apparatus for painting so brilliantly castigated by Howard Jacobson in *Seeing with the Ear* (1993): 'You cannot be transformed by the mere mention . . . of a painting,' Jacobson writes. 'Your participation in its experience is a drama of the eye.' For Cockrill there is the Word, and there is Light, and *then* he gets on with the real business of painting, and those great dramas of the eye.

The most stately, the most *ripened* of the whole series is an eloquent demonstration of this process. It is a study in scarlet, a colour which, for Cockrill, has a whole complex of allusions. It stands for blood, and bloodlines, for both catastrophe and continuity. He remembered 'Out, damned spot!' from *Macbeth*, how scarlet could also symbolise indelibility, and decided to call the painting *Anamnesis*, an archaic word that means an ordered recollection (and which was, more anciently, one of Plato's doctrines, according to which the soul pre-existed in a purer state and there gained its ideas).

But this was not a considered programme or even a 'set' for the picture. Even the very first workings of the ground are guided by the paint, not by Cockrill's intellectual premeditations. He has a remarkable sensitivity to gradations of colour, and scrapes away the scarlet where he glimpses a pallor or translucence. Then he begins to build the embryonic heart of the painting, and the darker crater in which it sits (and which in *Anamnesis* is wonderfully three-dimensional, like a opened fig). Quite soon the brushwork begins to acquire a momentum of its own. He works with fast strokes, letting his own physique (and maybe the memory of his father's) guide their rhythm and extent. He is fascinated by what paint does, and flecks and trickles are explored and extended, as stipples or threads, maybe. All the while he is eyeing the whole work, which by now he is unapologetically calling 'a being'. A transparent sac to the left of the central mass is filled with jellyfish-like shapes. A pair of cross-hatched grey diatoms floating in the red ground below are balanced by a grey 'hook' – maybe painted with the same brush – at the top.

Cockrill is fond of saying that these passages 'occur', as if they were spontaneously generated on the canvas. And there is clearly a painterly logic behind the way the paintings develop. Yet they are too warm and allusive to be confined within such a deterministic explanation, and they seem to be equally influenced by what I can only call eco-logic. Cockrill's 'beings' need food and shelter. They breed, erode rocks, form cooperative associations with other creatures. They evolve. They are not so much paintings of landscapes or creatures, as eco-systems in their own right. As John Berger wrote in *The White Bird* (1985): 'Art does not imitate nature, it imitates a creation, sometimes to propose an alternative world, sometimes simply to amplify, to confirm, to make social the brief hope offered by nature.'

This means that Cockrill's paintings need to be not just looked at, but explored, for their inner relationships, processes and rhythms, much as a field naturalist or archaeologist might browse through a terrestrial landscape. It also helps if some of the customary patterns by which we make sense of the world can be forgotten. Cockrill and I are both admirers of Annie Dillard's remarkable book about order and meaning in nature, *Pilgrim at Tinker Creek*. In her opening chapter she examines the act of seeing itself, and how people, blind from birth, who then gain sight are able to see patches of colour dissociated from the objects that generate them. Cockrill's beings are something like that – immanent forms, floated free of existing creatures, but still bound by the laws of nature:

Maurice Cockrill

I live now in a world of shadows that shape and distance colour, a world where space makes a kind of terrible sense . . . The fluttering patch I saw in my nursery window – silver and green and shape-shifting blue – is gone; a row of Lombardy poplars takes its place, mute, across the distant lawn . . . Why didn't someone hand those newly sighted people paints and brushes from the start, when they still didn't know what anything was? Then maybe we all could see colour-patches too, the world unravelled from reason, Eden before Adam gave names. (*Pilgrim at Tinker Creek*, 1975)

Andy Goldsworthy's *Végétal* (1996)

Someone once defined sculpture as 'frozen movement'. It's not exactly the description you would think of for Andy Goldsworthy's work, despite his startling piece in which a snowball, kept in a freezer till midsummer, melted to disgorge a cargo of fir cones and unseasonable daffodils. Goldsworthy's work – ice-bridges, wind-blown leaf patterns, bone-boulders bleaching in the Australian sun – is all about change and movement, but about releasing them, not freezing them. So it seems entirely natural that he should now have collaborated on a dance work, *Végétal*, with the French choreographer Régine Chopinot. We shared a drink before its Paris preview, and he explained how he has always seen affinities between dance and the kind of rhythmic physical work (stone-laying, withy-weaving) in which his own art is rooted. Dance also has obvious connections with the rhythms of the natural world, too; and that triangle – dance, work, nature – is the space in which *Végétal* is played out.

Beyond that, it is unclassifiable. Thirteen dancers – dressed for action in blue boiler suits – create Goldsworthy pieces on stage, sometimes using stones, leaves and wood as their raw materials, sometimes their own bodies. There is no music as such, but a *univers sonore* of orchestrated natural sounds (water dripping, woodworms boring) by Knud Victor. The five parts are entitled Earth, Seed, Root, Branch and Leaf, and inside each one, there are brilliant variations (and often improvisations) around a movement 'theme'. The dancers build a cairn, and on its unscripted collapse, start building it again. In 'Root' they shoot around the stage on their backsides, almost colliding with each other, but changing direction at the last moment until every possible combination of dancers has been used and every square foot of stage matted over. They weave a kind of hut from branches (dancing them onto the stage one at a time), dismantle it, build a wattle pen, and then an even wider stockade in which the rest of the work is performed. (This is where a tiny minority of the Parisian audience found the whole thing a sight too down to earth, and began cat-calling.) The final act, 'Leaf', silenced everyone. On a stage by now littered with stones, dust and foliage, the dancers become transpirers themselves, making their own rhythmic sound-track by hyperventilation and spectacular rib-cage work-outs. Even in these dramatic spells, it is Chopinot's genius for incorporating small, vernacular details of movement – the curve of a leaf's fall, the way a child plays with a stick while carrying it – that tells.

Meanwhile, for the whole two hours *Végétal* takes to perform, Chopinot herself moves imperceptibly round the edge of the stage – a prodigious act of discipline and balance. She is like the shadow of a sundial, a natural chronometer, reminding you of *the time things take*, and that repetition is an inherent part of work and growth.

Végétal is, as I said, impossible to label. At various times it is like an elaborate playground game, an aboriginal creation-myth, a square dance. It is also a kind of ecology of movement, a triumphant, enthralling celebration of the common language of motion shared by all living things. Pester your regional arts council to invite the show to Britain.

David Nash's Artistic Estate (1997)

The Victorian chapel where David Nash set up shop back in the mid-sixties sits in a row of quarrymen's cottages at the edge of Blaenau Ffestiniog in North Wales. From the outside it has a subfusc, municipal feel. But inside, the light filtering through the arched stained-glass windows picks out a space as bizarrely cluttered as the study of a nineteenth-century explorer or economic botanist. This is Nash's attic, his refugium. In it are many of the pieces made over the last thirty years – the prototypes, pieces unresolved, sculptures he does not want to be parted from, and new arrivals from projects overseas. There are roughly hollowed pods, charred towers and archetypal domestic forms: spoons, eggs, stoves. There are craning *Ubus* (titled after the playwright Jarry's caricatures of royalty) for which holes have had to be punched in the ceiling, which somehow heightens the gently satirical preposterousness of these giraffe-necked branchings. There is the almost pop-art *Comet Ball*, a charred exclamation mark, an assertion of gravity, which swoops powerfully down to its globular head, reversing the direction in which wooden growth normally leads the eye. But amongst these curved, organic pieces are many more angular forms – cracked cubes, ladders, massive seats. They are all plainly bits of trees, and their surfaces are wonderfully resin-scented and textured with the still legible marks of saw and axe. You can see how Nash responds to knots and warps and lines of natural splitting. But you can't miss their straight lines and hard diagonal cuts and often very unephemeral massiveness, qualities that in more than one sense go against the grain. David Nash, the best-known sculptor in wood in Britain, and the very model of a 'green' artist, has clearly not made an unconditional surrender to the idea of the tree.

But the diversity of this wooden congregation is compelling, and in the austere atmosphere of the old chapel, it reminded me of an idea from the old Judaic Cabbala, 'the Mystery of the Splintering of the Vessels', which if I understand it correctly refers to the containment of fundamental essences in the husk-covered forms generated by time. The slight air of ancient mystery is heightened by an epigram in high Welsh carved on the wall: 'Sancteiddrwydd a weddai i'th dy' – 'Sanctify this house with prayer'. They both seem rather Nashian notions, though I doubt whether his own commitment to spirituality in his work has any truck with out-and-out mysticism. He has found a common ground between nature and culture like few others, and done it without compromising what is, by any critic's standards, real sculpture. Yet beyond its purely aesthetic aims, he sees his work as a model or metaphor for the kind of relationship humans should have with nature. How has he been able to make his work stand for so much? It seemed to me likely that answers might lie in his most uncompromised pieces, the outdoor works *in situ* and made with living materials.

I had come up to Blaenau on a two-carriage train on a pitch-black January evening. It wasn't until next morning, drawing back the curtains, that I realised the town's infamous slate tip was almost in the front garden. Glittering with frost, the spoil heap rose into a clear sky like a parody of the real hills behind.

As it happened this was the place that David wanted me to see first. He climbed one of the quarrymen's paths some way in front of me, picking his way between the patches of frost on the grey stone like a mountaineer – or at least a man who knew his place, and was comfortable with it. He told me about how the slate used to be won, and showed me the tracks made by the miners when they still had to haul trucks by hand. He explained how slate rarely splits cleanly enough along its natural grain to produce viable roofing material, so that there are more rough blocks thrown away than finished slates. He was so immersed in – and awed by – the social history of this rock (its geological history – metamorphosed out of clay by massive underground pressure – is scarcely less symbolic) that I wondered why he had so rarely used it in his work. But he finds it an obdurate, uncompliant material, with none of the vitality and generosity of wood. Yet it plainly has an ambivalent meaning for him. Those diagonal marks that so characterise the tip – the angles of the slates' edges, the line of the tracks and pulley grooves, even the edge of the tip itself – are engraved in his imagination. He sees them as a motif for human work in nature, and they repeatedly appear in his own sculpture, cutting across the rough curves and pastoral sweeps of his wooden pieces. Yet the diagonal is a natural geometric device, too. The slope of the spoil tip itself is, ironically, a natural constant, never able to exceed about twenty-five degrees to the vertical at its steepest without becoming unstable, just as on natural scree slopes and shingle banks. The laws of geology and of the axe are close, and somewhere in here is the concept, central to understanding Nash's work, that wood is animated rock, the idea of stone expressed in plant tissue (just as rock is sometimes quite literally petrified wood).

David Nash is captivated by the idea of humans entering and benignly shaping the landscape, and his best-known work is all out-of-doors, from the great columns and ladders to the sky he has raised in Japan and North America, to the 'Sheep Spaces' of his home country. These little cocoons, worn out by animals simply by their continued presence, their habitation, are one of the fundamental particles of Nash's landscape cosmos, and he has both sketched them, and created them himself (for example, in an installation in Denmark in 1993):

> Animal traces are present across the land on many levels from the glossy trail of a slug to a fence rail gnawed by a horse. Such traces articulate the form and qualities of a 'place'. Sheep find shelter from wind, rain and sun wherever they can, lying by a rock, wall, bush or hollow. Lanolin from the wool oils the surrounding surfaces. They do not dig or scrape the ground but by their continued presence gradually erode an oval patch – a peaceful space, innocent and holy.

This sense of history being in-grained in a place is crucial to Nash, and to the form and positioning of his works (and is different from Anthony Caro's orthodox view that good sculpture should 'work' anywhere). When he was working in a forest in Poland in 1991, Nash found a group of unusually large alders which were growing in deep pits. They proved to be shell craters dating from a battle between German and Russian troops in the First World War. 'The fresh blood red of the alderwood and the doom of the charred oak took on a deeper significance being made in that place.'

From the slate tip we drove to one of Nash's own 'places', an evocative tree-lined, boulder-strewn hollow – the kind of place where humans would instinctively make a settlement. Here, close to the Rudolf Steiner school he helped set up, he is carving a giant redwood egg. It sits surrounded by pink chippings, as if it were creating its own nest, its own 'egg-space'.

The countryside round Blaenau is full of Nash's modest and mostly hidden marks. In the wooded valley Cae'n-y-Coed at Maentwrog, he has inherited a 4-acre plot of mixed woodland from his father. This is his sculpture nursery, a secular equivalent of the sacred grove, where he is taking his belief in working with nature to its logical conclusion and actually *growing* his pieces. It is an enchanting spot, in which it is hard to tell natural disorder from deliberate shapings. *Sabre Growth Larches* swirl in lissom curls towards the sky, like windblown plumes of smoke. Densely planted sycamore saplings have been knitted into the scroll-work of a *Celtic Hedge*. Nash is happy to see this aspect of his work linked to vernacular traditions like hedge-laying and the planting of oaks in forma-tion on village greens. This is typical of the eclecticism of his work – as is the shelter which sits amidst these figurative growths, built from split hazel wattle, and clothed with bitumen-painted plastic, all in the shape of the ancient Welsh coracle.

The defining work here is *Ash Dome* which Nash planted in March 1977. It was, he explains, a time of economic and political gloom. He felt that 'the cold war was very tense, and there was a general depression in the air, a feeling that we would not see the end of the twentieth century. *Ash Dome* was conceived as an act of faith in the future.' He had been wrestling with the problem of how to make a large-scale outdoor sculpture which was genuinely of its place, and which engaged with rather than defied the elements. He planted twenty-two ash saplings in a circle 9 metres in diameter, with the intention of slowly growing them into a domed space. Over the years, by persistent bending, pruning and grafting he has teased the ashes towards each other, so that in their first few feet of growth at least they are realising the domed form. But, two decades on, their growing tips have other ambitions, and Nash, having allowed nature a considerable hand in evolving the work, will now have to nego-tiate a settlement with it about how the dome develops. For its own project is to become an 'Ash Spire', as the leading shoots strain for the sun through the narrowing skylight afforded by the tree canopy around them. Would allowing them their head negate the whole project, tip the clump decisively into nature rather than culture's camp? Or would the progressively more intensive pruning (both of ashes and surrounding trees) that will be needed if the dome is to be completed, compromise the almost Buddhist principles of collaborating with nature that underlie the piece? Only time – along with place the other chief matrix in Nash's work – will tell. But I throw in my ecological ha'p'orth, and tell David about a recent discovery in the canopy of tropical rain forests. Instead of the fearful, snagging, mutually suffocating strife between trees that hard-line Darwinism conjures up, botanists actually working in this other world 200 feet above the earth have found that the growing tips of trees respect each other, allowing their neighbours their own space. It is a phenomenon which has been christened, with unusual sensitivity for scientists, 'crown shyness'.

Across the valley from Cae'n-y-Coed is the site of the extraordinary *Wooden Boulder*. In 1978, the occupants of a cottage close to the river were worried about a large overhanging oak tree. Nash agreed to cut it down for them, and the trunk became his first 'wood quarry', from which he subsequently made several sculptures. The chief one, echoing his early *Nine Cracked Balls*, was an immense hulk of wood faceted with the chain-saw until it was nearly spherical. It weighed half a ton. His original intention was to move it to the valley floor and then transport it back to his studio, but he then had the idea of using a nearby stream to move it for him, down through a succession of waterfalls and pools, so that its progress could also be a kind of narrative work. The wooden block was manoeuvred to the topmost set of falls, and let go. But it never made it to the bottom. It became wedged amongst the rocks halfway down, with water cascading around it. Nash realised at this point that this was the destiny for this piece, to become a wooden boulder, and in that realisation made what was to be a crucial decision not just for this piece but for all his future work. The block had been *released*, not just from the tree in which it had grown, but from the artist's control. He becomes a witness, a recorder, but no longer master of what had become a natural process.

Over the next twenty years it shifted gradually downstream. In the spring of 1979 Nash found it in a pool, washed down presumably by heavy winter rains. It lay there for eight years, capped by ice in winter, and packed around with dead leaves and wooden litter, then tumbling another hundred yards after a violent storm. In 1994 another flood sent it hurtling down, carrying a gate and part of a fence with it, until it wedged under a road bridge. Nash rescued it from here, and it now stands just a few yards away from the stream's junction with the River Dwyryd. It carries a remarkable charge poised here, one storm away from release into the river and then the Irish Sea. It is now almost indistinguishable from a real rock, stained brown by the acid in the water, its edges and corners worn smooth. The sense of an epic voyage already hangs about it, even though it has moved little more than 200 yards in two decades. Above all it seems a poignant symbol of freedom, and of the new egalitarian relationship David Nash has achieved with it. Now he recounts stories about it, not inscribes them *into* it.

That decisive human marking David Nash chooses more and more to add with chain-saws. Although one of his local friends likens their sound to 'all the evil things in the world having their own way' he keeps a suite of six lined up in echelon in his workroom, and prefers them to chisels and axes even for small-scale work. The power-saw, he says, is 'just a combination of all these simpler woodworking tools. I'm a sprinter. I like to get a sketch of the work done quickly.' He talks of the importance of 'feeling the tool work with your body' and anyone who has used a chain-saw will understand the bluff, heavy intimacy he is referring to. You get the feeling that he respects its directness, too, and that – as with the lifts he gave to the wooden boulder – he does not want to gloss over the 'natural' impetuosity of humans in his work. It doesn't seem at all contradictory to me that in Minneapolis in 1987 he used a horse to haul out oak timber from a wood, and was able to say of the experience: 'The presence of the horse brought a different quality to the work site and to the work itself. There was more sense of coaxing the form into existence rather than demanding it.' He is very much an empathetic, physically intuitive sculptor as well as a meditative philosopher.

This is also true when he is seeking out his raw material. He can 'spot' likely wood in the trunk, can visualise whole 'wood quarries'. He is frugal and demanding about timber, and would rather use a rough block that had served its days in a mine than anonymous and often profligate cuts from wood-merchants. 'Earlier I used the regular standard units from the woodmill, but I found them dumb as they did not tell of their origin, nor their destination. Now I get along better by going to the tree and responding to its time and space and to the circumstances of it being there and my being there.' When he was working in Barcelona he worked with – 'resurrected as sculpture' is the phrase he uses – the terminal cases in the municipal 'tree hospital', where ailing street trees are nursed back to health.

This is as much a moral as an aesthetic stance, inseparable from Nash's respect for trees as organisms and his concern for the importance of wood in human life. That he is able to express all these as aspects in a single relationship with wood is his great gift. His long series of boat-like *Vessels*, for example, begun in 1985, are full of associations. They are a response to the lip-like wounds that can open quite naturally on tree trunks; a homage to a universal human artefact (the series began after he had seen boat-like scars on gum trees in Australia, and subsequently learned that they were caused by native Australians cutting bark into boat-skins for fishing); and a reference to wooden boats as symbols of humans' journey through life. That these symbolic references never become solemn or overbearing may be a result of his Steinerist beliefs. 'I've always considered spirituality to be an immensely practical business,' he says. But I have a feeling that it is also a result of the qualities of his chosen medium itself. A tree is, so to speak, already a symbol, before it is worked or even conceptualised. Its solid heartwood and ephemeral leaves are, respectively, reflections of the long sweeps of history and the fugitive movements of daylight and the seasons. Its annual rings are figurative expressions of its whole experience – weather, drought, catastrophe, human intervention. The Chinese call wood 'the fifth element' yet it is already a synergistic combination of the other four. David Nash himself has described wood as a 'weaving of earth and light'. He has also said that 'the objects I make are vessels for the presence of the human being, aware and surrendering to the realities of nature'.

It is, I think, significant that in one of his most evocative indoor works,

Square and Branch, it is the branch that is growing from the square, not vice versa. We cannot escape from the human project, but it is not always the last word, the trump, even when its own origins are 'organic'. Nature, the weathering and softening of things, the new beginning, is what, paradoxically, humanises us.

A SENSE OF OCCASION

Devil's Meat (1993)

They are, as often as not, my first glimpse of autumn: a box of early, egg-yolk-yellow chanterelles, wrapped in moss and mailed from Scotland by a fellow fungophile.

This year [1993] they arrived in the middle of the Wimbledon fortnight heatwave, and for a day or two the smells of a summer kitchen were muddled with their fugitive apricot scent and the tangs of the peat and pine needles still clinging to them.

It was the eulogy on chanterelles in Dorothy Hartley's *Food In England* – 'sometimes clustered so close that they look like a torn golden shawl dropped down amongst the dead leaves' – that first made me notice the sheer sensuousness of fungi. Since then forays in search of them have become one of the more piquant seasonal pleasures, and about the only saving grace of dank weather.

At least sometimes they are. The behaviour of fungi during this extraordinary, sodden autumn has confirmed what capricious and cryptic creatures they are. I'm used to not finding chanterelles down south, but this year most of the big ground-growing species, from fly agarics to ceps, have been late, scant or maddeningly local.

Even an early October trip to the west of Scotland – usually a forager's nirvana – made me wonder if I had lost my instincts. It seemed a well-nigh perfect spot in perfect weather: a damp and venerable oakwood with the leaves already turning, and a day of pure Gaelic beauty, with Gulf Stream breezes clearing the morning mist from the sea lochs. But of toadstools there was barely a sign – except that the whole wood was draped with lichens, beard lichens and oak-moss festooning the branches, and membranous lungwort swaddling the trunks. These are all part fungi, part green algae, living in symbiotic partnership, so perhaps some of the woodland niches normally occupied by more obvious fungi were already full.

Now, a week later, I am back in the Chilterns, and it is monsoon weather again. I am wandering through a storm-racked beechwood, and it is raining so hard that I can see some of the fallow trees actually breaking up in the rain. The rotting heartwood, as crumbly as earth in patches, is dribbling down the trunks. Tiny wisps of peeling bark, prised off further by the black bootlace rhizomes of honey fungus, are being washed to the ground. Many of the wind-thrown trees – mostly casualties of the 1990 hurricane – are catacombs of fungi. Crimped-edge brackets range along the recumbent trunks, tiers of *Pholiota* and sulphur tuft sprout from the upturned rootplates. I can't put names to most of the vaguely buff bonnets that lurk in rot-holes and range in troops on the dead branches, but others are unmistakable: rashes of the tiny beads, purple and pink, of *Ascocoryne* and coral spot; miniature puffballs, the diaphanous caps of beech tuft (bone-china-white until they droop like Dali watches), gelatinous heaps of *Neobulgaria*, black and white spikes of dead man's fingers and stag's horn; and on still-standing stumps, ledges of dryad's saddle. The undersides of these bracket fungi are pitted with minute pores, like a sponge, and rain down spores continuously for half the year. Sometimes, against a low October sun, you can see them blowing from the undersides like wisps of smoke.

Then, on the ground, I spot a branch stained by *Chlorosplenium*. The wood has the same dull turquoise sheen as corroded copper, and oak logs infected by this species were once used in the manufacture of the elaborate veneer work known as Tonbridge Ware. But the fruit bodies exuding from cracks in the wood are something else – more like a ripple of fused cobalt glass than a plant. Inside the branch, thin mycelial threads – the main body of the fungus – will be probing the wood's capillaries, searching for damp patches and water seepage, secreting enzymes (and sometimes dye substances) that speed the dissolution of the wood and make its nutrients available. Having no chlorophyll, fungi are not able to manufacture their own foodstuff, and have to rely entirely on the detritus from other organisms, leached out by water – which is why they are so exquisitely sensitive to pollution carried in the rain. They are one of the vital agencies of natural recycling, permeating plants, soil and even the digestive systems of animals. And what we call toadstools are merely the occasional fruiting bodies of the fungus proper, the tip of an immense and intricate network of threads. Inside a hectare of wood which produces maybe 10 kilograms of toadstools each year, there is more than a tonne of this mycelium. In North America single individuals of honey fungus have been found whose mycelium pervades more than 15 hectares, and is probably 1,500 years old.

Why is it that there has been such a history of hostility towards these plants in Britain? Although hunting for edible varieties is going through one of its periodic spells of fashionableness, it is still a minority habit, and wild species are still too much the subject of popular suspicion to feature in ordinary markets in the way they do across much of the Continent. Our opinion has barely changed since 1627, when Francis Bacon denounced the whole tribe as 'a venereous meat'. By and large we still kick them to pieces in woods, and view their place in the great scheme of things as being roughly on a par with head-lice. And despite their crucial role as natural scavengers and recyclers, we have still paid almost no official attention to what is happening to them. (Unlike Holland, Germany and the former Czechoslovakia, for instance, where studies have revealed catastrophic local rates of extinction as a consequence of air pollution.)

That is not to say that, taken as a family, they are entirely benign. Some, of course, are poisonous, though these amount to less than one per cent of all the species that grow in Britain. Some are implicated in banes like dry rot, asthma and food poisoning. And people of sensitive or superstitious dispositions are sometimes disturbed by the striking similarities which many species show to human organs – brains, ears, tongues, livers and especially sexual parts. But this is true of fungi everywhere, and doesn't seem to have distanced them in other cultures. Robert Graves once argued that our national hostility was a hangover from the time when hallucinogenic species like liberty caps and fly agaric were the prerogative of a priestly elite and were surrounded by taboos. Yet it's a wariness that doesn't occur in other regions with prehistories similar to our own; and my own view is that its roots lie in our estrangement from woodland, the prime fungal habitat.

Britain was deforested earlier and more comprehensively than any other part of Europe. In the early sixteenth century, when our national tree cover was maybe no more than five per cent (less than it is now), the authors of one of the first popular manuals on plant use, *The Grete Herbal* (1576), divided fungi into just two kinds: 'one maner is deedly and sleeth them that eateth of them and be called tode stoles, and the other doeth not'. It was, to say the least, a highly functional distinction, and not exactly confidence-building. Even now forests are seen as symbolic of danger and lawlessness, and it may be no coincidence that the chief distinction in our culture between good and suspicious toadstools is made not between those that do or don't peel, or turn sixpences black, but between those that grow in fields and those that grow in woods.

What perplexed all early observers, though, regardless of their cultural background, was the question of where on earth fungi came from. Because their spores are too small to see with the naked eye, toadstools were, for nearly two thousand years, believed to be the products of some kind of spontaneous generation. In classical times, one belief was that they were produced by the action of thunder. Pliny, writing in AD 77, favoured a kind of natural fermentation of the earth. Pondering the origins of the most prized of continental species, Caesar's mushroom, he didn't seem the least put off by the possibility that they sprang 'from mud and the acrid juices of moist earth, or frequently from those of acorn-bearing trees'. In the sixteenth century, his compatriot John Baptista Porta reiterated in *Natural Magick* (1558) the belief that 'new kinds of Plants may grow up of their own accord, without any help of seed or such like'. But thirty years later he changed his mind, and insisted that 'from fungi I have succeeded in collecting seed, very small and black, lying hidden in oblong chambers or furrows [gills, that is] extending from the stalk to the circumference'. In 1751, Otto van Münchhausen – a real scientist, but with the imagination of his literary namesake – also found and collected fungus 'seeds', but testified that he had seen them hatch into small insects in water, and concluded that toadstools should not be regarded as plants but as the dwelling places of small animals.

Meanwhile the pioneering micrographer Robert Hooke had realised that moulds and mildews were 'nothing else but several kinds of small and variously figur'd Mushrooms'. But he failed to see spores at all, and believed that toadstools were created from 'putrifying bodies ... by the concurrent heat of the Air [and] excited to a certain kind of vegetation'. It was not until the early nineteenth century that the real mechanisms of fungal growth were understood. The spores are not so much seeds as minute samples of tissue, which expand laterally to become the mycelium – which, under the right conditions, throws up the fruiting bodies we call toadstools.

Despite the laboured progress of these revelations (they were, after all, flying in the face of centuries of mythology, as well as what seemed to be the clear evidence of the senses), the period between the Enlightenment and the mid-Victorian era saw an enthusiasm for fungi grow amongst the scientifically literate middle class in Britain. In the middle of the eighteenth century the first illustrated guides began to appear, culminating in Thomas Bolton's epic three volumes on the history of the fungi growing around Halifax. In 1758 'Sir' John Hill, who has since been generally regarded as a self-aggrandising charlatan, the court jester of eighteenth-century botany, wrote a meticulously observed and sympathetic monograph on one of the greatest oddities of the fungal world, the *Pietra fungaja*:

> An account of a stone ... which on being watered produces excellent mushrooms ... The rock-mushroom is a peculiar kind: and it is constantly this species and no other which the Italian stone produces ... The upper part is a mixed yellow and olive colour; and the surface is broken in a wild but beautiful manner, into a resemblance of scales or feathers. The under part is white; and in the pores lie the seeds. The substance of the mushroom within is firm and white as snow; and it is of a delicate and high flavour and perfectly

wholesome. A great deal of attention was used in gathering it to see in what manner it rose from the rock. The mould was removed, and its insertion made bare: it rose from the plain surface of the stone by a thick and irregular base which lengthened into a stalk, and thence proceeded to the expansion of the head. No roots were produced from this stalk in that part under the mould. So that it drew no nourishment from thence ... The mushroom consists of an expansion of that fungus substance which covered the stone: nothing more.

(The fungus stone is no fantasy. It is a conglomeration of earth or tufa held together by the mycelium of a bracket fungus, *Polyporus tuberaster*, and would be a sensation in the conservatory if it were more common.)

By this time the fungal scene was no longer so mysterious and alien, and even curates could trade saucy quips about priapic growths. In 1766 Revd Gilbert White of Selborne wrote to his friend Revd John Mulso about the 'Stinkhorns, or stinking morel, fungus phalloides' in one of the local woods, adding with a nudge, 'Linnaeus, for a certain reason, calls it phallus impudicus'. Mulso replied: 'I thank you for your learned Dissertation on the Canker or Stinkpot. I knew in general that all Flesh was Grass, but I did not know that Grass was Flesh before.' And at the turn of the century, the artist James Sowerby described a bizarre fungus (a *Clavaria*) he had found in a London cellar: 'It is remarkable for being luminous in the dark, when fresh, at the ends of the shoots. Mr Forster doubted whether this phosphoric appearance may not be owing to some vinous moisture imbibed, rather than a natural property of the fungus.'

This note of amused wonder was picked up by the Victorians. The first book devoted to edible fungi, Charles Badham's *A Treatise on the Esculent Funguses of England* (1847), is full of wry asides on the beneficence of these wonders of creation, from the use of birch polypore for razor strops to puffball spores for stupefying bees. (Though the best note on puffballs – and a classic vignette of Victorian frugality – comes from a slightly later text on edible fungi published by the Society for Promoting Christian Knowledge: 'We have known specimens to grow amongst cabbages in a kitchen garden, and when such is the case it may be left standing, slices being cut off as is required until the whole is consumed.')

The Victorians must also take credit for inventing fungus forays, those agreeable autumnal saunters where identification skills are shared and baskets filled. In October 1869, for instance, thirty-five members (including nine Reverends) of the Woolhope Naturalists' Field Club set out from Hereford on their annual foray. They ranged about the local landscapes by carriage, stopping off at likely hunting grounds, measuring fairy-rings, and identifying a remarkable variety of wild mushrooms: milk-caps, boleti, chanterelles, witches' butter, hedgehog fungi. More than sixty species are listed in the published account of the foray. The day ended at the Green Dragon in Hereford, with exhibits strewn out on the pub tables, and a late lunch of the day's trophies: shaggy parasol on toast, fried giant puffball, and fairy-ring champignons in white sauce. The puffballs especially were voted a great success, as was the day itself.

But in the twentieth century the fad collapsed, and the Victorians' enthusiasm and curiosity began to seem eccentric to the point of foolhardiness. I remember my own nervousness, as I moved on from fantasy chanterelles to real, mutable, mistakable toadstools. I stuck to the obvious for a long time: ink-caps cooked Geoffrey Grigson style (spread-eagled like a starfish over a fried egg); ceps dried in the airing cupboard; and above all, giant puffballs, whose magnetic appeal doesn't seem to have diminished one whit in the last hundred years. I never found a specimen as gross as the one spotted under an oak tree in Kent during the last war, which for a while was believed to be a new German secret weapon. But five-pounders, lurking like white rabbits under the hedges, were common and I have a pile of snapshots of my own and others' finds, posed on bars or alongside children and cats, as if they were a species of pet themselves. They were delectable to eat, with the silky texture of toasted marshmallow, but seemed to go on for ever, and I wish we had known that frugal Victorian cut-and-come-again tip.

In fact we had to learn many of the old knacks and wrinkles from scratch. I remember my first, belated hunt for field mushrooms on the north Norfolk marshlands, and my naive surprise that they weren't all standing stoutly up like fairy-story illustrations but were mostly hidden deep in the grass, so that you needed to keep your eyes focused just a few feet in front. I also discovered why folklore insists that you pick mushrooms early in the morning. It is nothing to do with them being new-sprung or 'dawnfresh' but a matter of first come first served. We had strayed that morning onto another group's gathering territory, and for the hour until breakfast our combined movements resembled a slow-motion formation dance. We never spoke, or acknowledged each other's presence, but somehow kept a steady twenty yards between us as we slowly quartered the marsh, sneaking hooded glances at each other between periods of intense scanning for the half-hidden white caps.

It was in 1976, the year of a long summer and a famous drought, that our national fungophobia began, at last, to show signs of cracking. When drenching rain finally arrived in mid-September, it fell on ground which had been baked hard, and created what seemed perfect conditions for fungal fruiting. I was quite convinced I could *smell* them growing: ceps in woods, parasols on road verges, and horse and field mushrooms in quantities that hadn't been seen for a generation. Foraging became such a craze that the BBC began issuing regular information bulletins on the radio. By the end of the month the wild mushroom mountain was so huge in my corner of the Chilterns that they were being hawked from door to door by enterprising children.

Those who have become aficionados since then – a growing number, to judge from the quantity of neatly cut stalks in British woods and the variety of species found on smart menus – will have found that foraging is a captivating business, a kind of vegetarian stalking. But I think it is sad that passions have been directed so single-mindedly towards edible species. The whole tribe is fascinating and more useful than we acknowledge – as the fortunes of the trees in Windsor Great Park demonstrate. The ancient oaks and beeches here have proved rather more disaster-proof than other sections of the royal fabric, and during the great storm of October 1987 not a single one was blown down, contrasting with the havoc wreaked amongst younger, apparently more healthy trees. This was partly because they had been hollowed out by fungal decay, turning the trunks into lightweight, wind-resistant cylinders. And the rotten, pulped wood helps feed their roots – meaning that, in almost mythological style, they are thriving on their own recycled heartwood.

Keats' 'Ode to a Nightingale' (1995)

> Forlorn! the very word is like a bell
> > To toll me back from thee to my sole self!
> Adieu! the fancy cannot cheat so well
> > As she is fam'd to do, deceiving elf.
> Adieu! adieu! thy plaintive anthem fades
> > Past the near meadows, over the still stream,
> > Up the hill-side; and now 'tis buried deep
> > In the next valley-glades:
> > Was it a vision, or a waking dream?
> > Fled is that music: – do I wake or sleep?

Keats surfaced from his reverie under a plum tree having composed eight of the most sensuous stanzas of the Romantic era in two or three hours. It was the last day of April, May Eve, and the luscious images that had poured from him – ecstatic, melancholic, elegiac by turns – seemed the ultimate evocation of the mixed emotions of a springtime night.

But it wasn't night-time as Keats wrote. He wasn't surrounded by 'embalmed darkness', or 'winding mossy ways'. He was in the garden of a friend's house in Hampstead, bathed by the sunshine of one of the memorable spring mornings of 1819. He may not even have planned to write that day, and the draft of the poem is scribbled on what looks like the end-paper of a book. It was no poetic licence to talk of a 'waking vision'. In those few hours he had voyaged through the crises of his own life, and through the symbolism of five centuries of writing about nature and the springtime.

The ode is not *about* a nightingale, in the manner of Coleridge's ebullient tribute, written two decades before. This 'conversation poem' as Coleridge tellingly subtitles it, plunges into the 'tangling underwood' of a deserted castle where multitudes of singing birds 'skirmish' with each other. The stanzas echo the piping and rattle of the song, and are the first since the medieval period to paint the bird as a symbol of freedom and joyfulness, rather than as a mournful familiar of the lovesick. ''Tis the merry nightingale', Coleridge insists, 'That crowds and hurries and precipitates/ With fast, thick warble his delicious notes . . .'

Keats' nightingale, though also a festive bird, could hardly be described so frivolously. It certainly isn't the focus of the poem but a pivot for

Keats' meditations on mortality, on hopes lifted and dashed, on the way the gift of consciousness could blight our experiences of beauty and nature by making us too aware of their earthly limits. The previous year, in his 'Epistle to Reynolds', he had written: 'It is a flaw/ In happiness, to see beyond our bourn;/ It forces us in Summer skies to mourn:/ It spoils the singing of the Nightingale.'

Yet the ode was prompted by a real nightingale's song, and ends with the bird's all too real flight from Keats away over the tangled scrub and bourns of Hampstead Heath; and if it is not a nature poem in the conventional sense it is one of the most penetrating reflections on our relationship with nature. We are graced by nature, share its earthliness and mortality, yet are never able to lose ourselves – our 'sole selves' – in it for more than a fugitive moment.

The twelve months that began in September 1818 were the most eventful in Keats' short life. He fell in love, produced much of his greatest work in an extraordinary burst of creative energy, but saw many of those close to him – and himself, eventually – stricken by illness. All of these experiences are reflected in the nightingale ode. In December 1818 his beloved brother Tom had died of tuberculosis aged just nineteen. John was grief-stricken, but also fearful for his own health. He had been a medical student at Guys Hospital for a while, and seen first-hand the TB wards 'where men sit and hear each other groan'. By the autumn of 1818 he had begun to notice symptoms of the disease in himself. His eyesight was failing and he had frequent and persistent sore throats. He toyed with the idea of emigrating to 'the warm South' – the only real remedy for consumptives. But he moved instead to Charles Brown's house, Wentworth Place in Hampstead, close to the Vale of Health (an address that doubtless played a part in Keats' belief, in his more optimistic moods, in a 'vale of soul-making' where poets could do therapeutic battle with the misfortunes of the world).

Hampstead also held another, more ambivalent healing influence. In the second week of April, Fanny Brawne, a sharp-witted, sympathetic eighteen-year-old, moved into the other half of Wentworth Place. Keats had met her the previous summer and fallen for her immediately. His love was reciprocated, but because of his health and precarious finances, he was guarded and diffident about expressing it.

Yet his family remained a source of stress and unhappiness. John's other brother, George, had emigrated to America in the summer of 1818, and was faring badly. It is an ironic coincidence that just as John was working on the nightingale ode, his brother was sinking into financial ruin after investing in one of the reckless business schemes of the bird-painter George Audubon.

But then something quite mundane and wonderfully English happens: the weather changes. In the middle of April 1819 there are the first intimations of what is to become one of the great springs of the early nineteenth century, a procession of balmy days that lasts until 18 May. At the beginning of May, John writes to George that 'everything is in delightful forwardness; the violets are not withered before the peeping of the first rose'; and to his sister in the same breezy mood: 'O there is nothing like fine weather . . . – and, please heaven, a little claret-wine cool out of a cellar a mile deep – with a few or a good many ratafia cakes – a rocky basin to bathe in, a strawberry bed to say your prayers to Flora in . . .' And as if the enlivening effect of the weather were not enough, he meets Samuel Taylor Coleridge in the flesh. On 11 April he is taking a walk towards Highgate, bumps into the now forty-seven-year-old Romantic pioneer by chance, and is drawn into a philosophical dialogue (or maybe more correctly a monologue) of seemingly cosmic range. It lasts all of forty minutes. This is part of Keats' own, probably biased, account of their stroll:

> I walked with him at his alderman-after-dinner pace for near two miles I suppose. In those two Miles he broached a thousand things – let me see if I can give you a list – Nightingales, Poetry – on Poetical Sensation – Metaphysics – Different genera and species of Dreams – Nightmare . . . Monsters – the Kraken–Mermaids – Southey believes in them – Southey's belief too much diluted – a Ghost story – Good morning – I heard his voice as he came towards me – I heard it as he moved away – I had heard it all the interval – if it may be called so.

It is an extraordinary prospect. Here are two of the greatest living English poets, on their one and only meeting, and the young Turk, twenty-five years Coleridge's junior, can barely contain his giggles.

But bombastic or not, Coleridge may well have sown the idea of a nightingale poem in Keats' mind that afternoon. Perhaps they had heard the song on their stroll, in a pause for breath between metaphysics and mermaids. In the nineteenth century 11 April wasn't an exceptional date for early migrants to arrive. They were certainly around in Highgate, where Coleridge was staying, and later became so noisy that they combined with his indigestion to keep him awake: 'Ah! PHILomel! Ill do thy strains accord with those of CALomel! [a stomach remedy]' he punned in a letter. Soon one bird had taken up residence in the secluded, high-hedged garden at Wentworth Place, and Charles Brown writes that Keats felt 'a tranquil and continual joy' at its song.

Yet he was still reading intensely, too, continuing his meticulous, annotated progress through Robert Burton's *Anatomy of Melancholy*, and rediscovering a favourite poem of his youth, the medieval pastoral fantasy 'The Flower and the Leaf', in a new version by Dryden. This is a spring-time poem centred on a nightingale, and its evocation of an enchanted wood of may-blossom and eglantine, and an entranced observer viewing the scene as an earthly paradise – 'all Elysium in a spot of ground' – leaves echoes and images in Keats' mind that he will soon be following as diligently as a map.

And so, on 30 April he goes out into the garden of Wentworth Place and sits under the plum tree. Fanny Brawne is a window-pane's thickness away. The nightingale is singing, that flamboyant, oratorical song, whose character relies so much on its pauses – pools of silence too tempting for an introspective like Keats. And soon he is sinking into them, drifting into the shadowed greenwood of 'The Flower and the Leaf' – and of all that he has read and felt this spring. He thinks of the nightingale's true home in the South, and yearns for that taste 'of Flora ... Dance, and Provençal song, and sunburnt mirth' that might just save his health, and make a future possible for him and Fanny. It might have saved his brother Tom, too, who had died 'pale, and spectre-thin'. All the while the bird carols on, a messenger from the living, from a world untouched by 'weariness ... fever and ... fret'. For a while Keats is half-tempted by 'easeful Death' ... 'To cease upon the midnight with no pain,/ While thou art pouring forth thy soul abroad/ In such an ecstasy'. Then, in the triumphant penultimate verse, this surrender is rejected. This small bird has survived for millennia; its song had buoyed up countless generations of the ill, the battle-weary, the displaced, back into biblical times. The poet, another modest singer, can hardly do less. And in three extraordinary lines whose rhythm catches something of the soulfulness of the night-ingale's song itself, Keats has a Gaian glimpse of the oneness of life: 'Perhaps the self-same song that found a path/ Through the sad heart of Ruth, when, sick for home,/ She stood in tears amid the alien corn'. Then, abruptly, he comes round. The nightingale becomes a real flesh and blood bird again, and flies off, its song fading across the Heath.

For me, it is the contrast between these last two stanzas, between the 'immortal bird' whose song has provided a chain of common experience and inspiration down through history, and the real bird, set free, as it were, from fantasy to be as frail and fugitive as the poet, that gives the poem its remarkable charge of honesty and *courage*.

But it has not always been seen in this light. In the late 1920s there was a famous critical row about the poem between Amy Lowell, the poet laureate Robert Bridges, and H. W. Garrod, the Professor of Poetry at Oxford. It centred on these final stanzas, on whether Keats was talking about a particular nightingale, or the idea of the nightingale, or 'the species' nightingale; and on whether the bird's abrupt, anti-climactic flight sabotaged the poem's mood. It seems a bizarre rumpus now, given how accustomed we have become to moving from particular experiences of nature to abstractions and generalisations – from 'a' nightingale to 'the' nightingale as it were. But Keats was in comparatively novel territory here, and the way he manages this movement in the ode again owes much to the ideas of a famous contemporary. In the spring of the previous year, 1818, Keats had attended William Hazlitt's course of 'Lectures on the English Poets'. He missed the first, by getting the time wrong, but met Hazlitt and the audience, many of whom he knew, on their way out. He dined with Hazlitt the following Sunday, and makes it clear in his letters that he had the highest admiration for him. He was clearly of a mind to be influenced by Hazlitt's clear and original thinking. In the fifth lecture, on Cowper and Thomson, there is a passage that is crucial to under-standing the origins of the nightingale ode – and of some of its most potent phrases. Hazlitt argues that what marks out the interest in nature from interest in other things is its 'abstractedness'. He goes on:

> The interest we feel in human nature is exclusive, and confined to the indi-vidual, the interest we feel in external nature is common, and transferable from one object to all others of the same class ... the cuckoo – 'that wandering voice' – that comes and goes with spring, mocks our ears with one note from youth to age; and the lapwing, screaming round the traveller's path, repeats for ever the same sad story of Tereus and Philomel.

'Self-same song'; 'same sad story': is the ode a bird poem or a purely metaphysical reflection, and a derivative one at that? I think it is both. Keats undoubtedly reworked influences and phrases from dozens of other writers – though this is hardly plagiarism, and he was on this occasion in the most fitting company: the nightingale itself often incorporates mim-icked phrases from other birds in its song. And Keats, by listening to other poets as well as the bird, succeeds in the poem in traversing the arc of feelings experienced by a listener, and the welter of associations the song has prompted over the centuries. There are allusions in it to the classical myth of the abused Philomel, metamorphosed into a night-ingale; to the medieval troubadours who saw the song as an emblem of spring and courtly love – and light-heartedness and lust, too; to the sickly, melancholic tones that were conventionally heard in the song in the sixteenth and seventeenth centuries; and of course to its reinstatement by the Romantics as an antidote to grief and decay. The tradition was carried forward by John Clare, who, though he rebukes Keats for paying insufficient attention to the real birds (which were all too easily 'trod down'), and who in his 'Nightingale's Nest' wrote a remarkably observed and intimate tribute to a fellow songster and fellow creature of the heath, also rejoiced in the bird's song, 'the happiest part of summers fame'.

The best-known nightingale lyric of our own times, 'A Nightingale Sang in Berkeley Square', also owes, I am sure, an unacknowledged debt to Keats. Like the ode it is set in London, but a London transformed by the wartime blackout into a magical Drydenesque landscape where the streets are 'paved with stars'. The mythical bird's song seems a benediction on the two lovers; but when their flight of fancy is broken by the dawn, one smiles and almost repeats Keats' closing phrase: 'Was that a dream, or was it true?'

Spring (1994)

It seemed for a while as if it might never come. Since September we had been suspended in what felt like a perpetual winter twilight, a bitter, corrosive mixture of wet and wind that promised nothing except more of the same. March [1994] was indistinguishable from November. April was dark and mizzling until its final week. Then, almost abruptly, we had our spring, four days of sublime, southerly weather packed into a single Bank Holiday weekend. On the last day of April there were swifts cruising high over Wembley Stadium after the Rugby League Cup Final. On May Day, there was May blossom foaming the verges all along the M4 – the second year running when it has been out from the start of its name month. In the centre of Bath on the holiday Monday, I saw speckled wood butterflies flitting amongst the august terraced gardens as if they were in dappled forest glades. When I got back to the Chilterns the following day the vegetation had run riot. Leaves and flowers that normally follow each other in orderly procession had burst open together, crab apple and garden lilac, cow parsley and sappy new beech foliage, the first horse chestnut candelabras swelling next to the last drifts of cherry blossom. On low ground even the oak and ash were leafing together – an occurrence which is simply not contemplated in weather lore. It was as if the entire landscape had been under a forcing frame.

And how we needed it. We were teetering on the edge of a mass pathetic fallacy, seeing the dismal weather as a reflection of the supposedly depressed and decadent state of the nation. Spring's business is to mark new beginnings, to purge gloom and self-deprecation, and we are in trouble when it gives us no signs to cling onto. I still keep, for comfort, the rhapsodic essay that Jan Morris wrote on the gilded spring and summer of 1990, which she saw as a fitting farewell to the decade that had given us Chernobyl and monetarism and an appalling sequence of assaults on the natural world. The hot seasons that year were full of serendipity and romantic associations. Mandela was freed, the Berlin Wall came down, and summer birds and prodigious insects swarmed through the halcyon days of May. In July and August, a giant Caribbean turtle was feasting off jellyfish in the Channel, and Morris watched seventy-seven pipistrelle bats fly out of their roost above the kitchen of her Welsh cottage. Those months, she wrote, were 'an allegorical moment of reconciliation; a window . . . through which all too briefly flickered a message that the worst might be over'.

Like the hopes of 1990, the brief spring of 1994 didn't quite come to fruition. It vanished as suddenly as it arrived. It was maddeningly condensed, with none of the slow, exquisite lightening, the savoured moments, of imagined (or remembered) springs. I was away from the home patch for just a short weekend, and still missed two seasonal rites of passage that I am sentimentally attached to: seeing my first swifts of the year over the parish church from my study window; and walking in a particular corner of my own wood on the day when the young beech leaves unfurl over the bluebells.

Some years ago I came across a scientific conceit that made me feel less disconsolate about these overdue springs. It was a measure of the advance of spring across the land, based on the average first dates at which common and widespread flowers first come into bloom. Different species flower at times determined by a combination of daylight length and temperature, and in general bloom later the higher and the further north they are. So, primroses come into flower a whole month earlier on the Devon coast than they do in the Cairngorms. As well as along the M4, May blossom will have been opening simultaneously on the Sussex Downs, the Pembrokeshire cliffs, and warm wasteland in the industrial Midlands. The lines joining these points are known as isophenes, and from them it is possible to calculate that spring travels inland and north at a rate of roughly two miles an hour.

That is remarkably close to strolling pace, and I used to toy with the fantasy of following the spring on foot, like a guest behind an unrolling carpet. But as anything other than an abstraction, the idea is of course a nonsense. The surfaces of Britain are so minutely and locally convoluted that every half mile has a sunny bank or shaded frost-pocket that can move first flowering dates two weeks either way. It is possible to join up regional first dates into wavy fronts and contours, but at a parish level the isophenes would cross like a mad cat's cradle.

Yet tracking the spring is something I seem to have been doing compulsively since I was a child. By the time I was a teenager I had a personal timetable of the 'proper' arrival dates and spots for summer migrants. Now, when things ought to be stirring and aren't, I get as fidgety as a migrant bird myself. I check out favourite parish plants, scan the skies over lakes, beat the bounds of my own territory. It is a ritualistic business, doubtless bolstered by nostalgia, but including a good deal of real nervousness. Ted Hughes saw the annual return of the swifts and their first madcap races around the house-tops as signs that all was well with the world: 'They've made it again,/ Which means the globe's still working, the Creation's/ Still wakening refreshed, our summer's/ Still all to come.' It's a heartlifting image, but over recent years I have found myself increasingly troubled by the awful corollary that lurks between its lines. What would it say about the state of creation if one year they *failed* to make it back? What if, one spring, leaves corroded by acid rain fell as soon as they had opened . . . ? That way lies real paranoia, which is why when the spring is held up, with plants in suspended animation and birds trapped on the other side of the Channel, waiting for the wind to change, I go hunting for reassurance further afield.

Henry Thoreau, in mid-nineteenth-century America, always walked westward, following the sun and the expanding frontier. 'My needle is slow to settle', he wrote, 'but it always settles between west and south-south-west. The future lies that way to me, and the earth seems more unexhausted and richer on that side.' I am not sure I share his transcendental views on rambling, but west is certainly the way you go to meet the spring. This year, on Solstice Day, 21 March, I was working in Devon, close to the balmy valleys south-east of Dartmoor. The rain fell continuously but the primroses were unbowed in the turf-banked lanes, and I decided to stay on for an extra day. It was not a wise decision, and I made things worse by walking a route that I had driven over last autumn, when I had been amazed at oakwoods clinging to sheer hills and corkscrew lanes like crevasses. But on foot the whole landscape seemed scaled down, and the spring flowers along the lanes were in incongruous order – the wild daffodils past their best, the woodruff and archangel out before the bluebells were barely in bud. Perhaps this is their way down here, but added to the gales it gave them a touch of uncomforting foreignness.

As March slipped into a grey April, I began making more urgent forays at home. There were chiffchaffs – the first warblers to arrive from Africa – singing in the woods, but little else. Our winterbourne, which had at least made something tangibly exciting out of the ceaseless rain, had slunk back underground. And on top of everything, it was the first spring our new bypass had carried traffic. I had learned to live with the road itself, which had been threaded neatly between our local woods and wild spots. I had even enjoyed the building of it, which had taken on the character of a rather intriguing natural disaster, a slow-motion earthquake or a glacier perhaps. But I had forgotten about the cars. Now it was roaring, and I stood in the woody common where I had spent a good deal of my adolescence, shocked at my own ability to blinker out the future for the sake of present excitement.

Selborne, the Revd Gilbert White's village, offered no succour either.

By the third week of April, a fortnight after their usual arrival, there were still no swallows in the village. I plodded the hollow lanes worn deep into the sandstone by centuries of use, and found their flowers as disordered as those of Devon. And one of their most ancient landmarks had vanished entirely. A patch of green hellebore, with vast jagged leaves and pea-green flowers, that had survived in the exact spot where White had described it for more than two and a half centuries, had finally succumbed, buried somewhere under farm rubbish and collapsed bank-top trees.

Oxford, I hoped, might be a bit more reliable. I go there every April to see the fritillaries in Magdalen College Meadow – one of the most beautiful and extraordinary sights of spring-time Britain. The snake's-head fritillary is, by a considerable margin, the most darkly glamorous and exotic of all our native flowers. It is rarely more than a foot tall with pale, grass-like leaves. But at the top of each stalk are suspended one or two crimped bell-flowers adorned with purple chequering. Close-to, the patterning becomes more complex, a mottle of lilac, plum and the rusty brown of dried blood, with the patches of colour laid over each other, as if they were scales. If you lie under a cluster of flowers they wave in the wind above you like cobras' heads – and you will see yet another reptilian feature: between the pointed, jaw-like petals, slip yellow and apparently forked stamens. No wonder fritillaries have picked up a remarkable and suggestive array of local names. In the West Country they were Lepers Lilies and Lazarus Bells, because of the similarity between the shape of the flower and the bells carried by lepers – and maybe between the livid blotches of the disease and the mottle of the petals. They were Toad's Heads in parts of Wiltshire, Dead Men's Bells in Shropshire, Snake's Heads widely across lowland England. Vita Sackville-West described them in a poem as 'Sullen and foreign looking, the snakey flower/ Scarfed in dull purple like Egyptian girls'.

And there have been writers – Geoffrey Grigson notably – who believed that they *were* foreign, an escape from cultivation, or a deliberate intro-duction into fashionably wild eighteenth-century estates. For there is an anomaly about their discovery in Britain. Despite their eye-catching flowers and a habit of growing in tens or even hundreds of thousands in the damp hay-meadows they favour, they were not officially recorded in the wild until 1736. The Magdalen colony was not explicitly com-mented on until 1785, causing the distinguished botanist Claridge Druce to sow the first seeds of scepticism about their origins a hundred years later: 'It is not a little singular that the Fritillary, so conspicuous a plant of the Oxfordshire meadows, should have so long remained unnoticed by the various botanists who had resided in or visited Oxford.'

There is a possibility that the flowers were introduced here and there.

But in most of their remaining sites in English river valleys they are growing in fields with unbroken histories as ancient hay-meadows. Many of the parishes where the flower used to grow had not just rich vernacular names for it, but annual festivals based around the plant. I think the failure to record it was confined to the botanical establishment, another episode of spring expectations gone awry. The plant grew largely in the kind of flat, wet, farming countryside that would not attract the average seventeenth- or eighteenth-century botanist. Its flowering period is short and fickle, and often in the coldest weeks of April. The botanists were by their firesides – or up more romantic mountains.

The fritillary is now reduced to a score or so of sites, having been all but wiped out by the ploughing, drainage and spraying of old meadows. But the Magdalen flowers survive, defiantly abundant, and were my first true taste of spring this year.

I drove back a circuitous way, via Greenham Common airbase in Berkshire. Since it was closed down two years ago Greenham has been going through a metaphorical spring of its own. The 2-mile-long concrete runway is already starting to dissolve, leaching calcium into the surrounding grassland, which is beginning to sparkle with chalk-loving flowers, wild carrot, eyebright, even orchids. Natterjack toads lie up under discarded ammunition boxes. The cruise-missile bunkers, Greenham's heart of darkness, have been colonised by bats. There is an even chance that Greenham may again become true commonland for local people and wildlife, which will make it a powerful symbol of regeneration and a real peace dividend. Late last summer I stood on that fearsome runway, the focus of so many communal nightmares, and watched swallows mobbing a family of young hobby falcons. So, on that warming April day, it was no real surprise to see, flitting over the thickets of razor-wire, my first swallow of the year.

It was a vanguard bird. Minutes later, as I was driving past Thatcham station, the air began to fill with swallows. They were strafing flies over the car park, drinking on the wing from the River Kennet and resting up in ever-increasing numbers on the telephone wires. More were materialising by the minute, dropping out of the clouds, until I counted more than a hundred. They had, I'm sure, just arrived after their Channel crossing, and I doubtless made a dreadful exhibition of myself welcoming them home.

That was 20 April, the first sign that the weather might change. The swifts arrived on the 30th, and by 3 May we were back in cool, wet Atlantic weather. Now it is mid-May, and I am walking in the high Chilterns, east of Watlington. There is a chill mist hanging over the hills, and it seems a day exactly in keeping with the drab procession of the past six months. Yet something has changed. In those intense few days at the beginning of the month, the landscape passed through its rites of spring. Now, despite the weather, it is in a different mode. The beeches are in full leaf, a fantastic luminous gauze that seems to glow against the mist. Troops of pure white, ectoplasmic slugs are crossing the lanes between the woods, bound on what business I do not know. There are swallows and house martins hawking for insects just inches above the pastures. And in the distance, heraldic above the ridge, I can just make out a soaring red kite, one of a population recently reintroduced here after the bird was wiped out across England by nineteenth-century gamekeepers. Life goes on in its own ways. The ordered, gentle march of spring is a human invention. For most species it is a convulsion, a time for the most urgent, compressed business of their lives. If this means they must fly by night, materialise out of the air, burst through concrete, find human help to reach new territory, and complete the whole rounds of migration and pairing, leafing and flowering in a few days, then that is how it must be, even if we are not there to see it. Keats was right to say that: 'It is a flaw/ In happiness to see beyond our bourn'. It is also a flaw to hang so desperately on what is to come, and fail to see survival enacted continuously under our noses.

Summer (1994)

It was one of the classic summers. It confounded all the forecasters and delivered the hottest July for three centuries. It sparked off a bumper crop of silly season visitations, from Mediterranean weaver-fish in the Channel to spontaneously combusting oil refineries. And it ended, much as the burnished drought of 1976 did, in torrential rains at the end of August.

It also generated a peculiarly English form of *mañana*, the slightly sceptical celebrations of a nation that knows it will never get very many of these festive summers: a mixture of gleeful, school holiday frolicking (with a rail strike as an excuse, too) and an underlying pensiveness that acknowledged that it couldn't last for ever. I found myself playing truant from the word processor more and more, yet still with a worried ear to the long-range weather forecast. At the tail-end of July [1994], I surrendered totally, and didn't think twice about driving halfway across the country for a working lunch on the north Norfolk coast. We ate oysters (without the slightest concern that there was no R in the month), walked through a haze of sea lavender to the dunes at Burnham Overy and paddled ritually in glittering water by a mile of almost empty beach. I think I spotted a Portuguese man-o'-war jellyfish (another hot weather phenomenon) sailing with the wind about twenty yards out, but it was probably a polythene bag, and I was only mildly ashamed that I couldn't be bothered to check.

But later that evening, faced with the long drive back, I paid for this lotus-eating with the first twinges of summer evening *tristesse*. There were swifts massing above Burnham Market as I sipped a beer on the green. They form these seething flocks quite late in their short stay with us, as they track insect swarms 50 feet or more up. This flock, a hundred or so strong, had built up over the Victorian east-side of the town and was now drifting over the green and the dried-out creek, towards the low hills beyond the church. The birds looked as if they were milling about haphazardly, like ash specks over a bonfire, but they were passing and crossing as artfully as a free-form aerobatics team, trawling the insect shoal from every direction. Then another ancient compulsion took over. At the edges of the flock, almost imperceptibly, birds began to fly in tandem, then in accumulating strands. The strands moved closer together until maybe fifty birds were careering together in a mass. It was a prodigious piece of flying, with birds repeatedly having to throttle back or increase their wing-beat rate to keep in formation. The ragged black comet screamed across rooftops, extruded itself through gaps between houses, gyrated round the church. Then, abruptly, the birds flung apart and were off flying leisurely in their own directions again. I suddenly remembered that this was the day when the largest chunk of a real comet, Shoemaker-Levy, was plunging into Jupiter, scattering hot organic chemicals all over the planet and probably changing its climate forever. It seemed a glib contrast between two kinds of chaos, cosmic explosion against the anarchic romping of the swifts, and I rather wished the thought hadn't surfaced right in the middle of my summer reverie. It was bad enough contemplating the swifts' departure for Africa in a week or so, without having to contemplate scales of time and distance that take one beyond birds and maybe beyond humans. This is always the one tiny flaw in peerless summers. These flat tops of the year, becalmed and seemingly endless, are of course anything but, and when bits begin to topple off the edge they can pull you down with them.

The poet Edward Thomas, depressive though he might have been, didn't seem to feel this at all. In 1906 he wrote that the two most satisfying places to be in high summer were 'the Bodleian Library and a little reedy, willowy pond'. Having experienced both I can't imagine two more stifling situations. I sympathise with his desire 'to be cool and at the same time to enjoy the sight and perfume of heat out of doors', but not with the way he regarded August, hanging betwen two seasons of uncertain weather, as 'the month of Nature's perfect poise'. The poise, I reckon, is precisely the problem. Unless you have a zen attitude to the seasons, you know it is an illusion. Even autumn, perversely, can seem more *promising*, the fall that uncovers the new buds. Summer, as you realise when it allows you to come back to your senses, is going nowhere but downhill.

Which is why water does help – not cooling pools or meditative depths, but moving, unpredictable, renewed water. It takes you somewhere else. In the first week of August I couldn't resist another day's truancy with two old friends who were nosing a narrow-boat along the Oxford Canal. It was a rare day of cloud and distant mist, brought on by the previous day's torrid humidity and temperatures in the top eighties. I had forgotten how hypnotic and relaxing canal travel could be. You glide so effortlessly between the banks that it sometimes seems as if they are moving – or perhaps rotating – past you. The Oxford Canal echoes the meanders of the River Cherwell whose route it dogs all the way between Woodstock and Banbury. Barns and cement-work chimneys slide up on one side of you, and half an hour later, reappear, making stately progress on the *other* side.

The canal is a tunnel of green in this flat and open landscape. One side is dense with reed and bulrushes, and the towpath side tousled with blossom – foams of white meadowsweet, valerian, and wild angelica, spiked with the pink spears of great willow herb (known as 'codlins-and-cream' in this part of the world), all wrapped up like a furbelow in a tangle of bindweed. Only the occasional angler's pitch gives you a view of the landscape beyond – and of the countless young swallows and house martins coursing the water meadows and stubble fields, and occasionally skimming the surface of the cut to drink. Just 40 miles to the east they have seemed almost extinct this summer. Then we round a corner, and a honey-coloured canalside church rises out of the reedbeds like an Arthurian fantasy.

Hot summers are always full of mirages and hallucinatory sightings like this. This summer it has been the turn of the dragonflies. Huge hawker species in shimmering shellacked coats of turquoise and black have been haunting our shrubberies for the past couple of months. Darting amongst the close-packed garden verticals they look unsettlingly alien. They are indifferent to people and to the cats that hurtle fruitlessly after them at the merest glimpse. They move with the rasping speed of animated cartoons, seeming to be first in one place and then another without ever having crossed the space between. I wonder if we would tolerate their brazenness and prehistoric shapes if they were just twice as big – the size of a blackbird, say, and preyed on butterflies rather than bluebottles. At dusk they take to the high branches of our neighbour's spruce tree, and the cats lie down underneath, gazing upwards as if they are starstruck.

In the last great heatwave, in August 1990, I found myself doing something rather similar. It was just before midnight on a Sunday at the beginning of the month. The temperatures had been in the mid-nineties that afternoon, and it was impossible to sleep. I was lying on the bed gazing out of the open window, when the sky suddenly became full of darting balls of orange light. They were roundish, fuzzy-edged and moving about in an oddly purposive way, turning on their tracks, crossing and swooping. It was the kind of movement made by living things, swifts and ants, say, not the brief random trajectories of sparks or meteorites. I was mesmerised at first, then alarmed. In front of my eyes was something my sceptical mind had always rejected – a swarm of unidentified flying objects. They sped about for about ten minutes, then vanished.

For the next few days I desperately tried to regain my equilibrium by dreaming up sensible explanations. I wondered if I had witnessed a bizarre electrical storm, or the Northern Lights come south, or a high altitude will-o'-the-wisp. I tried to imagine any creatures that could have given the undeniable aura the lights had of being alive. I toyed with the possibility that they were bats which had picked up phosphorescence from a roost in a rotten tree (as barn owls sometimes do), or that my sense of perspective had been warped by sunstroke, and they were tropical fireflies blown in on the Atlantic winds, and actually flying just a few feet from my windows. None of these explanations seemed the remotest bit probable.

Four days later the local paper saved me from panic, if not embarrassment. The lights had been seen all over the area, and weren't UFOs, or emanations from corn-circles, or luminous flying creatures, but a laser-show at a Tina Turner open-air concert at Woburn Park more than 15 miles away.

A more down-to-earth visitation is a regular enough event on our lawn to have become a kind of family occasion. We call it 'ant-rising day', the moment (almost always in August) when the black flying ants leave their nests for mating. It is a beautiful, chastening glimpse of a world whose pace we can barely comprehend, especially in this doldrum month. The few queen ants and the many smaller males fly up together from burrows all over the garden, and for a while the air is full of the glitter of their wings against the sun, like a slow shower of tinsel. They mate briefly, and about half an hour later the females return to earth, bite off their wings, and go underground to lay their eggs – provided they can run the gauntlet of predatory red ants who gather for the feast. The remarkable thing is that ant-rising occurs at exactly the same moment over a wide area. A few years ago I phoned round a circle of friends, and found that it was happening simultaneously (at 4 p.m. on 13 August to be precise) in patches of rough grass outside the theatre at Guildford, the High Wycombe telephone exchange and in the patients' garden at Hemel Hempstead General Hospital. This year, in keeping with the disordered nature of things, it seemed to occur twice, once in late July and again on 21 August.

Remembering these August ceremonials, I realise that what I like in summer is not so different from Edward Thomas' prescription after all: you sit in a bower and watch the world go by. When the weather is good enough I often spend whole days in the garden like this, writing fitfully under the shade of the beech tree, with papers clamped down by flints. Sometimes, close by, a robin sings its introspective autumnal sub-song. On the far side of the garden, the season shifts subtly in its supposed moment of 'perfect poise'. A late, solitary swift coasts towards the east, and not long after is followed by a hobby falcon, like a large swift itself. It is flying with relaxed, elbowy beats, coasting briefly on long rapier wings held out flat, and then banking in an almost vertical plane, so that I can glimpse its rufous leg feathers. They can catch swifts, and dragonflies, too, but this one is just cruising. Directly in front of me is the buddleia bush, the epicentre of all the garden's natural life in high summer. Buddleia came from China originally, but our native insects have come to adore its honey-scented purple flower-spikes. In some years I have counted up to fifty butterflies of ten different species on our bush at once. This year, the damp spring put paid to most overwintering tortoiseshells and peacocks, and there were fewer. But the bush still hums with life – bees, daytime moths, spotted flycatchers, the odd cat dreaming of its scrubland ancestors – all welcome ripples in August's stagnation.

The summer is almost over now, and I have come back to Norfolk, drawn to a walk along Blakeney Point, the 4-mile-long ridge of sand and tide-hurled shingle that splays out towards the Wash and encloses one of the most magical bays in eastern England. It is an exhausting plod on the bare shingle, like walking on a treadmill, and the saltmarsh that lies inland of the spit is not much easier. It is fretted with deep creeks, and barred here and there by tongues of shingle that have been sprayed into the marsh by storm tides. A mile to the south I can see the string of villages that marked the coastline a few centuries ago – Salthouse, Cley, Blakeney, Morston, Stiffkey.

So many of my *rites de passage* were played out along this coast. My teenage affair with nature was rekindled here, I dreamed up my first book, rented my very first cottage. My first night in north Norfolk, spent on a friend's converted lifeboat at Blakeney one August thirty years ago, was a transforming experience, changing the whole way I looked at and felt about landscape. I still have what I wrote about waking up the next morning: 'The whole landscape seemed to be on the move. Terns hovered feet above the water, and arrowed down for small fish. Spikes of cord-grass and sea-lavender bounced about in the tide-race. Swirling geometric figures opened up on the surface of the water, stretched and then closed again. Even the mud seemed to be alive, and slid out of the receding water with the moist shine of a new-born animal.' It was a liberating vision of being at the edge of things, and a sight that has kept me in thrall to this coast ever since.

I plod on over the pebbles, past a seemingly indestructible clump of sea-kale whose leaves I once tried to chew (not realising it should have been the stems) and decide to take to the marsh for a while. The tide is rising fast now, and I sit and watch the waders begin to move. On the last remaining patches of land, small groups of curlew, dunlin and grey plover sit it out until the water covers their feet. Everything is moving – yachts in the harbour, bird flocks, even plants bending with the current. I always find myself getting lost in tides, gazing at them much as one does at a fire, watching for the point of turning, for the first tuft of grass to resurface, for those damp runnels of sand to emerge scoured and sculptured in shapes that have never existed before.

I walk on to the Point. Out amongst the dunes here we used to enact our noble savage version of the English summer holiday. We dozed by the saltwater pools, ate samphire and shellfish we'd scrabbled out of the mud and played cricket with driftwood bats. Sometimes in high summer we would moor the boat out in the harbour and stay there, rowing to the Point or to the mainland when we fancied it. On warm August evenings the sea was full of phosphorescent algae, and each time we raised an oar it left a sparkler's trail in the air.

As the tide is ebbing I decide to walk back along the marshland edge, but it is almost impossible. There seem to be new pools everywhere. The rough tracks are covered with flashes of water and scuttling crabs, which shape up to me with their claws as I pass. Twice I go up to my knees in hidden creeks. After all these years I have begun to understand why I love this landscape so much. The tides are great renewers, greater influences on the life here than even the seasons. They soften and *contain* the seasons. This coastal strip, washed clean twice a day, already has the embryos of autumn, winter and spring within it. The samphire and sea-blite bushes are showing flashes of red. The winter waders are returning, white sanderlings scuttling about the beach, greenshank giving their lilting calls as they fly on to the newly exposed mud. And, deep under the tideline debris – the muddle of flotsam, shingle, dead birds, fish-egg cases and shells that forms new land here – the new shoots of buried shoreline plants are already reaching upwards.

I am nearly back at Cley now, and I spot a small swarm of sandhoppers on a patch of dry sand. As my footsteps get closer they begin to jump and throw themselves about in every direction. It used to be thought that this frenzied rush to escape was their normal way of moving. But now, a little less arrogant, we know better. I sit down, keep still and watch them begin to shift quite differently. They *swim* through the sand on their sides, in the gentle arcing motions of cruising swifts or Tina Turner's laser lights. Summer is on the move again.

Winter (1994)

All winter there has been an unfamiliar sound in my wood, just at the edge of my hearing. It is the lap of water running over stone. The stodgy clay which overlays this stretch of the Chilterns doesn't absorb rain well, and in the relentless downpours of the past months, the spill-off has been moving downhill like an incoming tide, fingering its way into every footpath and rabbit-run. It has carved out runnels down to the bare flint, piled up dams of woodland flotsam – beechmast, dock stems, dead leaves – and laid out terraces of miniature pools and rapids. For a few blissful hours on most days, I have had an upland river on my patch.

I have often felt this is just what the place needs. It's a muddled wood, full of lumpy medieval banks and straddling a sharp, dry valley that in the West Country would certainly have a stream as its focus. But underneath the clay this is chalk country, and whatever watercourse sluiced out the valley's profile fifteen thousand years ago, it has long since vanished hundreds of feet underground.

But rain of the kind that we have had this past year can bring it back to life. In something resembling a monsoon in the summer of 1992, when the ground was baked hard by drought, the downpours sent flash-floods rasping through the wood. Everywhere the water took short cuts, coursing down badger tracks, bursting through hedges from the fields next door, and occasionally taking off straight down the valley slopes. In the bottom a torrent built up that tore huge clumps of fern out by the root. It snapped off a 9-inch-thick branch from a fallen tree and drove it forward like a snow-plough, wiping a swath of ground 40 feet long clear of vegetation. All the water was doing, of course, was reclaiming the ancestral territory it had flowed over during the last years of the Ice Age.

This winter it has been like a war of attrition. Wildly different weathers have followed one another in dizzying alternations. Days of deluge are followed by abrupt freeze-ups, and old logs, as sodden as sponges, crack open as the water bulks up into ice. Dispiriting Atlantic depressions bring twilight at noon. Then there are gales. The whole wood is peppered with broken branches, speared into the ground like some last-ditch Saxon barricade. Only a few whole trees have been blown down, and they were already dying, but they have taken others with them. Just before Christmas, I stood in front of an immense column of ivy trellised on one of our last sickly elms, and held forth to a television camera about the great resilience and independence of ivy, and how it would unquestionably outlast the elms. At this point a tawny owl flopped tetchily out of the foliage, which I suppose I should have taken as a portent. Two weeks later the ivy, its stem as thick as an arm at the base, was flat on the ground, together with half a dead elm. Within days the leaves had been browsed off by the resident muntjac deer.

Everything seems to be in the process of being chewed or frozen or blown away. The badgers, which occupy a vast dynastic sett deep in the chalk at the bottom of the wood, are harrowing up the bluebell bulbs in their search for worms. The wild cherry trees have a fungal blight that turns the leaves prematurely brown and then stops them falling off the tree. They seem impervious to even the fiercest winds, and are still hanging on the trees like sagging tea-bags. And as if to underline the seasonal moral theme of dust to dust, cars have started to parachute into the wood, sliding gracefully off the S-bend in the lane and landing in the mud by the entrance gate. I have never seen one *in flagrante*, and all I find, the next day, are forensic hints of these events of the night: shards of red glass, bits of discarded rope, the prints of unsuitable shoes – the bric-à-brac of most small winter disasters.

In *Pilgrim at Tinker Creek* Annie Dillard wrote that to be 'frayed and nibbled' was one of the conditions of existence, but that it was all right, because 'the new is always present simultaneously with the old, however hidden'. That is reassuring, I suppose, but I have to say that I am feeling pretty frayed and nibbled myself. I have come up here to saw up some of the branchwood left over after the beeches were thinned last winter. It needs to be done, and I try to persuade myself that the exercise will also be an antidote to winter torpor. Always at this season, and more particularly this year, I feel bloated, irritable, immobile, crunched up inside myself. I suppose this may be partly a mild form of the fashionable disorder SAD (seasonal affective disorder), which is brought about by the lack of sunlight, leaving some crucial hormone levels close to the levels they are in sleep – or hibernation. Maybe this is not a disorder at all, and what is wrong is our attempt to buck our physiology. Oliver Sacks has argued that many psychosomatic disorders (migraine especially) might be civilised ornamentations of entirely natural states, especially of the biological response to stress that lies *between* fight and flight – what he calls 'vegetative retreat', playing dead, freezing. Perhaps I should give in and retreat to the wood-stacks, like the edible dormice that snooze away the cold months there. Certainly the alternative option – fighting languor with action – fills me with other dreads. What about the other perils of winter physiology, I muse to myself, feeling the cross-saw tighten up in a beech log. The blood steeped in fats, adrenalin levels soaring to try and soak them up, lungs grasping at polluted air? So I saw away in a slow and dignified way, find my head filling with hymns, and spend a lot of time pausing and pretending to gaze meditatively around at the prospects.

Or I pack up all this compulsive pottering and just go for a walk. And today I notice something that is the converse of Dillard's 'new hidden in the old'. The gales have piled up drifts of leaves all over the wood, obliterating old tracks and familiar views, and leaving enticing trails across newly bare ground. In places it feels as if I have never been here before. Strolling up the main track, I glance sideways and for the first time spot something that looks like a straight avenue tacking up the north-facing slope. I can't believe it is accidental. There are two big beeches and the oldest hawthorn in the wood all in a line down one side. The avenue is too wide for it to be a gap between planted rows – and I have never noticed it before. For a moment, I am seized by the conviction that I have at last discovered the route of the ancient track that I have been searching for for ten years. It is marked on an early nineteenth-century map, and was the chief trackway from the village down to the coach road. But in 1853, during the enforced Parliamentary Enclosure of the entire parish, it was closed off, along with twelve other old roads and footpaths. The notices of dispossession were posted all over the parish at the end of August, in the heavy type used on police 'Wanted' posters. The vicar who was appointed to the parish the following year was amazed at how patiently the 630 villagers accepted the enclosure, considering 'all the picturesque appearance of the place was gone, and perhaps the poetry . . . and considering of how many rights the enclosure deprived them'. Not a trace of the path survived, not even in aerial photographs. Now, maybe, some of it has resurfaced, a bit of an older, more congenial parish exposed by the new winter landscape.

It is odd how much we distance ourselves even from these more romantic aspects of winter gloom. During the great gale of 2 January 1976, I saw our churchyard yew with its foliage streaming sideways like bunting caught in a fan. In the heavy snowfalls of 1979 there were natural snow-balls ('snow-rollers') forming on our lawn as strong winds whipped over wet, slightly melting snow. And on the 23rd of that same month, I can remember the notorious 'glazed frost', when rain fell at sub-zero temperatures and froze so quickly that the raindrops rang as they hit the windows.

I suppose our problem is that we have a temperamental climate and a way of talking about it to match. As an eccentrically shaped island midway between two weather systems, we are stuck with a turbulent and unpredictable climate, whether we like it or not. It's rare that we get a chance to become acclimatised to anything. The whole business is made worse because acclimatisation is a physiological process as well as a psychological and cultural one. Winter really does get us down. The cold makes the blood clot more easily and nerve endings become less responsive. Levels of many of the substances that help combat infection fall. Bronchitis, arthritis and strokes are commoner in the winter. So is retinal detachment. We are buffeted every bit as much as ancient evergreens. The most dramatic effects happen during the complex cluster of changes that occur during the passage of a depression (the kind of condition that makes most people feel 'under the weather'). Blood pressure, phantom limb pain and migraine worsen, and rates of heart attack, appendicitis, suicide and industrial accidents, rise perceptibly. The Germans take this seriously enough to have a weather help-line for doctors, forecasting the kind of patients imminent weather changes are likely to bring to the surgery. We make things worse by going to extraordinary lengths to avoid accepting our weather. It is one of the great forces that shape our lives, and one we all experience in common, yet we sentimentalise its past, become obsessed about its future, and tetchy about what is happening now. We blame last year's mild winter for this year's bad summer, and with a typical piece of national masochism, expect we'll 'have to pay for it' when we do have a good spell. In something close to voodoo we have even begun to blame the forecasters themselves.

It was the fourth anniversary of the 1990 hurricane yesterday (25 January), the one the forecasters *did* get right. And with the extraordinary symmetry that the weather often shows, gales are again roaring in from the south-west. But they're taking a more northerly route this year, and all they do to my wood is give it a kind of grooming, raking dead wood out of the tops of trees and scattering it about the ground. The place seems full of new light, pouring down through the canopy and reflected off the gashed branches below.

The 1990 storm was a very different affair, far worse in the Chilterns than the great wind of October 1987. About thirty trees came down in the wood, chiefly birch, hornbeam and cherry. We left most of them where they fell. A few died, but others held onto their roots and put up sheaves of vertical shoots from the reclining trunks, so that we have a new landscape feature – miniature hedges inside the wood. One hornbeam we were able to winch halfway back into its root-hole. Relieved of most of its top branches, it has flourished as a miniature pollard, a stubby troll of a tree.

Thinning is really just a controlled gale. It creates gaps for new growth and leaves the ground deep in top-wood – which is what we're now slowly turning to firewood. I'm enjoying the sawing now, and forgetting my hypochondria. There is something satisfying about woodcutting that goes beyond the not terribly creditable human obsession with tidying nature up. Nine-month-old beech logs are already seasoned. They cut like loaves and smell of yeast. They produce a wild, xylophone clatter when you pile them on the stacks – an altogether more cheering winter sound than freezing rain ringing on windows.

My neighbours, who often work with me here, have discovered a book of photographs of woodstacks. It is a terrible indictment of our own dishevelled piles. In the Austrian Ausseerland, where they were taken, the peasants have a tradition of exquisitely customising their stacks. Some are symmetrical, framed, all of a piece; others are subtle counterpoints of colours and log-end shapes. In her commentary, the critic Yvette Wiener asks the obvious question. What is it all for, this compulsive searching for individual pattern in works which will be slowly deconstructed during the winter? 'Who is the mad man who meticulously reassembles in the stacking the log he has split apart beforehand, giving it back its original shape?'

We had something of the same fussy approach (though nothing like the imagination) when we first started work in the wood twelve years ago. After thinning and logging we would come close to hoovering the wood, gathering and burning up every stray twig as well as the logs. The bonfires were congenial affairs, but a terrible waste. Now we just gather the brushwood up into rough piles, and leave them for wrens and dormice and hibernating hedgehogs. And, years on, I have come to feel that culture should press lightly on nature in places like this, that our activities should be modest and appropriate as well as ingenious, rather like the tinkerings of bower-birds.

I take off for a walk. A tit flock is shuttling leisurely through the wood, hundreds of birds of half a dozen species strung out over acres of budding twigs. The birds keep the flock together with brief high-pitched calls, but already they will be forming pairs inside it. On the ground seedling ashes are popping up wherever there is a patch of light. The bluebell shoots are already 4 inches tall, only a month after the solstice. And when I break open a beech bud, as hard as a wooden skewer outside, I find it is full of leafy green tissue. I never cease to be surprised at how thin the husk between winter and spring can be. Then, quite suddenly, *two* muntjac deer spring out of a bramble patch at my feet and dash through the holly, white scuts sticking up like flagpoles. The possibility that muntjac fawns might be nibbling the rest of my ivy in a couple of months lifts my spirits more than I could have believed.

William Hazlitt, in his far-sighted essay 'On the Love of the Country', written in 1814, explains why experiences of this kind can be so affecting, so supportive. He suggests that, unlike our feelings for other humans, which are directed towards mortal individuals, there is a 'transferable' quality to our feelings for nature, which can be extended 'to the whole class'. He is right, of course, but it doesn't seem to lessen by one jot the sense of continuity provided by these new growths in the shell of winter; or the consolation they give me, sitting on my ramshackle woodpile, taking my pulse, and remembering I was born in the middle of a February snowstorm.

KNOWING MY PLACE

A Year's Turning in the Chilterns

'Jan 3: 1903. Am writing an essay on the life-history of insects and have abandoned the idea of writing on "How Cats Spend their Time".' So W. N. P. Barbellion began his classic *Journal of a Disappointed Man*. He was only thirteen at the time, and I have heartfelt sympathy with his sense of not being quite in control of the rudder. After a year of public journal writing I am struck by how haphazard the whole business is. Too few facts, too many rushed judgements, a marked tendency to make extravagant flourishes of private emotions.

But fits of self-doubt are endemic to writers. I sometimes try to assuage mine by pretending that writing is a legitimate rural trade, and prose a kind of alternative crop, yielding so many bushels of word to acres tramped. If so, I can report that there is little danger of a surplus word mountain building up in this corner of the countryside. To tell the truth the whole business feels more like hunter-gathering than farming. There is the same element of serendipity, of lucky finds and blank days; the same merging of roles, so that foraging becomes part of everything you do.

Which is why, in a rare spell of balmy weather in February, I found myself walking down a familiar track in a mood in which it was impossible to disentangle childish excitement and professional curiosity. The evening before I had seen the glint of running water where no running water had been for a decade, and I was off, chasing whole volumes of memory and possibilities.

I have walked these hills to the south of my home since I was a teenager, and the route has become almost a ritual beat. It is an unexceptional landscape of run-down parkland and narrow commons. But after thirty years you can come to love every fencepost. And in this unseasonable weather there was a wild *frisson* in the air – a thin gauze of green already in the hedges, rooks tossing over the copses, and gale-wrecked trees in every field, already seeming as cryptic and anciently rooted as standing stones.

At the edge of Icedell Wood was the most awesome collapse I have seen following the hurricane [in October 1987]; eight oak trees on a single root-plate 15 feet high and nearly 40 feet across. The branches on the two central trees had grown away from each other, forming a huge vaulted aisle now they were prostrate. I walked up and down this immense whale's gullet, counting my steps. It was more than 130 feet long.

I wriggled through the tangled branches into the wood. Drifts of tits and chaffinches, fellow foragers, rose and fell in front of me. Under the beeches by the old icehouse, the first green hellebores were already in flower, only days behind the celandines, and on the same site they were recorded in our first county flora in 1848.

I know their history, I rejoice in their continuity, yet I barely glance at them. I realise I have been racing through the wood, drawn by the lure of water and driven by workaday anxieties that I haven't yet unwound from. Just a few hours before I had been listening to a radio reading of Henry Reed's famous war poem 'Naming of Parts', in which he contrasts the stripping down of a rifle with the first stirrings of a garden after winter:

> And this you can see is the bolt. The purpose of this
> Is to open the breech, as you see. We can slide it
> Rapidly backwards and forwards: we call this
> Easing the spring. And rapidly backwards and forwards
> The early bees are assaulting and fumbling the flowers:
>   They call it easing the Spring.

Just a few hundred yards more and I am in the valley, barely able to stop running. That distant glint of water had been no mirage. Our local winterbourne, the Woewater, is up and flowing for the first time in a dozen years. The vast winter rains are bursting through the seams between the clay and chalk and charging down the valley. Within half a mile the stream is 4 feet wide and flowing as fast as I can walk. It has torrents and oxbows and eddies, and underneath them the young meadow grass is waving as silkily as waterweed. In one dip it has formed a pool by the edge of a wood, and bubbles rising from buried air pockets look like summer midges settling on the surface. I am time-warped, and for a few seconds am seized by a conviction that the first swallow will coast down the valley and begin hawking over the pool.

It doesn't, of course, but a mile or so further on I see something almost as wondrous. The stream has flooded the valley meadows, and flocks of fieldfares and redwings are feeding near the water's edge. A snipe jinks in the distance and, much closer, a heron flies up from a pond that has been a dry pit since I was a teenager. The water suddenly makes sense of the whole geography of the valley – the position of the farms, the ancient black poplar, standing again with its roots in water.

There is a legend here that the Woewater only flows in times of war and trouble, but it is hard to see how it could have brought anything but good to this dry valley.

Back home I check my diary to see if I had recalled the last rising accurately. I noted it on 12 April 1975 – a year memorable more for its wonderful summer than any particular woe, and for the fact that the fighting in Vietnam ended a fortnight later. I am not superstitious, but think that might be a better kind of legend to hang on to. The rising of water, like sap, is another kind of easing the spring.

[2]

I have lived in the Chilterns for most of my life, yet I still find it hard to bring the region into sharp focus. Familiarity can breed a kind of inconstancy, and over the years I have found a succession of different images coming to symbolise my home country for me. When I was a teenager they focused on a long, meandering valley which wound away towards the south and the sun till it vanished in a shimmering heat-haze over the distant hill country. Later came a more sober and reflective view: a common's edge in winter, and the tangle of old man's beard that knitted it to pale fields scraped out of chalk and flint. Most recently, perhaps, the almost oppressive silence of a beechwood in late summer, a woodland habitat so absolutely reduced to the essentials of greenleaf, trunk and earth that there is often nothing to register the sound of your footsteps.

These are all very partial views of the Chilterns, and if I was honest I would have to admit that each one is rooted in a quite specific place. But I've come to realise that this elusiveness, this refusal to be expressed by generalisations, is part of the region's basic character. It does not brandish its identity in the way the Cotswolds does its stone, or Sussex its huge downland vistas. The countryside round many of its main roads is such an undemonstrative variation on ordinary Home Counties themes that it is possible to drive across and not have the slightest idea you have been there. Yet this 400-square-mile tract was distinctive enough to be named 'Cilterne' (hill-country in Old Celtic) at least a thousand years ago, and to be designated an 'Area of Outstanding Natural Beauty' in 1964 – a fact which has led many sceptical through-travellers to enquire, quite simply, 'Where?'

The answer to this paradox lies partly in the essential geography of the Chiltern Hills. Guidebooks usually try to explain their inscrutable contours with the image of a westward-inclined fist, with Dunstable in the north as the little finger, the Thames between Goring and Windsor in the south, and the lines between the fingers and knuckles representing the gaps in which the few rivers and major roads run. But it is what lies between these main valleys that is the key to the Chilterns' character. Here is an intricate network of gulleys and combes that is almost completely invisible from the main roads. They are etched so deeply that many have a climate all of their own, humid in summer, harsh in winter. (One, near Rickmansworth, has the record for the greatest variation in daily temperature in Britain: 34°F at 6 a.m. to 84.9 at 2 p.m. on 29 August 1936.) Most are waterless, heavily wooded and hard to cultivate, and have generated a rural economy based on grazing and wood production. They are a kind of frontierland, and have nourished a long line of mavericks and dissenters, who, for their part, have helped perpetuate a landscape in their own image.

So don't believe any description of the Chilterns which reduces them to some stereotype of rural England. What makes them special and exciting is precisely that they are secretive, contrary, raggle-taggle and often quite wonderfully wild.

Even at their extreme eastern edge, where they merge with the flat country of the Middlesex Green Belt, you can sense the quirky, footloose spirit of the place. Go to Chenies, just 20 miles north-west of Hyde Park, and drop down to the banks of the River Chess. It is more like Dorset than the Chilterns in the valley, with a wide chalk stream, and sheep up to their ears in yellow flags. But on both sides of you the straggling scarp woodlands are beginning to climb away to the west and north. They are awash with cherry blossom in April, and later ringed by it, when the petals fall and settle on the margins of chalky clay that have been worn bare by sheltering animals. But all is not as mild and predictable as it may seem. Walk north up one of the side valleys (mostly known as 'bottoms' here) towards Flaunden, and after you pass a small chalk quarry buried among the trees, you come to the Green Dragon pub. But don't make this journey by car at dusk. Just before the pub there is a sharp corner, and halfway round, a huge wooden dragon, green and red, rears up behind the hedge. If this makes you think of Celtic whimsy and romance, you are beginning to understand the place.

Once, in one of these Chess valley meadows, I found two perfectly polished champagne glasses hidden in the cruck of a huge pollard oak. I like to think of the drinkers returning, once a year, and celebrating their anniversary 10 feet from the ground. Another time, just a few hundred yards from this spot, I met a class of sixth-formers on an outing from a Jewish school in London. It was their first visit, and they wondered if I could point them along an interesting route back to Chorleywood station. I did my best, and we went our separate ways. About half an hour later, I saw them again marching through the high wood, well on schedule, with their Hebrew songs ringing through the beeches.

The Chilterns are defined by their niggardly soils, their woodland and the imagination that centuries of coping with these frugal resources has called forth. The whole area rests on a deep bed of chalk. In some places this is so thick that the surface water takes more than twenty years to filter through to the aquifer, and what can be extracted from the deepest wells (as an enterprising bottling firm in Aldbury has recently discovered) is a kind of fossil water, stripped of all its usual modern pollutants. But chalk only appears in any quantities on the surface along the steep western escarpment between Luton and Watlington. This is where the last south-bound glaciers ground to a halt, and where the meltwaters eventually washed out the plain of Aylesbury. Here enough chalk is exposed to form the string of celebrated hills which includes Dunstable Downs and Ivinghoe Beacon. There are splendid orchids to look out for here, and gliders, but also more eccentric Chiltern specialities, like the herds of wallabies that bask in the spring sunshine on the west-facing slopes of Whipsnade Zoo.

But over most of the Chiltern plateaux the surface soils had their chalk leached out by rain long ago, and what remains is that stony, tacky mixture, the bane of local farmers and gardeners, known as clay-with-flints. It is flint, not the more amenable chalk, that is the quintessential Chiltern rock. I think we sensed this as children, and it was one of our youthful tests of endurance to walk barefoot over a newly ploughed field. Flintstones still seem inexhaustible in the fields, and after heavy rains the smaller pieces are washed out into the lanes and pile up in little shingle beaches, inches deep. Yet in some of the drier woods, huge unbroken lumps can suddenly appear on the tops of steep slopes, as if they had bobbed up through the clay.

The Chilterns have always been one of the most densely wooded regions of Britain. Indeed, on the most infertile of the clay soils, wood has probably been the only really practicable and profitable crop. In some reaches south of High Wycombe, between a third and half of the total area is under woodland, mostly beechwood of one sort or another. It is these beechwoods which, more than any other single ingredient, determine the look of the landscape today. They can be monotonous in high summer, when their deep shade seems to blanket out all other life. But catch them at their moments of change, when the sky is still just – or just about to be – visible, and there is nothing else quite like them. It is what their stone-smooth grey trunks do with sunlight that is so bewitching. In late October they frame and contrast with leaf colours that can range from bright yellow to darkest chestnut.

In the first two weeks of May, being in a beechwood is like wandering through a wood underwater. The newly opened leaves are almost translucent, and when the sun shines through them, the trunks are bathed in a dappled green light that shifts and ripples with even the slightest breeze. If the beeches are on an ancient, wooded site so much the better, for there may well be drifts of bluebells as well and a grass called wood melick, which, with the sun behind it, seems coloured a brilliant lime-green. It's a happy chance that so many of the Chiltern lanes run east-west: pick one of these – the Turville–Northend road, or Ashton Hill near Wendover – for an early evening stroll towards the sun and you will see what I mean.

But spare a moment, too, for some of the more ancient, mixed Chiltern woods. Go to Ashridge at cherry-blossom time, and to the gaudy thickets of maple, dogwood, spindle and a dozen other species that adorn the chalk slopes in autumn. Meander around the Happy Valley, near Ellesborough, where there are darkly humid and evocatively scented combes of native box. And remember that beech, though it is native here, has only been the definitive Chiltern tree for a hundred and fifty years. In the medieval period the area was covered with great tracts of mixed coppice, and was one of the major sources of fuel for London. The wood was taken by cart down to the Thames and loaded on to barges.

During the latter part of the eighteenth century, when coal became a cheaper alternative fuel, many of the Chiltern copses became redundant, and on the chalk were often grubbed out to make way for wheat. It was the rise of the furniture industry in the High Wycombe area that was the saving of them. The industry's demand for beech for chair-legs was insatiable, and over the first decades of the nineteenth century, many surviving woods – and new plantations – were devoted to growing beech timber. The account books of one (Hockeridge Wood) near Ashley Green, are preserved in the Hertfordshire Record Office, and actually document the change from fuelwood copse to timber farm in the late 1790s. Over a three-year period the entire wood was cut over, producing 120,000 faggots. Every sale was noted in the book, and the names of many local families that purchased wood – Geary, Redding, Pudephatt – are still common in this part of the Chilterns.

There has always been a close relationship between communities and woodland here, and a long tradition of free access to the land. Although pasturing in woodland and pollarding for firewood are no longer practised, many of the wooded commons where these rights were exercised still survive. Naphill Common, with its giant cherries and yews, Burnham Beeches and Frithsden are the finest, but fragments can often be found wherever there is a village place-name with 'Green' or 'End' in it. And the tradition finds another expression in the immense length of fiercely defended public footpaths that wind about the region.

The free-spirited atmosphere of the Chiltern combes has always attracted non-conformist political and religious movements. Amersham was a stronghold of the Lollards in the sixteenth century. The Chartist Land Company created a settlement of thirty-five smallholdings at Heronsgate, near Chorley Wood. Jordans, near Beaconsfield, began in 1919 as a Quaker-inspired village for craftsmen and women.

Does a landscape really help shape its inhabitants' behaviour? Faced with the ultimate Chiltern folly, the Watlington White Mark, one is tempted to say, simply, that they help make each other. H. J. Massingham used to believe the Mark was an authentic Celtic chalk carving, intended to register the summer solstice. In fact it was made by a local in the eighteenth century. He could see Watlington church from his window, and felt it would be improved by a spire. So he had the image of one carved in the chalk in Watlington Hill, in such a way that from his window, church and fake spire lined up as one.

[3]

Can a whole landscape be defined by something as inherently mortal as a single tree species? You might think so if you lived in the Chilterns. For a century and a half the region's woods – and they cover a vast area – have been dominated by beech plantations: pure stands of gracious, even-aged trees whose forerunners were planted for the Windsor chair industry. The guidebook description of these austere groves is 'natural cathedrals' and it is understandable that their current misfortunes are seen by many as a kind of desecration.

They are dying of drought and disease, being munched away by grey squirrels and blown over in gales. Nature seems to be giving a clear message that the beech is no tree for the current English climate. But the region's loyalty to it is unswerving, and an almost superstitious fear has taken root that if the beech goes, so will the entire woodland cover. So, more despairingly each year, the Chiltern beeches are propped up, put into intensive care and replanted when they succumb. The cost in ecological (and economic) terms is enormous. Natural woodland is bulldozed to make way for them; scrub suppressed by brushwood killers; poison laid down for the squirrels.

I grew up amongst the Chiltern beechwoods and share the widespread sadness at their plight. But they have been turned into totems here, mythologised to an extent that their real history and role do not warrant, and, when it comes to a choice, they have been repeatedly favoured at the expense of more ancient, indigenous woodland types. Our attitude towards them is typical of our desire to put living landscapes in aspic (or, in this case, ill-fitting corsets), and is an example of how, when it comes to nature, we forget the extent to which culture influences our views.

A taste for beech has always, I think, been a rather sophisticated, adult enthusiasm. When I was a child growing up in the Chilterns in the 1950s, it was certainly very low on our lists. It was useless for camps, impossible to climb, and really only good for carving your initials on. Our parents also seemed to have rather distant views of it, albeit more favourable than ours. They saw it as the epitome of elegance and classicism, a feminine foil to the ruggedness of the oak (fine timber beeches were always called 'queens', and singing about 'hearts of beech' would have sounded positively cissy). The undercurrent to this was the ambivalent suggestion that the tree wasn't a proper British native, but had been brought here from the Continent by the Romans, regarded in those post-war years as the fount of all civilisation.

The physical evidence of the beech's history tells a rather different story. The earliest remnants are pollen grains found in the Hampshire Basin, and date from about 6,000 BC – about two thousand years after oaks returned to post-glacial Britain, and five hundred years before the Channel opened up. The beech thus passes – just – the key test of nativeness, in being here before Britain became an island. But it was at the northern edge of its climatic range and by the Iron Age seems to have reached a natural limit south of a line between the Wash and Bristol Channel. Inside this zone it grew on all kinds of light, dry soils, though its well-known association with chalk and limestone may have depended on the opening up of these soils by early farmers.

And this is pretty much where it remained for the next two thousand years, give or take a few isolated colonisations and transplantings. In parts of south-east England it may even have become the commonest tree. But it would have grown then in more mixed woods, with sessile oak in some areas, hornbeam in others, and with ash, maple and elm on more calcareous soils. And the beeches themselves would not have borne much resemblance to the tall, straight trees we have come to associate with modern plantations. They were rarely used for building, and were not encouraged to become timber trees. Even in the Chilterns houses were framed in oak. The beech was valued historically as a more basic kind of workhorse. It was an energy source, producing firewood for humans, and mast for grazing cattle. Mixed beechwoods supplied fuel for many Roman ironworks. In the Sussex Weald, beech was the fuel of choice for the glass industry. And in the Chilterns wood cut from pollard oak and beech (and some coppice, too) was shipped up to London by barge, for the city's hearths and ovens.

The form of beech that develops under a regime of pollarding is squat and broad, with the mat of surface roots by which the tree braces itself on shallow soil echoed in a thick bushel of branches above. The trunk is adorned with intricate flutings, scars and knobs where the bark has grown back over the cut surfaces. Three or four centuries ago this was probably the most familiar type of beech in the southern English countryside. It is still visible in some of the ancient wood-pastures in the Chilterns – for instance at Frithsden, Burnham Beeches and Naphill Common – though with stouter and more gnarled branchings now that regular lopping is no longer practised.

During the eighteenth century, a new form of beech entered the currency. The Age of 'Improvement' had arrived, and tree-planting became a passion among the landowning classes. It was a convenient way of indulging in the contemporary taste for 'natural' scenery whilst producing a commercial crop. It also made a powerful statement about the planter's social status and its likely inheritance down the generations – for at least as long as the life of a hardwood tree. But in order for these underlying ambitions to succeed, no one else could be permitted to appropriate or 'disfigure' the trees, and from the eighteenth century on, common rights of pollarding began to be withdrawn in many woods. At the same time, plantations (often including conifers as nurse crops) began to replace mixed and naturally sprung woods. They coaxed into being a form of beech less familiar than the gnarled old pollards – a tall, straight-trunked, high-branching tree, a Palladian column in wood that soon found an apt economic role in the burgeoning furniture industry.

These changing economic and social roles influenced (and were influenced by) aesthetic judgements. The elegant, investment beech was looked on as beautiful precisely because it *was* economically desirable. (As late as the 1820s even Cobbett maintained that he had 'no idea of picturesque beauty separate from the fertility of the soil'.) It was then only a matter of time before plantation beechwoods were believed to be the correct, 'normal' vegetation of chalk-hill country, and in some ways more 'natural' than mutilated pollards – however Gothic and picturesque the latter might appear.

In the Chilterns they are *still* widely believed to be the 'natural' tree cover, despite the longer and historically richer ancestries of ancient, mixed woods and the few remaining stands of 'vulgar' pollards. I am fortunate in having one of the latter as a neighbour, the venerable waste of Frithsden Beeches, which has had such an eventful history as a wooded common. It was already predominantly beech in the mid-fourteenth century, and there is a telling record of the Black Prince looting some of the commoners' pollards, in order to pay for imported oak for a deer-park fence. And there was a famously unsuccessful attempt at enclosure in 1866, when Lord Brownlow's three miles of illegal fencing were torn down by London navvies. (The court case which followed marked a turning point in legislation to protect commonland.)

Even now the Beeches is a hectic place, a catacomb of immense, contorted pollards, fused and frost-cracked branches, aerial ponds, old graffiti, natural gargoyles and glowering faces glimpsed in the trunks. It is as far from being a 'natural cathedral' as you can imagine, and a lesson in how exciting woods can be when they are not kept under too close a rein.

Ironically, the cessation of pollarding in the mid-nineteenth century has led to the trees becoming top heavy, and more and more are blown over every winter. But natural regeneration of beech, birch and holly in the resultant gaps is spectacular (just as it is – with ash, cherry and maple – in the storm-blown plantations elsewhere in the hills). And, despite opposition from hard-line foresters, the National Trust (owner of the land) is experimentally pollarding some young beeches to replace them, in a fascinating marriage of rescue archaeology and woodland conservation.

I hope we can hang on to good numbers of beeches in the Chilterns – especially in historic and ancient woods. But I hope too that we remember how much their present status is a product of social posturing and commercial convenience in the not-so-distant past, and that we make room for more of the anciently indigenous mixed Chiltern woods. The identity of the region lies in the shape of the hills, in its hidden dry valleys and dark ridge-woods, in flint-drifts and hollow lanes, and in a long human tradition of commoning. It doesn't depend on maintaining one favourite tree as a virtual monoculture.

[4]

It was an almost trivial image, but it is the one from our local anthology of wartime memories that I know I shan't forget: the women cycling home 'in droves' from the munitions factory, down ice-bound lanes, lamps pointed downwards in the black-out, tyres half-deflated to hold the road, and carrying lengths of string to use as tow-ropes. It caught for me both the closeness and distance of those days. I know those twisting Chiltern lanes in winter, but nothing about what it must have been like to confront them – and six years of one's life – in an incongruous and unrelenting mixture of anxiety, camaraderie and sacrifice.

Now the VE anniversary is over, these stories will start to fade, and where will the memories live then? Almost every major event in our history has left enduring reminders engraved in the landscape. Vast parish churches and pagan hill carvings, tracks worn yards deep by centuries of trudging, massive Celtic boundary ditches, probably dug by slaves, running through my home hills, the sheer ubiquity of mud after winter rain – all tell uncompromising stories about the meaning of religion, labour and authority to our ancestors. They are, perhaps, even more than written records, the most dramatic records of the feel of the past.

The war itself was pure landscape to me, born as I was in its middle years. I remember gathering strips of radar-scrambling 'window' from the garden, and watching searchlights and barrage balloons. It is all I remember. War, like sex, seems to convey some intuitive sense of its importance to children long before they understand what it means. Now that I do understand, I have confused feelings of guilt and longing at having 'missed' it.

And the tangible evidence that it happened is vanishing inexorably. The emergency airstrips have mostly been dug up, the pill-boxes we played in as children in the late forties and fifties bulldozed away. What are left are vestiges: a couple of fields taken out of the common, and only now being allowed to 'tumble back'; a wood marked on the map as 'The Larches', but which locals call 'The Italian Wood'. It was planted by prisoners of war whom I remember walking in the lanes, with black patches on their sleeves and eyes a thousand miles away. They also looked after the wood I came to own. When they went home, they gave their neighbour in the village a strawberry basket woven from willow and hazel, split and chamfered with a pen-knife, and cut from trees I have coppiced myself half a century later. It passed to some friends on the neighbour's death, an exquisite reminder of one of the happier culture shocks of wartime.

The most solid relics are the road blocks – 'tank traps', as they were called – on a road up to the common, where my own dad's army did guard duty. They sit at the edge of a field, like bulky concrete pears, moss-bound and mysterious. A while ago, I found myself walking behind two ramblers who were theorising on the traps' origins as glacier-torn examples of a local rock, Hertfordshire puddingstone. They are drifting into the realms of mythology, like Avebury's standing stones. Perhaps this is how landscape humanises war.

[5]

It is just what you want to hear when the radio wakes you on a transcendental spring morning: the massed countryside management agencies out on another witch-hunt. This time the hapless victim is the muntjac, a shy, solitary deer from China no bigger than a retriever. Foresters are accusing them of browsing the tips of saplings. An English Nature researcher has quantified the percentage of bluebells they chew up in his standard woodland plots. And – whatever next! – they *bark*. From the tone of the interviews – 'this animal is like nothing else you are familiar with in the English countryside' – culling is not far away. Or perhaps a discreetly introduced virus, like myxomatosis.

We can claim some knowledge of the muntjac in the Chilterns. It was here the first populations began to build up after they escaped from local parks in the 1880s, and since then they've become, I suspect, our favourite visible large mammal. Not that they are obtrusive. They are rather retiringly suburban, glimpsed peeping through curtains of garden shrubs, or roaming along village pavements at night, red eyes picked out by the headlights. They have been in my wood for fifteen years, and have made not the slightest impact on the spectacular lakes of bluebells in April, preferring a diet of ivy, hazel and bramble leaves. I have watched them at even closer quarters in the garden. One stayed for several days a couple of years ago, much to the amazement of the cats, who took it in turn to rub noses, and in the evening sat round it like admirers at a salon. It gave the roses a pruning, and demolished a few geraniums. But it avoided bulbous plants – though not without 'sniffing' them first with its tongue.

Muntjacs do patchily graze bluebell flowers and leaves, though not as damagingly as badgers, which dig up the bulbs. They occasionally nibble young trees, but rarely kill them. In any case, perhaps these are the kind of tithes we should pay to have the privilege of wild creatures' company. The muntjac's most heinous crime, of course, is to be an 'alien', and successful to boot, for which we should be thankful, given how many of our native mammals haven't coped with the onslaughts of modern civilisation.

It will be sad if the Government's advisor, English Nature, joins in the hue and cry. In the 1947 White Paper which set out the principles of a national conservation policy, the drafters had a vision of constructing 'for the people a lasting and pleasurable resort'. Well, the people are not getting much pleasure these days. Although English Nature is putting out a blizzard of publicity about its commitment to conservation in the community, it (not, I must stress, its dedicated field workers) rarely sides with ordinary people's interests when conflicts arise. If it lines up with other rural lobbies to persecute this unassuming, accessible vegetarian, its standing with the public will sink even further.

[6]

Never go back, they say, but sometimes it is just too tempting. It was the birthday of an old friend from north Norfolk, where I'd spent some of the happiest times of my life. I'd met Mike and his wife Pooh this winter after a gap of a dozen years, but it was just as if we were all still running wild on the marshes as we had at the end of the sixties. A party in Blakeney in the spring felt like a chance to cock a snook at time.

It was, in the end, something special. Two birthdays, as it turned out, and Mike's 1994 vintage to celebrate as well. Somehow, in salt winds that blow straight from the Urals, he grows grapes; and a local GP, an alchemist, I suspect, turns them into wine. It was an extraordinary potion, a true *vin de pays*, dry as sand, with a nose uncannily like flotsam the day after a high tide. Most of the food had come from the shore. Mackerel, crabs and sea spinach. I hadn't tasted this for decades, and its ozone and iron tang would have made Proust faint. For me it brought back half a lifetime: the lilting calls of curlew, hot black mud on the legs, nights out at sea. The place drove the talk, which rapidly turned into yarning: tales of floods, fishing, trundling pianos down to the quay. We pledged resistance to the barbarian developers with their eyes on the local school's playing field, Mike took to reading a friend's poetry, and, with quite affecting courtesy, a prosaic eulogy I'd penned years ago to the culinary delights of the puffball. He made it sound like something from the Song of Solomon. Then the guitars came out, and I feared we were on the brink of maudlin nostalgia. But in a moment of pre-dawn clarity, I realised that this wasn't looking back; it was all still here, and they had kept faith with it.

Next morning the wind had switched to the south and the sky was so clear we could see Blakeney Point, four miles away. We walked down to the marshes, through bluebells and coconut-scented gorse, and I picked sea spinach again for myself. There were swallows flitting along the muddy creeks, and I felt so attuned that I bet my host the swifts would be back from Africa at 6.30 p.m. the next day, 1 May.

That day, home in the Chilterns in the early evening, I peered up at the sky with my binoculars. At 6.40 I made out the flickering crossbow shapes criss-crossing above the parish church. I rushed out to cheer them in, and within the hour there were a dozen strafing the supermarket car park. It was the first time I had seen swifts arrive on May Day since I was a schoolboy, when I used to walk about clutching my blazer collar, aching for them to materialise. I thought about their life since they had left last August, the half-million miles spent entirely on the wing – migrating, feeding, even sleeping. No wonder Ted Hughes wrote those exultant lines: 'They've made it again,/ Which means the globe's still working . . . our summer's/ Still all to come.' And for me, this spring, there was a new sympathy with this triumphant annual return to their motherlode.

[7]

It was almost midsummer and in the countryside it felt like mid-November. Rain-sodden branches cracked by the winds were scattered about the lanes like spillikins. Toadstools were already sprouting in the hedge-banks. It was time for a visit to the Chiltern Sculpture Trail's summer show – or perhaps, I should say, seasonal rehanging.

The Forestry Commission has been putting sculpture in its woods since the late seventies, and though some regard it as intrusive, it's usually made of the same mutable stuff as the landscape. And I was right in thinking that flameless June might have done some interesting editing in Cowleaze Wood. One of my favourite pieces, Bryan Illsley's *Raised Ash Line* – a long, curving rib of ash cutting the woodland verticals, like an aerial walkway for dormice – had been blown or taken down. But Paul Amey's *Fish Tree* was still standing, a skeletal metal tree with iron fish at the end of its branches. It had been on the receiving end of two years of rain since I last saw it. And it presented a bizarre and incongruous mixture of elements – autumnally rusty fish floating among spring green leaves. The jokiest piece in the wood, Robert Jakes' giant picnic table covered in a wooden check tablecloth, was also weathering impishly. It's a brilliant visual pun, the best place in the wood for having picnics *under*. And the tablecloth – now looking as if it was the arena for a frenetic tea-party – was covered with bracket fungi.

This is one of the points about environmental sculpture. Nature is expected to have a role in shaping it. It is ambiguous, hybrid, and challenges assumptions about the utility and durability of things. Many of the Cowleaze pieces are hard to find. They are hidden up dark tracks, lurking in hollows. All along the trail, serendipitously wind-thrown logs, dens, a polythene bag wrapped round a branch in the shape of a squirrel, make you wonder whether you are looking at a deliberate work or a natural happening. I thought that I'd at last found Illsley's other piece, *Broken Larch Circle*, only to realise that it was an extraordinary 'found tree' – a conifer bent over, split open like a mouth, and sprouting new shoots all along its upper lip. And were those symmetrical black collars round a stand of oaks caterpillar controls or Constructivism?

None of this is remotely 'arty'. It is in the great vernacular tradition of outdoor doodling, of name-carving, cairn-building and tree-decorating that has been going on for millennia. Halfway round the trail I glimpsed a stone structure topped with something red, and thought for a moment that I had tracked down Hideo Furuta's runic pink granite hump. But it proved to be a memorial from another generation, a tough stone memorial to the crew of a Halifax bomber downed in 1944, and still decorated with last year's Remembrance Sunday wreaths. Was Cowleaze Wood where the plane had crashed, or the pilot's favourite retreat?

Woods, even for the agoraphobic English, are still places of mystery and devotion as well as whimsy.

[8]

All summer the tousled sweeps of Tring Park had seemed to be thickening, like a cat's new coat. I'd catch glimpses of it from the bypass, and even from a distance could see the tide of young ash rising in the storm-blasted beech hangers and new shoots seeping up through the tawny stems of last year's ungrazed grasses. The whole prospect stirred perceptibly in the breeze. Something was going on in there.

It is a spectacular place, but I had stayed clear recently while it weathered one of its periodic crises. Back in the seventeenth century it was the north-west tip of Tring common, a tract of woodland, grass and heath that stretched over more than 3,000 acres. But gradually it was eaten away, one slice appropriated for a private park in the mid-eighteenth century, more for plantation woods, the last 300 acres filched and enclosed by Parliamentary enactment in 1853. The parkland area became grazing land and an unofficial public open space after the war, but a few years ago it was bought by Whitbread, who had ambitions to turn it into a golf course and country club. Fortunately it lies in the Chilterns' Area of Outstanding Natural Beauty, and the brewery's original schemes were summarily turned down by the planning authorities. So for the last eighteen months it has been a brooding and deliciously unkempt waste, getting its breath back.

I gave in to its new charms in June. I had just been to visit the Chilterns' soldier orchid site, and had been delighted by the spreading colonies which are no longer barricaded off, as they were in the 1970s. I remembered that Tring Park was probably one of the orchid's last Hertfordshire sites in the nineteenth century, when it grew 'abundantly' in sunny places by the edges of chalky woods, and I had a wild fancy that it might just have reappeared in the tangled west-facing slopes. Needless to say, I didn't find any, but the whole place had an invigorating sense of profusion. There were drifts of cowslips in seed, enough salad burnet to stain the steeper slopes claret and, in the half-shade along the wood-edge, a glimmering brocade of bugle and jasmine-scented valerian.

Then I began to hear the stories of the barn owls, which have not bred in this corner of the country for maybe twenty years. There were sightings by the village allotments, and one spotted on a path, munching a vole. They were all centred around Tring Park.

I took to going for dusktime walks amongst the overgrown paddocks and ragged hedges that lie between my wood and the Park. I didn't see the barn owls, but the smell of hay, the feel of rough grass on bare legs, and the low sun striping the beechwoods with shadows, conjured up the most powerful memories of enchanted evening walks as a teenager and of school holidays running wild as a boy. Our playground then was also an abandoned park, part of a long-demolished mansion. There were barn owls nesting in the old stables and they patrolled the lines of poplars and crumbling walls that marked our common boundaries.

Then, one evening in July, feeling lucky after watching two of the Chilterns' red kites circling a village further south, I stopped off for a quick look at the Park. It was about 8.15, and I saw the owls immediately, quartering the bleached, thigh-high grass that was now dotted with orchids and scabious, and the moon-discs of hogweed flowers. They were diving for prey roughly every thirty seconds, and catching something on about one strike in ten. I kept low and edged in the direction they were ferrying the food. They seemed quite unperturbed by my presence, so much so that I began to wonder if barn owls had slight tunnel vision. So when one flew straight towards me, I stood my ground. It sheared off with a screech when it was about twenty metres away, and went and hid in a tree. I hid too, in a hedge, and then followed them more discreetly to the nest tree, which proved to be an ancient beech with half its top blown out. Burying myself in a drift of hogweed nearby, I had the magical experience of the owls wafting past me just feet away, as silent as a breath.

I went back to the Park often over the summer, and each time the owls came out to hunt a little later. And each time I glimpsed, for just a few maddening seconds, the silhouette of a third owl. I thought at first that it was an unusually plumaged barn owl, but am now convinced that it was a short- or long-eared owl, which would be a testament indeed to the teeming mammal life in this Chiltern pampas. My last visit was on a moonless night before the rains began. It was almost too dark to see, but

I could just make out the adult owls dancing around amongst the branches, and I guess the young were on the point of leaving the nest.

One day, I suppose, the Park will have to be managed, otherwise it will all turn into woodland within a couple of decades (though all it really needs is a hurricane once a century and an occasional passing herd of bison). But I hope whoever has charge of it will have seen it this summer in its prime with the wild woods tumbling into the valley, and the owls beating over a mile of waving grass that looked less like tame old England than the Elysian plains of John Muir's California, before the ranchers came.

[9]

It is more than two decades since I wrote my first nature book, a guide to edible wild plants called *Food For Free*. It was a modest success in its own way, enabling me to risk becoming a full-time freelance, and I shall always be grateful for that.

But it had also the kind of oddball subject matter that gets one typecast. A few years after publication I was introduced to a well-known photographer at a party. 'Ah yes,' he mused, peering closely at me. 'You're the man that eats weeds. What an interestingly *earthy* face.' This, I felt, shrinking with embarrassment, was taking the idea that you are what you eat a little too literally, and ever since I have distanced myself slightly from that early guide to greens. I still enjoy feasts of seasonal crops: samphire from the north Norfolk marshes in summer, wild raspberries from my own wood, local hazelnuts for Christmas. But for the most part I have become a rather precious wayside nibbler, indulging in what the 1930s writer and fruit gourmet Edward Bunyard christened 'ambulant consumption' – single wild gooseberries (squeezed to test for ripeness first), sweet cicely seeds on walks before dinner as a kind of herbal aperitif, squidgy dewberries eaten on the stalk, like cocktail cherries.

This year, however, with an anniversary to celebrate and an odd pattern of weather whose effects on normal fruiting patterns I was curious to explore, I felt inclined to go for a proper, inquisitive foray, a working lunch, so to speak.

So I map out a route over familiar country near home which takes in some old hedges and one-time mushroom pastures, hoist a gathering bag over my shoulder – and then curse the fact that the mid-October day that I have carefully planned for this expedition turns out to be the most dismal of the autumn so far.

But half a mile on I find I am quite enjoying the mist and fine drizzle.

The berries on the trees, dust washed off at last, have an inviting dewy sheen. On the grassland, now thoroughly moistened, patches and rings of darker green grass that may be signs of underground fungal growth are materialising like watermarks.

I start browsing out of a sense of duty to begin with, and drench myself with showers of settled rainwater every time I reach into a bush. Things are already remarkably ripe, even though there have been no air frosts yet. I nibble a few agreeably soft haws, whose flesh always reminds me of underripe avocado, then start on the blackberries, which are still swelling in good numbers, despite all those saws about not picking them after Michaelmas. Even berries from adjacent bushes can taste quite different, with hints of grape, cherry, plum, and subtly different textures, reminding you that there are four hundred microspecies of bramble in Britain.

But I draw a blank with hazelnuts. It was not a good year for them to start with, and this year's explosion in grey squirrel numbers seems to have put paid to the few that did form. I try a few tricks, such as getting inside the bushes and looking out, hoping that any clusters will be more visible against the sky. But all I find are a few rather stale cobs already fallen to the ground. I munch some elderberries for consolation, but overdo it, and that slight cloying sensation, of having sucked fruit-flavoured frog-spawn, won't go away. There are clusters of miniature wood puffballs on the tree stumps, though, and I find that chewing some of the white flesh takes the elder aftertang away.

My route takes me up into the Chiltern foothills, and a labyrinth of green lanes. Long-tailed tits are dithering through the hedges, and the first chaffinch flocks gathering – though there is no beech mast either for them or me. I am heading for a wilding apple tree I discovered last year – sniffed out, actually, since its lemon-yellow fruits smelt deliciously of quince and scented the air for dozens of yards around. (They were too hard and acid to eat raw, but were spectacular roast with meat.) The tree has fruited quite well again, though it is too early for the fruits to have taken on their heady aroma. But there are plenty of other wilding apples about. I bite into one and it has the bitter-sweet, almost effervescent zest of sherbet. On another tree in the same hedge they are like miniature pippins. A third has long pear-shaped apples that have an extraordinary warm, smoky flavour behind the sharpness, as if they had already been baked. I ponder the huge genetic storehouse represented by these wayside wildings, all sprung from discarded cores and maybe cross-bred with true crab apples.

But I must be disappointed at how few fungi there are in the hedges and copses, as I start hallucinating them. A promising mound under an oak turns out to be a toy bubble car, and every white flash in the field is eventually an upturned flint. But as I turn for home through the valley meadows, with rooks massing above the woods on either side, I begin to strike lucky. There are freshly sprung field mushrooms, pink-gilled and unsullied by insects. There are fairy rings of 8-inch-diameter horse-mushrooms and of shaggy parasols (no good for eating raw, but I pick a bagful for later).

And in the ridgeway hedges on the last lap before home, the wild damsons are perfectly ripe and beginning to drop from the trees. The bushes line an old orchard and were, I guess, originally planted as a combination wind-break and pollinator for the cultivated plums. But they have spread some way beyond their original site, and suckers and seedlings (including a wonderful cherry-plum with round, thick, orange fruit) crop up for hundreds of yards along the hedge. There is one new taste sensation here. The hedge was cut in the summer with the fruit already formed, and the trimmings lie beneath it, covered with dry, wrinkled damsons that taste exactly like thin-fleshed prunes.

So this was my midday meal, ambulantly consumed but in strictly correct order: young field mushrooms and a few soft chestnuts, finished with wild plums and strips of lemony apple. After three hours of continuous nibbling it seemed, I will confess, rather on the acid and insubstantial side, and I began to yearn for a bowl of pasta. But never believe anyone who says there is no such thing as a free lunch.

[10]

For most of this century red kites have been one of the symbols of Welsh Wales. Embattled in a small but inexorably growing colony amongst the hanging oakwoods of Ceredigion, they have been seen by local naturalists as a satisfying snub to the English landed gentry, which exterminated them this side of Offa's Dyke in the nineteenth century. And sailing above the tourist traffic in the narrow lanes round Devil's Bridge, their tortoiseshell plumage touched with ermine, they do have an awesome, bardic presence.

This slice of Dyfed – recently christened 'Kite Country' by the Green tourist business – now has 120 breeding pairs, and it is easy to think of them as something uniquely and intrinsically Celtic. Yet the colony is, to tell the truth, more like a ghetto. The red kite was once a common bird across the whole of Britain. In the early fifteenth century, it made such a contribution to public health by scavenging carrion from the streets of London that it was made a capital offence to kill one – the first conservation law not solely concerned to protect hunting rights. Within not much more than two centuries the bounty was on the kites' heads, not the hunters'. They were persecuted for taking game birds, and, bizarrely, for stealing washing to ornament their nests. (Autolycus in *The Winter's Tale*, himself 'a snapper-up of unconsidered trifles', warns that 'When the kite builds, look to your lesser linen'.) The scale of the slaughter was enormous. The churchwarden's accounts in the village of Tenterden, Kent, for example, record the killing of 432 red kites in just fourteen years from 1677. With the spread of keepered shooting estates in the late eighteenth and nineteenth centuries it's no wonder the bird was driven into extinction in England and Scotland, and clung on only in the wild but less blood-thirsty hills of central Wales.

In the 1950s, a group of committed Welshmen formed the Kite Committee, and were able to nudge the population up from a dozen or so pairs to about a hundred by the beginning of the 1990s. But their expansion was laboriously slow, and there was some evidence that genetic interbreeding contributed to this. There certainly seemed little likelihood of their ever repopulating their old haunts over the border.

So in the late 1980s, the Royal Society for the Protection of Birds and the then Nature Conservancy Council set up a UK Red Kite Project Team, to consider reintroducing the bird to England and Scotland with nestlings from the large populations in Sweden and Spain. One of the release areas was in northern Scotland, another in the Chilterns, and the number of birds set free into the wild to date is over two hundred.

Although there have been echoes of the ancestral persecution of the bird (six illegally poisoned by farmers and two shot), the experiment has been a huge success. Since its beginning, 113 young have fledged in England and 42 in Scotland. This year [1995] has been the best ever, with 53 young birds flying from 23 nests around the Chiltern site. They have also become one of the great spectacles of this stretch of hill country. You are likely to spot individual birds gliding lazily over roads almost any-where east of Watlington. They are wonderfully adroit flyers: heading into the wind with wings shrunk back like a falcon, then wheeling like an eagle, and using their deep forked tails as rudders. No wonder that the kite gave its name to the flying toys that were introduced to this country in the seventeenth century.

But they are sociable creatures, too, and often form packs of up to a dozen, to be more efficient at finding carrion. They soar over village greens and stackyards – a vision of a wilder rural past. I understand purists' feelings that it would have been more satisfying to have let the indigenous Welsh population spread east naturally. But our new kites look uncannily at home hanging over the steep beechwoods, a confirmation of what many of us who live here feel – that the Chilterns is, in its history and character, a Celtic landscape itself.

[11]

I've never had a picnic to equal Rat and Mole's in *The Wind in the Willows* but I'm sitting in their Wild Wood, on a Badger sett, and munching wild redcurrants. It isn't, thank goodness, a Toad Hall Theme Park. The wood that was the inspiration for that thrilling thicket full of stoats and weasels and faces in trees really does exist. Bisham Wood stretches along the Chiltern scarp above the Thames near Marlow 'like a black reef in some still southern sea'. It has been through some tumultuous experiences since Kenneth Grahame knew it: infiltrated with conifers blown to pieces in the two great hurricanes, and, in 1990, finally rescued for locals and Wild Wooders alike by the Woodland Trust. Grahame lived above the wood between 1906 and 1910, in the then tiny village of Cookham Dean. It's a more sprawling commuter settlement now, but it possesses something I've not seen in a place like this before – a co-op pub: when the brewers put the Jolly Farmers up for sale in 1987, a group of more than fifty villagers clubbed together and bought it, for one equal share each. And *sans* fruit machines and muzak, it is doing very well. The talk inside was equally about investment deals and wood-burning stoves. The whole village struck me as a beguilingly contrary place, where merchant bankers come home from the City and turn into communards. I suspect that Grahame, an avowed pagan who was Secretary of the Bank of England in his day job, would still feel at home here. Back in the wood in the stifling heat things hadn't got quite the radiance of the chapter where Mole and Rat meet Pan, but were turning pretty hallucinatory. Dragonflies were materialising out of the heat haze. Shocks of deadly nightshade sprung out of the root-holes of windthrown beeches. Not exactly a wilderness, but pretty wild. Badger thought that their Wild Wood had 'planted itself' on the site of an old city, and in one sense he was right. Our imaginations can patch wildness over that deep sense of human occupation in the countryside.

[12]

Every late summer since the early 1980s I used to survey our local house martins. It was, to tell the truth, more in the way of a sample than a strict count, a meandering stroll along a fixed route past Victorian terraces and canalside cottages. It was a nerve-wracking business at times (peering through binoculars at other people's eaves is not recommended in these days of Neighbourhood Watch), but as funny and rewarding as the birds themselves. The nests would often be in bizarre and ingenious sites: spattering the ornate blinds of an Italian hairdresser and, once, audaciously slung under a burglar alarm above a jeweller's. But I hadn't the heart to do the rounds this year [1995]. I knew there were just two nests, the same number as 1994. They had been in a slow but steady decline since the mid-1980s, the number of occupied nests on my route dropping from fifty to twenty-two between 1989 and 1992. Then they plummeted to nine in 1993 and to two last year. The crash – worse than that of whitethroats in 1969 – has been repeated all over southern and eastern Britain. Ancestral colonies on farms and cottages have been deserted. Whole villages have been without a single nest for the first time in living memory. No one is sure of the cause yet, but for once it seems that it may not be our fault. Although people do still illegally knock down nests because the droppings spoil the look of pebble-dash, the unsettling fact is the birds simply haven't been returning. Which all points to some disaster in one of the martins' wintering areas or migration stop-off points. (Some distraught Suffolk friends blame Saddam Hussein's chemical sterilisation of the Iraqi marshlands.) Whatever the causes, we must pray it is only temporary, or we will have lost the most engaging and festive of all the birds that choose to live close to humans.

[13]

The winter solstice here was so gloomy that it was hard to tell where the shortest day ended and the longest night began. In any case, a few of us have long abandoned the solstice itself as the day to cling to for reassurance that the year has turned. It is far too late. For us 12 December marks the first chink in the sodden drapes of winter.

Because of the asymmetry of the earth's orbit round the sun, the relentless pincer movement of darkening mornings and afternoons doesn't conclude with a neat snap on 21 December. The mornings start lightening on New Year's Day, but the evenings on 12 December. The trouble is we can't think of a name for this first glimmer of new light – maybe because it is, to say the least, a notional shift. My wood seems utterly drained of colour and tangible life. Redwings – something of a euphemism in the gloom – shift through the black fretwork of the beeches like wraiths. The ground is pulped, clotted: a compost of leaves and rotting wood indistinguishable from the tones of clay and waterlogged trunks. Two years ago, the bluebell spears were showing through on Christmas Day. This year despite an autumn of Mediterranean warmth, there isn't a sign of them. But when I scrape away the sodden leaf litter, there they are, pallid and waiting. So are the bleached and optimistic shoots of the millions of acorns that fell in October.

This strange hinge in the year isn't dead, just becalmed. Perhaps we should revive that almost obsolete word 'fallow' to describe it. Francis Kilvert, I remember, used it for the far-from-dead condition of 'dead' (that is, turning back into earth) wood. Maybe 'Fallowmas Eve' would do for 12 December. It's not exactly bullish but does come close to catching the anticipatory feel of these three weeks of suspended animation.

On Stewardship (1990)

The notion of 'stewardship' became part of the ecological litany some time before Prince Charles gave it air-time. It is one of those intrinsically good sounding words, redolent of responsibility and doing one's duty. Yet it is, when you think about it, an odd choice for a form of relationship to supplant the discredited idea of human 'dominion' over nature. A steward, in anybody's dictionary, is simply a deputy, someone who manages or administers on another's behalf. On whose behalf are we the stewards of the planet? Not, presumably, its literal owners. God, then, or Gaia? I suspect that most of those who use the word might answer 'the planet itself', which at best is a piece of sophistry, and at worst a reworking of the patronising view that nature needs to be in human custody for its own good. This is asking for a warder, not a steward.

But its most dangerous undertone is precisely that subtle buck-passing, that denial of personal control. Managing nature not for yourself but for some unnamed or abstract other lifts you clear of the messy business of value judgement and political choice, and certainly from the need to consider whether the job needs doing in the first place. Altruism, as we are all taught, is its own reward and above such things.

When I bought a small Chiltern wood in 1981, I was still full of such blathering slogans. Doubtless there were sublimated personal longings, too, but mostly I dreamed of being the Good Woodward. I would return the wood to the community, preserve it for 'posterity' (another favourite beneficiary of the stewarding business), create a sanctuary. I could see it all so clearly: the parish out coppicing in the winter sun, the wood responding with floods of spring flowers and birds, the local hunt routed, the Greenwood restored to the People. Ten years later I am wiser about my own presumptuousness, and about the natural world's ability to look after itself. But chiefly I have learned that any conscious decision to intervene in natural systems involves a labyrinth of cultural assumptions, in which personal – or at least anthropocentric – objectives all too often masquerade as altruistic ones, done for 'nature's sake'.

The double standards were there from the outset, for in order to dis-own a wood, so to speak, I would first have to own it, and play the property owner. It was a role in which I felt decidedly uncomfortable, and when I finally signed the contract for 16 acres of ancient deciduous woodland just a couple of miles from my home, I wasn't at all sure what one was supposed to do next.

Fortunately Hardings Wood itself seemed full of prompts, at least at an ecological level. It was not so much one wood as three. Straddling a steepish valley that felt as if it ought to carry a stream was a mixture of tall ash, cherry and hazel. The slope flattened into a flinty plateau with free-range hornbeam, oak and holly. And to the north, separated from this old part of the wood by a wide bank and ditch, was a plantation of ninety-year-old beeches. There was a pond with frogs, a vast badger sett and a spectacular range of ancient woodland plants.

But, except for the six weeks when the whole wood was awash with bluebells, what struck me most then was its sense of dark and emptiness. No one walked in it. There were no paths and no undergrowth. There weren't even any seedling trees. It was a hollow, unwelcoming place, with only its spectacular ground flora to give a hint that inside was a real wood waiting to escape. What had gone wrong? As far as I could tell, Hardings, like many small woods, had been pretty well gutted of timber during the last war, and the closely packed trees that grew there now had regenerated naturally from the cut stumps or from seed. At some time during the 1950s the previous owner had interplanted these with stands of hybrid Italian poplars. It was a bizarre choice, given that these nursery-man's trees only really prosper on damp, rich soils. But in those days Bryant and May were sponsoring the growing of poplars for matchwood, and doubtless encouraged a lot of reckless planting.

After that the wood was virtually abandoned. There was no thinning of the dense mixture of wild and planted trees, and they grew leggy and tall. The poplars fared especially badly. They became infested with honey fungus, and on the dry steep slopes had already started to topple over. In many places they had formed mattresses of spongy rotting wood, which were blotting out all life beneath.

Given a hundred years or so the wood would have sorted itself out. The poplars would have rotted away, and the whippier trees been blown down. But I wanted to try and return it to a wilder, more varied structure *now*, to make it a more congenial place for human beings at the same time, above all to let in some light. That autumn, helped by a group of enthusiastic friends, I began canvassing the village about my plans to turn Hardings into a community wood. I talked to the local primary school, and distributed a newsletter through the Parish Council and WI. Responses were cautiously encouraging at first, and I only had one out-right protest – from a local taxidermist, of all people, who was irked at the possibility of 'community' involvement spoiling his private sojourns in the wood.

Not that many local people turned up for our first Sunday working party, but there were enough to start on what I had rather arbitrarily chosen as the first task, clearing the pond of generations of debris and opening up the area around it. With no real plan other than creating a clearing which would let more sunlight into the water, we simply sawed away at anything damaged or flimsy on the sunward side. But gradually personal preferences and sentiments began to find expression. One volunteer chose to pollard a broken oak instead of felling it. Others argued (for superstitious as much as sentimental reasons, I suspect) against the clearing of any holly trees, despite the fact that they are the most aggressive colonisers in the wood. I found myself pleading for two thorn bushes which a volunteer with forestry training had a predatory eye upon. In the end we ended up with a quite unexpected but communal landscape, not so much a clearing as a glade with groves.

Talking through the final details of work as we went along became a custom on working party days. But it became more difficult as the parish became more trusting and the number of volunteers grew. On fine Sundays as many as fifty people might spend some time working, and in the areas where trees were actually being felled and reduced to firewood, the activity could become frenetic. I am amazed, thinking about those early days, that no one was crushed or dismembered. There seemed to be something almost compulsive about people's desire to get to grips with the trees. No sooner had one been felled than it was stripped of branches, logged and stacked. It rarely took more than a few minutes, and when I paused to watch, it reminded me of those speeded-up films of jungle ants reducing a dead animal to a skeleton. I don't entirely understand the roots of this demented energy, but I know that I felt it myself. I don't think it is destructive, but has something to do with the phsyical exhilaration of working with trees in the open, with the smell and feel of fresh cut wood.

Not that it was all hard labour. Work days became very sociable events, helped usually by a large bonfire. And not everyone was gripped by the work ethic. Some older visitors were quite content to spend the day chatting and carrying the odd twig to the fire. But it was the children who had the most sensible attitude. They would saw or carry wood furiously for a while, then suddenly all take off at once, like a flock of birds. We would hear them in the distance, building camps amongst the old man's beard, or swings across the chalk pit. Half an hour later they would all come back to work again.

The big bonfires were one of the many mistakes we made in the early stages. They may have been welcoming but they scorched the earth and wasted tons of wood, and were really part of an almost reflex desire to tidy nature up that we all had to cure ourselves of. Now we just make dead hedges with tbe brushwood. They rot away in five or six years, and in the meantime make nesting sites for wrens and robins.

We still don't have a comprehensive 'management plan', cut and dried, and I rather hope we never will have. But the wood has begun to respond to our pottering, teasing it into patterns of growth that we – and it – both seem to enjoy. Frogs have returned in large numbers to the pond, and on mild March days there may be as many as a hundred mating and spawning in the water. The new tracks – not planned on paper, but just cut and trodden out by volunteers following their feet – are alive with butterflies in summer. And wherever we have let in more light, hosts of seedling trees – ash, maple and cherry chiefly – are springing up, and are already 8 feet tall in places.

The economics of the whole operation would make depressing reading for a monetarist. Our one purely capitalist enterprise, selling some timber beech thinnings from the plantation, made just about enough profit for us to buy some new saws, and put down a deposit on a second-hand pick-up truck. And although we have generated a formidable amount of small wood in, as it were, our 'current account', much of this goes out as free fuel, a perk for anyone who has helped cut it and can carry it away. The remainder we sell locally. Either way it is an exceptionally labour-intensive exercise. Roughly five hundred person-hours produce twenty-five tons of wood, which at current prices means a return of about 50p per hour's work.

But none of this takes account of the qualitative economics of the wood, or of transactions which have more to do with barter, and the commonland principle of purchasing a stick by cutting it. Moss is gathered by flower arrangers, pea-sticks by gardeners, wood-ash by potters. And people 'buy time' for the wood simply by choosing to spend their leisure there.

The return of people to the wood has been the most gratifying thing of all. Not so many people turn out to work, now the novelty has worn off, but they have been replaced by walkers and picnickers and out-and-out woodland hedonists. Bat-watchers, fungus-collectors, WEA evening classes all use the place. Once, at bluebell time, I chanced upon two lady watercolourists sitting amongst the flowers in immense white hats, and looking so utterly at home that I felt like an interloper myself. No one *possesses* a wood even if they do 'own' it.

It has partly been a distaste for playing the squire that has kept my private use of the wood in a low key. I have had plenty of fantasies about what I might do there. (I had a dream about an oil-strike there, and didn't feel the least bit bothered.) I am determined to spend a whole night there soon, something which plenty of local children have done. But I doubt if I will ever realise my most persistent fancy which is to go into semi-retreat there like a scholar-gypsy. I find I can write in the wood when the weather is fine, with my back against a tree in one of the glades, and every spring I fidget with the possibility of building a tree-house, or parking an old travellers' caravan down in the valley and turning it into a writer's den. Perhaps it is just laziness or a fear of vandalism that stops me doing anything about these whims. But somehow they feel too proprietorial, a kind of trespass, and I know that, for me, they would take away some of the surprise, the sense of 'otherness' of the wood.

'Managing' the wood can, ironically, also be a narrowing experience, although I now have skills I never dreamed of before. I know how to sharpen a chain-saw, cope with the chicken-bone springiness of holly wood, and how fast ash seedlings grow. But work can narrow one's view of nature as much as extend it. Sometimes, trying just to enjoy a stroll round the wood, I find I am trapped in a kind of managerial tunnel vision. I peer obsessively up at the canopy to see if we have let enough light in, scour the ground for regenerating seedlings. It needs a conscious act of will to relax, and remember that life has its own priorities here.

It is worth it. The wood has a wonderfully intricate and seasonal geography. After autumn and winter gales the whole interior of the wood is transformed. Drifts of leaves or snow obliterate the paths and leave new trails of open ground between the trees. I walk about as if I have never been in the place before, seeing the other sides of familiar trees. Snow and hoar frost weld the outer branches of the hollies to the ground, forming a kind of protective skirt, and woodcock sometimes shelter on the ground inside. If I get too close they shoot out at the last minute, quite silently, like a stifled gasp, and skim crankily away over the brambles until their chequered plumage merges with the shade.

In spring it is the moment for beech leaves and bluebells. The beech leaves don't grow gradually, like oak or birch. They unfurl, already full-sized and partly translucent, and can flood a wood within a matter of days. Up at the westernmost corner of the wood, a group of young beeches arch over a track through the bluebells, and most years leaves and flowers open in the same week. With the filtered sunlight dappling the trunks, and the bluebells rippling underneath, the whole corner takes on the submerged glow of an aquarium. Up to my knees in flowers I've found myself walking in slow motion here, amazed at the density of the light; and then going back and walking through it all over again.

But these are private pleasures, and I am aware that the community involvement in the wood may have been subtly directed by me to sustain them. One of the things we have uncovered over the past ten years is the extent to which the wood suffered from private ambitions in the past. In the mid-nineteenth century the entire parish was reorganised under a General Enclosure Award. I have read the minutes of the meetings the twenty-four local landowners held with the surveyor during the early months of 1853. They met in the Royal Hotel at Tring, about a dozen of them at a time, and systematically replanned the home country of 630 people. It says so much, that meticulously penned address at the top of the quarto sheets. The Royal was a commercial inn, outside the village, right next to Tring railway station and convenient for agents and absentee landowners. Here, over lunch, they argued about how much of the common each of them should be allotted, and, doubtless believing themselves to be stewards of a kind, recorded their belief that the scheme would lead to 'increased productiveness of the land, useful employment of labour . . . and an improvement in the morals and habits of the people'. And on 7 August, they agreed their plan for reshaping the parish's communication system. Two weeks later posters went up all over the village, printed in heavy block type like 'Wanted' notices. Thirteen existing ways and footpaths were to be completely closed, and replaced by two surveyors' roads leading to nearby towns. One of the footpaths stopped off was a track leading from Wigginton village to the valley, which passed through Hardings Wood. Not the slightest evidence that it ever existed remains.

By the end of the year the Enclosure was complete. The fences had been raised around the common, and the commoners and landless poor of Wigginton left with a 2-acre recreation field and 5 acres of allotment. Even by the standards of Parliamentary Enclosure it was a callous act, and it is odd that the people of the village did not resist (as they had, fiercely against an earlier attempt at enclosure, in the late seventeenth century). In the following year, 1854, the new curate at Wigginton – by no means a radical – set down some revealing comments on the consequences of enclosure:

All the picturesque appearance of the place was gone, and perhaps the poetry. Post and rail fences were right and left all over the place. But I believed the change would morally tend to the benefit of the people: they would be less rough, wild and uncivilised. I cannot judge whether this has happened; whether as some predicted 'wicked Wigginton would become virtuous Wigginton'. I cannot say that the people I knew as I knew them deserved the former epithet, or differed very much from other people of whom I have experience. But as I look back I am surprised that they accepted the enclosure as patiently as they did, considering of how many rights the enclosure deprived them.

The irony is that not a hint of the harshness of these events remains in the landscape itself; no sense of hurt or reproof; just, in winter sometimes, the slightest feeling of over-orderliness, of a loss of breathing-space in the hard geometry of the fields. But at most other times it seems to be in a state of grace, to be making a continual gesture of reparation. What were once the old rail and post fences are now hedges covered by wild roses, and along the new enclosure roads, the verges are thick with self-sown oak trees.

It was partly to try and restore a public route through the wood that we ended up doing some landscape reshaping ourselves. We also needed a track to get a vehicle into the wood, and carry cut wood out. We knew we would need a professional contractor to do the final excavation, as it would involve creating a cutting up one side of the valley, but we did most of the preparatory work ourselves. We looked over several possible routes, chose the one with the shallowest gradient, got our felling licence and cleared the few trees that lay along the track. The whole swath measured no more than 100 yards long by 4 yards wide. Then, in early October, we held a 'plant fostering day'. Numbers of local children and their parents turned up, dug up the ferns and primroses that lay along the path of the proposed track, put them in pots and took them home for the winter.

Two days later the Hymac 890 came into the wood. It was a huge yellow machine, normally used for digging agricultural drainage systems, and armed with an almost prehensile scoop. Its driver, Len, was a shy Londoner who used to make clock cases in Bethnal Green, and he seemed able to use it like a precision instrument. He could nudge trees over, then swoop to catch them before they fell. He could excavate scoopfuls of clay and deposit them *underneath* the machine, to raise his working platform. And all the while he was adding a subtle S-shape to the rather crudely straight route we'd marked out. I became fascinated by the machine, and took to watching it from a perch higher up in the wood. It shuffled back and forth behind the trees, purring gently, and with only the incriminating words 'Agricultural Improvers', forming whenever it passed into the open, to mark it out as a foreign force. In my diary entries for those days, Len and his familiar had already been gathered into the company of honorary forest creatures: 'When he is dragging soil back to level out the track he pulls it back and under himself, as badgers do when dragging bedding out of their setts . . . all the while the machine is being followed by small bands of robins, like tiny gulls after a woodland plough.'

The end product was a sinuous, unsurfaced road lying right in line with the autumn evening sun. And even after one week its hard edges were beginning to mellow into a moist, cheesy ribbon of clay and crushed chalk, crimped at the edges. The first frosts and rainstorms brought down drifts of debris over its bare surfaces – bluebell bulbs, moss, miniature landslides of flint. Within a month there was a green film of algae over the chalk. In the spring we put the fostered plants back. And one year later the bank was bristling with young birch seedlings, old man's beard, musk mallow and wild raspberries.

But it would be wrong to claim too much credit for what has become of the track. If it has any virtues they are due in only a very small part to our plans, more to Len's vision, and mostly to the immense recuperative powers of nature itself. It is (luckily perhaps) too small to be of any consequence for the long-term fortunes of the woodland ecosystem. But as a small *human* habitat, a bower built to accommodate our favourite plants and views, it has worked marvellously. Increasingly I feel that my feverish notes likening Len's machine to a badger were not so daft, and that a view of ourselves as partners in the planet, rather than stewards, is more helpful and honest. The consequences of our supposedly altruistic but arrogant grand stewardship schemes for nature form a hideous trail from English farmland to Amazonia. A modest and benign programme of self-interest might be a whole lot better. No one has ever accused badgers of being global vandals.

SOURCES

Genius Loci

'Spring Fever' is from *Birds*, 1978.

'Richard Mabey's Hertfordshire' appeared in *Illustrated London News*, 1982.

'Damp Humours' appeared in *The Countryman*, 1974.

'The New Forest' was first published in *Vole*, July 1979, as a review of *The New Forest: 900 Years After* by Peter Tate, Macdonalds, London, 1979.

'A Tide in the Affairs' was first published in *Places*, ed. Ronald Blythe, Oxford University Press, 1981.

'Paper Dreams' was written for the *Sunday Telegraph* (unpublished), 1981.

'The Tides of March' appeared in *Good Housekeeping*, 1982.

'Oxford: City of Greening Spires' appeared in *Harper's & Queen*, 1983.

'A Dales Diary' first appeared in *BBC Wildlife*, 1985 and as a longer essay in the Introduction to *The Yorkshire Dales* by Graham Noble, Colin Baxter, Grantown-on-Spey, 1996.

'A Walk Around the Block' is from *Walking in Britain*, ed. John Hillaby, Collins, London, 1988.

'A London Safari' appeared in the *Sunday Times*, 1989.

'A Seaside Town in Winter' appeared in the *Sunday Telegraph*, 1989.

'The Magnificent Severn' appeared in the *Sunday Times*, 1989.

'The East Anglian Badlands' appeared in the *Sunday Times*, 1991.

'Gilbert White's House' is from *Writers and their Houses*, ed. Kate Marsh, Hamish Hamilton, London, 1993.

Foreign Travel

'Winter in the Camargue' appeared in the *Sunday Times*, 1988.

'Green Crete' appeared in the *Sunday Telegraph*, 1989.

'The Lubéron' appeared in *The Times*, 1990.

'The Burren' appeared in the *Sunday Times*, 1991.

'Extremadura' appeared in *The Times*, 1997.

Politics in the Landscape

'Landscape: The Real Stuff' was first published in *Towards a New Landscape*, Bernard Jacobson, London, 1993.

'Living in the Past' was first published in *Vole*, 1978.

'The Promised Landscape' was first published in the series 'My Fantasy World' in *Good Housekeeping*, 1981.

'A Dorset Fable' appeared in the *Independent*, 1986.

'Anatomy of a Village' appeared in the *Sunday Telegraph*, 1988.

'The Roots of Civilisation' appeared in the *Sunday Times*, 1988.

'Dungeness: The Terminal Beach' appeared in the *Independent*, 1990.

'Filthy Images' appeared in *BBC Wildlife*, 1991.

'James Lovelock' was written for the *Sunday Times*, 1991 (unpublished).

'Lairds of Creation' appeared in *BBC Wildlife*, 1991.

'Flora Britannica' appeared in *The Times*, 1992.

'The Nature of Local Distinctiveness' is an edited version of a talk delivered at Common Ground's conference on Local Distinctiveness in September 1993.

'The Great Storm' appeared in *BBC Wildlife*, 1987.

Art and Ecology

'Art and Ecology' is from *Modern Painters*, 1991.

'Christo' is from *Modern Painters*, 1991.

'Don McCullin, *Open Skies*', appeared in the *Sunday Telegraph*, 1989.

'Tony Evans' was published as 'The Human Heliotrope' in *BBC Wildlife*, 1993.

'The Painter as Naturalist' is from *Modern Painters*, 1994.

'Maurice Cockrill' was first published as an essay in the catalogue to the exhibition 'Generation' at the Bernard Jacobson gallery, 1994.

'Andy Goldsworthy's *Végétal*' appeared in *BBC Wildlife*, 1996.

'David Nash's Artistic Estate' is from *Modern Painters*, 1997.

A Sense of Occasion

'Devil's Meat' appeared in the *Independent on Sunday*, 1993.

'Keats' "Ode to a Nightingale" ' was broadcast on BBC Radio in 1995.

'Spring' appeared in the *Independent on Sunday*, 1994.

'Summer' appeared in the *Independent on Sunday*, 1994.

'Winter' appeared in the *Independent on Sunday*, 1994.

Knowing My Place

'A Year's Turning in the Chilterns'

[1] is from *Landlocked: in Pursuit of the Wild* by Richard Mabey, Sinclair-Stevenson, London, 1994.

[2] 'The Chilterns: Home Country' is from *In Britain*, 1981.

[3] is from *Landlocked*, op. cit.

[4] appeared in the *Independent*, 1995.

[5] appeared in the *Independent*, 1995.

[6] appeared in the *Independent*, 1995.
[7] appeared in the *Independent*, 1995.
[8] is from *Landlocked*, op. cit.
[9] is from *Landlocked*, op. cit.
[10] 'Red Kites' appeared in the *Independent on Sunday*, 1995.
[11] appeared in the *Guardian*, 1995.
[12] appeared in the *Guardian*, 1995.
[13] appeared in the *Guardian*, 1995.
'On Stewardship' appeared in the *Guardian*, 1990.

INDEX